Space, Geography, and Politics
in the Early Roman Empire

By his will, Mr. Thomas Spencer Jerome endowed the lectureship that bears his name. It is jointly administered by the University of Michigan and the American Academy in Rome, and the lectures for which it provides are delivered at both institutions. They deal with phases of the history or culture of the Romans or of peoples included in the Roman Empire.

Frank E. Adcock, *Roman Political Ideas and Practice*

G. W. Bowersock, *Hellenism in Late Antiquity*

Jacqueline de Romilly, *The Rise and Fall of States According to Greek Authors*

George M. A. Hanfmann, *From Croesus to Constantine: The Cities of Western Asia Minor and Their Arts in Greek and Roman Times*

Claude Nicolet, *Space, Geography, and Politics in the Early Roman Empire*

Brunilde S. Ridgway, *Roman Copies of Greek Sculpture: The Problem of the Originals*

Mario Torelli, *Typology and Structure of Roman Historical Reliefs*

Cornelius C. Vermeule, *Greek Sculpture and Roman Taste: The Purpose and Setting of Graeco-Roman Art in Italy and the Greek Imperial East*

Paul Zanker, *The Power of Images in the Age of Augustus*

Jerome Lectures, Nineteen

Space, Geography, and Politics in the Early Roman Empire

Claude Nicolet

Ann Arbor
The University of Michigan Press

First paperback edition 2015

Published in the United States of America by
The University of Michigan Press
Manufactured in the United States of America

2018 2017 2016 2015 5 4 3 2

Library of Congress Cataloging-in-Publication Data

Nicolet, Claude, 1930–
[Inventaire du monde. English]
Space, geography, and politics in the early Roman empire / Claude Nicolet.
p. cm. — (Jerome lectures ; 19)
Translation of: L'Inventaire du monde.
Includes bibliographical references and index.
ISBN 0-472-10096-3 (alk. paper)
1. Geography—Rome. 2. Geography, Ancient. 3. Rome—Politics and government—30 B.C.–68 A.D. I. Title. II. Series: Jerome lectures ; 19th ser.
G86.N5313 1990
913.7—dc20 90-48168
CIP

ISBN 978-0-472-03623-3 (pbk: alk. paper)

Originally published as *L'Inventaire du Monde: Géographie et Politique aux Origines de L'Empire Romain.*

Also published as *L'Inventario del Mondo: Geografia e Politica alle Origini dell'Impero Romano.*

English translation by Hélène Leclerc.

The University of Michigan Press gratefully acknowledges the permission granted by the publishers of the Loeb Classical Library to reprint selected translations from volumes in that series.

Contents

Abbreviations

Note: the abbreviations for journal titles follow those set forth in *L'Année philologique*; citations to ancient authors follow the abbreviations set forth in *The Oxford Latin Dictionary*, ed. P. G. W. Glare (Oxford, 1982), and *A Greek-English Lexicon*, ed. H. G. Liddell, R. Scott, and H. Stuart-Jones (Oxford, 1968). Other abbreviations are as follows:

AC	*Antiquité Classique*
ANRW	*Aufstieg und Niedergang des römischen Welt*
BEFAR	*Bibliothèque des Écoles Françaises d'Athènes et de Rome*
BGU	*Berliner Griechische Urkunde*
BMCRE	*Coins of the Roman Empire in the British Museum*
BMCRR	*Coins of the Roman Republic in the British Museum*
CAH	*Cambridge Ancient History*
CIL	*Corpus Inscriptionum Latinarum*
CRAI	*Comptes Rendus de Séances,* Académie des Inscriptions et Belles-Lettres
CUF	Collection des Universités de France (Budé)
DE	*Dizionario Epigrafico di Antichità Romane*
DHA	*Dialogues d'Histoire Ancienne*
DP	*Le Droit Public Romain*
EFR	*École Française de Rome*
FHG	*Fragmenta Historicorum Graecorum*
FGrH	*Fragmente der griechischen Historiker*
FIRA	*Fontes Iuris Romani Antejustiniani*
FUM	*Forma Urbis Marmorea*
GGM	*Geographi Graeci Minores*
GLM	*Geographi Latini Minores*
GS	*Gesammelte Schriften*
HRR	*Historicorum Romanorum Reliquiae*
IG	*Inscriptiones Graecae*
IGR	*Inscriptiones Graecae ad Res Romanas Pertinentes*
ILLRP	*Inscriptiones Latinae Liberae Rei Publicae*
ILS	*Inscriptiones Latinae Selectae*
KS	*Kleine Schriften*
MDAI	*Mitteillungen des Deutschen Archaeologischen Instituts*

MEFRA	*Mélanges de l'École Française de Rome*
NS	*Notizie degli Scavi di Antichità*
OGI	*Orientis Graeci Inscriptiones Selectae*
ORF	*Oratorum Romanorum Fragmenta*
PMAAR	*Papers and Monographs of the American Academy at Rome*
QFGG	*Quellen und Forschungen zur alten Geschichte und Geographie*
REL	*Revue des Etudes Latines*
RE	*Real-Encyclopädie der klassischen Altertumswissenschaft*
RRC	*Roman Republican Coinage*
SB	*Sammelbuch Griechischer Urkunden aus Ägypten*
SDHI	*Studia et Documenta Historiae et Iuris*
TLL	*Thesaurus Linguae Latinae*

Map 1. The Italian regions established by Augustus

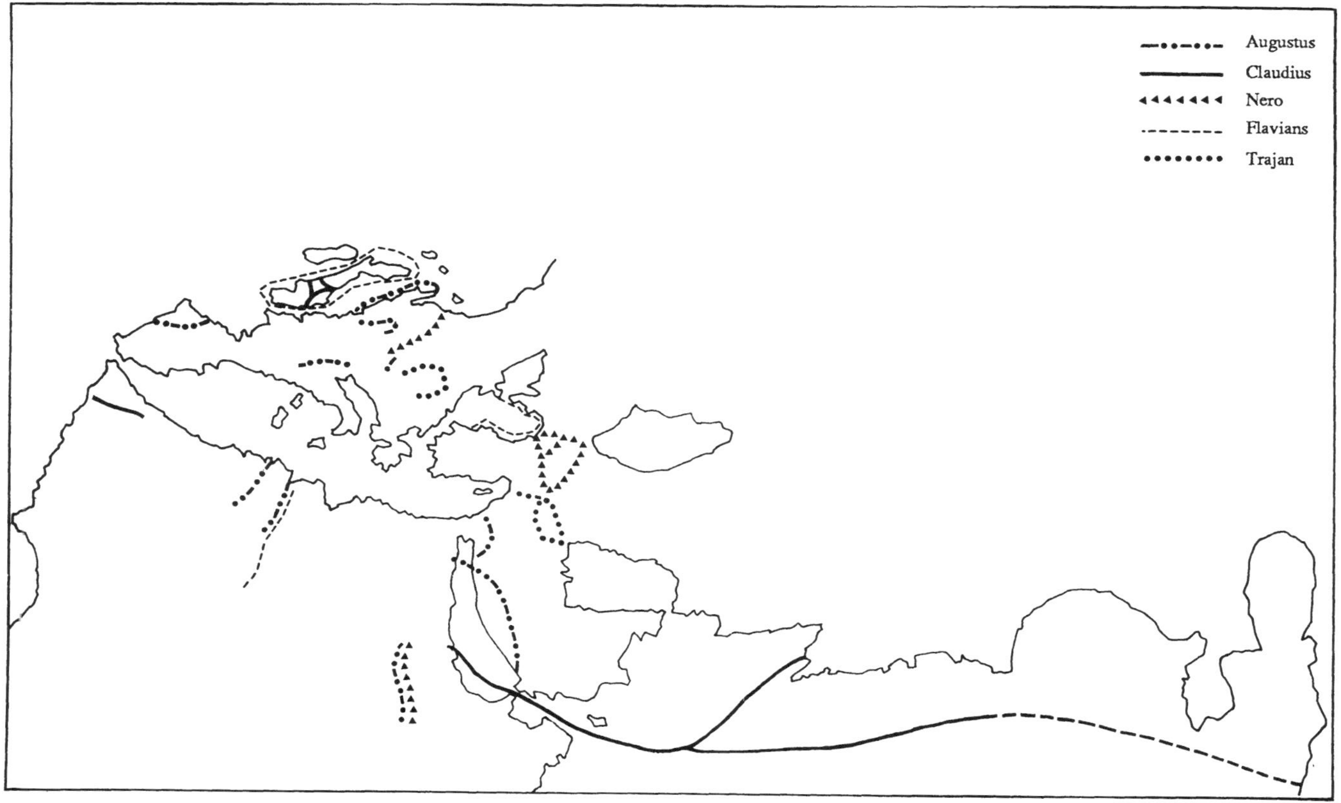

Map 2. Commercial explorations and connections from Augustus to Trajan

Introduction: The History of Geography, and Politics and Geography

The topic of this book is a historical reflection on space. As we know, Rome had an empire before becoming an empire. Of all the ancient cities (Athens, Sparta, Carthage, or Syracuse) it succeeded in conquering and preserving for at least two centuries vast territories dispersed over a wide area. Such expansion was felt by contemporaries to be inevitable and without bounds. After two centuries the republican structure of the Roman State, apparently incapable of adapting to this new territorial scale, collapsed in the turmoil of civil wars. The City became a monarchy: an emperor governed at Rome. It was what is known as the Roman "empire."

This book attempts to answer two very simple questions concerning this transition, crucial to the history of the world. First, why did the Roman conquest seem to come to a standstill at precisely the time when this transition took place with the reign of the first "emperor"? Augustus—rightly or wrongly—is not perceived as one of the conquerors who helped the empire make spectacular advancements (like Pompey or Caesar, and later Trajan). On the contrary, he is credited with a foreign policy that was one of caution, if not of inertia, as the historian Florus would later state. If this interpretation is correct, how can we explain this interruption?

The second question is different yet linked to the first. What happened on the political level, with the passing of the "free Republic" to the empire (which should be better termed the Principate), is evident. In spite of the caution and secrecy of its founder, of the ambiguity of the new political formulas, and of the ostentatious claim to restore the ancient institutions, it is a new monarchy—in great part hereditary—that is established. It is described as such by its Greek subjects who, unlike the Romans, did not have the same reasons to fear the word and its reality.

But if things are almost clear on the political plan, they are less so as regards the true nature of the new power in its contacts with citizens and subjects. In other words, has this empire, which expanded over a large distance (from a core which still functions in great part as a city), become—or is it becoming—a territorial state? Has it developed traits that are characteristic of this particular form of collective organization? Has it developed a territorial continuity in which the different parts of the state are entwined, from the center to the periphery, in a series of administrative districts where space is as important as men; a centralized and personalized power; a large and professional administration operating according to precise rules within the ranks of a well-defined hierarchy, in short, in a "bureaucratic" way; a single standing army and a unified and permanent fiscal system based on a coherent monetary system?

These two questions are in fact complementary and cannot be answered without showing a common denominator. Both are ways of considering the same reality: space. In order to set boundaries to their empire and to claim to have reached those that were marked out, the Romans needed a certain perception of geographical space, of its dimensions and of the area they occupied. Yet this space was forced upon them to the extent that they had to become or remain its master, to dominate its overwhelming distances, to recognize and exploit its resources, to gather information and convey orders from one end of the empire to the other, to assemble troops or have them patrol this space. The ineluctable necessities of conquest and government are to understand (or to believe that one understands) the physical space that one occupies or that one hopes to dominate, to overcome the obstacle of distance and to establish regular contact with the peoples and their territories (by enumerating the former and by measuring the dimensions, the surfaces and the capacities of the latter).

The objective is to know how the Romans, at a turning point in their history, became aware of this and adapted. With the notion of space as the central object, this book uses two corresponding approaches: a historical retrospect of the geography of the Romans and a history of the administrative use of geographical space. Who can deny that these two approaches have several points in common?

In fact, the history of geography is not synonymous with historical geography.[1] The latter aims at showing the geographical realities of a given space as they were at a given time: vegetation, clearings, cultivation, communication roads (in use or newly laid out), land possession, population, habitat, settlements, and boundaries (ethnic, political, or administrative). In short, it is a retrospective geography[2] that tends to recreate, on the same territory, the different phases of the imprint left by the peoples, not unlike pages or photographs that are superimposed and are to some extent erased. These changes from a historical geography are reproduced based on the actual terrain as projected by our knowledge; this is quite necessary, since what we wish to measure by comparison are the objective changes made with time.

This is neither the aim nor the approach of a *history of geography.* What interested me is not so much the spatial and territorial reality of the Roman Empire at its foundation, but the awareness of it possessed by the main players: the Romans and their adversaries, the ruling classes and the subjects. In a study such as this, geography should not be understood as a reality but as a representation of that reality. Like all sciences, in any case like history, geography is both the object of a study and the study itself, in its approaches and its results.

I mean "representation" of the earth and of the geographical space in the full sense of the word. Since it concerns geography, this representation offers the proper traits to the various processes of knowledge (intuitive or deductive, mythical or rational, practical or theoretical). It is transmitted by words, by *logos,* by discourse, by a speech given from the rostrum or read in the quiet of a reading room.[3] Like all sciences, it moves cumulatively: all sorts of progress, some empirical and others theoretical, slowly create a body of knowledge more or less imperfect and more or less accepted by society. But concerning geography, the frontier between the *known* and the *unknown* is first of all traced on a territory, in a space: the world is still a partly unexplored piece of land. Whence the fundamental notions, according to the concepts of that time, of the known and unknown world, of the inhabited or inhabitable earth. Geography—knowledge and representation of the earth—is still at the stage of voyages and discoveries: "inaccessible" spaces still remain. As for what is known, or rather surveyed, the first stage of understanding passes through different *descriptive* methods: such and such a thing in such and such a location, before or after such and such a thing—which is little else than an imaginary voyage.

At the same time the advancement of mathematics and science led another geography, based on astronomy and geometry, to remarkable results: to the identification of the world as a sphere (the globe), situated at the center of the celestial sphere and on which were projected "noteworthy circles and points": the poles, the equator and the tropics. In the third century B.C. it was even possible to measure the length of that sphere with stunning precision and to locate the "known world" with adequate exactitude, owing to some systems of projection of which the most perfected, those of Ptolemy (conform conical projections), are still in use. Hence a scholarly—and even theoretical—geography evolved that was able to trace the general frame of the planet that explorations, commercial links, astronomical and gnomonic observations, and measurements by geometers or military engineers would allow to be perfected, within the limits of the existing techniques.

This geography (representation through discourse, description, an account of a voyage, or an itinerary and geometric conceptualization) also comes with a cartography, or rather, it is cartography. In antiquity the same words specify *discourse* and *drawings*. Drawing and writing are complementary processes. The vocabulary of ancient geographers is a language similar to that of modern geographers.[4] It uses words, signs and pictures, symbols, and even colors. The distinction lies with two types of geography and cartography (a usage that lasted until the seventeenth century) that are differentiated essentially by scale. "Geography" traces the contours of continents and shores, on a small scale, and places regions or provinces—in a system of projection—by giving them form and dimension. "Chorography" is regional geography and cartography, on a larger scale and with far more details. Since the word also signifies (and definite proof of this does exist) the art of the geometers (military and civilian), we pass from regional chorography to "topography," which illustrates, and marks within a plan *(forma)*, the cadastre of a city or of a town.[5] It involves—from the planisphere to the cadastral survey—a series of representations that have a common geometric base, an assessment, and, supposedly, an exact representation of the surfaces. In brief, it is a source of reference that includes the areas by a gradual and uninterrupted series of transmissions, in the whole world and even in the cosmos.

Geometry and astronomy are equally indispensable to the geographer and to the geometer, as confirmed by the unanimous classical tradition from Polybius and Varro to Cassiodorus and Boethius. But other methods of seeing the world and comprehending space were also open to representation. Travel (by land or by sea), whose practical importance is evident, can also be expressed graphically. The route becomes a linear network with distances and intersections carefully noted in one dimension. Intercalary distances, like correct orientation, are less important than the actual mileage or the noting of ports, stopovers, lodgings, granaries, or other noteworthy spots. Whence the "painted itineraries," of which the Peutinger Table provides the most striking example. Certainly it is a way of understanding and representing space that follows *schemata* other than a map or a plan, but it is not incompatible and can be used jointly.[6]

Yet all these representations, soundly empirical or audaciously theoretical, depended upon the physical possibilities and techniques of men of that time. They were aware that these representations entailed considerable unknown territory and consequent error. It involved the inventory of a domain (the inhabited or habitable world), which had to be accomplished by continuous advancement. Worse yet, at the edge of the unknown, mythical thought prevailed over rational thought, although it was less marked than in other periods. After all, the realities of the cosmos (the heavens, the sun, the earth, and the ocean) were divine beings for the ancients. The scientific representation of the two concentric and identical spheres (the terrestrial in the center of the celestial) did not prevent the majority of people from feeling strongly about sensory illusions, to take metaphors more literally than we think: *"le soleil se couche à l'ouest, dans l'océan."* Whence the sacred nature of the mystery and, by a series of predictable shifts, the prestige attached to the survey or to the conquest of certain zones—in particular, the confines of the known world (represented as an island surrounded by the sea) towards its oceanic shores.

Since Alexander, the conquerors (candidates for the universal empire) dreamed (or pretended to dream) of retracing the steps of the gods or the demigods, e.g., Dionysos or Hercules. These pretensions rested on a number of evaluative errors, largely an underestimation of what is called the ancient world in its septentrional, meridional, and oriental regions. Therefore, to understand them or to affix certain otherwise inexplicable facts to them, we must make an effort to forget *our* vision, exact and *irrevocable,* of the physical world in order to attempt to reconstruct, recreate, and relive that of the ancients. That is to say that the history of geography, indispensable to us, would be that of errors of ancient geography rather than of its successes, since these have produced the most surprising affirmations or undertakings, as Roger Dion has so well demonstrated.[7] We must follow in his footsteps—seeing things in greater detail—if we wish to understand where Augustus wished to go and why he held himself back.

The history of Roman geography in the Augustan period that I would like to undertake is fundamentally a political history. Politics and geography were linked from the beginnings of this science. I do not mean geopolitics as understood by F. Ratzel and his emulators[8]—that is to say politics supposedly drawn from geography, from a geographic reality, unchanging and conclusive. On the contrary, I mean geography as science and representation, and the links are those that, far from setting a determinism with a single meaning between a "fact" of nature and the politics of states, have a double meaning between the will of an authority and the certainties, the errors or the illusions of a representation of the world.[9] These ambiguous bounds between "geography" (geographic science) and politics are evident if the graphic translation of geography is considered, that is, cartography.

The first maps in Western history appeared during the Persian Wars as visualizations of the distances that were destined to mark, or to mask, the balance of power. Even with reproduction made easy by engraving and printing, the map will preserve the rare and prestigious trait of a work of art used not only by the authorities but by sciences or pedagogy. It can easily be utilized as a monumental display in which the decorative effect is combined with ideological meaning, stressing the will to know, to conquer, to exploit or to convert: Renaissance Italy has left stunning testimony. As early as the fourteenth century, but especially in the fifteenth and sixteenth, the public authorities (commercial and imperial cities such as Venice and Florence, as well as independent princes and popes) wished to use and to display the geographic knowledge of their times[10] in the decorative form of painted maps within spectacular iconographic groups. Of this numerous collection some have disappeared, including the most ancient ones, at the ducal palace of Venice, at the Palazzo Pubblico at Sienna, and the Map of the World of the San Marco Palace at Rome for Paul II. But four magnificent and striking groups of the same period survive. First, there are the maps decorating the panels on the safes built in the *Guardaroba* of the Palazzo Vecchio at Florence, which was destined to preserve the collections of Cosimo de Medici. These panels derive in great part from the renowned scholar, cosmographer, and cartographer Egnazio Danti, who painted thirty of the fifty-two panels that to a certain extent form the earliest atlas.[11]

Then there are the geographic paintings of the Terza Loggia Gallery at the Vatican, which consist of a monumental map of the world (in two hemispheres) and two series of maps: one of the Old World, the other of regions recognized recently as the Turkish Empire, Japan, the Far East, and America. These paintings were sponsored by Pius IV (1559–61) and his successors and were carried out in part by the painter Antonio Vanosino of Varese and the cartographer Etienne du Pérac, who made use of contemporary maps.

Then—still in chronological order (ca. 1574) but in a different style—there is the extraordinary decoration found in the so-called room of the *Mappemonde* in the Palazzo Farnese of Caprarola.[12] In this aerie, built by Vignole into a Renaissance palace for Alexander Farnese, the decoration is entirely designed to exalt wisdom and science. After Philosophy and History, Cosmography follows in a series of panels surrounded by a mannerist decoration in which the image of the world alternates with sacred and profane geography, finally enlarged from the Ptolemaic system to its correct bounds because of the explorations of discoverers such as Vespucci and Magellan. These paintings, like those of the Terza Loggia at the Vatican, are also the work of Antonio Vanosino of Varese.

Finally, in 1580–81, the famous *Gallery of Maps* in the *Belvedere* at the

Vatican was sponsored by Gregory XIII. On a span of 120 meters, there are approximately forty panels distributed over the two walls and consecrated to Italy, *regionum orbis princeps.* Signed by E. Danti, who also provided an explanation in the accompanying texts,[13] the global map and the regional maps alternate with plans of battles or cities (among which there is a very beautiful plan of Rome revised or finished in 1631). In these works it is difficult to determine what is most admirable: the exactitude of the cartography (allowing for the knowledge of the times), the decorative beauty of the colors and the details, or the symbolical, pedagogical, and monumental character of these groups that express, in their own way, the enthusiasm for knowledge and discovery as well as the ecumenical pretensions of the papacy.[14]

Other examples of the functional association of science, art, and politics can be given. A century later the famous terrestrial and celestial globes, so-called de Marly, given by Cardinal d'Estrées to Louis XIV, were dedicated by their author Father Coronelli *à l'Auguste Majesté de Louis le Grand.*[15] Their author was certainly a professional cartographer from Venice, and he depicted no state secret. But the dedication, written by F. Charpentier, a member of the Academy, is revealing: the globe will be the symbol of power over a world *où mille grandes choses ont été exécutées et par luy-même (le Roy) et par ses ordres, à l'étonnement de tant de nations qu'il aurait pu soumettre à son empire si sa modération n'eust arresté le cours de ses conquêtes.* It must also be noted that the celestial globe was destined to glorify the king. It represented the state of the heavens *au moment de la naissance de ce glorieux monarque* and is nothing but *la figure en relief de la nativité du prince.* So the map, displayed in the palaces of the commercial cities and in those of sovereign princes or popes, is of a public nature.

In the period examined, the same association of politics and geography is striking. The first global map of the known world publicly displayed in Rome was initiated by Agrippa (the *Princeps*'s son-in-law and co-regent of the empire) and completed, after Agrippa's death, by Augustus himself. It was not the first map that the Romans had seen on the walls of their temples or on panels paraded during the triumphs. But it was the most complete (a map "of the world"), the most spectacular, and certainly the most exact for its day: Agrippa had traced it from numerous measurements taken on location, some of the results of which have come down to us. The study of its origins, conception, realization, and lineage (studied for more than a century by specialists) was already in itself a fascinating project. But it became evident to me that Agrippa's map was a special moment in an evolution that characterized the "crisis" of the empire; it was an element that needed to be combined with others in order to understand this obsession with space that was revealed by the successive phases of Augustus's politics.

First, it needed to be combined with the evidence of historians and the geographers of the period. It is not a coincidence that the most complete geographic work handed down from antiquity, that of Strabo, is from the Augustan period. Written by a historian and scholar, the work is a genuine survey of all the traditions of geographic writings. It is essentially from Strabo that we have knowledge of most of his predecessors: Eratosthenes, Hipparchus, Artemidorus, or Posidonius. At the same time it provides valuable information on the composition of the different types of maps, and good examples of the description of regions and peoples by way of narrative, accounts of voyages, or of itineraries. More striking yet, it gives a global vision of the world (and even the concurrent hypotheses in use) and the place the Romans assigned to themselves. This geography, by an Asian Greek who was in favor at Rome, is proclaimed openly as a "political geography" written mainly for the use of the ruling groups and destined to give an account of the state of the world (considered as satisfactory) at the beginning of Tiberius's reign: opened, on the one hand, by recent and direct commercial links with India, closed, on the other, by the *pax romana.*

With the objectives of my inquiry thus defined, the approach was obvious. A history of geography implies reading, or rereading, geographic sources: Greek and Latin geographers, whether preserved well or poorly, whether major or minor. The approach can only be philological. Fortunately, German science had paved the way in the nineteenth century, but not everything has been said. A continuous edition, translation, or commentary on most of the chapters of Strabo, Pliny, and Ptolemy is sorely needed. But if one seeks to study the connection between politics and geography, acknowledged or not, one must query all the sources. It is a well-known fact that poetry of varied kinds uses evocative names, myths, propaganda, or famous achievements. There is, therefore, a geography of Virgil, of Horace, and of Ovid. Indeed nearly all literature is open to a geographic reading, particularly history. The history of Rome, that of the conquest of a world empire, can be written in the linear style of an annalistic narrative. Yet it can also be written according to a rhythm linked to geographic space: first, the expansion of Rome connected to defensive or offensive wars more and more distant, describing a sort of spatial and temporal spiral reaching the real or symbolic limits of the world; then, as a direct consequence of this extension, the civil wars and finally the establishment of unity with Augustus's victory accompanied immediately by a resumption of the conquest ending temporarily under Augustus and Tiberius, followed by Trajan's renewal of the offensive. Such is the ternary rhythm of the history of Rome for the historians of the second century A.D., Florus and Appian. Yet for the attentive reader this new way of seeing and of writing is already evident among Augustus's contemporaries, Livy in his last books, the geographer Strabo, and the historian Velleius Paterculus. Therefore, in this period geography begins to *influence* history.[16]

A significant point will demonstrate this. The importance of different maps in the geographic representation of the period has already been shown. This is not a new notion, since the role played by geographers in Alexander's circle is commonly recognized. But Velleius, in a striking yet curious passage,[17] proves indirectly that Roman staff officers in A.D. 6 while preparing their great offensive against Maroboduus, king of the Marcomanni (who occupied Bohemia), were using maps oriented northwards that indicated the distances from the boundaries of Italy.

These sources have to be seen in a new light. But there is more: Augustus's posthumous work, the "account of his achievements" or *Res Gestae,* the solemn text over which he had pondered for many years and which was published and posted near his Mausoleum after his death, can be considered at least in its second half as a genuine geographic survey. The names of areas and peoples, locations, and the indications of distance punctuate the *princeps*'s catalog of his conquests (or of his conquests' moderation) in such a way that its pedagogical and political insistence is striking. The text appears almost as a commentary to a map and to require the guidance of a drawing. That drawing, Agrippa's map, was not far off: the portico where it was displayed was a few hundred meters from the Mausoleum. It was also not far from the imperial forum, inaugurated in 2 B.C., whose famous decoration (statues of founding heroes, of great men of the Roman homeland with their *elogia* and, as I believe, of representations of the provinces and of non-Roman peoples) contributed to the glorification of Rome and the emperor. This was done in the double register of history and geography according to a rhythm and plan that inspired, at the other end of the empire, the extraordinary *Sebasteion* of Aphrodisias, which has recently been rediscovered. To comprehend the importance of geography for the mentality and the ideology of this period, it is important not only to reread and to scrutinize maps, authors, and official texts, but also iconographical and architectural works—in short, archaeology.

Is it possible to discern an administrative geography of the empire at its foundation?[18] Curiously enough, this second question has practically never been approached in a manner that interests me. Roman administration has been dealt with extensively. As to its history (following Mommsen, Hirschfeld, or Pflaum), the preoccupation was with personnel and its recruitment rather than its function and activities. Epigraphical and papyrological sources directed scholars in their research. This led to a minute and indispensable understanding of organization and the *cursus honorum*. In addition, scholars have identified the different provinces of the empire and studied their towns, roads, and military or nonmilitary settlements—but always according to modern maps.

Yet this history of administration has had little interest in the real administrative workings of so vast a territorial empire; that is, how the contacts between the adminstrators and the administered were organized and handled; how information necessary for decision making was gathered and circulated, and how commands or instructions reached their destination. It is not a matter of considering the judicial basis or content of administrative acts, nor is it a matter of competence or hierarchies. It is necessary to question concrete procedures inasmuch as they fit into space and time.

As it applies to people (i.e., transportation by land or by sea, and communication), this study is related to the history of techniques; its basic points were stated at the beginning of this century in an excellent book by W. Riepl.[19] The history of administrative documents, when considered precisely with its links to space and time, is of more interest. The contents, and even diplomatic aspects, of the few extant administrative documents have for a long time been scrutinized by historians and jurists. Their archival relevance has been more neglected. How were they distributed, how were they classified, how many copies existed and where? These questions are crucial to the problems of the territorial organization that interest me.

The functioning of the ancient city rested ultimately on the physical presence of citizens in a privileged nucleus within the confines of civic space. Even when the census, the vote, or the military levy required the assistance of written procedures, these were reduced to a minimum since the displacement and the presence of people had preceded them.

The fundamental classifications of a city are personal and not territorial, and this arrangement cannot endure when the territory is too large. Even if the civic link is felt as strongly as before, it will be expressed and organized in a different manner. Therein lies the new importance given to the written word. People and their possessions, as statistics, will be *represented* by documents whose originals or copies will travel back and forth between the center and the periphery. Once listed, classified, and stored, these documents will constitute, at the center of power, an administrative memory and picture of the world that will correspond more or less to those geographic images that we have studied.[20] It is natural for the census of populations and the inventory of landed properties to insert themselves into the measurement and representation of space about which the government had taken the initiative, and which it used for its glory and justification. But here again there are emblematic synchronisms. It is not a coincidence, I am convinced, that this new organization (a topographic organization of the "territories," until then very ambiguous, of the City and of Italy: the fourteen urban and eleven Italian regions) appears precisely in the reign of Augustus. I have studied its emergence in relation to the centralization and the classification of archives.

The outline of this work is as follows. Two chapters consider the ecumenical and ostentatious claims of the founder of the empire in his posthumous *Res Gestae,* by restoring them to the cosmocratic tradition of the Roman *triumphatores.* The next two chapters deal with the state of geographic knowledge (and of errors) in the Augustan period and the increase in spatial reports (explorations, surveys by land and by sea, and cartographic accounts) of the Roman Empire at its peak. The fifth chapter studies the main achievement in which mythical, scientific, and political elements converged: the famous map of Agrippa. Two other chapters focus on the techniques and attempts at controlling space (e.g., the census of people and the cadastres of land). The eighth chapter considers the (false) problem of the "geographic work" of Augustus, and finally, the last chapter attempts to explain the modifications of the administrative landscape and the reason for the introduction of the urban and Italian regions.

An inquiry such as this at least has the advantage of forcing the historian to venture onto the less familiar grounds of related disciplines: geography in its spatial realities and methods, and also in its history. In short, I borrowed a considerable amount of information from specialists who have helped me with their science and their advice, and of whom I can thank but a small number: Mr. Philippe Pinchemel, who allowed me the use of the excellent library in the Centre d'épistémologie de la géographie on Mahler Street; Mrs. Monique Pelletier and Mrs. Pastoureau from the Department of Maps and Plans at the Bibliothèque Nationale; Professor G. Kish at the University of Michigan, who introduced me to his university's admirable Clements Library; finally, those renowned experts on the history of ancient geography, Mrs. G. Aujac (who contributed her unpublished critical edition of Ptolemy's texts at the Gustave Glotz Center), and above all, my colleague and friend, Jehan Desanges, to whom I owe numerous and useful comments on the first version of this manuscript (several of which I have quoted with his initials).

Yet cartography touches on the history of art and archaeology; Mrs.

Nathalie de Chaisemartin and Professor Kenan Erim provided many documents or unpublished information on the *Sebasteion* of Aphrodisias; Mrs. Agnès Rouveret with her knowledge of ancient painting and sculpture helped me in my attempts to interpret the Forum of Augustus; Miss Patricia Falguière, a member of the French School at Rome, kindly and competently guided me through the Gallery of Maps at the Vatican and, on a very Stendhalian winter day, through the Farnese Palace of Caprarola. The students in my seminar at the École des Hautes Études gracefully undertook for three years to discuss geography as well as history, and to them I owe many pertinent comments and criticisms. Mr. J.-L. Ferrary, with his usual kindness and wide knowledge, accepted the ungrateful task of revising the manuscript that Mrs. Micheline Courteix, secretary at the Gustave Glotz Center, patiently typed. Finally, I wish to thank Professor John D'Arms and the University of Michigan, for, by honoring me with the invitation to participate in the prestigious Jerome Lectures, they encouraged me to write this book and provided me with the opportunity to sojourn at Ann Arbor and at Rome.

To all I express my gratitude.

Paris, Ann Arbor, Rome
July 1986 to May 1987

NOTES

1. Regarding these distinctions, albeit trivial, cf. for example the remarks made by Ph. Pinchemel, "Réflexions sur l'histoire de la géographie: histoire de la géographie, histoire des géographes," in *Histoire et épistémologie de la géographie, Bull. Com. Trav. hist.*, Sect. de géographie (1979), 221–31; P. Claval, *La pensée géographique* (Paris, 1972), and, for antiquity, the introduction by Fr. Prontera, *Geografia e geografi nel mondo antico* (Bari, 1983), ix–xxxiii.

2. According to the accurate comment by R. Dion, "La géographie humaine rétrospective," the introductory lecture of a course on the historical geography of France at the Collège de France, 1948 in *Littérature gréco-romaine et géographie historique,* ed. R. Chevallier (Paris, 1974), 15–30. The continuity or modifications of land possessions and of exploitation on similar sites appear, for example, in the numerous scholarly researches of Louis Robert on Asia Minor; taking place, if I may add, on a very large scale at the level of the territory of the city (easily spotted and known as early as antiquity). These studies stress the judiciousness of the surveys and of the ancient descriptions rather than their errors. On the scholarly methods of historical geography of Asia Minor, see L. Robert, *Villes d'Asie Mineure*[2] (Paris, 1962), 427–36.

3. It is natural for those who are inclined to study the links between myth and history to have been tempted by the links between image and geographical reality: for example, the studies of M. Détienne and Christian Jacob. Cf. C. Jacob, "La mimèsis géographique en Grèce antique," in *Espace et représentation—Penser l'espace* (Paris, 1982), 53–80.

4. According to the famous distinction made by F. de Dainville, *Le langage des géographes* (Paris, 1964), x–xii.

5. Ibid., 1–3.

6. Cf. the recent and provocative work of P. Janni, *La mappa e il periplo, cartografia antica e spazio odologico* (Rome, 1984). (See my reservations, below, chap. 3, n. 45).

7. I owe much to the works of R. Dion that are devoted to geography in antiquity, particularly in the time of Augustus. See the tribute to R. Dion by R. Chevallier (see n. 2). Since I had the good fortune to buy some books from R. Dion's library (i.e., his editions of Strabo, of Ptolemy, of the *Geographi Graeci Minores,* etc.), I can realize the scope and the meticulousness of his knowledge concerning the authors and ancient history in general. Since the latter is my specialty, I had to (and was able to) make in-depth philological or archeological studies. His *Aspects politiques de la géographie antique* (Paris, 1977), although not as detailed, is not unworthy of a place among the works of the German scholars such as Müllenhoff, Detlefsen, Kubitschek, O. Cuntz, A. Klotz, E. Norden, etc.

8. F. Ratzel, *Anthropogeographie,* 2 vols. (Stuttgart, 1882–91); *Politische Geographie*[3] (Munich, 1903). Cf. the comments made by Cl. Raffestin, *Pour une géographie du pouvoir* (Paris, 1980), 9ff.

9. On the ambiguities of the links between nature and culture, and the dangers of narrowminded determinism, see Clarence J. Glacken, *Traces on the Rhodian Shore* (Berkeley, 1967), in particular 429ff.; on the links between theology, cosmology, cosmography, and geography at the simultaneous rediscovery of Ptolemy's work and the discovery of the New Worlds see W. G. L. Randles, *De la terre plate au globe terrestre, une mutation épistémologique rapide, 1480–1520* (Paris, 1980).

10. See G. Kish, *La carte, image des civilisations* (Paris, 1980), in particular 50ff., plates on pp. 80–81, "La carte, élément décoratif à la Renaissance"; Numa Broc, *La Géographie de la Renaissance* (Paris, 1980), 202, 204ff. But the most complete summary (on wall paintings) is still in the two monumental publications of R. Almagià, *Monumenta Cartografica Vaticana,* vol. 3, *Le pitture murali della Galeria delle carte geografiche* (Rome, Vatican City, 1952), 11ff., Appendix (on the groups from Venice, Sienna, and Rome, which have preceded these and have disappeared); and vol. 4, *Le pitture geogr. murali della Terza Loggia e di altre sale Vaticane* (Rome, Vatican City, 1955). Following the work of R. Thomassy, *Le papes géographes et la cartographie du Vatican* (Paris, 1852), which I have not seen, the tradition was to attribute to Ligorio the responsibility for the maps on the third floor: R. Almagià (p. 27) disproves this hypothesis and also rules out that E. Danti held this same responsibility. The article of M. Besnier, "Les cartes vaticanes. Une vue de

Rome en 1631," *Mél. Arch. Hist.*, 1900, 289–98, is cursory, ill-informed regarding Danti, and deals with only one *tableau.*

11. Regarding Egnazio Danti, see the entry by Almagià in *L'Enciclopedia Italiana,* and J. del Badia, *E. Danti, cosmografo e matematico* (Rome, 1898), *non vidi.*

12. Regarding this group, see the recent publication of M. Praz and I. Faldi, *Il Palazzo Farnese di Caprarola,* SEAT ed. (Rome, 1981); G. Labrot, *Le Palais Farnèse de Caprarola. Essai de lecture* (Paris, 1970); on the geographical paintings, in addition to the first works of Almagià, in *Riv. Geogr. Italiana* (1919), 133–37, (1952), 131–34; cf. G. Kish, "The Mural Atlas of Caprarola," *Imago Mundi,* 1953, 51–56; and R. Amalgià, "Sugli autori delle pitture geografiche del Palazzo Farnese di Caprarola," *Rend. Accad. Lincei*[8] 11, nos. 5–6 (1956): 129–33.

13. Danti explains how this work had been entrusted to him in a letter to the Dutch cartographer Ortellius dated December 24, 1580, as quoted by Besnier and Almagià. A comment on the vocabulary: in the gallery, he writes in Latin: *In conficienda hac Italiae chorographia;* in the letter in Italian: *Mi ha poi condotto in Roma a fare une descrittione d'Italia in une galleria.* Cf. below, p. 172.

14. On the links between theology, cartography, and missionary undertakings, see F. de Dainville, *La géographie des Humanistes* (Paris, 1940), 106ff., 146–49.

15. M. Pelletier, "L'Amérique septentrionale du globe de Louis XIV," in *Imago et mensura Mundi,* Atti del IXo Congr. Intern. di storia della cartografia (Roma, 1987), 393–407; see also his general study in *Imago Mundi* 34, (1982): 72–89.

16. See my comments, "L'Empire romain: espace, temps et politique," *Ktèma* 8 (1983): 163–73, in particular 171.

17. Velleius Paterculus 2.109: "[Marobod] was also to be feared on this account, that, having Germany at the left and in front, Pannonia on the right, and Noricum in the rear of his settlements. . ."; cf. Cl. Jodry, "L'utilisation des documents militaires chez Velleius Paterculus," *REL* (1951): 265–84.

18. From this notion came the idea and the writing of this book, between 1984 and 1986, in accordance with the preliminary works of a thematic action planned by the C.N.R.S. on "La genèse de l'Etat moderne," in which medievalists and modernists in charge were willing to include specialists on antiquity. Whence my two papers from the colloquia in Aix-en-Provence ("L'Empire romain est-il un 'Etat moderne'?") and in Rome ("Centralisation d'Etat et problème du recensement dans le monde gréco-romain,") published in the corresponding *Acta,* and which I expanded upon and completed in this text.

19. W. Riepl, *Das Nachrichtenwesen des Altertums, mit besonder Rücksicht auf die Romer* (Leipzig, 1913).

20. There is no deliberate link, but merely a coincidence, with the undertaking of Pierre Nora, *Les lieux de mémoire,* vol. 2, *La Nation,* 3 vols. (Paris, 1986–87).

I

The *Res Gestae* of Augustus: Announcing the Conquest of the World

When we speak of the "Roman Empire," it is a play on words. Empire—*imperium*—suggests first of all a domination, a hegemony, the outcome of a conquest, or a successful diplomacy. The Romans did have such an empire while still a "free Republic," that is, before they had an emperor.[1] The system known as the empire was never so named in antiquity: its title (unofficially of course) was the Principate.

It is not incorrect to make a semantic link between the territorial and political meanings of empire or between empire and emperor. For the new system, formally and solemnly established by Augustus in 27 B.C., is firmly associated from the beginning with the destiny of the empire, that is, with the domination of Rome.[2] The conquest began well before him. His predecessors—Pompey, then Caesar his father—had extended its boundaries almost to infinity. But at their deaths, Rome still had dangerous rivals or potential adversaries. In the last century B.C., foreign wars had always ended in internal conflicts that culminated in civil wars, in which Rome had almost perished. The *princeps,* founder of the new system, averted all these dangers. First, he completed the conquest by extending it over most of the world: one could not, nor should, go beyond these boundaries. Then he restored peace and harmony to the state. He had, in a sense, founded Rome for a second time. Finally, he had established a new system (*status reipublicae*) that allowed him during the long years of a prosperous principate to complete the conquest and pacification, to organize and to govern that world henceforth enclosed in a harmonious and everlasting way.[3] Thus, his achievement was spatial, temporal, and political. It was considered the accomplishment of a divine will that had assigned to Rome the destiny of conquering, of dominating, but also of pacifying and organizing the whole world: *Tu regere imperio populos, Romane, memento.*[4] Imperial Rome, that is the Rome of the empire (territorial), and Rome of the emperor (who governs), "absorbs in its fate the fate of mankind."

To Augustus we owe the clearest and most striking *expression* of this slowly ecumenical conception of the Roman Empire. This emerges after an attentive reading of the key document he left to posterity: the *Res Gestae.*[5] My aim is not to repeat the exegesis after so many others (in particular Mommsen!), but to recognize that the text, solemn and meaningful, not only recounts the actions of one statesman among many but also describes a geographic and social area that was henceforth fully defined. Thus, for its last stage it was enrolled in that movement that had assigned the conquest and control of the inhabited world to Rome. We must recall the circumstances of its posthumous publication, willed by Augustus and entrusted to Tiberius under the direction of the Senate and the people.[6] It was one of three (Suetonius, *Aug.*, 101) or four (Cassius Dio 56.33.1) documents that Augustus had sealed the year before his death and deposited with the Vestal Virgins. The first contained the directives for his funeral (cf. infra); the second, called *Index rerum gestarum* by Suetonius and *τὰ ἔργα ἃ ἔπραξε πάντα* by Dio, is none other than our text; and the third, the famous *Breviarium totius imperii,* summarized the number and placement of the troops under arms, the state of the treasury (*aerarium* and other coffers), and the accounts of the public revenues. This fundamental document, the earliest of its kind attested, will be discussed later. A fourth document (disputable) may have consisted of advice on foreign and domestic policy given to the Senate and, indirectly, to Tiberius.

The *Index rerum gestarum* was to be engraved on bronze tablets and placed before the Mausoleum.[7] Nothing had been left to chance. Even the site chosen by Augustus for his text—the Mausoleum was begun in 28 B.C.—shows that it was conceived as a part of a monumental and symbolic topography in Rome itself, which he had carefully planned and completed over several years and whose significance was clear to his contemporaries, as is attested by numerous sources. The Mausoleum, in clear imitation of the tomb of Alexander at Alexandria, was designed to fix the life and death of the founding *princeps* permanently at Rome, far from the influence of oriental illusions, and at the same time was intended to reinforce his dynastic scheme. By A.D. 14 at Augustus's death it had been used several times for the princes of his household. But between 13 and 9 B.C. it had indirectly acquired a new meaning. It was integrated as a reference point in a new colossal complex formed by the *Ara Pacis,*[8] erected after the pacification of the West, and by the huge *Horologium* whose *gnomon* consisted of an obelisk brought from Egypt (*Aegypto in potestatem populi Romani redacta*).[9] The *Ara Pacis* was positioned so that it marked the equinoctial line that coincided with the birth of Augustus (September 21 / 23), thereby establishing a direct link between the *princeps*'s birth and world peace.

But the line passing through the axis of the Mausoleum and the obelisk also was at right angles with the one joining the obelisk and the altar. The birth, the death, and the horoscope of Augustus were therefore permanently linked to the topography of the new Rome at the *Campus Martius*. It is clear that a symbolic system (familiar to the ancients) of cosmogony and astrology prevailed throughout the conception of this complex, thanks to the *mathematicus* (astrologer) Facundus Novius (Pliny, *NH* 36.72). The *Pax Augusta,* the conquest of Egypt, the emphasis on Capricorn (Augustus's zodiacal sign) associated on his coins with the globe (symbol of universal domination),[10] and the link with the Mausoleum, all had an obvious cosmocratic significance. The fact that Augustus had wished (and no doubt for a long time) to have the *Index rerum gestarum* located in front of the Mausoleum after his death is an invitation to place this document within the same context. The same request is found in his first sentence: *rerum gestarum divi Augusti, quibus orbem terrarum imperio populi Romano subiecit . . .* (the authenticity of this formula will be discussed below).

Closer scrutiny is required. The *Res Gestae* is not a text with symbolic or astrological inclinations; rather, it is a factual exposé of great sobriety. If it claims the conquest of the world for Rome's advantage under Augustus's influence, it proves it without the slightest reference to symbolic concepts, and without metaphors. On the contrary it uses geographical, historical, and political concepts that were precise and, I would say, indisputable.

The three sections of facts, connected yet distinct, that are recalled by the *Res Gestae* have often been noted:[11] the political activity of the early years and the *honores* (the first fourteen chapters); the expenses (*impensae*) and the generosities (*largitiones*) (chaps. 15–24, and 25–33); the foreign activities, the conquests, and the victories or diplomatic achievements that constitute the explanation and the justification of the initial formula for the conquest of the *orbis terrarum*. Two brief and condensed concluding chapters (34–35) come back to the establishment of the new regime in 27 B.C. and culminate with the bestowal of the title *Pater Patriae* in 2 B.C., which was inscribed on the base of the quadriga of victory (among others) that the Senate dedicated to him in the *Forum Augustum*.

Let us examine in some detail the outline of the important chapters that deal with the subjection (I deliberately use an ambiguous word to translate *subiecit*) of the inhabited world (*orbis terrarum*), using Mommsen's summary:

Chap. 25
5.1–3: Pacification of the sea as a result of the war against Sextus Pompeius.

3–8: Those who took the oath of allegiance to the emperor prior to the war at Actium.

Chap. 26
9–10: The provinces whose boundaries were extended.
10–12: The pacified Gauls, Spains, Germany.
12–14: Submission of the Alpine peoples.
14–18: Naval expedition on the Ocean. Embassies of the Germanic peoples.
18–23: Military expeditions in Ethiopia and in Arabia.

Chap. 27
24: Egypt added to the empire.
24–31: The Armenian affairs.
31–34: The provinces recovered from Mark Antony and Sextus Pompeius.

Chap. 28
35–36: Military colonies established in the provinces.
36–38: Military colonies established in Italy.

Chap. 29
39–43: The recovery of standards taken by the Parthians and other enemies.

Chap. 30
44–49: War waged against the Pannonians and the Dacians.

Chap. 31
50–53: Embassies received by Augustus.

Chap. 32
5.51–6.3: The kings who had taken refuge with Augustus.
6.3–6: The Parthian hostages.
6–8: Other embassies.

Chap. 33
9–12: Kings assigned by Augustus to the Parthians and to the Medians.

The chapters invoke in a logical order the pacification of frontier provinces (such as Gaul or Germany), or strategic provinces (the Alpine regions); the naval explorations in the Northern Ocean and land explorations in Ethiopia and Arabia; the annexations or protectorates carried out in the East; victorious diplomatic relations with traditional enemies like the Parthians, the Pannonians, and the Dacians; the flattering embassies from foreign peoples such as the Indians; and the veterans' colonies sent out to populate the world. In brief these chapters constitute a detailed commentary and a justification of the opening formula. Let us note that they also constitute the last part, almost the ending, of the *Res Gestae,* and that they are followed by the very short chapters 34–35 that provide the famous official definition of the Principate, about which much has been said. The spatial extension of the conquest to the limits of the world is shown as being linked directly to the new order that was established and guaranteed by Augustus.

The final version of the *RG* was completed and finalized some time in A.D. 13 as Augustus repeatedly affirmed. It has been observed that there are traces of revisions and that one or several original versions are of an earlier date.[12] The scarcity of allusions to events later than 2 B.C. is particularly noticeable. There are only a dozen (and perhaps less if, as I believe, the naval expedition of chap. 26.4 should be dated to 9 B.C. rather than to A.D. 4.) And if there are traces of awkward revisions (e.g., that about Germany at 26.2), the silence concerning major events (i.e., Varus's disaster in A.D. 9 or the revolt of Pannonia in A.D. 6)—although explicable—shows that the triumphal account that is given is likely to have been prepared for the fateful year of 2 B.C.: Augustus's sixtieth anniversary, which was astrologically significant.[13] This is the year in which he received the title *Pater Patriae* and in which he dedicated the temple of Mars Ultor, where he inaugurated his Forum—both monuments being full of imperial symbols—and where, in order to prepare the great Eastern mission of Gaius Caesar, he held a *naumachia* recalling the victory of the Greeks over the Persians. Just as the *Res Gestae* is topographically linked to the Mausoleum and to the zone of the *Horologium,* so it is chronologically and politically identified with the martial sphere of the Forum of Augustus. This point should not be overlooked.

Chapters 25–33, clearly dedicated to the subjection of the world, relate to the military and diplomatic themes that were connected to the temple of Mars and to the Forum[14] (such as the title *Pater Patriae,* the site that stored the retrieved Parthians standards, the triumphal atmosphere of the Forum's *elogia* and the deliberations over war and victory linked to the temple). These chapters have a remarkable feature: they are a lesson in political and military geography. This trait has already been noted, but it must be considered in more detail and in its entirety. No doubt such a trait is inherent in the very nature of the text. The *Res Gestae* (a unique monument) recalls several types of documents known from antiquity[15] without identifying itself with them. These documents include the great inscriptions commissioned by Oriental kings to celebrate their conquest and composed, as was the *Res Gestae,* in the first person; the *cursus honorum* listing positions or honors, and the *elogia,* a tradition of Roman dynasties. Augustus himself had composed the *elogia* of the statues of venerable ancestors in his Forum. But also there were the rarely mentioned *tituli,* which might be more elaborate or less, and often were accompanied by allegories, paintings, and even *maps.* As early as the second century B.C., especially in the first, Roman *triumphatores* (Sulla, Pompey, and Caesar) had exhibited these *tituli* during their triumphs and then had dedicated them (cf. below for Pompey). The *Res Gestae* combined all of these but on a scale never achieved before. Its importance lies less in the number of victories or countries listed (Pompey's records according to Pliny were difficult to surpass) than in the global, and geographically significant, character of the facts and names listed.

The document contains no less than fifty-five geographical names divided into four large categories. First come Rome and Italy along with the names of fourteen provinces: Achaia, Aegyptus, Africa, Asia, Cyrenae, Galliae [*sic*], Germania, Hispaniae [*sic*], Illyricum, Macedonia, Narbonensis, Pisidia, Sicilia, and Syria. Secondly, there are the names of countries and peoples: peoples defeated and annexed, peoples subjected, countries to which expeditions or exploratory missions were sent, ancient enemies or peoples with whom Augustus was the first to have contact, distant peoples who sent deferential embassies, and finally peoples who requested or received kings from the Romans. There are twenty-four such peoples or countries: the Adiabeni, Aethiopia, the Albani, Arabia Eudaimon, Armenia, the Bastarnae, the Britanni, the Charydes (or Herudes), the Cimbri, the Daci, the Dalmati, the Germani, the Hiberi, India, the Marcomani, the Medi, the Pannoni, the Parthi, the Sabaei, the Sarmatae, the Scythae, the Semnones, the Suevi, and the Sugambri. Thirdly, there are the names of the four rivers: the Albis, the Danuvius, the Rhenus,and the Tanaïs (the Don); one mountain range, the Alpes; three seas: the Oceanus (the one in the northwest), the Hadrianum mare and the Tuscum mare, and the Oriens; and fourthly the names of towns (or of *oppida*) numbering six: Actium and Ariminum, Gades, Mariba, Meroë, and Nabata.

This collection is itself impressive. The familiarity of the Roman public with the names of these places or peoples should not be underestimated, for it would mean ignoring their use, and even their abuse, in poetry. Roman political speeches were no doubt filled with foreign names. Many of the names and, above all, the names of provinces mentioned by Augustus, had to be relatively familiar to most Romans, although whether they could place them accurately is another matter.

However, the conclusions are slightly different if we study the nomenclature and geography of the other names. Many of these peoples or names are mentioned in Latin for the first time during the Augustan period. Some were already known—at least since Pompey's triumph in 61 B.C. or because of Caesar's *Commentaries.* Such is the case of the *Daci* (Caesar, *BG,* 6.25.2), the *Charudes* (*BG,* 1.30; 37, etc.), the *Sugambri* (*BG,* 6.35; 4.16), the *Suebi* (perhaps known since the 60s; cf. Pliny's anecdote about the Indians of the Northern Ocean at *NH,* 2.170), or the *Marcomani* (*BG,* 1.51, in Ariovistus's army). This is very recent knowledge and science indeed.[16]

In the case of other names, the *Res Gestae* provides the first sure testimony in the Latin language. For example, the *Adiabeni* (*RG,* 32.1: their king is Artaxares) are not mentioned before Pliny (6.25; 28, etc.), unless in Strabo (11.503 C etc.; 16.736). The most obvious example is that of *Arabia quae appellatur Eudaimon,* to use Augustus's own words (26.2). Here again, there is no other mention except in Strabo (16.4. 2, etc.). The use of the Greek word instead of its Latin equivalent, *felix,* proves that the name of that region, familiar to Greek geographers, had not yet been latinized and perhaps was not even known to the Romans.[17] It is found in a later geographical text, the *Divisio orbis terrarum,*[18] which is assumed to derive from Agrippa's work because of its striking textual affinities with the authentic fragments of his *Commentarii.* It is probable that certain names listed by Augustus were unfamiliar or unknown to his contemporaries. From this the conjecture arises that they would have needed the help of illustrations in order to appreciate those names.

There is even more striking evidence to support this hypothesis. The first was noted twenty years ago by R. Dion in some pioneering studies.[19] His work deals with passages on the boundaries of the world, as understood by the geography of the period, that have a prestigious significance for those who, since Alexander, have aspired to universal domination. The first boundary was the Ocean, which surrounds the earth but which Rome was the first to reach and control, towards Gades in the time of the Scipios and then into Gaul and the Rhine at the time of Caesar.[20] According to Polybius and others, Alexander's failure was to die before turning his attention towards this part of the *oikoumene.* Hence the profound meaning and solemn nature of the passage (*RG,* 26.2–4) in which Augustus narrates his successes (hiding the failures) in the regions that Rome, *suo ductu,* was the first to approach: the Gauls, the Spains, and the "oceanic" part of Germany, pacified as far as the Elbe. There is also the naval expedition between 12 and 9 B.C. (cf. below) to the *fines Cimbrorum* (which we know from Pliny to have been the *promontorium Cimbrorum* or Jutland). This northern coast of the *oikoumene,* which the geographers of that period erroneously believed to be shorter and further south, and which they believed some Indi[21] had reached by some easy circumnavigation, was one of the borders of the world, a *terminus.* This explains the reference to the pacification of the Alps, inserted between two allusions to the boundary of the *oikoumene*; from Italy the Alps are the essential passage towards these boundaries. But in the following lines there is another implicit allusion to another boundary, this time to the south: Ethiopia (that is, the African countries south of Egypt) and Arabia (*RG,* 26.5). Finally, the eastern boundaries are also clearly indicated in 31.1, in reference to the embassies of the Indian kings "never seen before with any Roman commander" (*non visae ante id tempus apud quemquam Romanorum ducem*). These passages follow a precise geographical scheme.

But there is more. I have stated that the *Res Gestae* included names of four rivers and six towns or *oppida.* Here again some names appear for the first time in the text: the Albis, the Germanic river beyond the Rhine (which for Strabo still marks the limit of the known world, but this is problematic); the Tanaïs, well known and marking the traditional boundary between Europe and Asia (Mela, 1.8) and the Danuvius. We shall see later that the identification of the upper course of this river (which the Greeks called the Ister in its lower course) and the progress of the conquest to its banks are among Augustus's greatest undertakings and among his most important contributions to the science of geography in his day. But this was far from being familiar to the Roman public: the inaccurate identification of this river would remain long after his time. Some precise geographic indications, textual or visual, would have been necessary for the public to appreciate fully what Augustus meant in his writings.[22]

The fact is even more explicit if Augustus's words in certain key passages are considered in detail, where the topographic precision of his expression would not be understood without such indications: "My fleet sailed through the Ocean eastwards from the mouth of the Rhine to the territory of the Cimbri" (*classis mea per Oceanum ab ostio Rheni ad solis orientis regionem usque ad fines Cimbrorum navigavit . . .* ; 26.4). The point of departure, the direction, and the limit reached would have no meaning for those who could not actually see them: "In Ethiopia we got as far as the city of Nabata, close to which is Meroë; in Arabia, to the confines of the Sabaeans, to the city of

Mariba" (*in Aethiopiam usque ad oppidum Nabata*[23] *perventum est, cui proxima est Meroë; in Arabiam usque in fines Sabaeorum . . . ad oppidum Mariba;* 26.5).

In this case the topographic description is even more visual. This is carried out by the precision of the names of the *oppida* that mark the outer limits reached by Aelius Gallus's military expeditions in Arabia in 25–24 B.C. (Strabo, 16.4.22; Dio, 33.29; Horace, *Carm.*, 1.29.2; Pliny, *NH,* 6.169) and by those of Petronius against Queen Candace in the Sudan in 24–22 B.C. (Strabo, 16.1.54; Dio, 54.5; Pliny, 6.181–82), and finally by the location of the town of Nabata in relation to Meroë. All these names, and especially the latter, were known to the Hellenistic geographers (Pliny, 6.183: Timosthenes, Eratosthenes, Artemidorus), but they were certainly less familiar to the Romans. They could not have been appreciated without some illustration. They must have been mentioned in the reports sent to Augustus by the leaders of expeditions, Aelius Gallus and Petronius, two prefects of Egypt. Since these events were prior to 23 B.C. it is more than likely that Augustus himself had mentioned them in his *Autobiography,* completed around 23 B.C. (Suetonius, *Aug.*, 85.1). But this does not help the understanding of the text of the *Res Gestae*. Most of the rare or specific names mentioned by the emperor are found only in Strabo, Pliny, or later in Ptolemy—that is, in specialized writers (geographers) whose works would not likely be well known to the public for whom Augustus's posthumous text was destined. Is it to be believed that the emperor was resigned to speak in a void, and not to be understood by his public when he employed a rare toponym, or when he described, in a subtly rhetorical manner, the Roman Empire extending over almost the entire region bounded by the northern Ocean ("from Gades to the mouth of the Elbe") or stretching towards the southern portion of the *oikoumene,* to the "Ethiopian" border? Surely not. The *Res Gestae* asserts from the very first line that there was Roman control of the inhabited world (*orbis terrarum*). And it proves this methodically, without symbolism, by using a series of topographic lists that correspond to precise geographical knowledge—knowledge that reflects the science of the times, but that also surpassed the vague beliefs of the common man. Concerning particular points (e.g., the survey of the mouth of the Elbe and the upper Danube, or the penetration as far as Nabata and Mariba), Augustus shows that he is clearly aware of having combined a sponsor's indirect glory in geographic expeditions with military glory. Since Alexander's time this had been the tradition of Hellenistic rulers. Antiochus had sponsored a naval expedition on the Caspian Sea and the Ptolemies had sought routes to India. Like them, Augustus could boast "never before me, never as far." For him, as is clear from the *Res Gestae,* the empire was a world, almost a new world which had been discovered, explored, and mastered. It is within a real geographic context that it came about. And it is within this context that the *princeps* should be recognized and admired by his readers.

NOTES

1. For some useful historiographic summaries see J. Linderski, "*Si vis pacem, para bellum:* Concepts of Defensive Imperialism" in *The Imperialism of Mid-Republican Rome,* ed. W. V. Harris, Papers and Monographs of the American Academy at Rome 30 (Rome, 1984), 133–64; E. Frézouls, "Sur l'historiographie de l'impérialisme romain," *Ktèma* 8 (1983 [1986]): 141–62; E. Badian, *Roman Imperialism in the Late Republic* (Ithaca, 1967). For a good approach in terms of geopolitics see P. Veyne, "Y a-t-il eu un impérialisme romain?" *MEFRA* (1975): 793–855; the best geographical history of the Roman Empire remains Mommsen's volume 5 (Book 6) of his *Histoire romaine,* published in 1885: "Les provinces sous l'Empire," which can be read in a translation (reprint, Paris; 1985), 503–962. For the institutional continuity (pompous and misleading) between the *libera respublica* and the *principate* see Mommsen, *Römisches Staatsrecht* (Leipzig, 1871–87, 2:745ff.); F. De Martino, *Storia della Costituzione Romana,* vol. 4 (Naples, 1974); H. Castritius, *Der romische Prinzipat als Republik* (Husum, 1982); D. Timpe, *Unters. zur Kontinuität des früher Prinzipats,* Historia Einzelschr. 5 (1962); and P. Brunt, "*Lex de imperio Vespasiani,*" *JRS* (1977): 95–116.

2. P. Brunt "*Laus imperii,*" in *Imperialism in the Ancient World,* ed. P. A. Garnsey and C. R. Whittaker (Cambridge, 1978), 159–91.

3. On the notions of "foundation," of "*saeculum,*" see the tremendous bibliography and useful summary in D. Kienast, *Augustus* (Darmstadt, 1982), 67–84; J. Gagé, "*Romulus Augustus,*" *Mél. Arch. Hist.,* 1930, 138–81; A. Magdelain, *Auctoritas Principis* (Paris, 1947), 54ff. (also Suetonius, *Aug.,* 28.3, for the "edict of foundation"); P. Grenade, *Essai sur les Origines du Principat* (Paris, 1961), 100ff.

4. Virgil, *Aen.,* 6. 851.

5. See Mommsen, *Res Gestae Divi Augusti*^{2} (Berlin, 1883); J. Gagé, *Res Gestae Divi Augusti*^{3} (Paris, 1975); H. Volkmann, *Res Gestae Divi Augusti*^{3} (Berlin, 1969); H. Malcovati, *Imper. Caes. Aug. Fragmenta*^{4} (Turin, 1964), LII-LXV; Z. Yavetz, "The *Res Gestae* and Augustus' Public Image," *Caesar Augustus,* ed. F. Millar and E. Segal (Oxford, 1984), 1–36.

6. Regarding Augustus's testamentary documents see E. Hohl, "Zu den Testamenten des Augustus," *Klio,* 1937, 323–42; J. Ober, "Tiberius and the Political Testament of Augustus," *Historia,* 1982, 306–28; H. Schmitt, "Tacitus und die nachgelassenen Schriften des Augustus," *Mél. H. Bengtson,* Historia Einzelschr. 40 (1983): 178–86; for the testament itself (the largesses to be distributed) see C. Nicolet, "Plèbe et tribus: les statues de Lucius Antonius et le testament d'Auguste,"

MEFRA, 1985, 799–839. Regarding the "advice" see Tacitus, *Ann.*, 1.11: *quae cuncta sua manu perscripserat Augustus, addideratque consilium coercendi intra terminos imperii, incertum metu an per invidiam; Agr.*, 13.3: *ac longa oblivio Britanniae etiam in pace: consilium id divus Augustus vocabat, Tiberius praeceptum.* Ober ("The Political Testament of Augustus," 321) considers the fourth *biblion* mentioned by Dio to be a forgery attributed to Tiberius, who would have merely received verbal instructions (that is overlooking Tacitus).

7. The Mausoleum, still visible at the west of the Corso, is striking for its size and for its name; Augustus, at the age of thirty-five, chose the site and the appearance of his tomb. His blatant or secret intentions have been scrutinized thoroughly: is it to "imitate" Alexander or to dissociate himself from him? E. Kornemann, *Mausoleum und Tatenbericht des Augustus* (Leipzig, 1921); id., *"Monumentum Ancyranum," RE* 16 (1933): 211–31; M. L. Bernhard, "Topographie d'Alexandrie: le tombeau d'Alexandre et le Mausolée d'Auguste," *Rev. Arch.* 47 (1956): 129–56; R. Ross Holloway, "The Tomb of Augustus and the Princess of Troy," *AJA*, 1966, 171–73 (Trojan origins); K. Kraft, "Der Sinn des Mausoleums des Augustus," *Historia*, 1967, 189–206 (the author, based on Suetonius, *Aug.*, 81 and Dio 53.30.5, showed that the tomb was begun three or four years before any steps toward monarchy were taken, in the anti-Antonian atmosphere previous to Actium); D. Kienast, "Augustus und Alexander," *Gymnasium*, 1969, 430–56; J. C. Richard, "Mausoleum: d'Halicarnasse à Rome, puis à Alexandrie," *Latomus* 29 (1970): 370–88 (who suggested that it was a dynastic tomb as early as 28 B.C. inspired not by Egypt but by the legendary Caria); contra, F. Castagnoli, "Influenze alessandrine nell'urbanistica della Roma augustea," *Riv. Fil. Istr. Class.*, 1981, 414–23.

8. *RG*, 12.2: *cum ex Hispania Galliaque . . . Romam redi, Ti. Nerone P. Quintilio consulibus, aram Pacis Augustae Senatus pro reditu meo consecrandam censuit ad campum Martium;* this altar was decreed on July 4, 13 B.C. (*Fasti Amitern., CIL* 1^2, 244) and dedicated on January 30, 9 B.C. *(Fasti Praen., CIL* 1^2.212; Ovid, *Fasti*, 1.709–10). See Erika Simon, *Ara Pacis* (Tübingen, 1967); E. La Rocca, *Ara Pacis Augustae* (Rome, 1983).

9. Ref. in general Sharon L. Gibbs, *Greek and Roman Sundials* (New Haven, 1976). The use of monumental sundials was not new. Any monumental group could be used: for instance, the whole of the *comitium* during the archaic period (Pliny, *NH*, 7.212). The first public sundials appear at the beginning and in the middle of the third century B.C. (id., 213–15): an example being the one brought back from Catana by M. Valerius Messala in 263 B.C., which could not function at Rome's latitude! Pliny provides the essential text regarding the *horologium* built on the *Campus Martius* by order of Augustus (*NH*, 36.72–73). The obelisk was found on its original site in 1748 but was subsequently moved to the Piazza Montecitorio. It bears the following inscription: (*CIL*, 6.701–2 = *ILS*, 91): *Imp. Caesar Divi / f. Augustus / pontifex maximus / imp. XII. cos. XI. trib. pot. XIV / Aegupto in potestatem / populi Romani redacta / Soli donum dedit.* The dedication to the sun is important: it alludes to Apollo of Actium; it recalls the role of *gnomon* given to

the obelisk and Augustus's birth on the day of the fall equinox (September 23). Since 1976, the studies and the excavations on the site of the *horologium* have shown the accuracy of Pliny's text, which mentions the existence of a drawing to represent the lines and the hours; see E. Buchner, "*Solarium Augusti* und *Ara Pacis*," *Mitt. Deutsch. Arch. Inst. Rom* 87 (1980): 355–73; id., *Die Sonnenuhr des Augustus* (a collection of these articles) (Mainz, 1982), esp. 37 (= *Mitt. Deutsch. Arch. Inst. Rom*, 1976, 347). For the symbolic meaning of this monument: La Rocca, *Ara Pacis*, 55–56. It is meaningful (but not surprising) that Augustus's funeral pyre, located east of the Mausoleum, is also linked with the Altar of Peace and the obelisk that recalls Augustus's birth.

10. Cf. below, chap. 2, n. 31; J.-B. Giard, *Bibliothèque Nationale, Catalogue des Monnaies de l'Empire romain*, I. *Auguste* (Paris, 1976) 203, no. 1403 (12 B.C.).

11. Concerning the composition of the *Res Gestae* see essentially W. Ensslin, "Zu den *Res Gestae Divi Augusti*," *Rhein. Mus.* 81 (1932): 335–65; J. Gagé, *Res Gestae Divi Augusti*, 13–23.

12. Kornemann's theory linking the *Res Gestae* to a text (the first four chapters) dated from 28 B.C. (before the inauguration of the new regime) and to which Augustus would have made successive additions, is no longer accepted. A first draft is in fact attested by the insertion of *cum scribebam haec* in chapter 4. Yet if the given number of consulships (*consul fueram terdeciens*) brings us to 2 B.C. (or later), the number of *tribunicia potestas* (37 = A.D. 14) proves a later revision. The scarcity of evidence for a revision later than 2 B.C. is interesting. The *RG* would not have mentioned bitter defeats such as the *clades Variana* in Germany in A.D. 9; yet the awkward and embarrassed composition of chapter 26.2 has the marking of a clumsy correction: "I have pacified the provinces of the Gauls, the Spains, and Germany, bounded by the ocean from Gades to the mouth of the Elbe" (U. Wilcken, in *Hermes*, 1903, 618 and in *Sitz. Preuss. Akad.*, 1932, 225–46; J. Gagé, *Res Gestae Divi Augusti*, 22, n. 2; but cf. below, chap. 4, n. 18, the different opinion of R. Dion.)

13. R. Syme, "The Crisis of 2 B.C.," *Sitz. Bay. Ak. Wiss.*, 1974, 3–34 (= *Roman Papers*, 3: 912–36, esp. 920–21) (also Seneca, *De brev. vitae*, 4.3); R. Syme, *History in Ovid* (Oxford, 1978), 192ff. Augustus had turned sixty in 3 B.C. (age of "retirement") and might have wanted to avoid the fearful passage of his "climacteric year," the sixty-third (Gellius, 15.7.3) by preparing the Parthian expedition of the eldest of his grandsons.

14. Concerning the temple of Mars, the Forum, and the *naumachia* of 2 B.C., cf., below, chap. 2.

15. J. Gagé, *Res Gestae*, 28ff., 32ff. regarding the "oriental inscriptions" (and the third ed., 216, on the parallel with the *Res Gestae Divi Saporis*, cf. A. Maricq, *Syria*, 1958, 304–31; J. Gagé, *La montée des Sassanides* [Paris, 1964], 281ff.); concerning the Pompeian and Caesarian "precedents" of the *Res Gestae*, see below, chap. 2.

16. This inquiry (which has not been undertaken before to the best of my knowledge) on the most ancient occurrences of some geographical names in Latin must

take into account the loss of a great deal of Latin literature (including geographical works such as Varro's—see below, chap. 3). The study of the names of Germanic and Nordic peoples has been done by German scholars, especially by K. Müllenhoff, *Deutsche Altertumskunde,* vols 1–4[2] (Berlin, 1890–29); and recently N. H. Sitwell, *The World the Romans Knew* (London, 1984), 200; G. Kossack, "The Germans," in *The Roman Empire and its Neighbours,* ed. F. Millar (London, 1967), 294ff. and 351. E. Norden's book on the sources of Tacitus, *Die germanische Urgeschichte in Tacitus' Germania*[2] (Leipzig / Berlin, 1922), is still crucial.

17. The oldest reference to this name is found in Diodorus's famous description 2.49 (2.48 for the whole of Arabia "sheltered from the Romans"): Diodorus wrote in Caesar's time.

18. Concerning this text, see below, chap. 6. It was edited for the first time by E. Schweder in 1876, following the *Vat. Pal.* 1357 and reedited by P. Schnabel, *Phil.* (1935), 432–39; A. Riese, *Geographi Latini Minores* (Heilbronn 1878), frag. 21: *Arabia Eudaemon / flecmea (Phlegmaea i.e., combusta,* Letronne; *Pe⟨tra⟩ea,* Schnabel) *inter duos sinus Arabicum et Persicum itemque extra Arabicum sinum Trogodyt⟨ic⟩e Arabia Aegypto proxima.* For the military expeditions on the Red Sea in the Augustan period (Aelius Gallus and perhaps C. Caesar), see below, chap. 4.

19. R. Dion, "Explication d'un passage des *RGDA,*" in *Mél. Carcopino* (Paris, 1966) 249–69 and, more general, some studies in *Aspects politiques de la géographie antique* (Paris, 1977).

20. In the geopolitics of the times, the symbolism of rivers is linked to their practical use as a ditch and a frontier. The Nile and the Tanaïs have a cosmographic importance: they mark the frontier between Asia and Africa and Europe respectively. The Rhine and the Danube are "ditch rivers"; it is one of Augustus's glories to have pushed the limit of the empire that far : Tacitus, *Ann.,* 1.9: *mari oceano, aut amnibus longinquis saeptum imperium.* Cf. M. Cary, *The Geographical Background of Greek and Roman History* (Oxford, 1949), 274–86; R. Syme, "The Northern Frontier," *CAH* 10 (1934): 361ff.

21. Mela 3.44–45; Pliny, *NH,* 2.170 (following Nepos); J. André, "Des Indiens en Germanie," *Journ. Sav.* 1982, 45–55. Concerning all these points, see below, chap. 4.

22. See also *RG,* 27.3: *provincias omnis, quae trans Hadrianum mare vergunt ad Orientem . . . .*

23. Regarding this city (and its spelling) refer to the Greek text of the *Res Gestae:* Ναβάτη; Pliny, 6.184: Nataba, etc., J. Desanges, *Recherche sur l'activité des Méditerranéens aux confins de l'Afrique* (Rome, 1978), 312ff. For the identification of Mariba see J. G. Anderson, in *CAH* 10 (1934): 877 and, more recently, H. von Wissmann, "Die Geschichte der Sabäerreichs," *ANRW* II, 9, no. 1 (1976): 398. The city was known and mentioned since Eratosthenes (Strabo, 16.4, 768 C) and Artemidorus but here again the *Res Gestae* is the most ancient Latin text.

II

Symbolism and Allegories of the Conquest of the World: Pompey, Caesar, Augustus

The *Res Gestae* affirms and proves the direct or indirect completion of the conquest of the *orbis terrarum* in geographical terms. It is likely that Augustus's text contained, in his introduction, this formula (absent from the Greek translation). In any case, it was implied. Chapter 3 deals with civil and foreign wars fought victoriously "throughout the world" (*toto in orbe terrarum*), chapter 13, with the peace secured by victories "by land and by sea throughout the whole empire of the Roman people" (*per totum imperium populi Romani terra marique*). The collection of geographical data—for those who understood geography—resulted in the same affirmation. This is not surprising, since the literature and art of the period often used this theme. Let us refer to a number of texts and well-known facts, after the examples of H. D. Meyer and of P. Brunt, who improved Meyer's work.[1] Since the 30s B.C. official, or at least semiofficial, poetry claims universal domination as Rome's destiny: e.g., Virgil's "temple" planned at Mantua in Augustus's honor (*Georg.* 3.25–33) recalls, in its decoration, the trophies captured "over both extremities of the world."[2] Jupiter's famous prophecy in Book 1 of the *Aeneid* promises Rome an empire without end (*imperium sine fine;* 1.278), which may be understood in a spatial as well as a temporal sense. "Augustus's eulogy"[3] in Book 6 promises Rome an empire over "the (whole) world" (6.780), and ends with the famous distribution of historical destinies: it is left for some (the Greeks) to understand and to describe the world in scientific terms, but for the Romans to conquer and to govern it.[4] As P. Brunt pointed out (*pace* H. D. Meyer), these proud demands for universal pacification (through domination) were consistent with Augustus's plans and politics, at least until the last few years of his reign—and certainly until the campaign against the Marcomanni in A.D. 6. Horace,[5] although refusing to write an epic poem about this political position, celebrated (or anticipated) this imperial dream[6] in all his work. Ovid's testimony is perhaps the most striking—even if we can detect some provocative irony (as did R. Syme) in *Ars Amatoria,* 1.174 (in the irreverent prophecy of a future Parthian triumph) but not in the *Fasti,* 2.130; 683.[7] Despite his bitter preface, Livy asserts (1.16.7) that someday Rome's destiny was to be the head of the world (*caput orbis terrarum*). In short, the Augustan peace, as P. Brunt demonstrated, is one of conquest and not of renunciation. The desire to reach the ends of the world—to Britain, across the Rhine, to the East—and to confirm Rome's direct domination or supremacy, was no mere assertion.

Yet Augustus's solemn and introductory assertion, so abrupt, is paradoxical for at least two reasons. First, despite its peremptory character, it is far from being new. In spite of Augustus's claims, the notion of Rome's universal domination had been expressed—albeit unofficially—by historians or orators some two centuries earlier.[8] In ca. 160–150 Polybius[9] asked in his preface how Rome had been able to subjugate (ἐπικρατηθέντα) nearly the whole inhabited world (σχεδὸν ἅπαντα τὰ κατὰ τὴν οἰκουμένην) under one rule (1.1.5). Polybius explained this clearly: unlike the other great hegemonies of the past comparable to it (Persia, Sparta, Macedonia), the Roman Empire succeeded in expanding over all parts of the inhabited world, in Europe as well as in Asia and Africa, in the East as well as in the West. Rome demonstrated her superiority (over Alexander) by her successes in the West over "peoples who were not even known" to the Macedonians: "they subjugated almost the whole inhabited world" (σχεδὸν δὲ πᾶσαν πεποιημένοι τὴν οἰκουμένην ὑπήκοον αὑτοῖς).

Thus this is universal domination, or close to it, for in regions not truly under its domination, there is no power that can seriously oppose it. This idea is even more plainly asserted at the beginning of Book 3 ("all the known parts of the inhabited world have come under the δυναστεία of Rome"), and again elsewhere (15.9.5; 6.50.6).[10] So, in Polybius, domination does not involve a ready-made expression without geographical meaning: Polybius had extensive geographical knowledge (he is one of the geographers referred to and criticized by Strabo), and he devoted several important digressions and an entire book (34[11]) to geographical questions, namely, to the different kinds of geography—astronomy and mathematics, general or specific, and descriptive. As concerns this study, he clearly established (3.59) a link between the Roman conquest and the improvements in geographical knowledge that this conquest made possible—particularly in the West, through surveys and exploratory expeditions not unlike the one he undertook in Africa for Scipio (Pliny, *NH,* 5.9). It is clear that Polybius—who was aware of the eastern dimensions ascribed to the *oikoumene* by Eratosthenes (Strabo, 14.2.29, 663 C)—cannot mean that the Romans dominated the entire area of the *oikoumene,* but rather that they were present in each of its parts and—at this date—had no serious rivals. Although based upon geography, Polybius's assertion is therefore essentially political.

Had this been stated before him? The comment that Livy attributes to Ti. Gracchus after the trial of the Scipios may not be authentic: "[L. Scipio] had spread the domination of the Roman people to the extreme confines of the earth" ([*L. Scipio*] *imperium populi Romani propagaverit in ultimos terrarum fines;* 38.60.5). It certainly represents an audacious exaggeration:[12] Rome "has (only) conquered the wealthiest king in the world."

However, it seems that the expression "masters of the *oikoumene*" (*κύριοι τῆς οἰκουμένης*), referring to the Romans, was already in use as early as 133 B.C., since Plutarch puts it in the closing remarks of a famous speech by Tiberius Gracchus that is considered authentic.[13] It is possible that the Romans of this period had actually used this kind of expression. Q. Fabius Maximus may have done so in his funerary *laudatio* for Scipio Aemilius: "it is quite natural that there, where he had lived, had been the center of the domination of the world" (*necesse enim fuisse ibi esse terrarum imperium ubi ille esset*),[14] but this would then be the only example found in the second century.

One must resist the temptation of placing in this period the mysterious Aemilius Sura,[15] historian (?) and author of *De annis populi Romani,* known only from a gloss at the end of Velleius, 1.6.6 that was first noted on the Aldine edition of 1591. Sura proposed the theory of the "four empires" (*rerum potiti*) (three of which were Eastern) that preceded Rome: Assyria, Media, Persia, and Macedonia. He also placed Rome's supremacy (*summa imperii*) after the subjugation of Carthage.[16] But it does not follow from this that Sura was writing around 190 B.C.! In fact, it was much later that the Romans concerned themselves with these eastern chronologies. Indeed, it was towards the beginning of the first century B.C. that the slogan based on the expression *orbis terrarum* (*orbis* by itself dates from the Augustan period) appeared in Roman political terminology, although it did not yet appear in official documents (cf. below p. 34).[17] If the speech[18] quoted in the *Rhet. ad Her.*, 4.13 is authentic, it must date to the time of the Social War (ca. 90 B.C.), and it pompously defines Roman power as "the empire of the world, the empire to which all nations, all kings, all peoples have consented" (*imperium orbis terrarum, cui imperio omnes gentes reges nationes . . . consenserunt*). But as early as 81 B.C. Cicero can say about Sulla: *cum . . . orbemque terrarum gubernaret* (*Sex. Roscio*, 131). But of course it was primarily during Pompey's time and especially after his triple triumph in 61 B.C. that the expression and the idea came into popular usage—this is well known.[19] Pompey had not failed to promote the idea himself. First it is seen on an inscription (ἀντίγραφον) that was perhaps dedicated in the temple of Venus on the day of his triumph, and that recalled his πράξεις (or *res gestae*) in the East since his campaign against the pirates. It must be quoted in its entirety since it seems to be one of the most typical precedents for the *Res Gestae* of Augustus (Diodorus, 40.4 = *Const. Exc.*, pp. 405–6):

> Pompey had inscribed on a tablet, which he set up as a dedication, the record of his achievements in Asia. Here is a copy of the inscription: "Pompey the Great, son of Gnaeus, Imperator, having liberated the seacoast of the inhabited world and all islands this side [of the] Ocean from the war with the pirates—being likewise the man who delivered from siege the kingdom of Ariobarzanes, conquered Galatia and the lands and provinces lying beyond it, Asia, and Bithynia; who gave protection to Paphlagonia and Pontus, Armenia and Achaia, as well as Iberia, Colchis, Mesopotamia, Sophenê, and Gordyenê; brought into subjection Darius king of the Medes, Artoles king of the Iberians, Aristobulus king of the Jews, Aretas king of the Nabataean Arabs, Syria bordering on Cilicia, Judaea, Arabia, the province of Cyrenê, the Achaeans, the Iozygi, the Soani, the Heniochi, and the other tribes along the seacoast between Colchis and the Maeotic Sea, with their kings, nine in number, and all the nations that dwell between the Pontic and the Red Seas; extended the frontiers of the Empire to the limits of the earth; and secured and increased the revenues of the Roman people—he, by confiscation of the statues and the images set up to the gods, as well as other valuables taken from the enemy, has dedicated to the goddess twelve thousand and sixty pieces of gold and three hundred and seven talents of silver."[20]

We see that the *orbis terrarum* (οἰκουμένη) is mentioned twice, the borders of the empire (ἡγεμονία) being confused with those of the *oikoumene*. This text is slightly different from Pliny's versions that on the one hand record the inscription that accompanied Pompey's booty dedicated at the temple of Minerva, and on the other set forth the *praefatio* of his triumph. Both of these are quoted more precisely by Pliny, *NH*, 7.97–8:

> Cnaeus Pompeius Magnus, Imperator, having completed a thirty years' war, routed, scattered, slain or received the surrender of 12,183,000 people, sunk or taken 846 ships, received the capitulation

of 1538 towns and forts, subdued the lands from the Maeotians to the Red Sea, duly dedicates his offering vowed to Minerva.

This is his summary of his exploits in the East. But the announcement of the triumphal procession that he led on September 28 in the consulship of Marcus Piso and Marcus Messala was as follows:

After having rescued the sea coast from pirates and restored to the Roman People the command of the sea, he celebrated a triumph over Asia, Pontus, Armenia, Paphlagonia, Cappadocia, Cilicia, Syria, the Scythians, Jews and Albanians, Iberia, the Island of Crete, the Bastarnae, and, in addition to these, over King Mithridates and Tigranes.

This text does not mention the *oikoumene,* unlike the version given by Diodorus. But there is no reason to doubt the latter because Pompey had proudly proclaimed in a speech[22] that he had received Asia as a "frontier province" and that he had made it the center of the empire—a formula that Cicero would borrow from him.[23] Cicero elaborated on this theme on several occasions.[24]

But as Pliny noted (*NH*, 7.99), the same could be said of Caesar since he went even further—towards the North this time—towards the ends of the world: *C. Caesar [. . .] in iis est nunc locis quae regione orbem terrarum, rebus illius gestis imperium populi Romani definiunt* (Cicero, *Pro Balbo,* 64). This point is so well taken that in the time of the Triumvirate, Nepos could clearly state that *in ea urbe in qua domicilium orbis terrarum esset imperii* (*Att.*, 3.3), or note that Antony and Octavian each wanted to be the first "not only of the City (*Urbis*) but of the world" (*orbis terrarum*) (ibid., 20.5). Thus Nepos outlined for the first time a *iunctura* that would become famous, but only in the Augustan period. Now firmly entrenched, this theme would become commonplace through its encouragement by the highest authority, and it would foster the nostalgia of ecumenism until Byzantium or Charlemagne, in spite of all obstacles.

The second reason for our surprise before a text like the *Res Gestae* is political: at least one power existed that was well known to the Romans and that remained independent and outside the empire: Parthia.[25] If Augustus, in his *Res Gestae,* claimed that this independence was nothing else but a type of vassalage, the opposing view could nevertheless be put forth during his lifetime. The historian Trogus, perhaps inspired by Timagenes, insinuated as much when he stated that the Parthians and the Romans "shared" the world. He is not alone, as the same tradition is found in Strabo[26] alongside the orthodox thesis of the identification of the borders of the empire with those of the inhabited world. Better yet, Augustus claimed to have "subjected the world" to the empire of Rome. But he should have known that this was not the case, since his posthumous advice to his successor who according to Tacitus made it a principle or a doctrine was that henceforth one must "never venture beyond the frontiers of the empire" (*consilium coercendi intra terminos imperii*).

It is one thing to find assertions by historians or orators who are expressing themselves in private; it is quite another to see these appear officially in diplomatic documents or in the form of symbolic representations set up by the state. Several types of documents attest to this official usage, albeit somewhat later than the unofficial assertions. First, there are formulas used in *senatus consulta,* then monetary symbols, and finally, figurative representations—sculptures or *tableaux*—displayed during the triumphs or solemnly placed in official and monumental arrangements. We have seen the triumphal inscriptions of Pompey, but we do not know if these had the official sanction of the *senatus consultum* granting his triumph. This is likely. We are certain that during this period two official texts expressed—in the name of the Roman state—the assertion of Rome's universal domination. The first is the *lex Gabinia Calpurnia de insula Deli*[27] (58 B.C.), preserved in a bilingual inscription on Delos (*CIL,* 1^2.2500). This consular law, granting various fiscal and jurisdictional privileges to Delos, unusually includes a preamble that copies the *senatus consultum* authorizing—or inviting—the consuls to propose it. The whole world (*orbis terrarum*) is mentioned twice in this inscription. In the first instance (l. 14) it is to recall that it was devastated by pirates for several years (*praedon[es q]uei orbem [ter]rarum complureis [annos vastarint]*); in the second (l. 19), to recall—without naming him—Pompey's pacificatory undertaking: *[re publica pulcer]rume administrata imperio ampli]ficato [p]ace per orbe[m terrarum confecta]*. Even if the coasts of the Inland Sea are clearly referred to in this context, the ecumenical pretension is evident.

The second reference also concerns Pompey. In September of 57 B.C. he was given an extraordinary *cura* for the provisioning of Rome. The proposed motion drawn up by the consuls—the one which will have become law—entrusted to him *omnis potestas rei frumentariae toto orbe* (Cicero, *Att.,* 4.1.7). Such must have been the terms of the law, confirmed by the Greek sources that report them (later, of course). Still it is worth noting the way in which these later sources translate or interpret this Roman phraseology. Dio (39.9.3), like Plutarch (*Pomp.,* 25), is careful to specify that this *orbis terrarum*[28] was indeed *orbis Romanus: τῆς οἰκουμένης τῆς ὑπὸ τοῖς Ῥωμαίοις οὔσης* (Dio); *ἡ ὑπὸ Ῥωμαίων οἰκουμένη* (Plutarch).

Let us consider the coins. It is striking to see that the appearance on Republican coins of the first symbols that can definitely be interpreted as those of "universal" domination (with the aforementioned ambiguities) of the Roman people is contemporary with the first textual testimonies (cf. above). These consist of a globe associated with other subjects on the obverse or, more often, on the reverse.[29] It is important to be cautious in the interpretation of such symbols. For example, it is futile to attempt to distinguish "celestial" from "terrestrial" globes on such tiny and sometimes awkward documents. Occasionally the representation is sufficiently precise. The drawing on the globe of zodiacal signs (semicircles on the inner circumference) or the zodiacal band, or sometimes the intertwining of circles that almost certainly represent the armillary sphere (a symbol of astronomical studies), are clearly distinguishable. But inversely, if the globe is or seems to be smooth, or if it seems to be decorated with irregular lines, it is futile to interpret it as the terrestrial globe, still less to see the illustration of the *oikoumene,* or even of the four *oikoumenes* of Crates of Mallos. In fact the distinction is artificial from the point of view of the ancients: for them the two spheres were concentric and naturally associated with each other.[30] The celestial sphere, whether armillary or not, was the most common; it was the one that best represented the cosmos in its entirety.

Conversely, it is known that the strictly geographic sphere (the one most striking for its pertinence), which should have represented the planet and on it the known *oikoumene* (and the other possible "worlds"), was a cumbersome object, and few in number (if any replicas ever existed after those constructed by Eratosthenes or Crates). Strabo dismissed the creation of such an object as inconvenient and improbable (2.5.10, 116 C). It is thus likely that the representation of a globe, in order to have the maximum symbolic value, had to refer to the most useful and widespread object.

For all that, the distinction is of little importance, for the globe is less the sign of the concrete domination of space easily located on the surface of the earth than of a sovereignty the more recognizable for being general and "cosmic," even more than geographic. No empire, no universal monarch could in antiquity reasonably wish to dominate the entire terrestrial sphere. Three-quarters of it remained literally unattainable in ancient cosmogony, out of the reach of all human enterprise.[31] A universal domination could not claim more than the one known *oikoumene.* Nevertheless, they could claim to fit in the order of the cosmic destiny—either they were under the protection of or they held a covenant with the gods, or they were in some way divine. They become therefore an element, or the guarantee, of world order. This is then the visual symbol of the "elevation" of the globe. The globe could have numerous meanings and various applications depending on the context.

Nevertheless, with these precautions in mind, the ever-more-frequent appearance of the globe on Roman coins[32] from about 76 B.C. or 75 B.C. leaves little room for doubt concerning the meaning of its pretensions. We must leave out a purely allegorical example: the presence of a globe at the side of Urania on a coin struck by Q. Pomponius Musa (in 66 B.C.). The entire issue, playing on the moneyer's cognomen, represents the nine Muses (*RRC,* 410; cf. 409, no. 2: M. Plaetorius Cestianus [67]: Cybela and the globe). In the other cases, the globe symbolizes a universal domination following a typology that was set after its first two appearances. Either the globe is associated with other symbols of domination, or it serves as a support for symbolic figures that in this way reinforce the truth of the assertion of possession. On the oldest example (a denarius of Cn. Lentulus; *RRC,* 393), the globe appears between a scepter with a wreath on the left and a ship's rudder on the right; on the obverse, the head of *G(enius) P(opuli) R(omani).* The scepter and the rudder clearly illustrate the formula *terra marique* (by land and by sea), Hellenistic in origin and applied to Alexander and to the monarchs who claimed to be his successor.[33]

The first literary reference to an empire or to a victory "on land and on sea" in broad sense of on *all* lands and on *all* seas occurs, as far as Rome is concerned, in 66 B.C. However, this applies to the *lex Gabinia* of 67 B.C., which had entrusted to Pompey a universal command against the pirates on the sea and on all the coasts: "One law . . . sufficed to make us finally seem the true masters of all the peoples and all nations on land and on sea" (Cicero, *de imp. Cn. Pomp.,* 56). In fact the symbol corresponding to this expression appeared ten years earlier, on the reverse of a coin. One wonders then (at the expense of a slight chronological disorder) whether this coin of Cn. Lentulus (like that of P. Lentulus; *RRC,* 317) was not meant to celebrate another universal comand against the pirates, that of M. Antonius in 74 B.C.[34] The coin of P. Lentulus bears also the *genius populi Romani* on the reverse, but this time in magisterial pose—crowned by Victory, holding the scepter and the cornucopia, placing his right foot on a globe and his left on a prow of a ship.

The image of the globe as symbolizing the domination *terra marique* is seen in 42 B.C. on a denarius struck—for the glory of the triumvirs—by

L. Mussidius Longus; the globe appears together with the laureate head of Caesar (*RRC,* 494/39 A), and again in 44 B.C. on a coin struck by L. Aemilius Bucca (*RRC,* 480/6), also in association with Caesar. The globe is either seen beneath an allegorical figure or trampled underfoot, as for example under *Roma* (facing the figure of *Italia*) in 70 B.C. (*RRC,* 403); likewise, under a seated figure of *Roma* in 48 B.C. (*RRC,* 449/4); or under Venus in 44 B.C. (*RRC,* 480/3); or under Victory in 31 B.C. (*RRC,* 546/4). In this last case, it is already an "Augustan" type.[35] In all these cases the symbolism is so obvious that it makes little difference, all in all, if what is represented is really the celestial globe (as on *RRC,* 393).

But the geographical character is undisputable on a famous and more significant coin. It is a denarius struck in 56 B.C. by Faustus Sulla, the son of the Dictator and the son-in-law of Pompey.[36] The four types of that coinage impartially glorify Sulla on the one hand and Pompey on the other. Concerning Pompey, one type represents three trophies that commemorate his three triumphs (in 79 B.C. over Africa, in 71 B.C. over Spain, and in 61 B.C. over the East). But the other type is far more interesting. In the center there is a globe (with no trace of the zodiac or of the armillary bands), surrounded by three small crowns and a larger crown above. On the left there is an *aplustre* (an ornament for the prow of a boat); on the right, an ear of corn. This is thus a condensed illustration of all of Pompey's famous deeds: the three triumphs over the three parts of the world (Africa, Europe, and Asia); but also the *imperium terra marique* granted to him in 67 B.C. against the pirates. It is quite likely that the ear of corn on the right symbolizes not only his command on land but also the *cura annonae* of 57 B.C., whose universal nature was no doubt recognized officially in the proposal (Cicero, *Att.,* 4.1.7). It is evident that these three successive triumphs on the three continents had drawn the attention of contemporaries: Cicero had affirmed their ecumenical character on several occasions (*De domo,* 110; *Sest.,* 67; 129; *Balb.,* 9; 16). Under these conditions, and on this one occasion, the globe (maintaining its sovereign value) is probably meant to recall these triumphs over the *orbis terrarum.* This is confirmed by Pompey's own open assertion. At the time of his last triumph in 61 B.C., he not only recalled his victories over the pirates and over thirteen Asiatic or eastern nations (Pliny, *NH,* 8.98) but he also summed up his previous victories:

> He celebrated his triumph in honor of all the campaigns which he had ever led, all together; he had very numerous and beautifully decorated trophies carried by for each of his feats of arms, even the smallest; but

> following these there came one that was larger, magnificently adorned, bearing an inscription indicating that this was the *oikoumene.* (Dio 37.21.2)

The exceptional character of this triumph no doubt justified the extraordinary honor of the gold crown that he could wear on certain occasions, in particular to the theater (Velleius, 2.40.4). The words *orbis terrarum* (a translation of *oikoumene*) had certainly been uttered and, for that matter, been inscribed beneath a summarizing trophy by Pompey himself.[37] This time it was in its concrete geographical extent that the universality of the Roman Empire was asserted. And Pompey clarified his own words in a speech by explaining that when he had received Asia as a province, it had marked the edge of the Roman Empire; when he restored it, it was at its center (Cicero, *Prov. Cons.* 31; Pliny, *NH,* 7.99; Florus, 1.40.31). Let us note this essential idea in passing: it is in protecting provinces that until then had been frontier, by means of new conquests (thereby forming a new buffer zone), that one extends the limits of the empire to those of the world, as though by successive contacts. This will be Augustus's reasoning in one of the culminating passages of the *Res Gestae: omnium provinciarum populi Romani quibus finitimae fuerunt gentes quae non parerent imperio nostro fines auxi* (26.1).

While these claims had been symbolically declared by Pompey in 61 B.C. with the inscriptions of his triumph and trophies, he also wanted to have them displayed permanently in certain sections of the decor of his theater, finished in 55 B.C. (thus the coin type issued in 56 B.C. by Faustus Sulla was topical). Pliny, quoting Varro (36.41), indicated the statues of "fourteen nations" (a number that coincides with the *praefatio* of his triumph; Pliny, *NH,* 7.98). In the same theater complex there was a statue of Pompey himself (preserved today, considerably restored, in the Palazzo Spada) in the heroic nudity of an *imperator,* with sword and cloak, and holding a globe in his left hand.[38] This is no doubt the famous statue that was located in the *Curia* facing the theater, at the foot of which Caesar was murdered. The comparison with the coin of 56 B.C. made by F. Coarelli is conclusive. Certainly, the theater in the *Campus Martius* is not, as he says, "in the sacred center of the city"; and the statues, if they are those of the nations of the *praefatio,* recalled only Pompey's Eastern victories. But the globe, like his trophy, discreetly recalled that he had in principle "conquered the world," in the name of the Roman people.

Caesar went even further.[39] He too—but more directly—wished to assert an ecumenical domination by a symbolic representation. This was done by means of a statue, or rather a group, erected this time on the *Capitolium* and dedicated by the Senate, among the other honors for his triumphs of 46 B.C. Unfortunately, it is difficult to get a clear idea of the composition of this group. It is mentioned in an obscure manner in two passages of Dio, whose translation is difficult and which can give rise to false interpretations.

> The Senate also decreed [says Dio at 43.14.6] that his [triumphal] chariot would be dedicated on the Capitolium, facing Jupiter and that he [Caesar] would tread on a bronze image of the *oikoumene,* the whole bearing an inscription calling him "demi-god."

Farther on (43.21.2), returning to the descriptions of the ceremonies of the quadruple triumph (over Gaul, Egypt, Pontus, and Africa), Dio recalls an ostentatious act of devotion on Caesar's part.

> On this occasion, he climbed the steps of the Capitolium on his knees, neither casting his eyes upon the chariot dedicated to Jupiter in his honor, nor upon the image of the *oikoumene* lying beneath his feet, nor upon the inscription which it bore; but later he had the word "demi-god" erased from the inscription.

These texts[40] cannot be translated without a preconceived reconstruction of the monument. Most scholars (from Vogt to Hoelscher and D. Michel) have pictured a statue of Caesar with both feet or one foot on the globe, like the *genius populi Romani* on the coin of P. Cornelius Lentulus, or like Roma, Venus, or Victory on somewhat later coin types.[41] But there are difficulties with this explanation. Dio uses the expression ὑπὸ τοῖς ποσὶν αὐτοῦ κειμένην, "lying beneath his feet," which is not particularly apt for a globe. Further, the word εἰκών usually implies a statue rather than a mere object, even a symbolic one such as a globe.

Another possible iconographical model was sought elsewhere. *Oikoumene* must, in fact, be represented by an allegorical figure. This is already attested in the Hellenistic period, in the form of a woman wearing on her head a turreted crown or a tower (somewhat similar to Tyche).[42] She appears at Cronos's side, crowning Homer on the relief of Archelaus of Priene in the British Museum. According to Libanius (8.529),[43] she crowned Alexander in a group at the *Tychaion* of Alexandria. She appeared in a painting (and not in a statuary group) that served as the decor in the theater at Athens during the *Demetria* in honor of Demetrius Poliorcetes. The text of Douris of Samos cited by Athenaeus (12.50, 536 a, = Müller, *FHG*, ii, p. 477; Jacoby, *FGrH*, 76 F 14) must be read in detail; Demetrius was represented "driving his chariot" (ὀχούμενος) "against, towards, over (ἐπί) the *oikoumene*."

Two hypothetical reconstructions of Caesar's statue have recently been proposed, independently of each other. The first, proposed by S. Weinstock,[44] presumes a statue of the *oikoumene* kneeling before Caesar, who raises her up in a gesture of *restitutio;* this reconstruction relies on two interesting documents. The most striking is a coin of Hadrian (*BMCRE*, 3.418, no. 1211) that bears the legend *Restitutori Orbis Terrarum:* at the feet of the standing Hadrian is the figure of *Orbis* (a woman with a turreted headdress), with her right knee on the ground and the globe in her left hand. The other and more controversial document is a terracotta relief from the Muzeo Nazionale Romano, dated (tentatively) to Caesar's time. On it an *imperator,* crowned by a Victory to the left of a trophy, holds out his hand to a kneeling figure similar to the *Orbis* on the coin mentioned above; the globe is on the ground between them. But leaving aside the uncertainty about the date, there are still many difficulties. In particular, the figure is helmeted and holds a spear, and this would better suit *Roma* or *Italia* than *Terra*. In any case, this reconstruction of Caesar's "statue" on the *Capitolium* eliminates a central element: the presence of the chariot.

G. Picard's reconstruction[45] rests on the chariot. Recalling that the painting of Demetrius Poliorcetes represented him "driving his chariot towards" or "over" the *oikoumene,* Picard compares it to another monument, a plaque from the Antonine altar of Ephesus preserved in Vienna. The plaque depicts an emperor (L. Verus) climbing into a chariot that looms over a prostrate figure (*Tellus*). He hypothesizes therefore that the monument of Caesar on the *Capitolium* was of this type, except that the prostrate figure would have been the *oikoumene*.

It is unfortunate that this type of representation of *apobates,* frequent enough in ancient art, should not be attested for a triumphal chariot by any imperial coins. No doubt this reconstruction is by far the most satisfactory, since it is the only one to take into account both the expression ὑπὸ τοῖς ποσὶν αὐτοῦ κειμένην and the presence of the chariot. The globe on its own, given the general and often cosmic nature of its significance, could not have been so precisely defined by *oikoumene*. In 46 B.C. Caesar had triumphed over the three parts of the world and it is certainly with reference to, and in opposition to, Pompey that he had this group erected on the *Capitolium*. But there was a considerable difference: Pompey, in 61 B.C., was a mere mortal, an *imperator* (though unrivalled) of the Roman people, to whom he brought back his conquests (cf. above). By 46 B.C., Caesar was almost a monarch and even, according to the attested inscription, a demi-god or at least a "hero." When Pompey decided upon a monumental representation, he did not dare to depict himself blatantly as the *triumphator* of the *oikoumene:* he was content to be represented globe in hand amidst the fourteen nations over which he had triumphed in 61.

Augustus certainly had not hidden his ecumenical claims.[46] The *Res Gestae* clearly begins with this pretension (above p. 29): *quibus orbem terrarum imperio populi Romani subiecit,* which is—for the most part—its explanation and justification. At first glance, the claim is confirmed, indirectly at least, by iconography; first, by the symbolic use of the globe on Augustus's coin types.[47] Before 29 B.C., some denarii from the mint at Rome depict the *Princeps* nude with a foot on the globe (Giard, 12–17; he holds a spear and an *aplustre*) or else he holds the globe (Giard, no. 5); elsewhere his bust is beside a globe (Mattingly, *BMCRE,* 1.42, no. 217; 7 B.C.); or Victory is standing on the globe (Giard, nos. 49, 67, 68, etc.). The globe is also associated, as are the cornucopia and the rudder, with Capricorn, Augustus's astrological sign (Giard, pp. 186–88). But is difficult to say whether these coin types are derived from any actual monument.

The Augustan architectural program must certainly be considered along the same lines as the precedents set by Pompey and Caesar, since it clearly conveys the same ecumenical character, as we see in the Forum of Augustus. This was inaugurated in 2 B.C. at the same time as the Temple of Mars Ultor, which was promised during the battle at Philippi.[48] The ageing emperor wanted to make this inauguration a true ideological and dynastic manifesto, profiting from his approaching sixty-third birthday and from the presentation to the consulship of the eldest of his grandsons, Gaius Caesar. In this same year, on 5 February, the Senate bestowed upon him the title of *pater patriae* (*RG,* 35). Both facts are connected. The Senate, as Augustus recalled, decided that the title should be inscribed over the porch of his house, on the *Curia Julia* and in the Forum of Augustus "under the quadriga placed there in his honor." This quadriga probably faced the entrance to the Temple and thus would bring to mind Caesar's monument on the *Capitolium;* only the inscriptions differ.

Apparently, this chariot (certainly trimumphal) had nothing about it that was specifically ecumenical. Yet, upon closer examination, it definitely had that aspect, for it was manifestly at the center of a monumental complex that aimed to glorify, by its functional designation, the political achievements of the *princeps,* not only as "avenger" but also as "founder" of a new order provided with heirs.

The decoration of the Forum speaks for itself. Augustus had gathered there the statues and the *elogia* of the founders of Rome, of his *gens,* and of all the most famous *triumphatores* in Roman history "to serve as an example to himself and to the princes who would succeed him" (Suetonius, *Aug.*, 31.8). These *elogia,* although they are much shorter, are in a sense the models, the archetypes of the *Res Gestae.* As seen above, scholars agree that this work was written by Augustus, in a preliminary form nearly complete, around 2 B.C. For this reason some assumed that this first draft, or at least some excerpts, had been posted in the Forum, completing the series of *elogia* from the past, and perhaps, associating with the triumphal statue of the new *Pater Patriae.* The statues of the founders and of the *triumphatores* were located under the two porticos with the *titulus* underneath and the *elogium* above. But there was something more. Velleius, in his excursus devoted to the survey and to the origins of the provinces, writes of those that were pacified or created by Augustus, (their "creation" is problematic but this is not important here):[50]

> in addition to the Spains and other nations (*gentes*), whose inscriptions (*tituli*) adorn his Forum, Augustus made Egypt a tributary . . . (2.39.2).

The interpretation of this crucial sentence is delicate. Taking up a suggestion by Degrassi[51] (*Inscr. Ital.,* 13.3, *Elogia Fori Aug.*, p. 5), L. Braccesi[52] (followed by P. Zanker, p. 12) thinks that the word *tituli* (in the plural) means only *one* inscription and not *many,* one perhaps spread over several columns, and specifically the one mentioned by Augustus in connection with the quadriga and the title of *pater patriae: idque . . . inscribendum . . . et in Foro Augusti sub quadrigiis quae mihi ex S.C. positae sunt censuit* (*RG* 35). This inscription would not have consisted merely of a few words recalling the title, but would have included (in keeping with the surrounding *elogia*) a lengthy *elogium* of Augustus, perhaps the first draft of the *Res Gestae.* This is a seductive hypothesis, which has the merit of linking the first draft of the *Res Gestae* (clearly revealed by all the editors since Mommsen, Kornemann, and Ensslin) in a close relationship with the dedication of the Forum and the Temple of Mars. But could Velleius have used *titulis provinciarum* (in the plural) to mean: "an inscription where the names of the provinces appear"? The expression *titulus (provinciae)* usually means "an inscription that designates a province." This would more readily bring to mind a series of statues, or of allegorical representations, of the provinces and of the conquered peoples. Certainly only the *elogia* of great men (mentioned in the texts, especially in Suetonius) have been found in the Forum of Augustus; there is no effigy of a province or representing a people. But the second level of the porticos was decorated with caryatids—a precise and deliberate imitation of the Acropolis in Athens.[53] A well known passage in Vitruvius (1.1.4) shows that the caryatids (women of Karya) are seen as allegories of conquered cities (*exempla servitutis*) in the architectural symbolism of the period, even if derived from a false etymology. Any direct relationship is debatable. Nothing indicated that the caryatids of the Forum might have been individualized. But there were other elements in the decoration in the Forum that could represent provinces or *gentes*. Ovid writes (*Fasti,* 5.545; 561) that the weapons of the conquered were exhibited on the doors of the Temple in the Forum: *prospicit in foribus diversae tela figurae armaque terrarum milite victa suo*. But there were also the *clipei* between the caryatids, two of which have been found (Zanker, p. 13), and which served perhaps an allegorical function. Is it not possible that Velleius's phrase described allegorical sculptures decorating these *clipei,* and that there were inscriptions (*tituli*) identifying them?

Be that as it may, the parallels between the two accounts are striking. Velleius begins with the *Hispaniae*. In the *Res Gestae* 26.2, Augustus mentions the Gallic and the Spanish provinces first: *Gallias et Hispanias provincias, item Germaniam, qua includit Oceanus a Gadibus ad Ostium Albis fluminis pacavi*. Velleius mentions the *alias gentes*. In 26.4, Augustus cites the names of peoples: "*alii Germanorum populi,*" but in 30.1, the *Pannoniorum gentes;* in 30.2, the *Dacorum gentes;* in 32.3, the *plurimae aliae gentes* who had friendly relations with the Roman people during his reign; and in 33, the *gentes Parthorum et Medorum*. As will be shown these enumerations in the *Res Gestae* are charged with significance. They clearly begin (in 26.4–5) by mentioning the reconnaissance expeditions and explorations towards the edges of the world. And by showing the subject status of peoples further and further away, as far as the Indians (31.1), they give credence to the idea of at least an indirect universal domination.

This interpretation is by no means farfetched. Mars Ultor was not only the dynastic avenger of the assassinated Caesar; he was also, in some way, the avenger of Crassus: the *signa recepta* were in his temple (*RG,* 29.2; Ovid, *Fasti,* 5.579).[54] The title of *Pater Patriae* could, by an explicit analogy to the Father of the Gods, suggest a universal terrestrial domination. Ovid clearly states this in Book 2 of the *Fasti* (1.130), when he mentions it (on 5

February): "for a long time now, you (Caesar) have been like a father to the Universe (*res tamen anti dedit, sero quoque vera tulisti / nomina: iampridem tu pater orbis eras*); and further on: *hoc duce Romanum est solis utrumque latus . . . quodcumque est alto sub Iove, Caesar habet* ("all that exists beneath the canopy of Jove is Caesar's own"). The same significance can be given to the famous formula in reference to Terminus at the end of the same Book 2 (l. 683ff.): *gentibus est aliis tellus data limite certo: Romanae spatium est Urbis et orbis idem* ("the land of other nations has a fixed boundary: the circuit of Rome is the circuit of the world").

Does this imply that this assertion of ecumenical triumph in 2 B.C. was without its problems? The return of the standards in 19 B.C., and their final dedication to Mars in 2 B.C., was certainly not sufficient. In spite of the dispatch of embassies and of hostages (in 10 B.C.),[55] the relations with the Parthians had become strained. As R. Syme[56] stated, "an expedition to the East . . . was in the air," and its leader would naturally be C. Caesar. Among the spectacles accompanying the dedication of the Temple of Mars Ultor, there had been a famous *naumachia* (*RG* 23) of which Dio (54.10.7) and Ovid (*Ars Am.* 1.171) reveal the highly significant theme, the re-enactment of the Persian Wars. The commentary (perhaps out of place in an erotic work) that Ovid gives us in his evocation also reveals a turning point in the imperial policy that may have been forthcoming: in order to accomplish the domination of the *orbis*, which until that time (as pointed out in the first draft of the *RG*) had been only theoretical, it would be necessary to take hold of the waiting East:

> Lo! Caesar is preparing to add what was lacking to the conquered world. Now, farthest East, shalt thou be ours; Parthian, thou shall pay penalty. . . . Your avenger is at hand . . . valor falls early to the lot of Caesars.
>
> Ecce, parat Caesar, domito quod defuit orbi
> Addere. Nunc, Oriens ultime, noster eris.
> Parthe, dabis poenas . . .
> Ultor adest . . . Caesaribus virtus contigit ante diem. (1.177–84)

This theme is emphasized throughout the passage so much that one wonders whether it does not convey an irreverent irony. The reverses and the death of C. Caesar would render this irony cruel in retrospect, for example when it anticipates (l. 213ff.)[57] Gaius's "Parthian triumph" with its tableaux, its maps, or its allegorical figures—among which there was a woman representing Persia: *haec est Danaeia Persis.* Let us hope, for the sake of Augustus's vanity, that the statue of Persia did not yet figure among those in his Forum.

Be that as it may, at the climax of his life, Augustus had combined two different traditions in order to assert in the Forum the ecumenical pretensions later related in his *Res Gestae.* One tradition was that of Caesar who placed his own triumphal chariot with the "reasonable" title of *Pater Patriae* opposite the god Mars, and apparently without crushing the *oikoumene;* the other tradition was Pompey's, who (on a monument that showed fourteen conquered nations in a cosmically or geographically symbolic order) had also placed in a now-unknown location a statue of himself as the *triumphator* of the world.

In fact, Augustus was equally interested in these two statues, which offered him respectable precedents. In 44 B.C. he had dedicated a statue of his father on the *Capitolium* bearing, legitimately this time, the epithet *hemitheos*[58]—a fact that is not often mentioned. And, as early as 32 B.C., he had had the statue of Pompey removed from the *Curia* and placed at the apex of a marble arch that was *contra theatri eius regiam* (Suetonius, *Aug.*, 31.9). The Theater of Pompey and the Forum of Augstus were therefore made to complete each other. And both were proof, in their own way, of the ecumenical pretensions of the Roman domination (cosmic or historical). The Theater asserted that Pompey had nearly left the world of the living by reaching its edges from East to West. Augustus, without the slightest claim to immortality, showed concretely in his *Res Gestae* that his campaigns, his explorations, and his diplomatic successes had extended the domination or the influence of the *imperium populi Romani* to the known limits of the *oikoumene.* It is not surprising[59] therefore that it is *Oikoumene* (with her crowned head), flanked by *Oceanus* and *Tellus,* who crowns him on the *Gemma Augustea* in Vienna. The occasion, it is true, is a triumph of Tiberius's; the globe, decorated with Capricorn, appears above Augustus's head and recalls the prediction of Nigidius Figulus.[60] It is also not surprising that numerous monumental groups, here and there throughout the empire, should have reproduced in several ways these Roman monuments as a mark of loyalty. I will not elaborate on the theater built by Herod in Jerusalem (Josephus, *A.J.*, 15.8.1) that, on the exterior of its *cavea,* bore ἐπιγραφαὶ Καίσαρος and the trophies of the peoples whom he had conquered.

More important attention must be given to the astonishing and recently discovered *Sebasteion* of Aphrodisias.[61] It makes little difference that it was dedicated somewhat later, towards the end of Nero's reign: in its exaltation of the Julio-Claudian family, Augustus's share is predominant. The double gallery of the *Sebasteion* (eighty meters long) displayed, on the one hand, low-relief panels representing princes of the Julio-Claudian dynasty in various attitudes: some clearly are linked with specific conquests (Claudius and Britannia, Nero and Armenia), while others are more general. For example, one represents Augustus (?) with the celestial veil receiving tributary offerings from the earth and the sea (Erim, *RA* [1982] 166, no. 7), another shows Earth (*Gè*) with her hands extended towards Rome, which, in conjunction with the "victory of the Augusti," clearly alludes to her universal domination (Reynolds, *ZPE* [1981] 323, no. 7).[62] In the northern portico, there were panels representing provinces or nations surrounded by cosmic allegories that are definitely identified by the inscriptions that accompany them. One can see *Hemera* (Reynolds, no. 12) and *Oceanos* (no. 13), then Crete, Cyprus, and Sicily (nos. 14, 15, and 16), and finally several peoples or *gentes*. J. Reynolds listed four of them in 1981: Ἔθνους Δακῶν (no. 17), Ἔθνους Βεσσῶν (no. 18) Ῥαιτῶν (no. 19), Ἔθνους Τρουνπειλῶ[ν] (no. 20), and more than likely as G. Bowersock suggests, Ἔθνους [Ἀρα]βῶν.[63]

Since Reynolds's publication other allegorical figures have been found: K. Erim ([1983] 279) listed the *Iapodes*, the *Dardani*, the *Andizetti*, and the *Pirystae*[64] (a woman with a round shield). These series of names of peoples naturally raise a few problems of interpretation: the attribution of an ecumenical conquest to Augustus seems to contrast with the celebration of later victories over Britain and Armenia (as in Strabo and Pliny). But Britain was one of Augustus's defeats, awkwardly concealed by Strabo. It is one of the characteristics of the Roman vision of the world that this is not considered a real contradiction. But what is striking, as the first editors saw, is the similarity between the details of the decoration and the Augustan texts. The choice of the countries and especially of the *gentes* represented seems completely arbitrary, yet there are two noticeable parallels. The first parallel is the presence at Aphrodisias of precisely the same *gentes* mentioned in the *Res Gestae,* in the form of Ἔθνους + genitive plural: the Daces (*RG,* 30.2) or, in any case, those *gentes* conquered or beaten by Augustus, his sons, or his lieutenants; the Rhaeti, who evoke the campaigns of Tiberius; the Bessi, already conquered by Augustus's father, C. Octavius, and by M. Primus and M. Lollius (Dio, 54.3; 20; 35); the Trumpilini, one of the Alpine peoples listed on the *Trophy of the Alps* (Pliny, *NH,* 3.136; *CIL,* 5.7817; cf. *RG,* 24); and the Arabs (rather than the Suevii), who take us back to the *RG* and to the expedition of Aelius Gallus (or to the one planned for C. Caesar?).

All of these can be assigned with confidence to a group of Augustan victories. The second parallel, the other series of names or of personifications of nations, concerns the Balkans, the Iapodes, the Dardani, the Andizetti, and the Pirystae. Some of these peoples no doubt had been in contact with Rome before Augustus, and their names may appear in some of our isolated sources. But it is striking to note (Erim [1983] 279) that the complete series can be found only in Strabo's *Geography* (7.5.314ff.). Strabo's intentions, in writing his geography, are clearly political. His description of the world, when seen as a whole, is constructed so as to lead to Rome's pretended universal domination. We know of his partiality for Asia, his homeland. But if later decorators (?) of the *Sebasteion* may have taken inspiration from historical or geographical texts in order to celebrate the cult of the masters of the world, one can wonder about the prototype of a decoration that visualizes the conquest of the world, in allegories both cosmic (the Earth, the Ocean, and the Sun) and geographical (the *gentes*), might not this prototype have been simply the Roman monument where the *Pater Patriae*—who is also the Father of the World, as Ovid recalls (*Fasti,* 2.130: *iampridem tu pater orbis eras*)—had gathered the statues or the emblems of the innumerable countries that he had conquered, in the order in which he named them in the *RG* (cf. Ovid, *Fasti,* 1.599)? For Strabo, the monarchy of Augustus is quite simply that of a father. At Rome as at Aphrodisias, allegorical geography joined the cosmological myths of the sovereignty to mark the accomplishments of the times.

NOTES

1. See the recent summaries on Augustus's foreign policy in D. Kienast, *Augustus* (Darmstadt, 1982), 274ff.; H. E. Stier, "Augustusfriede und romische Klassik," *ANRW* II, 2 (1975): 3ff. esp. 16–20. In antiquity, opinions concerning the true nature of the foreign policy of Augustus and of his successors were divided: either it was *inertia Caesarum* (Tacitus, *Ann.*, 1.11.4; *Agr.*, 13.2; Florus, *Praef.*, 4) or aggressive. A useful examination of this question is found in C. Wells, *The German Policy of Augustus* (Oxford, 1972), 1–13. Dio (53.10.4–5; 54.9.1; 56.41.7) is the only ancient source to state that Augustus's policy was strictly defensive; among the modern sources, H. D. Meyer supports this statement ("Die Aussenpolitik des Augustus und die augusteische Dichtung," (*Köln. Ist. Abh.* 5 [1961]) but cf. contra P. Brunt's book-review in *JRS*, 1963, 170ff. R. Syme maintains (*History in Ovid* [Oxford, 1978], 151–53) his noncommittal views regarding sites and chronology (*CAH* 10 [1934]: 351ff.): prudence and withdrawal in Britain, in the East (against the Parthians); aggressivity along the Upper Danube, to assure communications with the Balkans and, in Germany, up to the unsuccessful campaign against Maroboduus and the Marcomanni in A.D. 6. The "moderation" of Augustus's aims, as opposed to the

notion of "the conquest of the world," has been defended, especially by W. Oldfather and H. V. Canter, "The Defeat of Varus and the German Frontier Policy of Augustus," *Univ. of Illinois Studies* 4, no. 2 (1915), in particular 60ff. (a good historiographical exposé).

2. Virgil, *Georg.*, 3.32: *Et duo rapta manu diverso ex hoste tropaea / bisque triumphatas utroque ab litore gentis.* See A. Degrassi, "Virgilio e il foro di Augusto," in *Scritti Vari di Ant.* 1:283ff. The *Georgics* were written in 30–29 B.C. (Donatus, *Vita Verg.*, 91–95). Concerning all these texts, see D. Little, "Politics in Augustan Poetry," in *ANRW* II, 30 (1982): 357.

3. Virgil, *Aen.*, 6.781: *En huius, nate, auspiciis illa incluta Roma / imperium terris, animos aequabit Olympo . . .* ; 792: *(Augustus Caesar) aurea condet / saecula . . . super et Garamantas et Indos / proferet imperium.*

4. Virgil, *Aen.*, 6.849ff.: *(alii) / orabunt causas melius, caelique meatus / describent radio et surgentia sidera dicent: / tu regere imperio populos, Romane, memento. . . .* In the latter verse, the plural *populos* surely has a universal connotation. *Aen.*, 6.794–95 alludes to the campaign of Balbus, who spread the *imperium* over the country of the Garamantes (I owe this observation to J. Desanges).

5. "Letter to Augustus" (*Epist.* 2.1.253ff.: *tuisque auspiciis totum confecta duella per orbem*); cf. E. Fraenkel, *Horace* (Oxford, 1957), 383ff; R. Syme, "Poetry and Government," in *History in Ovid* (Oxford, 1978), 171ff. (who dates this epistle after Agrippa's death). Regarding the links between a work written in epic style and Agrippa's map, see below, p. 114.

6. E. Fraenkel, *Horace,* 426ff.; R. Syme, *History in Ovid*, 48ff. (= "Forgotten Campaigns"). Concerning the irony or clumsiness of Ovid, who had added, in an erotic book, the passage on the *naumachia* and the Parthian triumph wished for C. Caesar, see R. Syme, "The Crisis of 2 B.C.," *Sitz. Münch.*, 1974 (= *Roman Papers,* 3:921–23; cf. Sven Lundstrom's recent work, *Ovids Metamorphosen und die Politik des Kaisers* (Uppsala, 1980).

7. Ovid, *Fast.*, 2.130: *sero quoque vera tulisti / Nomina: iampridem tu pater orbis eras[. . .]/ Quodcumque est alto sub Jove, Caesar habet* ("yet didst thou also receive, though late, thy title true; long time hadst thou been the Father of the World"). 2.683: *Gentibus est aliis tellus data limite certo: / Romanae spatium est urbis et orbis idem* (the land of other nations has a fixed boundary: the circuit of Rome is the circuit of the world).

8. Concerning this theme, see J. Vogt, "*Orbis Romanus*" (Tübingen, 1929) (= *Vom Reichsgedanken der Romer* [Leipzig, 1942], 179–207; and = *Orbis* [Freiburg im Bresgau, 1960], 151–71; P. Brunt, "*Laus imperii,*" in P. Garnsey and C. Whittaker, eds., *Imperialism in the Ancient World* (Cambridge, 1978), 159–192, esp. 168–172.

9. For Polybius's "universal" vision, see P. Pédech, *La Méthode historique de Polybe* (Paris, 1964), 119, 497, 509 (the ἐπιβολὴ τῶν ὅλων). To my knowledge there is no specific study on the notion of οἰκουμένη in Polybius; it is necessary to read P. Pédech's excellent studies on Polybius's geography, op. cit. 515–97; F. Walbank, "The

Geography of Polybius," *Class. et Med.* 9 (1948): 155–82, and his scattered remarks in *Polybius* (Berkeley, 1972), 70, 103, 108, 114, 127, 157.

10. Polybius's Book 6 is devoted entirely to the analysis of the social and political causes of Rome's preeminence. See C. Nicolet, "Polybe et les institutions romaines," in *Polybe,* Entretiens de la Fond. Hardt 20 (Genève, 1974), 209–65.

11. F. Walbank, *Commentary on Polybius* (Cambridge, 1979), 3:583ff. It has been suggested the Polybius, sensitized to geography because of his later voyages, could have added, much later, the twelve or more geographic *excursus* that we encounter in his work. Both Strabo and Pliny used Polybius's work. Regarding his geographical sources, see F. Walbank, *Commentary on Polybius,* 3:567 (Dicaearchus, Eratosthenes, and Pytheas).

12. Concerning this episode, see P. Fraccaro, "Ancora sui processi dei Scipioni," *Athenaeum,* 1939, 3ff. (= *Opuscula,* 1:393–416). Livy is sceptical; refer to H. Malcovati, *ORF*[4] (Turin, 1976), 98 (Livy, 38.56.1–6).

13. H. Malcovati, *ORF*[4], 199 = Plutarch, *T.G.*, 9.6: "they are styled masters of the worlds."

14. Malcovati, *ORF*[4], 199 = Cicero, *Mur.*, 75.

15. Velleius, 1.6.6: *Aemilius Sura de annis populi Romani: Assyrii principes omnium gentium rerum potiti sunt, deinde Medi, postea Persae, deinde Macedones; exinde duobus regibus Philippo et Antiocho . . . haud multo post Carthaginem subactam devictis, summa imperii ad populum Romanum pervenit. Inter hoc tempus et initium regis Nini Assyriorum . . . intersunt anni MDCCCCXCV.* See M. Schanz and C. Hosius, *Geschichte Röm. Literatur,* 2:587–88; H. Bardon, *La littérature latine inconnue,* 1:195. Mommsen, "Mamilius Sura, Aemilius Sura," *Rh. Mus.*, 1861, 282 (= *GS,* VII, 70–76), noted the coincidence between the numbers and the Hellenistic chronographers from the East (those of Ctesias); he distinguished Aemilius Sura from Mamilius Sura quoted by Pliny. He made the former an author of a universal history during Sulla's time. The only reason to date him prior to Velleius's time is the passage in Velleius; but this is no doubt an interpolation placed in the edition of 1591 by Delbenius; most scholars agree. However, contra, J. W. Swain, "The Theory of the Four Monarchies: Opposition History under the Empire," *C P* 35 (1940): 1–21 (who makes Aemilius Sura an author in second century B.C.). Cf. H. Peter, *Hist. Rom. Rel.* 2 (1906): 210; and D. Mendels, "The Five Empires: a Note on a Propagandistic *topos*," *AJP,* 1981, 330–39, who claims it to be a *topos* that appeared only in the first century B.C.

16. No doubt this is Ζαμα, according to the chronological account given from the beginning of the reign of Ninus. This is the chronology of Eratosthenes and Ctesias; Diodorus, 2.22.2.

17. The principal pieces of evidence were collected and commented upon by J. Vogt, "*Orbis Romanus*" (cited above, n. 8): but he did not have Bohnenkamp's *TLL* article, "*orbis*" (Leipzig, 1978) 906–21, at his disposal, which I used (cf. Friedrich, *Materialen zur Begriffsbestimmung des o.t.* [Leipzig, 1887] *non vidi).* For *orbis (nude dictus)* = *orbis terrarum, TLL* col. 917, l. 32 (Virgil, *Aen.*, 4.231; Horace,

Carm., 1.12.57, etc.). See also the famous *iunctura urbs* and *orbis, TLL* col. 916, l. 15 (and below, p. 55), which only appears under Augustus, except for examples in Cicero (*Cat.*, 4.11) and Nepos (*Att.*, 3.3).

18. *Rhet. ad Her.*, 4.13; G. Calboli in his edition (Bologna, 1969), 291, finds this to be the oldest example of the Roman "ecumenical" claims. Calboli attributes the *Rhet.* to Cornificius; the speech, if authentic, came from a partisan of Q. Varius Hybrida.

19. Texts and facts in Drumann-Groebe, *Gesch. Roms*², (1908) 4:491ff.; Van Ooteghem, *Pompée le Grand bâtisseur d'empire* (1954), 281; R. Seager, *Pompey, a Political Biography* (Oxford, 1979), 77–78. Concerning the cosmocratic symbol of his triumph, see S. Weinstock, *Divus Julius* (Oxford, 1971), 38–39, 43.

20. Diodorus Siculus, 40.4: Ὅτι ὁ Πομπήιος τὰς ἰδίας πράξεις ἃς συνετέλεσεν ἐπὶ τῆς Ἀσίας ἀναγράψας ἀνέθηκεν, ὧν ἐστιν ἀντίγραφον τόδε. Πομπήιος Γναΐου υἱὸς Μέγας, αὐτοκράτωρ τὴν παράλιον τῆς οἰκουμένης καὶ πάσας τὰς ἐντὸς Ὠκεανοῦ νήσους ἐλευθερώσας τοῦ πειρατικοῦ πολέμου . . . καὶ τὰ ὅρια τῆς ἡγεμονίας τοῖς ὅροις τῆς γῆς προσβιβάσας, καὶ τὰς προσόδους Ῥωμαίων φυλάξας, ἃς δὲ προσαυξήσας, τούς τε ἀνδριάντας καὶ τὰ λοιπὰ ἀφιδρύματα τῶν θεῶν καὶ τὸν λοιπὸν κόσμον τῶν πολεμίων ἀφελόμενος ἀνέθηκε τῇ θεῷ χρυσοῦς μυρίους καὶ δισχιλίους ἑξήκοντα, ἀργυρίου τάλαντα τριακόσια ἑπτά.

21. H. Malcovati, *ORF*⁴, 362 = Pliny, *NH*, 7.98: *summa summarum in illa gloria fuit (ut ipse in contione dixit, cum de rebus suis dissereret) Asiam ultimam provinciarum accepisse, eandemque mediam patriae reddidisse.*

22. Pliny, *NH*, 7.97ff.: *Cn. Pompeius Magnus imperator bello XXX annorum confecto fusis fugatis occisis in deditionem acceptis hominum centiens viciens semel LXXXIII depressis aut captis navibus DCCCXLVI oppidis castellis MDXXXVIII in fidem receptis terris a Maeotis ad Rubrum mare subactis votum merito Minervae.*

23. *De. Prov. Cons.*, 31: *Asiam imperium antea nostrum terminabat;* cf. Florus, 1.40.3: *sic Pompeio duce populus Romanus totam, qua latissima est, Asiam pervagatus, quam extremam imperii habebat provinciam mediam fecit.* Unfortunately, this is not the place to comment on the rest of the sentence for it implied geographic conception.

24. *Sest.*, 67: *imperii populi Romani orbis terrarum terminis definisse;* 129: *vir is qui tripertitas orbis terrarum oras atque regiones tribus triumphis adiunctus huic imperio notavit;* cf. *Balb.*, 9; 16; *De domo*, 110: *Pompeium principem orbis terrae*, etc.

25. As early as the Augustan period, Pompeius Trogus (= Justinus) had noted this: Justinus, 41.1.1: *Parthi, penes quos, velut divisione orbis cum Romanis facta, nunc Orientis imperium sit;* the same notion is in Florus 1.40.31: *exceptis quippe Parthis, qui foedus maluerunt* (however, this passage dates to Pompey's time rather than to Augustus's reign). On these points, see O. Seel, *Eine römische Weltgeschichte* (Nuremberg, 1972), 204 (regarding the manner in which Justinus reconciles this apparent acceptance of the division of the world with his theory regarding the "succession of [universal] empires"). Lastly, the posthumous article by O. Seel,

"Pomp. Trog. un Universalgeschichte," *ANRW* II, 30, no.2 (1982): 1363–1423; G. Forni and M. G. Angeli Bertinelli, "Pompeo Trogo come fonte storica," *ANRW* II, 30, no. 2 (1982): 1298–1362. It is possible that the source for this assertion was Timagenes of Alexandria; M. Sordi, "Timagene: uno storico ellenocentrico e filobarbaro," *ANRW* II, 30, no. 1 (1982): 755–97.

26. Strabo, 11.9.2, 515 C; 17.3.24, 840 C; but contra 6.4.2, 288 C. About these contradictions, cf. below p. 73.

27. J.-C. Dumont, J.-L. Ferrary, P. Moreau, and C. Nicolet, *Insula Sacra, la loi Gabinia de Délos (58 av. J.-C)* (Rome, 1980), 73–75.

28. The expression *orbis Romanus* (to indicate that part of the world under the control of the Romans) appears only in Lucan (8.441; 10.456, cf. 8.211: *orbis qua Romanus erat*); *imperium Romanum* had been used instead.

29. The symbolism of universal domination and, in particular, of the globe has been studied; see A. Schlachter (and F. Gisinger), *Der Globus, seine Entstehung und Verwendung in der Antike,* Stoicheia 8 (Leipzig/Berlin, 1927), especially Rome, 64–89; A. Alfoldi, *Die monarchische Repräsentation im romischen Kaiserreiche* (Darmstadt, 1970), 235ff. and "Insignien und Tracht der romischen Kaiser," *MDAI(R),* 1935, 1–171; and more recently, P. Arnaud, "L'image du globe dans le monde romain," *MEFRA,* 1984, 53–116.

30. In order better to understand the concentric character and the assimilation of two spheres (celestial and terrestrial), see G. Aujac's excellent summaries: "La sphéropée, ou la mécanique au service de la découverte du monde," *Rev. Hist Sc.,* 1970, 93; "L'image du globe terrestre dans la Grèce ancienne," *Rev. Hist. Sc.,* 1974, 193; "Sphérique et sphéropée," *Historia Mathematica* 3 (1976): 441; "Le ciel des fixes et ses représentations en Grèce ancienne," *Rev. Hist. Sc.,* 1976, 289; "Regards sur l'astronomie grecque," in *L'astronomie dans l'Antiquité classique,* ed. G. Aujac and J. Soubiran (Paris, 1980), 35–56, and his introduction to *Géminos, Intr. aux Phénomènes* (Paris, 1975), LXV–LXXVII.

31. This is the lesson on modesty that Cicero draws from the "contemplation of the sphere" in his famous passage "The Dream of Scipio" (*De rep.,* 6.20: *a quibus exspectare gloriam certe nullam potestis*), with a commentary by Macrobius (*Comm.,* 2.5), in accordance with the whole scientific tradition of the Greeks—even if the hypothesis of the four "inhabitable worlds" of Crates of Mallos is not accepted by all (cf. J. O. Thomson, "Marcus Aurelius and the Small Earth," *JRS,* 1953, 47–48).

32. Henceforth, see M. H. Crawford, *Roman Republican Coinage,* vol. 2 (Cambridge, 1974); I identified the coinage according to his catalog. It is pointless here to provide a bibliography of the arguments for each of these types. Regarding the globe, refer to the works of S. Tabaronni, "Sfere celesti sulle monete romane," *Caelum* 26 (1956): 7–16, and "Globi celesti e terrestri sulle monete romane," *Physis* 7 (1965): 317–53, which have been rightly questioned by P. Arnaud.

33. A. Momigliano, "*Terra marique,*" *JRS,* 1942, 53–64 (= *Secondo Contrib.,* 431–46).

34. M. Antonius Creticus had a famous *imperium infinitum* (Cicero, 2 *Verr.*, 2.8; Velleius, 2.31, esp. 3); in order to interpret these symbols, M. H. Crawford believes that it is an attempt to justify the war against Sertorius (*RRC*, 1:409).

35. Mark Antony also used this symbol in 40 B.C. (Grueber, *BMCRR*, 2:495, nos. 114–15).

36. *RRC*, no. 426, 4a. The different types of the issue concern Sulla on the one hand (no. 426, 1), Pompey on the other; A. Alfoldi mistakenly linked all these types to a Sullan propaganda: "Symboles syllaniens et propagande pompéienne," *REL*, 1950, 54–55. The three small crowns recall the three triumphs; the bigger crown is the golden one voted for Pompey in 63 B.C. (Velleius, 2.40.4; Dio, 37.21.4, who erroneously writes "of laurels").

37. Regarding the new cosmic symbolics, spectacular and refined, of this colossal complex, see F. Coarelli, "Il complesso pompeiano del Campo Marzio e la sua decorazione scultorea," *Rend. Pont. Acc. Arch.* 64 (1971–72): 99–122; G. Sauron, "Le complexe pompéien du Champ de Mars: nouveauté urbanistique à finalité idéologique," *L'Urbs: espace urbain et histoire,* Colloquium of the French School in Rome (Rome, 1985), 456–73; E. Frézouls, "La construction du *theatrum lapideum* et son contexte politique," *Actes des Colloques du CRPOGA* 7 (Strasbourg, 1983), 193ff.; P. Gros, "La fonction symbolique des édifices théâtraux dans le paysage urbain de la Roma augustéene," in *L'Urbs* (quoted above), 319–46. Concerning the group of statues, see Pliny, *NH,* 36.41: [Varro] *et a Coponio quattuordecim nationes quae sunt circa Pompeium factas auctor est* (cf. Suetonius, *Nero,* 46). These were perhaps later surrounded by a portico (the *Porticus ad Nationes?*).

38. D. Falenna, "Il Pompeo di Palazzo Spada," *Arch. Class.* 8 (1956): 193ff.

39. Regarding Caesar's cosmocratic claims, besides D. Michel, *Alexander als Vorbild für Pompeius, Caesar und Marcus Antonius. Archaeologische Untersuchungen,* Coll. Latomus 94 (Brussels, 1967), see S. Weinstock, *Divus Julius* (1971) (for the statue on the *Capitolium,* refer to pp. 40–59).

40. Dio, 43.14.6: *ἅρμα τέ τι αὐτοῦ ἐν τῷ* Καπιτωλίῳ *ἀντιπρόσωπον τῷ Διὶ ἱδρυθῆναι, καὶ ἐπὶ εἰκόνα αὐτὸν τῆς οἰκουμένης χαλκοῦν ἐπιβιβασθῆναι, γραφὴν ἔχοντα ὅτι ἡμίθεός ἐστι . . . ἐκέλευσαν.* 43.21.1: . . . *μήτε τὴν εἰκόνα τῆς οἰκουμένης τὴν ὑπὸ τοῖς ποσὶν αὐτοῦ κειμένην. . . .*

41. J. Vogt, *Orbis Romanus,* (Tübingen, 1929), 158, n. 22; T. Hölscher, *Victoria Romana* (Mainz, 1967), 23 n. 120; D. Michel, *Alexander als Vorbild,* 73 and 85.

42. Concerning these personifications, see J. Schmidt, *Oikoumene* (2), *RE* 17 (1936): 2174; D. Pinkwart, *Das Relief des Archelaos von Priene und die Musen des Philistos* (Kallmunz, 1965), 34–42. Regarding the painting that served as the decor during the *Demetria,* see Schlachter, *Der Globus,* 65 n. 4, who rightly leans toward a personification and not a globe: contra J. Vogt, *Orbis Romanus,* 158 n. 22; P. Arnaud, "L'image du globe," 114 (inexact); S. Weinstock, *Divus Julius,* 42, 47.

43. An image of Ge with Hemera, Nyctè, Ouranos, and also the East and the South, had been carried to Daphnae at the famous "triumph" of Antiochus IV Epiphanes in 167 B.C.: Polybius, 31.3 = Athenaeus 5, 195.

44. S. Weinstock, *Divus Julius,* 50 (and pl. 5, 5) [cf. our fig. 12 for the coin of Hadrian]; 45 for the low relief of the *Via Cassia* (Fuhrmann, *MDAI(R),* 1949, 23), actually at the Museo Nazionale. Concerning *orbis terrarum* on imperial coins, see a coin of Vespasian with a turreted head and *Paci orb(is) terr(arum) Aug(ustae)* (*BMCRE,* 2:96, no. 459). Another coin, interesting if authentic, is mentioned by Miller, *Mappae Mundi,* 3:130; *Pax orbis terrarum / M. Cocceius M. f. Nerva III vir / Asi(a) Eur(opa) Afr(ica);* unfortunately it is cited following a seventeenth century collection (*Caroli ducis Croyiaci et Aschotani . . . numismata* [Anvers, 1654], pl. 15, fig. 18). In fact this coin does not exist.

45. G. Picard, "Le monument de César Cosmocrator au Capitole," *Rev. Arch.,* 1973, 261–72. This is the famous low relief of the "Parthian altar" at Ephesus, probably dedicated by an Ephesian supplies-manager for the Parthian expedition of L. Verus. Besides the apotheosis of the emperor, it consisted of a series of historical panels (the adoption, the battle), and allegorical figures, either cosmic (the Sea, the Night, the Moon) or geographic (towns and provinces); see B. Andreae, *L'art de l'ancienne Rome* (Paris, 1977), 249, 435–35; F. Eichler, "Zum Partherdenkmal von Ephesos," *Oester. Jahrb.* 9 (1971): 102–36; and more recently, W. Oberleitner, ed., *Funde auf Ephesos und Samothrake,* Kunsthistor. Mus. (Vienna, 1978), 66–93. On this low relief surely the reclining figure carrying the *cornucopia* in her left hand and with a child near her is *Tellus* and not *Oikoumene.*

46. See J. Rufus Fears, *Princeps a diis electus, PMAAR* 26 (1977): 205ff.

47. J. B. Giard, *Bibl. Natl. Catal. des Monnaies de l'Empire Rom. vol. 1: Auguste* (Paris, 1976).

48. Cf. below p. 55; P. Zanker, *Forum Augustum* (Tübingen, 1974), and A. Degrassi's extensive introduction to his edition of the *Elogia* of the *Forum, Inscr. Ital.* 13, no. 3 (1937): 2–8; H. Jordan, *Topographie der Stadt Rom* (1885), 2:443ff.; O. Gilbert, *Geschichte und Topogr. der Stadt Rom*[2] (1901), 110ff.; Platner-Ashby, *Topographical Dictionary of Ancient Rome* (London, 1929) 220–23; G. Lugli, *Roma Antica, Il centro monumentale* (Rome, 1946) 258–69, and F. Coarelli, *Roma*[2] (Rome and Bari, 1981), 104ff.

49. Last, M. Bonnefond, "Le Forum d'Auguste et le Capitole: transfert de fonctions et mutations idéologiques" in *L'Urbs: Espace Urbain et Histoire* (Rome, 1987), 251–78. The Forum fits in the famous dossier of the links, albeit ambiguous, between Augustus and the myth of Alexander (cf. below p. 56). A summary and an earlier bibliography are found in G. Cresci Marrone, "Alessandro fra ideologia e propaganda in età Augustea," *Giorn. Ital. Fil.,* 1978, 245–59. Augustus had dedicated in his Forum spoils taken from Alexandria, the golden statues of Victory that had served as columns to the cenotaph in which Alexander's ashes had been borne from Susa to Alexandria (Pliny, *NH,* 34.48: *Alexandri quoque Magni tabernaculum sustinere traduntur solitae statuae ex quibus duae ante Martis Ultoris aedem dicatae sunt;* cf. Diodorus, 8.26.6). Moreover, he had placed, no doubt under the porticoes, two paintings by Apelles, one which represented Castor, Pollux, and Alexander, and the other *belli imaginem restrictis a terga manibus Alexandro in curru triumphante*

(Pliny, *NH,* 35.93–94). Surely it involves an "allegory" of war (Bellona?), and not simply of the captives, as believed by R. Dant ("*Belli facies et triumphus,*" *MDAI(R),* 1984, 115ff., based upon Statius, *Theb.,* 12.519), which Mrs. Agnes Rouveret pointed out to me.

50. Velleius, 2.39.2: *Divus Augustus, praeter Hispanias aliasque gentes, quarum titulis forum eius praenitet, paene idem, facta Aegypto stipendaria, quantum pater eius Galliis, in aerarium contulit* (cf. A. G. Woodman, "Questions of Date, Genre and Style in Velleius: Some Literary Problems," *CQ,* 1975, 272–306; J. Hellegouarc'h, *Velleius Paterculus,* CUF, (Paris, 1982), 1:24, 53–59). No doubt, there was a creation not of the provinces of Raetia and Pannonia under Augustus but of new districts attached to the old provinces: see H. Braunert, "*Omnium provinciarum populi Romani . . . fines auxi,*" *Chiron,* 1977, 207–17 (comm. to *RG* 26.1).

51. In fact, this interpretation goes back at least to Mommsen, in *CIL,* 1 (1863), p. 281 (taken as such by Hulsen, *CIL,* 1^2, 1, p. 1187, no. 2: *quibus sub quadrigis ad exemplum statuarum in porticibus collocatarum res ab Augusto gestas inscriptas fuisse arguit Vellei locus . . .*). This interpretation is taken up again in all the handbooks on topography cited above, n. 48. Mommsen also quoted Horace, *Carm.,* 4.14.2–5: *tuas / Auguste virtutes in aevum / per titulos memoresque fastus aeternet;* but Horace died in 13 B.C.: see A. Degrassi, "Virgilio e il foro di Augusto," in *Scritti vari di ant.,* 4 vols. (Rome, Trieste, 1962–71) 1:283. Yet if the work on the Forum, inaugurated between 6 and 2 B.C., was already well advanced at this date, this cannot be a first draft of the *RG.*

52. L. Braccesi, "Una ipotesi sull'elaborazione delle *RGDA,*" *Giorn. Ital. Fil.,* 1973, 25–40, taken up and expanded upon in *Epigrafia e storiografia (interpretazioni augustee)* (Naples, 1981), 11–38, esp. 17–18: "il plurale *tituli* potrebbe tanto riferirsi a una singola iscrizione incisa su piú colonne, quanto a una pluralità di epigrafi continue . . . Propenderei, decisamente, per la prima ipotesi." Kornemann puts forth the same hypothesis in *RE* 16, no. 1 (1933): 225.

Another hypothesis was put forth, too readily and contradictorily (and long since forgotten), by R. Lanciani, "Il Foro di Augusto," *Bull. Comm.,* 1889, 27–32. He gives an account of the discovery of the base of a golden statue of Augustus offered by the province of Baetica in Augustus's Forum (Gati, *NS* [1889] 16; *CIL,* 6.31267 = *ILS,* 103): *Imp. Caesari / Augusto P.P. / Hispania Ulterior / Baetica quod / beneficio eius est et / perpetua cura / provincia pacata / est auri / p(ondo) C(entum).* Lanciani, who held the common view ("the quadriga on the base of which was engraved the narrative of his warlike expeditions"), then ingeniously linked this inscription (later than 2 B.C.) to Velleius's text. And the golden statue can prompt this opinion. But the base—actually in the reserves of the Casa dei Cavalieri di Rodi—is very small: some thirty cm high. It is not known whether golden statues dedicated by other provinces or *gentes* exist. Would Velleius have used *titulus* to signify a golden statue of Augustus offered by a province?

53. B. Wesenberg, "Augustusforum und Akropolis," *Jahrb. Deutsch. Arch. Inst.,* 1984, 161ff., esp. 172, 183–84, n. 141: "Kennzeichnende Waffen [sicher aber nicht die Kopien der Erechteionkoren] Konnten die *tituli* durchaus sinnvoll erganzen."

54. Mommsen's theory concerning the first Temple of Mars on the Capitolium, which Augustus would have built in 19 B.C. before the one in the Forum, must be rejected: see J. Simpson, "The Date of the Dedication of the Temple of Mars Ultor," *JRS*, 1977, 91–94, who quotes Horace's undisputable testimony (*Carm.* 4.15.4): *Tua, Caesar, aetas . . . / et signa nostro restituit Jovi:* between 19 and 13 B.C. the standards were still in a temple of Jupiter (Jupiter Tonans or Feretrius?).

55. *RG* 33.2, about 10 B.C. (Gagé, *RG*, 142).

56. R. Syme, "The Crisis of 2 B.C." (= *Rom. Pap.*, 3: 922).

57. Ovid, *Ars Amat.*, 1.213–28:

Ergo erit illa dies, qua tu, pulcherrime rerum,
Quattuor in niveis aureus ibis equis;
Ibunt ante duces onerati colla catenis,
Ne possint tuti, qua prius, esse fuga.
Spectabunt laeti juvenes mixtaeque puellae,
Diffundetque animos omnibus ista dies;
Atque aliqua ex illis cum regum nomina quaeret,
Quae loca, qui montes quaeve ferantur aquae,
Omnia responde, nec tantum si qua rogabit;
Et quae nescieris, ut bene nota refer:
Hic est Euphrates, praecinctus harundine frontem;
Cui coma dependet caerula, Tigris erit;
Hos facito Armenios, haec est Danaeia Persis
Urbs in Achaemeniis vallibus ista fuit;
Illa vel ille duces, et erunt quae nomina dicas,
Si poteris, vere, si minus, apta tamen.

[Therefore that day shall dawn whereon thou, fairest of beings, shalt ride all golden behind four snow-white steeds. Chieftains shall go before thee, their necks laden with chains, lest they be able to save themselves by the flight they used before. Joyous youths shall look on and maidens with them, and that day shall make all hearts o'erflow. And when some girl among them asks the names of the monarchs, or what places, what mountains, what rivers are borne along, do you answer everything, nor only if she asks you; ay, even if you know not, tell her as if you knew it well. That is Euphrates, his forehead fringed with reeds; he with the dark blue locks downhanging must be Tigris. These, say, are Armenians, here is Persia, sprung from Danae; that was a city in the Achaemenian valleys. That one, or that, are chieftains; and you will have names to give them, correct, if you can, but if not, yet names that are fitting . . .]

The interpretation that recognizes Ovid's insolence or clumsiness was shown above. *Contra* G. Williams, *Change and Decline* (Berkeley, 1978), 79.

58. Servius, *Ecl.*, 9.46: *etiam in Capitolio statuam super caput aueream stellam habentem posuit: inscriptum in basi fuit:* καίσαρι ἡμιθέῳ; cf. H. Malcovati, *Imp. Caes. Aug. Fragm.*[4] (Turin, 1962), 87–88.

59. Concerning these questions, see J. Rufus Fears, *Princeps a diis electus . . . ,* 206–15. Regarding the *gemma Augustea* of Vienna, see Furtwängler, *Antike Gemmen,* 56; H. Kahler, *Die Gemma Augustea* (Berlin, 1967) (which would celebrate Tiberius's triumphal return in A.D. 9–10); D. Kienast, *Augustus,* 108.

60. Suetonius, *Aug.,* 94.5: *nota ac vulgata res est P. Nigidium, comperta morae causa* [the late arrival of Octavius, Octavian's father, to the Senate in September 63 B.C. due to the birth of his son], *ut horam quoque partus acceperit, affirmasse dominum terrarum orbi natum . . . ;* the same Figulus linked the sign of Capricorn to a cosmic conception of the royalty: Fears, *Princeps a diis electus . . . ,* 210.

61. Since 1979, information of the finds made on this famous site and in subsequent digs was given in K. Erim's *Revue Arch.,* 1982, 163–69; *Aphrodisias 1982,* V. Kazi Sonuçlari Toplantisi (Ankara, 1983), 275–83; *Aphrodisias 1985* (Ankara, 1986), 541–45; or S. Mitchell, "Archaeology in Asia Minor," *Arch. Reports, JHS* 31 (1984–85): 70–105. See also the provisional and wonderfully edited synthesis by K. Erim, *Aphrodisias* (London, 1986), 106–23. Concerning the history of Aphrodisias and its links with Rome (other than the latter), see J. Reynolds, *Aphrodisias and Rome* (London, 1982) (a collection of the documents from the "wall of the archives" of the Theater).

62. Regarding the *Sebasteion,* see Fr. Hueber, "Der Baukomplex einer Julio-Claudischen Kaiserkultanlage in Aphrodisias" in *Aphrodisias de Carie,* ed. J. de la Genière (Paris, 1987), 63–68. The inscriptions that accompany certain panels and statues (known in 1980) have been published by J. Reynolds, "New Evidence for the Imperial Cult in Julio-Claudian Aphrodisias," *ZPE* 43 (1981): 317–27. The *Sebasteion* (a name attested by an inscription previously known, see *IG,* 3.2839) is a double portico (81 m long by 14 m wide) with three stories that led to a sanctuary "of the august gods." Aphrodite was represented, Προμήτορα θεῶν Σεβάστων (Erim, *Aphrodisias,* 111), as well as the mythical ancestors of the Julio-Claudians, among them Aeneas. Concerning the expression προμήτωρ, see a dedication to Trajan in J. Reynolds, *Aphrodisias and Rome,* no. 55; and L. Robert, *AC,* 1966, 417. I do not know if the figure (Erim, 115) really represents Augustus. It is worth noting a representation of two young *principes* (Gaius and Lucius rather than Drusus and Germanicus), one of whom (Gaius) carries the globe and the aplustre, both symbols of universal domination. Concerning *Roma* and *Ge,* see J. Reynolds, "New Evidence for the Imperial Cult in Julio-Claudian Aphrodisias," *ZPE* 18 (1981), no. 7.

63. G. Bowersock, *Roman Arabia* (Cambridge, Mass., 1983) 49 n. 15.

64. Most of these names—for example the *Andizetti*—are known only by Strabo and Pliny; Strabo, 7.5.3, for the 'Ανδιζῆτοι and the Πειροῦσται.

III

Errors and Truths: The Geographical Knowledge of the Time

It has been shown how the ecumenical claims of Roman domination, from Pompey to Augustus, were ostentatiously expressed through architectural or iconographic programs by way of an allegorical and religious transposition. The personifications of nations (which are sometimes more symbolically than realistically identified), the recourse to cosmological allegories (the Ocean, the Earth, or the *Oikoumene*), and the use of astrology on a monumental scale (in the *Horologium* placed within Rome itself) could all be interpreted as corresponding to the emphatic exaggerations of commissioned poetry. However, none of this could be proven.

But it has also been shown how the *Res Gestae* of the *princeps*—conforming to the tradition of triumphal inscriptions and *elogia*—wanted to be viewed as didactic and almost as pedagogical. Its geography was factual and not allegorical. It was based upon the actual lay of the land, marking precise boundaries, indicating directions and almost including distances. This leads to the inevitable question: what is the relationship of this text to contemporary geographical knowledge and, particularly, to the knowledge prevalent at Rome?

Despite the loss of so much ancient science and literature, the stages of knowledge can be reconstructed with enough precision.[1] It is worth noting that the ancients themselves took pains (more often than we think) to assess and to recapitulate, in a very pedagogical way, the successes—or sometimes the errors—of their predecessors. When scholars, philosophers, geographers, or historians speak of the world or of geography, they often begin with some criticism of their predecessors. In order to reconstruct the fragmentary and successive visions of these men, one has to consult Herodotus, Aristotle, Polybius (partially lost), and in particular Strabo or Pliny for the broader outline. Moreover, Ptolemy adopted the same procedures, and because of him, we know his predecessors: Marinus of Tyre, and the sailors or travellers who brought back new information. And this is enough to reconstruct—at least approximately—the progress and the changes in the representation of the world by the ancient Greeks and Romans (the views of the Orientals, Indians, or Chinese, although no less interesting, present different problems). It would be fascinating to compare these, as was recently done by J. André and J. Filliozat.[2]

This progress evolved on two slightly different planes. The Greeks, first of all, (like the Phoenicians and the Egyptians before them) gained knowledge of nations with which they were directly or indirectly in contact by sea rather than by land. Sailors and merchants had written more or less elaborate descriptions, often anonymous, with or without the intention of being published and handed down to posterity. Such texts represent inventories of remarkable locations and areas, coordinated along lines of communications. Naturally these accounts can convey other information, such as directions according to the cardinal points or the compass-card, or observations of peoples encountered, frontiers, and goods.

In brief, the genre of *periplus* in its elaborate form (which may have been assumed quite early, just as the short versions would last for a long time) has two possibilities. On the one hand, the account can be a visualization (eventually graphic) of regions so extensive that it becomes a "drawing of the world," a graphic and global representation (on a small scale) of the world (known, inhabited, or accessible, as the case may be). On the other, the account can be an ethnography, a description of peoples combined with their history and their myths. As early as the fifth century B.C., Hecataeus of Miletus had written a *Periegesis*, or *γῆς περίοδος*. Herodotus, who had simply entitled his work "Inquiry," or Ἱστορία, had also combined ethnography and geography. As will be shown, neither of these two original methods of representing and of describing the world was abandoned. At every phase of ancient history, each would undergo new developments, with the extension of voyages of discovery. Such voyages were important and diverse: some of them were maritime and exploratory, like that of Pytheas in the western and northern Ocean (one of the great mutations in the knowledge of space), while others were military or political, like all the surveys, official or otherwise, that followed Alexander's conquests in the East, in India and Bactria.[3]

But from the outset, knowledge of the world had also evolved on a second plane, which can either be labelled scientific or theoretical. By that, I mean that it aimed at global knowledge, on a small scale, and at giving an account as completely and satisfactorily as possible of the size, the nature, and even the origin or characteristics of the physical universe. In this way, the inquiry (or the theoretical construction) fell within the scope of more general knowledge.[4] It was attached to what we would call cosmography, physics, meteorology, etc. (terms that Aristotle would popularize in the fourth century B.C.): that is, to connections between the elements (earth, sea, air), links with astronomy, and an explanation of natural phenomena whether celestial or terrestrial. This double trend is evident from the beginning, even before the flourishing of Greek science in the Hellenistic period. For example, it is very early (among the Pythagorians, perhaps in the fifth century B.C.), that the hypothesis of a spherical terrestrial globe was formulated, by means perhaps more philosophical than rational or empirical. But it would take a long time—until Plato (*Timaeus*, 63a), Aristotle (*De caelo*, 2.14 298a), and above all, Eudoxus of Cnidos (fl. ca. 368–365)—for this idea to take root and supplant other views such as the Ionians' flat disk or Anaximander's cylinder.[5] It was also very early that attempts were made to represent visually on a tableau (*πίναξ*) the whole known world (and the Ocean); that is, this was early cartography,[6] for it involved total representations in two dimensions, rather than merely linear summaries. Anaximander, ca. 550 B.C. (Agathemeros, *Geographias hypotyposis*, 1.1), is credited with the first map, the prototype of those "Ionian maps" or "old maps" of which Strabo and Geminus speak five centuries later, and which Herodotus (4.36) and Aristotle (*Mete.*, 2.5 362b) criticized. Furthermore, these were "speaking" maps, or maps accompanied by texts, as is shown by the ambiguity of the terms that describe them: *γῆς περίοδον γράφειν* or even more simply *γεωγράφειν* which indicates a drawing of an outline, but one that also sometimes includes distances and lists of countries or seas. Of these first graphic (and hence metric) attempts, we have only echoes in historians or philosophers, and not in writers of the *periploi*. Therefore, there must have been contact.

These two different directions would both undergo a truly quantitative and qualitative mutation in the Hellenistic period, under the influence of the great expansion of the horizon that was recognized by the Greeks, and of the development of astronomical and geometrical science. The beginnings of astronomical geography—that is, based on the terrestrial and celestial spheres considered as concentric—are due, before Alexander, to the geometer and astronomer Eudoxus of Cnidos (fl. ca. 368–365),[7] who had also "described the world," that is, drawn a map and written a text of this title (Agathemeros, 1.1; *RE* VI, col. 947), and put forward the concepts of latitude, the equator, and the tropics. He was the first to provide astronomical methods for determining the latitudes and to try to measure the length of the meridian (Agathemeros, 1.1; Aristotle, *De caelo*, 2.14 298a). But, from another perspective, the actual knowledge was greatly extended by Pytheas's journeys[8] to the West and North, by Alexander's officers—Nearchus and Patrocles—to the East, and then, by the voyages and expeditions to the Red Sea and Ethiopia ordered by the Lagidian kings.

Henceforth, the majority of these expeditions were undertaken or joined by scientific observers: Pytheas made astronomical surveys of the latitude and wrote, based on his journey, at least two works, *On the Ocean* (Geminus, *Eisag.*, 6.9), and *Description of the Earth* (Schol. Apollonius Rhodus, 4.761–65 = frag. 15 Mette). Some sources acclaimed this scholar as a "philosopher," and his books included notes on physics as well as ethnography. The same holds for the officers and scholars in the circle of Alexander and his successors.

This encyclopaedic spirit, e.g., of Aristarchus of Samos[9] and of Dicaearchus,[10] marks all of Hellenistic culture. To Dicaearchus, a philosopher and an historian, we owe decisive progress in the construction of maps, since he was the first to conceive of the projection plane based on geometric data. There were two perpendicular axes, of which the first (the *diaphragma*) corresponding to a main parallel (from the Pillars of Hercules to the Himalayas, passing through Sardinia, Sicily, the Peloponnesus, the southern coast of Asia Minor, and the Taurus Mountains), while the other was a meridian. Dicaearchus had also joined to it a geographical work (Περίοδος γῆς, Lydus, *De mens.*, 4.107, p. 147 Wünsch). But this is truly the case for the veritable father of ancient scientific geography, Eratosthenes of Cyrene (273–192),[11] the fourth director of the Library at Alexandria—a polymath, mathematician, philosopher, astronomer, and grammarian—who was perhaps the first to entitle one of his works "Geography" (Γεωγραφικά or Γεωγραφούμενα: Strabo, 1.29); but another of his writings, more "geometric," was entitled "Measurement of the Earth" (Περὶ τῆς ἀναμετρήσεως τῆς γῆς: Heron, *Dioptra*, 35).

While Eudoxus and Dicaearchus had calculated the terrestrial meridian on the basis of astronomical measurements (Pédech, 97), Eratosthenes had substituted for it the well known measurements of the meridian between Syene and Alexandria based on the measurements of the difference in the latitude of these two cities on a given day (specifically, the summer solstice, which allowed him to observe that Syene was situated on the Tropics). Further, knowing the distance (given by royal *bematistai*) he was able to deduce the measurement of the degree of latitude and hence the entire circumference. Eratosthenes, despite the factual errors on which his measurements were based, arrived at 252,000 *stades,* which (using the Egyptian *stade* of 157.5 m) equals 39,690 km—an amazingly accurate result but the subject of dispute, since it depends upon contradictory errors and since it is not known which *stade* Eratosthenes used (see Pliny, *NH,* 12.53 who gives 47,500 km!).[12]

It is not by chance that Eratosthenes's geographical work is relatively well known to us. One might suppose that this is due only to the preservation of the work of Strabo (p. 384 Berger), an author who was curiously isolated. But in reality Eratosthenes, though he was criticized by his successors, was always cited and recognized as the starting point for every discussion (including those of Hipparchus and Polybius). He was also one of the Greek geographers (along with Artemidorus or Posidonius) who was most frequently quoted by Latin authors such as Cicero, Varro, and Vitruvius, and above all by Pliny, Mela, and Macrobius. This is because discussion of every question began with him: the development of the map with new measurements of the Earth, the adoption of a plane projection system with meridians and parallels, and the conception of the outline of the *oikoumene* as a vast island entirely surrounded by Ocean to the north, south, east, and west, which was located in the northern hemisphere (cf. below) yet occupied less than half its surface.

To Eratosthenes, the *oikoumene* was basically elliptical, twice as long as it was wide (or a little more), or shaped like a *chlamys:* a rectangle rounded at its two ends and punctuated by various seas or gulfs. He estimated that the *oikoumene* was 38,000 *stades* wide; it was bounded in the North by the latitude of Thule reached by Pytheas, in the South (at 3,400 *stades* from Meroë) by the latitude of the "cinnamon country," and calculated (in degrees of latitude) from the observations by Pytheas and by Philo for Meroë.[13] Its length was, according to him, almost 70,800 *stades,* from Cape St.-Vincent to the mouth of the Ganges, and about 78,000 *stades,* if the land to the east of the Ganges was taken into account. If his *stade* equals 177 m,[14] it exceeds the actual length by 3,000 km. But two things should be noted: firstly that to Eratosthenes no lands existed farther east than India (except several islands, among them Taprobane—that is, Ceylon); and secondly, that in his conception of the world with its overestimated length (though smaller than it is in reality), the overestimation of the length of the Mediterranean compensated for this supposed lengthening. Thus, the eastern coast of the Mediterranean—a world known to and taken over by the Greeks—was a bit less than half of the total length. Therefore, despite the illusory lengthening, the northern, southern, and eastern boundaries of the *oikoumene* did not appear inaccessible. We will return to this point later.

Men still had to draw their information correctly on a map. Eratosthenes invented (or perfected) a drafting system that completed the reticulation by his cylindrical projection: the division of the Earth into *sphragides*,[15] i.e., into simple, easily traceable geometric figures such as squares, rectangles, and parallelepipeds—that would generally correspond to parts of the world but not to natural regions or nations. They are purely a cartographic convention. This did not prevent Eratosthenes from writing an excellent regional geography in his other work (Strabo, 16.4.2–4). The word *sphragide* also apears in the vocabulary of surveying and of the fiscal geography of Egypt; etymologically it means a "seal" or "signet." The total number of *sphragides* is unknown, and Strabo mentions only four, of unequal size. Eratosthenes's system, although criticized, would remain the fundamental viewpoint of the ancient world for three centuries—until Marinus of Tyre and Ptolemy. The contemporaries of Augustus, Strabo in particular, retained the essentials of this system. It would only be contested, or completed, on two levels.

First of all, it was contested from a theoretical or mathematical view, mostly by the geometer and astronomer Hipparchus of Nicaea (190–120),[16] in his three-book geographical work, devoted solely to criticism of Eratosthenes. He was the first to urge and to attempt to use purely geometric methods in order to improve Eratosthenes's map, on the one hand by relying upon precise measurements—astronomical or from journeys—and on the other, by systematically using triangulation (Strabo, 2.1.27–34). He had, no doubt, included a table of latitudes modified by astronomical observations (Strabo, 2.5.34–43). Despite the way in which Strabo has transmitted them (length of the day to the solstice), Hipparchus probably was the first to translate them into degrees equal to 1/360 of a circle (see Dicks, 148–49; Strabo, 2.5.34, 132 C). And he modified the old theory of climates (κλίματα) by constructing regular zones around each degree of latitude. He spaced his half-hourly zones in half-hour increments, relative to the latitude expressed in the hour of the longest day, that is, 400 or 700 *stades* large. In any event, the astronomical phenomena did not change in this space (Dicks, 160). But Hipparchus himself did not attempt to draw up a map—and he certainly did not propose,[17] much less practice, any other system of projection than the cylindrical system of Dicaearchus and Eratosthenes (contra Berger, *Erdk.*, 476 and *Hipp.*, 35–37; cf. Dicks, 206).

Such was the view of the *oikoumene* achieved by Hellenistic science in the third and second centuries B.C., which combined the new observations and measurements of sailors and soldiers in the East and West, and the astronomical and mathematical elaboration of this data on the sphere. It was at the same time amazingly accurate in its representation of the vast zone appropriated by the Greeks—from the Gades to the Ganges, from Meroë to Thule—and inadequately limited.

This feeling of insularity of the *oikoumene,* and of its smallness compared to the vastness of the successfully measured globe—struck the ancients sufficiently strongly that a theory was born which, from the second century B.C. to the fifteenth and sixteenth centuries of our era, did not cease to haunt its students (whether accepted or rejected by them) and which has influenced our vocabulary and our subconscious. It was the theory of the "plurality of the inhabited worlds," coming from the scholar and grammarian Crates of Mallos (ca. 168 B.C.[18]), who was also concerned with the sphere (*sphairopoiia*). He used it as the only acceptable system of projection to represent the globe.[19] But in this way the isolation of the island *oikoumene* in the midst of the Ocean was suddenly apparent. And Crates also put forward the hypothesis (plausible but unverifiable) that there were three other *oikoumenai* in the other three sections of the world, which he called the *perioikoi,* the *antoikoi,* and the *antipodes* (Geminus, 16.1; Strabo, 1.4.6; 2.5.13, 118 C).[20] But in fact these three other worlds were inaccessible. This was made so particularly by the climate of the equatorial zone, but also by the distances to be covered (although on this point optimism was higher: see Strabo, 1.4.6, 64 C: it was possible to sail westward from the Iberian Sea to India).

Crates's more or less schematic representations of the sphere derive from this: the oceans cut across the sphere in a broad swathe, forming a cross and isolating the four continental landmasses that float on it (see fig. 25).[21] This cosmographical and geographical vision of the globe—which according to Strabo the geographers neglect, concerning themselves only with the inhabited world (*oikoumene*)—was a popular one in the culture of the time. It lent itself to the cherished considerations of Stoicism concerning the relativity of things that, in short, preached modesty. At Rome, Cicero popularized it in his introduction to the theory of the immortality of statesmen, which he ascribes to Scipio Africanus in Book 6 of *De republica* (at 20–21, *obliquos, transversos, adversos*). Following Macrobius, the theory would last into the Middle Ages, strongly opposed nevertheless by the return to the flat-earth theory. Philosophy adopted this doctrine,[22] but the geographers, as we have seen, disregarded it. It could be adapted to all sorts of metaphors—for example, in pretending to wonder if the furthest limits of the *oikoumene* (Britain or Taprobane) were not, in fact, the outposts of the underworld.[23]

These, then, are the essentials of the spatial and mental data in which was included the geographical vision of the ancients, until the revolution brought about in the first and second centuries A.D. by Marinus of Tyre and especially by Ptolemy.[24] This is not to say that no progress was accomplished between Hipparchus and the Augustan period. But it involved corrections to bearings or distances, discoveries on the borders or on the flow of certain rivers, or about routes newly surveyed or opened; in short, it involved an expansion of the well-known and measured zone. It was not a change in the general knowledge about the *oikoumene*. All in all, men of this era were filling in a picture whose outlines were already traced.[25]

Although the result of this new knowledge was for the most part assimilated and transmitted by Greek authors—Polybius, Artemidorus, Agatharchides, and Posidonius, and still others like Alexander Lychnos and Serapio—it must be stressed that they were aware (from Polybius to Strabo) that these improvements were largely made possible by the Roman conquest.[26] While the eastern campaigns of the second and first centuries B.C.—including those of Pompey—were fought in lands already known, the situation was not the same in the West.

The Greeks, mainly for political and military reasons, had only a general and approximate idea of the western part of Europe and Africa—especially of the northern and southern coasts of the Ocean. If Polybius and then Posidonius were able to describe Spain and Gaul anew, it was because they were able to travel there and because the commercial contacts and relations (official or unofficial) had increased. The merchants and the Roman armies opened up the routes and took measurements and notes (see the latitude measurements taken by Caesar in Britain with the *clepsydra, BG* 5.13.4); the geographers (polymaths or historians) tried to adapt these novelties to existing literature. This marked a general tendency, which was pointed out by the historians of geography: the development of a detailed descriptive geography (which, following Strabo, can be called "chorography"), which was largely devoted to history and to human geography (ethnography). Agatharchides's *On the Red Sea* is the best example.[27] While certain works—like the *geographoumena* of Artemidorus of Ephesus[28] (ca. 100 B.C.)—included in their introduction (Book 1) general corrections to the map of Hipparchus and Eratosthenes, and therefore dealt with the *oikoumene* in general, most of these works involved descriptions in the form of *periegesis*, or itineraries, spanning the world in vast, crudely circular movements and describing in detail, in an inventory, the coasts or overland routes (Strabo, 14.2.29, 663 C). This was not, as was stated, a regression, but rather a close coexistence of two complementary visions of space. This would be both Strabo's and Pliny's plan—as in fact it is the type of plan necessitated by all work of regional geography.

It should also be noted that henceforth most (Greek) authors of geographical works are men who had ties (official or unofficial) with the Roman authorities: Polybius of course, but also Artemidorus who pleaded at Rome on behalf of his fellow-countrymen against the publicans; Posidonius, a friend of Pompey and Cicero; and soon, as we shall see, Juba, Isidorus of Charax, or Strabo.

Yet, we must also note the special importance and influence of the work of Posidonius (ca. 135–50 B.C.).[29] He too was an encyclopaedist—mathematician, physicist, philosopher, historian—and a man of his time interested in the development of Roman politics in the world. Born in Syria (whence came important information concerning the East, which the Parthian conquest was cutting off from the Mediterranean), he traveled from Egypt to southern Gaul and to western Spain. Only one geographical work, Περὶ Ὠκεανοῦ, is formally attested if we disregard the *periplus* or *periegesis* mentioned in Pliny's index (15), but his *Histories after Polybius* (according to the *Suda*) contained many numerous and thorough passages of descriptive geography. Many of his fragments—which are often essential for us since they deal with mathematical geography (Edelstein 180–81, following Agathemeros and Cleomedes), with cosmography of the globe (the zones), and with physical geography (the hydrology of rivers, volcanoes, etc.)—cannot be positively attributed to either of these two works, but could be from his work on physics (*FHG,* 3.248–49) or on geometry. It has even been postulated that he wrote a monograph on the Celts.

At any rate, Posidonius's importance was considerable and undoubtedly well deserved because of the coherence, the breadth, and perhaps the originality of his doctrine. But as far as our study is concerned, we must stress two essential points. The first is in connection with mathematical and astronomical geography and with cosmography, and that is that he used a method—different from Eratosthenes's—to measure the terrestrial meridian that was based on the observation of the height of the star Canopus at Rhodes and at Alexandria (Cleomedes, *De motu,* 1.10.50–52 = frag. 202 E). His uncertainy about the actual distance between these two cities led him to calculate 180,000 *stades*—a figure too low no matter what length of *stade* he used. Nevertheless, this figure, unlike that of Eratosthenes, would have greater success and would be accepted by Ptolemy (this would have important consequences though they are not relevant to this study).[30] Next, he proposed a different and famous definition of the global zones, which henceforth were fixed by precise gnomonic lines corresponding to those actually used, that is, the arctic circle and the tropics (Strabo, 2.5.43, 136 C). These had the advantage of being detached from the circle of stars always visible in the sky, which varied depending on the place of observation

(Aujac, 158). Posidonius gave another definition of the zones that was climatic and even ethnographic. He had the originality to think (as Eratosthenes and Polybius before him) that the intertropical zone was neither uninhabitable nor uninhabited—which allowed, at least in theory, the possibility of voyages to the temperate zones of the Southern Hemisphere (Strabo, 2.2.3, 95 C = frag. 49 E.; 2.3.3, 98 C). He was also interested in marine phenomena, especially the ocean tides, which he himself observed at Gades.

The second essential point is that a developed human geography appears in Posidonius: his *Histories* included invaluable information about the Celts that we would not otherwise have (Athenaeus, 4.151 e-152 f = frag. 67 E., etc.). Strabo and Pliny borrow greatly from his works (whether from some unknown geographical book or the *excursus* to his *Histories*) for their regional descriptions of Spain and Gaul.[31] In short, all the elements of a complete geography, both physical and human, were certainly evident in Posidonius's manifold work.

It is a widespread error to believe that the Romans did little else than explore, measure, and conquer, thereby leaving "science" to the Greeks. There would be no Latin geography before attempts (usually spurned) by Pliny or Pomponius Mela.[32] This rests on a few, often misunderstood, shreds of evidence. Three or four passages in Cicero's letters to Atticus, from April to July of 59 B.C., mention Cicero's vague desire to write (or translate) a geographical work; but he eventually found the subject monotonous and not conducive to development. He jokes with Atticus, "I have hardly understood one line in a thousand" in Serapio's work (*Att.*, 2.4.1); but in fact he had read Eratosthenes, Serapio, and Hipparchus (who criticizes Eratosthenes), as well as contemporary authors such as Alexander Lychnos (*Att.*, 2.22.7) and Tyrannio, his host (*Att.*, 2.6.1). We have seen that Cicero knew the cosmography of Crates of Mallos; who could doubt that he had read Polybius and Posidonius?[33]

We are so convinced of Roman incompetence in this field that some editors of Caesar—especially Meusel and Klotz—have suppressed all *excursus* of a geographical character from their editions, claiming that "traces of Hellenism"[34] would be detected there. It is easy to reply, as some scholars fortunately have done, that if there is proof that Caesar made some precise and personal efforts to be informed, there is also proof that he collected data or had them collected (it amounts to the same thing): he quotes Eratosthenes (*BG*, 4.13; 6.24) and must have been aware of Posidonius. Moreover, the man who would reform the calendar with the help of Sosigenes knew how to make latitude measurements by the length of the days and the nights.

This is not, in fact, a real problem: at the end of the second century and in the first century B.C., "opposition" between the Greeks and the Latins was fast fading in favor of the appearance, at least in the educated classes, of a truly cultural *κοινή*. Higher education was certainly conducted in both languages; the Latins perforce had read the Greek authors for a long time, but better still, they associated with them and often included them in their circles.[35] The world vision—which varied according to the author, the level, the style, and the context—as conveyed by all types of geographical writings is neither Greek nor Roman: it is one and the same. Nevertheless, it is true that strictly speaking, geographical literature appeared later in Rome, towards the middle of the first century B.C. Therefore, it is a relatively recent phenomenon in Augustus's time.

But we do have at least two authors whom we must cite: Caesar and Varro. We have seen that the former's geographical *excursus* in his *Commentarii* about Gaul, Britain, and Germany make up coherent and pedagogical passages; there is no serious reason to consider them late interpolations. Caesar prepared them, or else had them prepared, on the basis of his readings of earlier writers (Eratosthenes, Polybius, and perhaps Posidonius; cf. the dimensions of Gaul: Strabo, 4.1.1; 4.5.1, 198–99 C = *BG,* 1.1.5–7). They must also have been based on more recent accounts such as those of the merchants whom he questioned about Britain (*BG* 4.20–21). What is interesting is the insertion of these documentary passages in texts that were like reports—even if these reports (which had no precedent) were published and aimed at a public larger than the normal senatorial circle. Though these passages are brief and succinct, because they were they must have seemed striking to his contemporaries and widened their knowledge of those regions that for a long time were known only indirectly—but that were finally reached and soon conquered, pacified, and measured. Alexander himself had had surveys conducted and had left in his archives a vast amount of new information about unknown worlds, but he had not written an account and a *tableau* of his conquests (the *Ephemerides* is a private journal). Later geographers—in particular Strabo—will have owed much to Caesar.[36] This new knowledge was probably also diffused by the more traditional historical works (or poems) glorifying the conqueror, for instance the poem of Varro Atacinus[37] (a Roman from Gallia Narbonensis) concerning the war with the Sequani, or the work of that Apollonius *libertus* who is quoted by Cicero (*Fam.,* 13.16).

But from a geographical viewpoint, the most complete (if not the most up-to-date) summary for the Roman public was found in the work of Varro of Reate.[38] Or rather, in his works: it is known that there was no purely geographical title in Jerome's incomplete catalogue (Jerome, *Ep. ad Ruf.,*

2.20), yet an unmistakeably geographical work, *De ora maritima,* is mentioned and quoted by Servius (*Ad Aeneidos,* 1.108, 112; 5.19; 8.710). Other sources (Solinus, and some *Itineraries*) refer to some works (?) on estuaries, or naval *Ephemerides* (Schanz–Hos. 1.569). But, as we know, Varro is frequently quoted by Pliny (fourteen times by name and even more often without being named, *pace* G. Sallman). Some of these quotations give distances (like Artemidorus or Agrippa) for Spain (Pliny, 4.115), Pontus (4.77), and Italy (3.95); these measurements might come from geographical or autobiographical works (the *De legationibus)* or from the *De geometria,* which certainly included development in the art of the *agrimensores.* Sallman tried to reduce to this core Varro's contribution to geography just as Pliny uses it. But this is hypercritical, and we should keep an element of Detlefsen's and Klotz's old hypothesis, which sees Varro as one of Pliny's three main sources: the source for his littoral descriptions with a series of toponyms and coastal cities—a striking characteristic of his geographical works. This is the case for the regions outside of Italy (cf. below p. 175 for the latter), for example Africa, as J. Desanges has recently shown.[39] Be that as it may, for Varro's lost works in which geography was definitely found, and for Varro himself, who certainly had read the available literature (since he was a librarian and an encyclopaedist), it is certain that geographical elements are present in his extant works: see for illustration the famous eulogy of Italy in *RR,* 1.2.3–7 (which was perhaps also found in Book 11 of his *Antiquitates,* according to R. Reitzenstein's hypothesis in *Hermes* [1885] 514–51).

Both Posidonius and Varro were providing a picture of the state of prevailing knowledge and geographical representations at the time when Rome, with Augustus, was examining the world now conquered. Is it then justifiable to speak, as has been done for so long, of a contrast—indeed of a division—between the "scientific"[40] spirit of the Greeks and the "practical" spirit of the Romans? We do not get that impression when reading Vitruvius,[41] a younger contemporary of Varro. This architect also sees himself as an astronomer, a geometer, and a geographer. He mentions and cites many Greek scholars, e.g., Eratosthenes, Hipparchus, and Posidonius. In fact, he understands the notion of latitude and informs us about sundials, including the portable ones. He has a theory of climates (independent of Posidonius's) and he knows and mentions the use of drawn maps. It is clear that technical literature (in Greek, and in Latin, insofar as it had begun to appear) was known among the Roman ruling class and, particularly, among highly skilled technicians like himself. Certain scientific fields (theoretical mathematics, for example) were still at this date expressed essentially in Greek, but their circulation began, directly or not, among a chosen Roman public, that of the *principes* and of high-ranking officials who felt the need to surround themselves with Greeks, either for political reasons or for their own prestige. After all, since we have lost Varro's geometry, the extent to which these subjects were being expressed in Latin is unknown.

Nevertheless, caution is necessary when dealing with geography itself. Greek geographers before Augustus, from Artemidorus and Agatharchides to Posidonius and Menippus of Pergamum (who wrote between 35 and 25 B.C.), either did not know at all or knew only vaguely the regions of the Northern Ocean: the Celtic region, Brittany, Germany, the "ocean shores" as far as the "Northern Pillars of Hercules," and the supposed outlet of the Caspian Sea. However, they described more fully the regions of the South—to Ethiopia, the Red Sea, Media, and India. While certain names, which in the *Res Gestae* (cf. below p. 85) mark the furthest limit of Augustus's conquest or fame, appear in certain of these geographers, such as the Sabaeans of Arabia Felix in Agatharchides, they are ignored by the Latin sources and are transmitted only by the Greeks (Diodorus, 3.47ff.). For example, it is almost certain that Theophanes of Mytilene, who had in his *Mithridatica* recorded the victories of his protector Pompey, provided geographical information (*FHG,* p. 315, frag, 5; *FGrHist,* 188 F 6 = Strabo, 11.14.11, 530 C, etc.) Yet this text, in Greek, is cited only by Strabo: those new geographical names were known to the Romans only through Pompey's triumphal inscriptions. The absence of these names in Latin texts is certainly an interesting indication of the limits of Roman geographical literature before the time of Augustus and Varro. This is not to say that they were unknown at Rome, at least in the circles in which Greek and scholarly literature were accessible; but, I think, no one had yet seen them written on an official document or in a public place.

To the Romans of that time, what was known concerning the general representation of the *oikoumene* was the world of the Greeks. They knew it with its remarkably correct results: an awareness of the globe's spherical shape, of its true dimensions, and of its latitudes (and the methods to calculate them). They were aware of the general location, on this globe, of an *oikoumene* measured approximately from the Atlantic coast of Europe and North Africa to almost the meridian of the mouth of the Ganges—that is, of an *oikoumene* much smaller than it is in reality, and in which (taking into account the inevitable errors in measurement of longitude) the inhabited part, or the part known to the Mediterraneans, obviously took on proportions larger than in nature, which gave it an added importance—indeed, a centrality.

They also knew it with its distortions and its errors:[42] the first being its width. They believed that towards the north, in the region of Pontus Euxinus and of Palus Maeotides, the depth of the European and Asiatic lands did not extend much further than the latitudes that they knew, in the west, to Brittany or the mouths of the Rhine. Thus the Northern Ocean seemed navigable and, so to speak, within reach. Likewise, to the south, Africa was believed to be a stretch of land longer than it was wide, which meant that the ocean bordering it—Ethiopian or Indian—was at a fair distance from the Mediterranean coast. Whence came their belief in all the accounts (incredible in our eyes) of possible circumnavigation westwards to the north or the south. According to Strabo (2.3.4ff.), Posidonius related at length, giving credence to its truth, the accounts of the "merchant-adventurer" Eudoxus of Cyzicus[43] who claimed to have found in the Red Sea a shipwreck identified by him (and by some Egyptian shipowners) as typically Gaditean; whence sprang his unfortunate attempts to circumnavigate Africa along the western shore, sailing from Gades. What is interesting is that, despite his failure, Posidonius believed that it could be done. Similarly, it was believed—according to Patrocles's inaccurate reports—that the Hyrcanian Sea (the Caspian) was connected to the Northern Ocean by a passage sometimes called the Northern Pillars of Hercules[44] (Strabo, 2.1.17; 7.2.4; 11.6.1; Tacitus, *Germania,* 34; Lucan, 3.278).

The reasons for this quite remarkable mixture of correct information, errors, and illusions are neither mysterious nor amazing. We should not put forward a "natural" difference between the ancient way of thinking and ours.[45] In the name of the anthropological reading of the ancient texts, their conceptions and representations of space have been implacably compared to our own. Unable to organize space into a two-dimensional format—cartographical if you will—they remained bound to the *periplus,* to a linear vision as if along an itinerary. This linear view, even if it records distances correctly, takes little account of true orientations, remains without depth, and juxtaposes a succession of points without placing them truly in space. In short, it produces a grossly distorted universe, as seen in the Peutinger Table.[46]

Of course, there is some element of truth in this conception. The spatial distortions and the incommunicability between one itinerary and another in the Peutinger Table have long been noted. The importance of itineraries, from seamark to seamark or stage to stage, is seen clearly in the ancients' daily life and their direct vision of the world—and, indeed, it has not altogether disappeared in our day. This is adequately explained by the technical conditions of these journeys. This mentality must not systematically be set in opposition to a cartographic mentality, which only appeared in modern times and which brought about a totally new vision of space in two dimensions, through complete charts based on astronomical measurements and on actual triangulation.

We have seen (and we will see) that this awareness of the surface extension of space, oriented according to the cardinal points and able to be represented or drawn with a truly geometrical accuracy, is found amongst the Greeks as early as the fifth century B.C., and is greatly perfected during the third and second centuries. In its principles, this awareness developed to such an extent with the work of cartographers of the imperial era, Marinus of Tyre and Ptolemy, that it was not surpassed until the seventeenth century.[47] They elaborated refined systems of projection that tried to account for the spherical nature of the globe, and the map was drawn with a large number of points (8,000) whose coordinates were given, like ours, in degrees of latitude and longitude. From then on, intangible principles are accepted. Naturally the practical realization left much to be desired: first there were the problems with the exactitude of the observations (when these could be entrusted to experts) and even, more fundamentally, the opportunity to make them. The sighting instruments (the diopter and perhaps the astrolabe) were either imperfect or tardy. But above all, the measure of the longitude was problematic without the help of chronometers, especially for maritime distances, which was not the case with the measurement of latitude. Consequently, in Ptolemy many coordinates stem not from direct observation, but from deductions or calculations that were based on data gathered from official or unofficial itineraries, which were more accurate in *relative* numbers but difficult to appreciate in absolute terms.

Therefore the "map" existed from the beginnings of Classical civilization. Along with it, the concept of "surface," that is, of space in two dimensions, is sufficiently attested by the *sphragides* of Eratosthenes, Hipparchus, and Posidonius, and the "lengths" and the "widths" of regions as given by Agrippa. Therefore, it is a lasting and close contamination, rather than an opposition, between the two "mental structures" that is noted in antiquity. At the same time, there is a remarkable progress in conceptualization—from the "Ionian maps" to Ptolemy, by way of Eratosthenes, Hipparchus, and Marinus of Tyre.

It is true that the character of the actual diffusion and destination of these maps is questionable. The ones just described are global maps of the *oikoumene*—comprising one third or one half of the surface of the hemisphere. They are maps on a small scale, despite the dimensions given by Strabo (2.5.10, 116 C, following Eratosthenes: a πίναξ seven feet long). A detailed cartography certainly existed in Greece and especially at Rome (see below p. 149), for the purposes of mapping lands belonging to cities or the cities themselves. This cartography was on a larger scale and was very accurate, being based on plotting and centuriation of the terrain. Between these two extremes, there is no testimony except fleeting and inconclusive references (like that of Varro's to the map (?) of Italy) to a regional cartography on an intermediate scale.

The second category is clearly official in function: it involves public documents of a cadastral type (see below). On the contrary, the general cartography is of a scholarly genre. It was the work—we know, when evidence is available—of astronomers or geographers who no doubt had drawn the maps or had them drawn, an impractical yet precious document that could only be drawn by a specialist (as it is today) but that could not be mechanically reproduced.[48] The notion of breaking up such a monument into panels, whose connection causes problems of projection (as still today), is apparently tardy: it perhaps goes back to Ptolemy or his later "editors."[49] Nevertheless, the pedagogical use of these panels in philosophical or other types of schools is attested for more than eight centuries, from the fourth century B.C. to the fourth century A.D. It will be shown that there was a public use for these maps, or "graphic representations" of countries, at least at Rome, but one of a very specialized nature: ostentatious, connected with triumphs or with temples, and therefore linked in one way or another to a mythical way of thinking or to collective interests.

The itineraries were definitely of a practical use. But destined for whom? Some were surely for private use, by sailors, merchants, or pilgrims (see the goblets by Vicarello); but others were for military use, such as those drawn by Alexander's *bematistai* or those mentioned in the Roman period by military writers such as Vegetius. Others still were perhaps used by certain administrations, such as the model of the Antonine itinerary.[50]

All these comments also apply to geographical literature. Moreover, graphics and writing are closely linked and often undistinguishable in antiquity: an itinerary is sometimes merely a list, a text; the coasts are not drawn on a *periplus,* unlike on the Genoan *Portulans.* Inversely, if the texts of the geographers shown above—up to and including Strabo and Pliny—sometimes spread out from the global vision of the *oikoumene* and of the "parts" of the world (the *sphragides* or other divisions), they often amazingly resembled itineraries. They enumerated the names of areas and of towns often in a topographical order (for example, along coasts or a route); thus a detail viewed at first as nonsensical can be explained. Their vocabulary itself appears sometimes borrowed from the *periplus,* in its concrete and visual character: "we find," "we reach," "beyond," etc.

All these remarks are important; but is it certain that such habits exclusively characterize a "noncartographical" mentality? Here again the answer greatly depends in part on the nature of the public at whom it was aimed and on the diffusion of geographical literature. There is no answer to this question, at least within the scope of this work: our sources are too fragmentary and the pieces of evidence too scattered. What is known of the aims or of the real public of Artemidorus, of Posidonius, or of Varro? One can only reason by analogy, remembering (for example) the essential role, more symbolic than practical, of geographical writings (a geography of discovery) in the circle and among the successors of Alexander.

But indeed the ancients themselves have given us the answer in a most formal and most unequivocal manner. It was not by chance, evidently, if the answer appeared precisely during Augustus's time through an Asian Greek, a representative of those intellectual notables who were thoroughly Hellenized and completely won over by the new Roman power, or who—better yet—rubbed shoulders with the governing class and especially with those entrusted with the administration of the vast empire, indeed, with its expansion. I mean of course Strabo,[51] the sole author of a general geography whose text we possess, along with Pliny and Ptolemy. (It is a mystery why his is the only work completely transmitted from antiquity). But Strabo's writing is unequivocal: for him, geography is indeed the science of the appropriation of the land by man, the inventory of his home, of his resources, and of the traces that he had left behind him. This geography is strictly political; it is essentially aimed at the rulers in order to allow them to govern better; but it also determines the types of government—at least for Strabo's time—and explains the beginnings of the empire.[52] Its geography is neither especially practical nor theoretical (mathematical), neither public nor private, but rather all of these together, because knowledge is needed for action, and no doubt understanding must precede obedience.

And this is why it is first of all a great inventory of everything. This in turn explains the importance in Strabo of notations concerning the "resources," the economy, alongside historical notations.[53] But which economy? It is the local resources, for the inhabitants, but it is also, and perhaps especially, the fiscal resources gathered by the rulers. We must realize that only Strabo's passages inform us about affairs as crucial as the slave-trade at Delos in the second century, the rapid development of the port of Puteoli, the silver mines in Spain (also mentioned by Diodorus), the wine consumption in Gaul, the duty paid in Gaul for trade with Brittany, the census numbers for Gades and Padua, the sudden development of trade with India by the Red Sea, and other data important to our knowledge of economic history in the Augustan period. To be persuaded of this, we need only consult Tenney Frank's index. This inventory, dominantly geographical, is a heroic undertaking, and it is more complete than those attempted by his predecessors because, for the first time, it is universal. Its only equivalent is the yet more heroic and more integrated attempt by Pliny the Elder, for whom cosmography and geography are the introduction, the "mental frame" (geometrical and at the same time political) that would allow the perception and the classification of an inventory of Nature in its entirety. It is an amazing inventory in itself, but it is even more amazing because this Nature, in Pliny's eyes, is henceforth universally accessible from a focal point, simultaneously the center of government and the matrix of civilization, "which gives humanity its meaning," and towards which the resources and the knowledge of an almost-enclosed world converged with its ensuing grandeur and its happiness.

In the preceding chapters, it has been shown how the *Res Gestae,* the political text *par excellence,* which Augustus had sealed before his death, came to crown and to explain rationally—this time for the benefit of the whole world—everything that he himself, and in particular his urban program at Rome itself, had proclaimed, using for that the symbolic and metaphorical language of architecture and of religion, throughout his reign: the *pax* that spread throughout the world though it was definitely centered on Rome; the conquest of prestigious borders deliberately pursued and achieved; the majesty of the Roman people, in victory and in peace; the *orbis terrarum subiectus.* In short, all this converges on a truly ecumenical geographic vision. This was in some ways an appeal to geography for his own interests and the needs of Rome. Strabo (to our knowledge) was the first author of this period to answer this call. But would Strabo have done so if the government had not set the first example? This inventory of a world finally completed (at least, so they thought) and henceforth unified—it is in reality Roman power that from the moment the new regime was established—and perhaps even from Caesar's victories at the beginning of 44 B.C.—had conceived and undertaken it. Each could make use of the other: politics could serve geography, and vice-versa. This will be the onus of our study henceforth.

NOTES

1. The great nineteenth-century syntheses on the history of ancient geography: P. F. Gosselin's *Recherches sur la géographie systématique et positive des Anciens* (Paris, 1813); A. Forbiger's *Handbuch der alten Geographie,* 3 vols. (Leipzig, 1842–48); M. Vivien de Saint-Martin's *Histoire de la géographie et des découvertes géographiques* (Paris, 1873); even C. R. Beazley's *The Dawn of Modern Geography,* 3 vols. (1896–1906), are outdated, especially on the philological point of view (for the ancient and medieval cartography, cf. below, chap. 5). The basic works of reference are still E. H. Bunbury, *History of Ancient Geography,* 2 vols. (London, 1879); and (concerning the Greeks) H. Berger, *Geschichte der wissenschaftlichen Erdkunde der Griechen*, 4 vols. (Leipzig, 1887–91; 2d ed. 1903), which also deals with the Greeks "under Roman influence"; J. O. Thomson, *History of Ancient Geography* (Cambridge, 1948); and various articles in *Real-Encyclopädie:* F. Gisinger, "Geographie," *RE,* suppl. 4 (1924), 521–685; "Oikoumene," *RE,* XVII, no. 2 (1937), 2123–74; W. Kubitschek, "Karten," *RE,* X, no. 2 (1919), 2022–2149 (regarding articles on certain authors, cf. below); the excellent book by C. Van Paassen, *The Classical Tradition of Geography* (Groningen, 1957); recent and useful syntheses by experts on Polybius and Strabo: P. Pédech, *La géographie des Grecs* (Paris, 1976), and G. Aujac, *La géographie dans la monde antique* (Paris, 1975). It should be noted that C. Müller's collection, *Geographi Graeci Minores,* 2 vols. (Paris, 1855–61) only contains the texts that have come down to us in complete form. Fortunately the fragments of the first geographers, from Hecataeus to Hipparchus, Eratosthenes and Posidonius, are found (when these have not been edited separately by modern scholars, cf. below) in the collections of C. and T. Müller, *Fragmenta Historicorum Graecorum,* 5 vols. (Paris, 1841–69), and of F. Jacoby, *Fragmente der griechischen Historiker* (Berlin/Leiden, 1926–58). Finally, see the various studies (shedding light on modern methods and points of view) collected by F. Prontera, *Geografia e geografi nel mondo antico: Guida storica e critica* (Bari, 1983), esp. V–XXXIII. Regarding the geography of the Romans, cf. below n. 32.

2. Concerning Indian geographers or cosmographers, see the recent work by J. Filliozat, *Appendice* in J. André, *Pline l'Ancien,* VI, 2 (Paris, 1980), 143–165 (cf. especially id., "Sur une série d'observations indiennes de gnomoniques," *Bull. Com. Tr. Hist.,* Sect. géogr. (1952): 11–13); regarding the geography of Near-Eastern empires, see P. Goukowski, "L'espace impérial de Darios Ier," in *Essai sur les origines du mythe d'Alexandre* (Nancy, 1978), 1:221–24: an oriented space, divided in great concentric circles, containing lists of peoples described in a coherent circular motion; add to his bibliography the work of P. Calmeyer, "Zur Genese altiranischen Motive, VIII, Die statistische Landcharte des Perserreiches II," *Arch. Mitt. aus Iran* 16 (1983): 141–222.

3. P. Goukowki, "Kosmokrator," in *Essai sur les origines du mythe d'Alexandre* 149–161, and 341–51, esp. 347 n. 81 (concerning Alexander's geographical knowledge); see also the studies by Roger Dion cited below, n. 42.

4. This led to the use of works on the history of the sciences; for example see the great syntheses by P. Tannery, *Mémoires scientifiques* (Paris, 1912–37), vols. 1–3; *Pour l'histoire de la science hellène*² (Paris, 1930); *Recherches sur l'histoire de l'astronomie ancienne* (Paris, 1893); P. Duhem, *Le système du monde: Histoire des doctrines cosmologiques de Platon à Copernic,* 5 vols. (Paris, 1913–17); O. Neugebauer, "The History of Ancient Astronomy: Problems and Methods," *Journ. of Near Eastern Stud.* 4 (1945): 1–38; the most important texts are found in E. H. Warmington, *Greek Geography* (London and New York, 1934); and in M. R. Cohen and I. E. Drabkin, *A Sourcebook in Greek Science* (Cambridge, Mass., 1948), 89–181. On all these points, refer to the excellent discussions and summaries in G. Aujac, *Strabon et la science de son temps* (Paris, 1966), 147–216; and in her two editions on Strabo, Book 1 (with Fr. Lasserre) (Paris, 1969), 3–49, and especially Book 2 (Paris, 1969), supplementary notes.

5. The famous map of Aristagoras, tyrant of Miletus, used to convince the Spartans: Herodotus, 5.49.51; regarding the Ionian "round maps," Herodotus, 4.36; but especially the brief survey of Agathemeros, 1 and 2 (in C. Müller, *GGM* 2:471); regarding the great precursor Anaximander of Miletus (ca. 611–546 B.C.), several versions of his cosmography: sphere (Diogenes Laertius, *Vita Phil.,* 2.2); cylinder, column (Hippolytus, *Ref. of all Her.* 1.6.3 = Cohen and Drabkin, *Sourcebook,* 92).

6. For ancient cartography in general, see K. Cebrian, *Geschichte der Kartographie,* vol. 1 (Gotha, 1922); K. Miller, *Mappae Mundi, die ältesten Weltkarten,* 6 vols. (Stuttgart, 1895) studies the late-classical and medieval documents that have come down to us: but see 6.114–147, *Gemessen Karten* (from Eratosthenes to Pliny); and especially the excellent and recent summary of O. A. W. Dilke, *Greek and Roman Maps* (London, 1985).

7. Fr. Lasserre, *Die Fragmente des Eudoxos von Knidos* (Berlin, 1966).

8. For important, albeit uneven, bibliographies on this famous Marseillais, see first of all the work of H. G. Mette, *Pytheas von Massilia* (Berlin, 1952) (Introduction, 1–16); and R. Dion, "Où Pytheas voulait-il aller?" in *Mél. Piganiol* (Paris, 1966), 1315–336; and "Alexandre le Grand et Pythéas," in *Aspects politiques de la géographie antique* (Paris, 1977), 175–223 (perhaps more controversial but contains the complete dossier).

9. Aristarchus (ca. 310–230 B.C.) presented, perhaps with Heraclides (ca. 390–310 B.C.), an innovative heliocentric theory of the solar system: see Th. Heath, *Aristarchus of Samos* (Oxford, 1913), 260–75; Cohen and Drabkin, *Sourcebook,* 105–14 (Simplicius, *Comm. on Aristotle, De caelo,* 444–45 Heiberg); see the explanations, on 107–8, with Archimedes's text, ed. Heath, 222.

10. See his fragments in F. Wehrli, *Die Schule des Aristoteles,* vol. 1 (Basel, 1967). Besides his work on the map and his use of the *diaphragma,* Dicaearchus took an interest in altimetry: W. Capelle, *Berges- und Wolkenhöhen bei griechischen Physikern,* Stoicheia, vol. 5 (Berlin, 1916); R. Baladié, *Le Péloponnèse de Strabon* (Paris, 1980), 131–35; H. Berger, *Erdkunde,* 3: 41–56.

11. H. Berger, *Erdkunde,* 3: 57–117; Berger has also edited the fragments, *Die*

geogr. Fragm. des Erat. (Leipzig, 1880) (the source index, 383–84, clearly shows our dependence on Strabo, Pliny, and Cleomedes); R. M. Bentham, *The Fragments of Eratosthenes* (Ph.D. [London, 1948]), *non vidi;* Dilke, *Greek and Roman Maps,* 32–35; for details on the measurement of the meridian, Cleomedes, *On The Circular Movements. . .,* 1:10ff. (translated, following Heath, in Cohen and Drabkin, *Sourcebook,* 149–53); regarding the map, the *oikoumene* in the shape of a *chlamys,* etc., Strabo, 2.1–3.

12. The following observations come from J. Desanges: "je ne sais si la distance de Méroë à la latitude correspondant au pays produisant la canelle a déjà été prise en considération par Eratosthène ou provient d'Hipparque, postérieurement: cf. mes *Recherches sur l'activité,* p. 74, n. 214. Sur le problème de Philon (dont je ne suis pas sûr qu'il séjourna à Méroë), cf. ibid., pp. 248–251. Indiscutablement les observations d'origine ont été effectuées par des marins en mer Rouge, et non dans la vallée du Nil nubien, cf. Pline, 6.171: *res ingentis exempli locusque subtilitatis immensae, mundo ibi deprehenso, cum indubitata ratione umbrarum Eratosthenes mensuram terrae prodere inde conceperit.* On aura posé l'équivalence grossière: Bérénice (des Troglodytes) = latitude de Syène; Ptolémaïs des Chasses = latitude de Méroë. Pour le point sur l'axe nilotique marquant la latitude du pays de la Canelle (Somalie du Nord, ex-italienne), on voit aussi que la référence d'origine est empruntée aux marins de l'ocean Indien."

13. (Comment by J. Desanges:) "Pline réduit donc aussi le stade d'Eratosthène au système commode: 8 stades font un mille romain (c'est le 'stade romain' d'Artémidore). Cela permet à Pline de dire sans sourciller (5.40) que 'Polybe et Eratosthène, que l'on tient pour les plus exacts, ont compté. . .onze cents milles. . .etc.' Il cite dans l'ordre inverse de la chronologie les auteurs, parce qu'il a lu Polybe approuvant Eratosthène (et non directement Eratosthène). Or les spécialistes estiment que le stade de Polybe est différent de celui d'Eratosthène (cf. G. Aujac, *Strabon,* t. II de la CUF, pp. 191–92; sur le stade attique, H. Prell, *Die Vorstellungen des Altertums von der Erdumfangslänge,* Berlin, 1959, p. 62). Il en résulte que Pline accumule les mesures données par divers auteurs grecs pour une même distance, sans se préoccuper de l'existence de divers stades et les transforme toujours en milles romains suivant la même recette, ce qui est assez étonnant pour un moderne. Reste à savoir si Polybe se souciait de transformer dans son système les stades d'Eratosthène, s'il est vrai qu'il employait le stade attique, sensiblement plus long que celui d'Eratosthène, d'ailleurs évalué différemment par G. Aujac et H. Prell. Ce problème mériterait une étude critique. Cf. en dernier lieu, à ma connaissance, D. Engels, 'The Length of Eratosthenes' Stade' dans *AJP* CVI, 1985, pp. 298–311, qui ne simplifie pas le problème."

14. There is nothing more confusing than the question concerning the evaluation of the Greek *stades* (see F. Hultsch, *Griechische und römische Metrologie* [Berlin, 1882], 57–64; H. Prell, *Die Vorstellung des Altertums von der Erdumfangslänge* [Berlin, 1959]; G. Aujac, *Strabon,* 2.192). See below the French works by A. Berthelot on Agrippa.

15. H. Berger, *Die geogr. Fragm. des Erat.*, 222ff.; Strabo 2.1.22–39 (see G. Aujac, *Strabon, Livre II*, 192–93). Concerning the fiscal meaning of *sphragis*, "governmentally defined and numbered area of land," *Pap. Oxyr.* IX, 18, 11, 8; *Pap. Fay.*, 339; *BGU*, 831, 6; *SB*, 4325, 11, 4.

16. See the excellent edition with an introduction and comment by D.R. Dicks, *The Geographical Fragments of Hipparchus* (London, 1960), more complete than that of H. Berger, *Die geogr. Fragm. des Hipparchos* (Leipzig, 1869).

17. A highly obscure fragment of Synesios, *Epist. ad Paeonium*, 311 B (*de dono astrolabi*), ed. Terzaghi, II, 138, 18 (Dicks, fr. 63) indicates that Hipparchus was preoccupied with the projection of the sphere. A few modern scholars attributed the stereographic projection to him (F. Joly, *La cartographie* [Paris, 1976], 61–62); Berger (*Erdkunde*, 476–79; and *Hipp.*, 35–37) thought that the systems of projection, visibly conical, to which Strabo alludes (2.5.1, 109 C; 2.5.10, 116–17 C) were those of Hipparchus. This is possible but not proven.

18. "Krates," *RE*, XI no. 2 (1922), no. 16 (W. Kroll); H. Berger, *Erdkunde*, 3:113ff., 123–26; Agathemeros, *GGM*, 2:471: his *oikoumene* was semi-circular.

19. Strabo, 2.5.5, 112 C, for the shape and division of the globe: the *oikoumene* would occupy one quarter of the sphere; 6, for the "artichoke head," his *spondyle:* 10, 116 C for Crates's sphere that should have been at least ten feet in diameter to be intelligible.

20. Geminus, 16.1; Strabo, 1.4.6; 2.5.13, 188 C; this is a widespread tradition in antiquity as seen above: in addition to Cicero and Macrobius, *Comm.*, 2.9, quoted above, cf. for example Ampelius, *Liber Mem.*, 6.1: *orbis terrarum, qui sub caelo est, quattuor regionibus incolitur. Una pars eius est, in qua nos habitamus* etc.; *orbis terrarum, quem nos colimus, in tres partes dividitur* . . . (the double meaning of *orbis terrarum*, the globe and the *oikoumene*, is obvious) (p. 5, Woelfflin); J.-J. Reinaud has already shown the importance of this theory for the ancients, *Relations politiques et commerciales de l'Empire romain avec l'Asie orientale* (Paris, 1863), 64ff.; concerning the Middle Ages and the Renaissance, see W. G. L. Randles, *De la terre plate au globe terrestre, une mutation épistémologique rapide (1480–1520)* (Paris, 1980), 10, 64.

21. A. Schlachter, *Globus* . . . , 54, 66–69; P. Arnaud, "L'image du globe dans le monde romain," *MEFRA* 96 (1984): 64.

22. Lucretius, *De rer. nat.*, 1.1057ff. seems opposed to the (correct) vision of the *antipodes* (also mentioned by Cicero, *Acad.*, 2.123); in Book 2.1075, the *alios aliis terrarum in partibus orbis* are not the inhabitants of the other *oikoumenai* of the globe but those of other, plausible terrestrial globes: see J. O. Thomson, *Hist. of Ancient Geography*, 216–17.

23. Mela, 3.70; Pliny, 6.81; Seneca, *Medea*, 1.378; but Servius, *Ecl.*, 1.66, formally states that it is a metaphoric and poetic usage; Velleius 2.46.1: Albinovanus Pedo, 19, for the North Sea, cf. below p. 87; Pliny, 10.19; see 8.7; Florus, 1.45.2; 16.

24. It is impossible to tackle the immense and fascinating problems raised by

Ptolemy as geographer. In addition to the fundamental synthesis by E. Polaschek, "Ptol. als Geographer," *RE,* suppl. 12 (1965), 681–833, see Dilke, *Greek and Roman Maps,* 72–86 and 154–66; A. Diller in his introduction to the reprint of the Nobbe edition of the *Geographia* (1966); and recently G. Kish, "Claudius Ptolemaeus und seine Werk," in *Die Cosmographia des Claudius Ptolem. Codex Urbinas Latinus 277* (Basel, 1986), 17–24 (and 87–90). It must be recognized that Ptolemy is more of an astronomer and a cartographer than a geographer, and that the apparent precision of the coordinates of his 8,000 "remarkable locations" is purely graphic. In fact, he is a compiler, in geography as in astronomy; see R. Newton, *The Crime of Claudius Ptolemaeus* (Baltimore, 1977) (with a book-review by H. A. Lewis in *Imago Mundi* 31 (1979): 105–7). I will deal elsewhere with the problem of the existence of maps in the ancient editions of Ptolemy—generally denied. Regarding Marinus of Tyre, see E. Höningman, *RE,* XIV, no. 2 (1930), 1767–96; and N. G. Photinos, *RE,* suppl. 12 (1970), 791–838; regarding the width of the Earth and certain measurements in Africa, refer to J. Desanges, *Recherches sur l'activité des Méditerranéens aux confins de l'Afrique* . . . (Rome, 1978), 197–98, 330–31.

25. Concerning the progress and regression in the knowledge (and in the measurements) of certain parts of the world, see A. Berthelot, *L'Asie ancienne . . . d'après Ptolémée* (Paris, 1930), and "Les données numériques fondamentales de la géographie antique d'Eratosthène à Ptolémée," *Rev. Arch.,* 1932, 1–34.

26. Polybius, 3.59; Strabo, 3.4.19, 166 C; Pédech, *La méthode historique de Polybe,* 565.

27. D. Woelk, *Agath. von Knidos über das Rote Meer* (Bamberg, 1966); S. Gozzoli, "Etnografia e politica in Agatharchide," *Athenaeum,* (1978), 54–79. Fragments in C. Müller, *FHG,* 3:190–97; and *GGM,* 1:111–95, concerning the *περὶ τῆς* Ἐρυθρῆς θαλάσσης.

28. Fragments published by R. Stiehle, "Der geograph. A. von Ephesos," *Philologus,* 1856, 191–244; concerning the man, an influential leading citizen who intercedes with the Romans, see M. Rostovtzeff, *Soc. and Econ. Hist. of the Hell. World* (Oxford, 1939), 1039–40 (with Strabo, 14.1.26).

29. K. Reinhardt, "Poseid. von Apamea," *RE,* XXII, no. 1 (1953), 558–826 (republished with corrections [Stuttgart, 1954]); L. Edelstein and I. G. Kidd, *Posidonius,* vol. 1, *The Fragments* (Cambridge, 1972), 180ff. concerning geography; M. Laffranque, *Poseidonios d'Apamée* (Paris, 1964); W. Capelle, "Die griechische Erdkunde und Poseidonios," *N. Jahrb. Kl. Altertum* 45 (1920): 305–24. His links with Pompey and Cicero are well known.

30. G. Kish, "Claudius Ptolemaeus," quoted on 23–24 and nn. 17–18; Numa Broc, *La Géographie de la Renaissance* (Paris, 1980), 9–19.

31. See Fr. Lasserre, *Strabon,* (Books 5 and 6) (Paris, 1967), 3:18; *Strabon* (Books 3 and 4) (Paris 1966), 2:5ff. concerning Spain, 106–10 regarding Gaul (the use of Caesar's *Commentaries* through the reading of Asinius Pollio)

32. *For us,* the extant Latin geography begins with these two authors: what preceded them depends on the uncertain *Quellenforschung.* In addition to the his-

tories of Latin literature (Schanz-Hosius, *Gesch. röm. Literatur,* vol. 1 [Munich, 1927]; vol. 2 [Munich, 1935]; H. Bardon, *La Littérature latine inconnue* [Paris, 1952–56]), there are few syntheses on Roman geography; however, see L. Canesi, "La produzione geografica latina e gli influssi letterari," *Historia* (St. Stor. per l'Ant. Clas., 1931), 145–68, 330–50, 511–32, who overstresses its rhetorical aspect; R. Almagià, *Gli studi geografici in Roma nell' epoca di Augusto, Quaderni Augustei, Studi Italiani IV* (1937); see especially the series of valuable publications in W. Sieglin, ed., *Quellen und Forschungen zur alte Geschichte und Geographie* (Berlin, 1901–20) (replaced in 1938 by *Q. F. zur Gesch. der Geogr. u. Volkenkunden*) in which German and Austrian specialists in the ancient ethnography of German peoples or of authors such as Pliny, Agrippa, or Mela (among them, A. Klotz and D. Detlefsen) have written some famous monographs (quoted below). Before them, K. Müllenhoff, *Deutsche Altertumskunde* (Berlin, 1890–1929), whose specialty was German antiquities, had in the 1870s masterfully dealt with most Latin authors, especially Caesar, Pliny, and Tacitus. See G. Oehmichen, *Plinianische Studien* (Erlangen, 1880). G. Guarnieri's *Le corrente del pensiero geografico nell'antichità classica,* 2 vols. (Milan, 1968) was not available to me. Some useful information on various authors can be found in R. Chevallier, ed., *Littérature gréco-romaine et géographie historique* (Paris, 1974), 105–245; but the best guide (whether one agrees with his conclusions or not) on Latin authors up to Pliny is unquestionably K. G. Sallmann, *Die Geographie des älteren Plinius in ihrem Verhaltnis zu Varro* (Berlin, 1971), who systematically studies Pliny's Greek and Latin sources. K. Langlouis's thesis (typed), *Raumauffassung und geographische Weltbild in der röm, Politik von Pompeius bis Traian* (Tübingen, 1951) adds little to the work done by Vogt, if only to take into account the explorations (see below), or the various studies on the sea (W. Burr), or the "natural frontiers" (J. Sölch, 1924). On Roman cartography, see below, chap. 5. Concerning Mela, P. Parroni, *Pomponii Melae de chorographia* (Rome, 1984) and A. Silbermann's forthcoming thesis.

33. J. Wikajak's article, *"De M. Tulli Ciceronis opere geographico quid judicandum,"* *Meander* 35 (1980): 541–46, is incomplete (see J. O. Thomson, *History of Anc. Geogr.*, 217). Concerning Cicero's projects in 59 B.C., see *ad Att.*, 2.4.1: Serapion's book had been sent to him "of which, between ourselves, I hardly understand one line in a thousand": Serapion of Antiocheia (see Klotz and W. Kroll in *RE,* II A, no. 2 (1924), 1666; Pliny, *NH,* ind. 1. 4 and 5), a mathematician and an astronomer; *Att.*, 2.6.1: *γεωγραφικὰ quae constitueram magnum opus est;* Alexander's books are also mentioned (2.20.6; 2.22.7) i.e., Alexander Lychnos, from Ephesus, known by Strabo, 4.1.25 (Knack, *RE,* I, no. 2 (1893), 1448), a rhetor, statesman, author of astronomical poems, and Strabo's contemporary; he added Tyrannio (2.6.1): in fact, Theophrastus of Amisos (Tyrannio is a nickname), a grammarian, who was well known by him, by Caesar, and by Pompey, and who also may have written geographical works (C. Wendel, *RE,* VII, no. 2 [1943], 1811–19).

34. There is a good synthesis of the controversy on the geographical interpola-

tions in Caesar in O. Seel's edition, *C. Julii Caesaris commentarii* (Leipzig, 1961), liii ff. (bibliography lxxxiv); and in J. Harmand, *ANRW* I, 4, 525–26.

35. G. Bowersock, *Augustus and the Greek World* (Oxford, 1965), 1–13 concerning the Republican period; and recently E. Rawson, *Intellectual Life in the Late Roman Republic* (London, 1985), 54 (concerning Greek writers and technicians, 250ff. regarding geography). For general information, on the κοινή, see J. Kaimio, *The Romans and the Greek Language,* Commentat. Human. Litter. 69 (Helsinki, 1979); M. Dubuisson, *Le Latin de Polybe* (Paris, 1985).

36. A. Klotz, *Cäsarstudien, nebst einer Analyse der Strabonischen Beschreibung von Gallien und Britannien* (Leipzig, 1910).

37. H. Bardon, *La littérature latine inconnue* (1952), 1:368–70.

38. Schanz-Hosius, *Gesch. röm. Liter.,* 1:569; R. Reitzenstein, "Die geographische Bücher Varros," *Hermes* 20 (1885): 514–51; D. Detlefsen, "Vermutungen über V.'s Schrift *de ora maritima,*" *Hermes* 20 (1886): 240–65; H. Dahlmann, *RE,* suppl. 6 (1935): 1172–1227; and especially K. G. Sallmann, quoted above n. 32, esp. 113ff. (but see J. Desanges's laudatory but cautious review in *REL,* 1971, 447–49; Sallmann does not believe in a geographical work, of the *periplus* genre, which was Detlefsen's and A. Klotz's old hypothesis; Pliny owes him much but he used of all kinds of works).

39. J. Desanges, *Pline l'Ancien. NH, V, 1–46* (Paris, 1980), 11–20; it is true that Varro knows Greek and that the "description of the coastline" of Octavian's time, common to Mela and Pliny, abounds in Greek toponyms or in a form still Greek (J. D.).

40. The importance of this false contrast for the interpretation of Agrippa's work will be shown below; this does not mean that Latin authors such as Pliny were not moralists or statesmen as well as scholars; see the accurate remarks of A. Dihle, "Plinius und die geographische Wissenschaft," *Tecnologia, economia e società nel mondo romano* (Como, 1980), 121–37, esp. 136; also W. H. Stahl, *Roman Science* (Madison, 1962) (Ital. trans. [Bari, 1974], esp. 87, 161ff.).

41. See for example Book 9 on "gnomonic" with its references to geometry, astronomy, etc. See J. Soubiran, *Vitruve,* I, IX (Paris, 1969), introduction and comments. Whether he is identifiable with the *praefectus fabrum* Mamurra, Vitruvius is certainly an *eques* who served as an officer.

42. Regarding those errors of representation, see R. Dion, *Aspects politiques de la géographie antique,* 248ff. ("Les postulats géographiques de la propagande romaine"), who correctly notes (278) the progress, or the corrections that are made precisely in the time of Augustus and the Julio-Claudians.

43. J. H. Thiel, *Eudoxus of Cyzicus,* Hist. Stud., 23 (Utrecht, 1966).

44. Strabo, 2.1.17; 7.2.4; 9.6.1; Lucan 3.278; Tacitus, *Germania,* 34; see below, chap. 4.

45. Excellent reflections on the nature of *works* and *maps* of ancient geography are found in F. Prontera, "Prima di Strabone, materiali per un studio della geografia

antica come genere letterario" in F. Prontera ed., *Strabone, contributo allo studio della personalità e dell'opera* (Perugia, 1984), 189–259. Cf. the recent work of P. Janni, *La mappa e il periplo, cartografia anticae e spazio odologico* (Macerata, 1984) (and his previous article "Orientamento," in *Quaderni Linguistici e Filologici* [Macerata, 1981], 53–70), who, setting down the elements of a physiology (and a sociology) of the spatial perceptions and representations, and distinguishing between those linked to the itinerary and *periplus,* and those which suggest a global vision, superficial and therefore abstract, attributes, almost exclusively, the latter to the ancients and the former to the "moderns." In fact, as Kubitschek, "Itinerarien," *RE,* IX, no. 2 (1916), 2310, has already shown, the two types coexist more or less always even in remotely complex civilizations (some scholars already contrast the spatial conception, cartographic in character, of the first sedentary civilizations with the linear ones of the nomads: A. Leroi-Gourhan, *Le geste et la parole,* La mémoire et les rythmes [Paris, 1965], 2:150–59). Better still, according to technical or cultural changes, ancient models can reemerge: the automobile resurrected the linear vision of the ancient nomads in an era of triangulation and even of maps by satellite. Furthermore, Janni, who undertakes excellent semantic studies on words used in geographic discourse (favorable to his thesis), somewhat neglects the Latin authors (neither Agrippa nor Ptolemy are found in the *Index*). In the eagerness to deal in antithetical pairs and in the research of "structures" raised to the standard of systems, the influences, the drawbacks, the overlaps—in brief, the *continuum* of history—are forgotten.

46. It is beyond the scope of this book to examine the various types and evolution of Greco-Roman cartography up to the Byzantine period and beyond, into the Middle Ages and the Renaissance. See P. Arnaud's thesis, cited below, p. 91; concerning the Peutinger Table (which, in my opinion, was not inspired by Agrippa's work—see below, p. 102—but which also had, in its own fashion, a "system of projection"), see the recent work of A. and M. Levi, "Map Projection and the Peutinger Table," in ed. L. Casson, *Coins, Culture and History in the Ancient World, Studies in Honor of Bluma Trell* (Detroit, 1981), 139–48.

47. *History of Cartography,* ed. J. B. Harley and D. Woodward (Chicago, 1988). See L. Bagrow, *History of Cartography,* revised by R. A. Skelton (London, 1964); and a few useful and recent works: I. Kupčik, *Cartes géographiques anciennes* (Prague, 1980; Paris, 1981); *Cartes et figures de la Terre* (a collective work) (Paris, Centre Pompidou, 1980); and especially G. Kish, *La carte, image des civilisations* (Paris, 1980), esp. 53ff., for the "reform" of cartography in France.

48. Whence the link between "painting" and cartography—a link that would be found even in the twentieth century. The semantics is revealing: the expressions *orbis pictus, itineraria picta* and *tabula* (the translation of πίναξ) mean both a map and a *tableau.* But are the maps of the Palazzo Farnese of Caprarola (G. Kish, *La carte,* pl. 82) maps or *tableaux?* Concerning the "vignettes" of the *agrimensores,* see below p. 156. A fanciful theory, stemming from a misinterpretation of Pliny, *NH,* 35.11,

attributes the invention of a mechanical process for the reproduction of portraits to Varro.

49. It is not within the scope of this book to examine the delicate problem of the "maps" that accompany Ptolemy's manuscripts: a general map and twenty-seven (or sixty-four, according to written traditions) specific maps (regional); do the latter really correspond to the chorographies of a Strabonian type? See below, p. 172, for the meaning of this word. The prevailing theory (for example Bagrow), which claims that Ptolemy's older maps are Byzantine (due to Maximus Planudes) is, in my opinion, overly critical. For the invention of the modern atlas, see Numa Broc, *La Géographie de la Renaissance,* 173ff. The first work thus named is that of Mercator (1595), but the representation of Atlas carrying the terrestrial globe already appeared on the title page of the *Tavole moderne di geografia . . . di diversi autori raccolte e messe secundo l'ordine di Tolemeo,* published at Rome, ca. 1575, by Antoine Lafrery. But the first "atlas," that is to say a book of geographical panels, is without doubt the *Theatrum Orbis Terrarum* by the Dutchman A. Ortelius (1570). See N. A. E. Nordenskjöld, *Facsimile Atlas to the Early History of Cartography* (Stockholm, 1889), 117–36; Ph. L. Phillips, *A List of Geographical Atlases in the Library of Congress* (Washington, D.C., 1914), 3:81–92 (I owe this reference to Mr. J.-L. Ferrary).

50. Clarification is found in K. Miller, *Itineraria picta,* indeed an edition of the Peutinger Table (Stuttgart, 1916); M. and A. Levi, *Itineraria picta: contributo allo studio della T.P.* (Rome, 1967); W. Kubitschek, "Itinerarien," *RE,* IX, no. 1 (1916), 2308–63. Regarding the Antonine itinerary (O. Cuntz, ed., *Itineraria Romana,* vol. 1 [Leipzig, 1929]), see N. Reed, "Pattern and Purpose in the Antonine Itinerary," *AJP,* 1978, 228–51, and the general but very sensible comments of R. Rebuffat, "Le Bouclier de Doura," *Syria* 63 (1986): 85–103, but this document is *not* an itinerary, as shown by R. Uhden and P. Arnaud in *CRAI,* 1989, forthcoming.

51. We have recently justly insisted upon the firmly political (that is, stemming from the art of good government) character of Strabo's geography. One needs only to read it in order to accept it (see 1.1.18: *Πρὸς τοὺς ἡγεμονικοὺς βίους καὶ τὰς χρείας*; see C. Van Paassen, *The Classical Tradition of Geography* (Groningen, 1957), 1–32; E. C. L. Van Der Vliet, *Strabo over Landen Volken en Steden* (Amsterdam, 1977) (see "L'ethnographie de Strabon, idéologie ou tradition?" in *Strabone, I, Contributi . . . ,* ed F. Prontera [Perusia, 1984], 27–86); F. Lasserre, "Strabon devant l'Empire romain," in *ANRW* II, 30, 1 (1983), 867–96.

52. Strabo is one of the rare authors of the period who explains the change of regime that Rome has undergone (from the *libera res pubica* to the empire), recalling also the problems of physical dimension and of distances; see the topical passage 6.4.2: *χαλεπὸν δὲ ἄλλως διοικεῖν τηλικαύτην ἡγεμονίαν ἢ ἑνὶ ἐπιτρέψαντας ὡς πατρί.* The same idea is found only in Dio (= Maecenas?), 52.15.6, but also 44.2.4, which is much clearer because here Dio writes his own opinions. I will study that theme elsewhere. For the time being, refer to G. Mancinetti-Santamaria, "Strabone e

l'ideologia augustea," *Ann. Fac. Lettere di Perugia,* n.s. 16, no. 4 (1978–79) 129–42.

53. Useful comments are found in M. Clavel-Lévêque, "Les Gaules et les Gaulois: pour une analyse du fonctionnement de la "Géographie" de Strabon," *DHA 1* (1974): 87–88; and "La domination romaine en Narbonnaise. . . ," in *Modes de contacts et processus de transformation dans les sociétés anciennes,* École Française de Rome (Rome/Paris, 1983), 608–9.

IV

Explorations and Expeditions during the Roman Empire

In general, the great voyages of discovery in antiquity are attributed to the Greeks both before and after Alexander: from Pytheas, who traveled to the extreme northwest, to Nearchus, who passed along the coast of the Indian Ocean, the record is indeed impressive.[1] The Romans, although latecomers, did not remain unfamiliar with these discoveries. We have seen that Polybius (3.59) and Strabo (3.4.19, 166 C) give the Romans credit for having made journeys and surveys possible in many regions, particularly in the West, as an indirect result of their political domination and pacification.

But on this point the foundation of the Empire brought about considerable changes. First of all, it led to the exploration and surveying of areas as yet unknown or unexplored. Most of these attempts, some of which were remarkable, either prepared for or accompanied military expeditions; others were accomplished more peaceably, as official missions or private commercial ventures. This does not mean that the former were not also of an economic or financial nature. The desire for prestige and the concern for the *imitatio Alexandri* are evident for some of these expeditions—especially those commissioned by Augustus and Nero. Before considering their documentary aspect and their exploitation, I will review quickly the principal expeditions known to us up to the Antonine period, using recent updates on the subject (J. Desanges and R. Sherk).[2] The outline will surely exceed the specific chronological framework of this book but it will better demonstrate the substantial place held by the reign of Augustus in the expansion of the world as a whole.

I. Africa along the Nile toward the Red Sea and Arabia

1. In 29 B.C., the prefect of Egypt, Cornelius Gallus, leads the Roman army into Thebaid, further than any king has previously done.[3]
2. In 25–24 B.C., his successor Aelius Gallus leads a difficult expedition along the Arabian coast of the Red Sea as far as Arabia Felix (Strabo, 16.4.22; Pliny, 6.160; Dio, 53.29).[4]
3. A short time later, C. or P. Petronius, his successor, leads a campaign

in Meroë, 870 miles south of Syene (Strabo, 17.1.54; Pliny, 6.181–85).[5]

4. Strabo places in the Augustan period the (controlled) expansion of trade to India, definitely by taking advantage of the monsoon (2.5.12; 17.1.13).[6]
5. During this period, rather than during the reign of Claudius, the voyage of discovery by a freedman of Annius Plocamus (publican of a *portorium* in the Red Sea) brings him directly to the Deccan.[7]
6. In A.D. 1, Gaius Caesar, Augustus's grandson, leads a campaign against some Arabs who are not only Nabataeans but also from the Red Sea[8] (*ultra finis extremas populi Romani: CIL,* 11.1421).
7. In A.D. 61–63 under Nero, an exploratory and cartographic expedition, entrusted to a praetorian detachment, surveys the route between Syene and Meroë (Pliny, 6.181; 12.19; Seneca, *QN*, 6.8.3–4; Dio, 63.8.1).[9]

II. *Northern Africa and the Sahara*

1. In 20 B.C., Cornelius Balbus, proconsul of Africa, reaches the Fezzan, south of Tripoli, for a distance of 910 miles, a distance known to Agrippa (Pliny, 5.38; 6.209).[10]
2. Valerius Festus, legate of the *legio III Augusta,* opens another road to the land of the Garamantes in A.D. 70 (Pliny, 6.38).[11]
3. But under Titus and Domitian (between A.D. 76 and 82–83), two expeditions, one military under Septimius Flaccus, the other civilian under Julius Maternus, reach "the land of the rhinoceros," no doubt south of Tibesti. It certainly was not as far as Marinus of Tyre had imagined (according to Ptolemy, 1.8.4, etc.), but it was a journey of three or four months (perhaps 1,500 or 2,000 km).[12]
4. Finally, in Mauretania during the reign of Claudius, C. Suetonius Paulinus explores and crosses the Western Atlas Chain for the first time (Pliny, 5.14).[13]

III. *The Eastern frontier of the Empire and the Persian Gulf*

1. In preparation for the great Eastern expeditions of Gaius Caesar, between 2 B.C. and A.D. 2, two scholars and geographers, King Juba II and Isidorus of Charax, are "commissioned" to undertake two geographical studies (Pliny, 6.139–41).[14]
2. Corbulo's campaigns in Armenia under Nero are conducted with geographical updates (Pliny, 5.83 on the course of the Euphrates; 6.40 on the Caspian Gates—which Pliny says are incorrectly identified and named, because they are in fact the Caucasian Gates).[15]
3. Under Hadrian, Arrian, then legate of Cappadocia, undertakes an

inspection tour of the eastern coast of Pontus Euxinus as far as the Bosphorus kingdom, and submits his report in Latin and Greek (Arrian, *Periplus*, 6, 10).[16]

IV. Northern Europe and the Danube

1. The attempts to conquer Germany, led with perseverance under Augustus from 12 B.C. to A.D. 9, include among other things expeditions as far as the Elbe's mouth and middle and upper reaches (by Cn. Domitius Ahenobarbus between 6 B.C. and A.D. 1: Dio, 55.10),[17] and naval expeditions along the coasts of Frisia and Germany. One of these expeditions is remarkable and exceptional: mentioned by Augustus himself (*RG* 26.4), it leads the fleet "up to the frontiers of the Cimbri" (that is, the tip of the Jutland peninsula), a point never before reached (Pliny, 2.167); but ice and fog force it to turn back. This was no doubt a grandiose attempt to circumnavigate the North Sea to the Pillars of Hercules in the Caspian Sea, as stated by Tacitus (*Germania*, 34). Should this expedition be attributed to the Elder Drusus (Suetonius, *Claud.*, 1), or to Tiberius in A.D. 4–5 (Velleius, 2.106) or even to Germanicus in A.D. 14 (a fragment of Albinovanus Pedo, Seneca, *Suas.*, 1.15)? A text of Dionysius (ca. 7 B.C.) supports the first date, since it mentions regions of the ocean "where it is possible to navigate" and which were reached by the Romans.[18] In any case, the name and location of the Vistula were known to Agrippa (but not to Strabo).[19]
2. Under Nero, a fiscal procurator from Rome sends an *eques* to explore and to travel a new amber-route from Carnuntum (Pliny, 37.45).[20]
3. In A.D. 83–84, after his final victories in Britain, Agricola orders a circumnavigation of the island: he is able to explore the Shetlands (Tacitus, *Agric.*, 38, 10).
4. And finally the Danube: great progress is made during the reign of Augustus with the identification of the sources of the Ister (Strabo, 7.3.13).[21]
5. During the Dacian campaigns, Trajan finally has precise topographical surveys done (Balbus *mensor*, 92–93 Lachmann).[22]

When plotted on modern maps, these expeditions determine exactly the regions where most of the improvements in distance estimation occurred, in measurement of astronomical coordinates or in topography. They mark the progress of geography between Posidonius (ca. 60 B.C.)—the last stage, or almost the last stage, of Strabo's map—and the great cartography of the second century—with Marinus of Tyre and Ptolemy. The Romans at that time had not discovered any unknown lands, but they effectively penetrated, surveyed, and publicized lands of which the Greek had heard. Besides, any dichotomy between Greek science and Roman practical knowledge is illusory for this period, so complete is the cultural symbiosis on both the practical and the theoretical levels.

But this expansion of knowledge and relations denotes something else as well: a system of relationships, an "opening up" between the world of the empire or the *orbis Romanus* (when considered closed or completed), and the rest of the world, entirely new and very different from the world that had been passed down by the Hellenistic period. It involves the western world, tamed, known, and penetrated; it includes new commercial and cultural links with India and Southeast Asia by the Red Sea and the Ocean (no longer through the Parthian intermediary)—and soon (as Ptolemy assures us) by the trans-Caspian routes of Central Asia. Rome certainly had not, strictly speaking, "conquered" the ancient world: but all the ancient world could come to it.[23]

NOTES

1. The history of ancient explorations is mainly dealt with in the general works of the history of geography and of discoveries (for example Vivien de Saint-Martin or Bunbury). The best are those of M. Cary and E. H. Warmington, *The Ancient Explorers* (London, 1929) and, especially, that of R. Hennig, *Terrae incognitae, Eine Zusammenstellung und kritische Bewerkung der wichtigen vorkolumbischen Entdeckungsreisen. . .*, 4 vols. (Leiden, 1936–56) (vol. 1, to Ptolemy), which provides a German translation of all the sources and a discussion, and which has the advantage of also including the Eastern sources (mentioning Indian and Chinese explorations); see also the recent work (more journalistic, but sometimes useful) of N. H. Sitwell, *The World the Romans Knew* (London, 1984).

2. R. T. Sherk, "Roman Geographical Exploration and Military Maps," in *ANRW* II, 1 (1974), 534–62; regarding North Africa and the Nile, as well as the Red Sea, J. Desanges, *Recherches sur l'activité des Méditerranéens aux confins de l'Afrique* (Rome, 1978).

3. Cornelius Gallus the poet; see *CIL*, 3.14147, 5 = *IGR*, I, 1293 = *OGI*, 624 = *ILS*, 8995: *exercitu ultra Nili catarhacte[n transd]ucto, in quem locum neque populo Romano neque regibus Aegypti [arma ante] sunt prolata. . .*; Strabo, 17.1.53, 819 C. Gallus was recalled and condemned by Augustus (Dio 53.23.5; Suetonius, *Aug.*, 66.2). A Latin papyrus containing one of his elegiacs, no doubt abandoned by an erudite officer between 25 and 20 B.C., was found recently at Qasr Ibrîm near the second cataract; R. D. Anderson, P. J. Parsons, and R. Nisbet, "Elegiacs by Gallus from Q.I.," *JRS*, 1979, 125–55.

4. Gallus was preparing a maritime expedition but it was by land that he attempted to reach the strait of Bad el-Mandeb. The land expedition reached Mariba (in the Yemen?), which Augustus points out, *RG* 26.5; this is certainly the most southern point ever reached by Roman troops (for a discussion of the text in the *RG*, see above, chap. 1, p. 23). Strabo, a friend of Gallus (2.5.12, 117 C), witnessed this expedition (ibid.) whose commercial significance is obvious: to control trade to the Arabian coasts of the Indian Ocean and to India, which at that time was flourishing (2.5.12, 118C). He provides the principal accounts (16.4.22–24); Dio, 53.29.3–8, names 'Αθλούλα as the farthest site reached by the Romans, which would be Vatil, slightly north of Mariba: on the date, see S. Jameson, "Chronology on the Campaigns of Aelius Gallus and C. Petronius," *JRS*, 1968, 71–84; and especially H. von Wissmann, "Die Geschichte des Sabäerreichs und der Feldzug des Aelius Gallus," *ANRW*, 9, 1 (1976), 308–544.

5. *Res Gestae* 26.5: *in Aethiopiam usque ad oppidum Nabata perventum est, cui proxima est Meroë;* Strabo, 17.1.53–54; Pliny, 6.181–85; Dio, 54.5; Hennig, *Terrae incognitae,* 254; J. Desanges, *Recherches sur l'activité*, 309–16.

6. This opening is, on a historical scale, an important event, which increased contact between the Indian continent and the Mediterranean; see henceforth M. Raschke's important update, "New Studies in Roman Commerce with the East," *ANRW* II, 9, 2 (1978), 604–1378 (663 and 671 on the excavations at Arikamedu where Arretine pottery was unearthed; 1260ff.).

7. Pliny, *NH*, 6. 84 recalls the adventure of this freedman who reaches Ceylon "in the time of Claudius"; but a bilingual inscription from Nubia, dated in A.D. 6, mentions another freedman belonging to the same patron or to his family (J. Meredith, *JRS*, 1953, 38–39 = *SEG*, 13. 614): see M. Raschke, "New Studies in Roman Commerce," 644 and 849–50.

8. The inscription on the cenotaph at Pisa (*CIL*, 11.1421 = *ILS*, 140) in Gaius's honor indicates that he had "held his consulship leading a successful campaign beyond the farthest frontiers of the Roman people." Therefore, this is not the Armenian campaign of A.D. 2 (G. Bowersock in *JRS*, 1971, 227). Pliny also mentions a campaign in the land of incense (2.168; 6.160; 12.55); G. Bowersock, *Roman Arabia* (Cambridge, Mass., 1983), 56–57; for the expedition's preparation recourse was made to the works and science of Juba II and Isidorus of Charax (for Juba, see Pliny, 6.136; 12.56; 32.10; for Isidorus, and not Dionysius, of Charax, Pliny, 6.141; Jacoby, *FGrH* III.1.130–31).

9. This episode is particularly interesting for our purposes here because it demonstrates the use of the army for scientific surveys and the type of documents that followed. Pliny (7.181, 184–86) tells of a survey expedition (*explorandum*) led by the praetorians under the command of a tribune ordered by Nero (who "was thinking" of an Aethiopian expedition), and who wrote a report. This report, at least as regards the distances from town to town, is cited below (184–85), but it also includes some notations on the fauna and flora, and on the inhabitants. Seneca (*QN*, 6.8.3–4) chatted of this expedition with two centurions: Nero, he says, had sent them "in

search of the source of the Nile." In spite of the mention of bellicose projects by Pliny (and by Dio, *Epit.*, 53.8.1), surely it involves the one and only enterprise. In Book 12.19, Pliny provides valuable information: the expedition resulted in the drawing up of a *forma Aethiopiae*, which was given (*allata*) to Nero, and which showed (*docuit*) that there were few trees, from Syene to Méroë, over 996 miles (?). *Forma Aethiopiae*: the expression recalls quite clearly the famous *forma Italiae* in the Temple of Tellus mentioned by Varro. *Forma* is also one of those words that designate large-scale maps and (see below p. 158), those of the *agrimensores* or of the urban *mensores* (e.g., for the waterworks), which indeed could include, to some extent, symbolic illustrations. See R. Sherk, "Roman Exploration and Military Maps," *ANRW* II, 1 (1974), 559; P. Arnaud, *Imago Mundi*, unpub. thesis (Paris, 1984), 300; concerning the link with the *situs depicti* of the Caucasus sent by Corbulo (Pliny, *NH*, 6.40) see below n. 15.

10. See Pliny, *NH*, 5.36–38, for the expedition and triumph of Balbus, who in 19 B.C. displayed on this occasion the *simulacra* of the known towns and tribes along with their names. Surely there was an Eastern expedition, in the Garamantes country, in the direction of Fezzan—for a distance of 910 miles from north to south; a distance given as new by Agrippa and cited by Pliny (*NH*, 6.209). It is not surprising that not one of those *oppida* or *gentes*, known to the last senator to have triumphed under his own auspices, is mentioned in the *RG:* Augustus could not make this claim. Regarding the reach of this expedition, see J. Desanges, *Recherches sur l'activité*, 189–95. Agrippa's borrowing of this proves on the contrary that—although based on dynastic inspiration—his map was essentially a scientific work.

11. Pliny, 5.38; Tacitus, *Hist.*, 4.50.

12. See J. Desanges, *Recherches sur l'activité*, 197–213. Ptolemy's passage, on which I will not dwell, is a good example of how the cartographers (Marinus, and Ptolemy who corrects him) distort the sources at their disposal so that they correspond with their own purely cartographical preoccupations.

13. See J. Desanges, *Pline l'Ancien* (Paris, 1980), 135ff., on *NH*, 5.14–15. Regarding Pliny's indifference concerning the geographical curiosity and activity of Roman officials (whom he distinguishes from private merchants), refer to *NH*, 5.12 and the commentary by J. Desanges, *ibid.* 124ff.

14. Concerning Juba, see n. 8; Pliny, *NH*, 6.141 mentions the birth at Charax of a *Dionysium, terrarum orbis situs recentissimum auctorem,* not mentioned elsewhere; with Bernhardy (*ad Den. Per.*, 496) the amendment is *Isidorum*. Isidorus's texts are found in C. Miller, *GGM*, 1:224–56 (thirteen references are found in Pliny, not including the one stated above). W. H. Schoff, *Parthian Stations of Isidore of Charax* (reprint, 1976); Weissbach, in *RE*, IX no. 2 (1916), 2064, who has reservations concerning this identification.

15. *NH*, 5.83: (*Euphrates oritur*) . . . *ut prodidere ex iis qui proxime viderant Domitius Corbulo in monte Aga* (quoted in the *Index* of Book I *Domitio auctore*); no doubt these are his *commentarii;* see H. Peter, in *HRR*, 2:134 (Tacitus, *Ann.*, 13.8), see 99–101; Pliny, 6.40, deals with the common confusion between the "Cas-

pian Gates" and the "Caucasian Gates": according to Pliny, Nero's orders were aimed at the latter. The maps drawn and sent by Corbulo incorrectly gave them the name of Caspian (*situsque depicti et inde missi hoc nomen habent*); regarding those *situs depicti,* see P. Arnaud, *Imago Mundi,* 303–4. The correct sense of the word *situs* can surely be questioned: "landscape," "locations"; but *situs* is found in definite descriptions of maps (Eumenius, *Pan.,* 5.20), and Pliny's style is often affected. All that can be noted is that the document had to be different from that which Pliny called the *forma Aethiopiae* undertaken by soldiers.

16. Concerning Arrian, see the recent work by P. Vidal-Naquet, "Flavius Arrien entre deux mondes," *Arrien, histoire d'Alexandre,* trans. P. Savinel (Paris, 1984), esp. 311–21; R. Sherk, *ANRW,* II, 1 (1974), 542–43.

17. This question has given rise to an immense bibliography in Germany and elsewhere: K. Müllenhoff, *Deutsche Altertumskunde* (Berlin, 1870); see E. Norden, *Die germanische Urgeschichte in Tacitus' Germania* (Leipzig, 1920); O. Montelius, *Le relazioni fra l'Italia e la Scandinavia prima di Augusto* (Rome, 1903); R. Hennig, *Terrae incognitae* 1:261, 266, 276, 280 (concerning his chronology, see below); R. Syme, "The Northern Frontier under Augustus," *CAH*, 10 (1934):358–64; C. Wells, *The German Policy of Augustus* (Oxford, 1972); K. Christ, "Zur augusteichen Germanienpolitik," *Chiron*, 1977, 149–205.

The question is hampered by the chronological and topographical imprecision of the sources. The earliest is Augustus himself, who said, first of all (*RG* 26.2): "I brought peace to the Gallic and Spanish provinces as well as to Germany, throughout the area bordering on the Ocean from Cadiz to the mouth of the Elbe" (*Gallias et Hispanias provincias, item Germaniam, qua includit Oceanus a Gadibus ad ostium Albis fluminis pacavi*), which naturally could only have been said before Varus's disaster in A.D. 9. Then, he mentions the naval expeditions: "My fleet sailed through the Ocean eastwards from the mouth of the Rhine to the territory of the Cimbri, a country which no Roman had visited before either by land or by sea, and the Cimbri, Charydes, Semnones and other German peoples of that region sent ambassadors and sought my friendship and that of the Roman people" (*classis mea per Oceanum ab ostio Rheni ad solis orientis regionem usque ad fines Cimbrorum navigavit, quo neque terra neque mari quisquam Romanus ante id tempus adit, Cimbrique et Charydes et Semnones et eiusdem tractus alii Germanorum populi per legatos amicitiam meam et populi Romani petierunt*); an event which is therefore prior to A.D. 14. This text is often linked to a passage in Velleius (2.106), which surely concerns Tiberius's second campagin in Germany in A.D. 4–5: "There [on the Elbe] with . . . a close watch upon the seasons, the fleet which had skirted the windings of the sea coast sailed up the Elbe from a sea hitherto unheard of and unknown, and . . . effected a junction with Caesar and his army" (. . . *et eodem mira felicitate et cura ducis, temporum quoque observantia, classis, quae Oceani circumnavigaverat sinus, ab inaudito atque incognito ante mari flumine Albi subvecta, plurimarum gentium victoria, cum abundantissima rerum omnium copia, exercitui Caesarique se iunxit*). Certain of Velleius's expressions ("never before") are surely rhetorical exaggerations (see R. Syme, *Danubian Papers*, [Bucharest, 1971]) 33 n. 23, who recalls that the Elbe had already been reached twice, by Drusus in 9 B.C. and by Cn. Domitius Ahenobarbus between 6 B.C. and A.D. 1: Dio, 55.10; see Woodman, "Questions of Date, Genre and Style in Velleius," *CQ*, 1975, 304 n. 1; Hellegouarc'h, *Velleius*, 2:248–49). But a link with the *RG* is impossible simply because Velleius states formally that the fleet (coming from the Rhine) had not gone beyond the Elbe, since it followed its course: on the contrary, the navigation ordered by Augustus to the east (it should be noted) had inevitably to go beyond it.

On the other hand, Pliny (2.167) certainly alludes to the same facts as Augustus: "Today the whole of the West is navigated from Cadiz and the Columns of Hercules, all around Spain and Gaul. But the larger part of the Northern Ocean was explored under the patronage of Divus Augustus, when a fleet sailed round Germany to the promontory of the Cimbri, and thence, saw or learnt of, a vast sea which reached the region of Scythia and localities numb with excessive moisture" (*A Gadibus columnisque Herculis Hispaniae et Galliarum circuitu totus hodie navigatur Occidens, Septentrionalis vero Oceanus maiore ex parte navigatus est auspiciis divi Augusti Germaniam classe circumvecta ad Cimbrorum promontorium et inde immenso mari prospecto aut fama cognito Scythicam ad plagam et umore nimio rigentia*). The order in which the Spains, the Gauls, and the navigation among the Cimbrians are mentioned attests to a source common to the *RG*, confirmed in its mention by Augustus himself. We are far beyond the mouth of the Elbe. Pliny wants to prove that the *oikoumene* is entirely surrounded by Ocean: he therefore reports the results of the most recent and furthest expedition to the North Sea, that is, in the ancient views, the one that flows into the Caspian Sea, then into the Indian Ocean: there is no *continent* to the North (only islands, i.e., Scandinavia, as he recently learned, 2.246: *immensas insulas non pridem conpertas cognitum habeo*). Thus, this is an expedition prior to A.D. 14. This helps to reject, unlike others, the hypothesis that could attribute the expedition to Jutland (*promontorium Cimbrorum*) to Germanicus in A.D. 15–16.

The third crucial text is a passage in Tacitus, *Germ.* 34: "Nay, in that quarter we have essayed the ocean itself, and rumour has published the existence of pillars of Hercules beyond our range: whether it be that Hercules visited those shores, or because we have agreed to enter all marvels everywhere to his credit. Nor did Drusus Germanicus lack audacity, but Ocean vetoed inquiry alike touching itself and touching Hercules; and next the attempt to inquire was abandoned, and it was voted more religious and more reverent to believe in the works of Deity than to comprehend them." (*ipsum quin etiam Oceanum illa temptavimus; et superesse adhuc Herculis columnas fama vulgavit, sive adiit Hercules, seu quidquid ubique magnificum est, in claritatem eius referre consensimus. Nec defuit audentia Druso Germanico, sed obstitit Oceanus in se simul atque in Herculem inquiri. Mox nemo temptavit, sanctiusque ac reverentius vesum de actis deorum credere quam scire*).

As was shown by Roger Dion ("Explication d'un passage des *RGDA*," *Mél. Carcopino*, 1966, 249–69, and *Aspects politiques de la géographie antique* [Paris, 1977], 216–22), those northern "Pillars of Hercules" are none other than the Caspian straits believed as such in all ancient geography up to, but excluding, Ptolemy (see Strabo, 2.1.17; 7.2.4; 11.6.1; Mela, 1.2; 3.5; Pliny, *NH*, 2.168). Lucan also refers to them by this name (3.275–79).

Of course, others were also placed elsewhere; in Pontus (Servius, 11.262; see Müllenhoff, *Die Germanie des Tacitus* [Berlin, 1900], 430); or in Helgoland (yet without ancient texts; see D. Detlefsen, "*Die Entdeckung des germanischen* Nordens," *QFGG* (Berlin, 1904), 8:43ff.; E. Norden, *Die germ. Urgeschichte*, 469–71, for more ancient and modern features). Tacitus's expressions (*temptavit*) show that this is not only a military expedition but an exploration. Who was its leader? Elsewhere, Tacitus (*Hist.*, 5.19) gives, like so many other ancient sources, to the Elder Drusus the double name *Drusus Germanicus*, which was decreed to him posthumously by the Senate (Suetonius, *Claud.*, 1.3; Dio. 55.2.3; Florus, 2.30.28; *Consol. ad Liviam*, 337, 457; Ovid, *Fasti*, 1:597, etc.; see *PIR* 2.198). He never refers to Tiberius and Germanicus in this way. We are therefore led to date this maritime expedition to the time of the Elder Drusus, between 12–9 B.C. Suetonius also attributes to this Drusus, the father of the emperor Claudius, the glory of having been the first to navigate on the Northern Sea (*Claud.*, 1: *is Drusus in quaesturae praeturaeque honore dux Raetici, deinde Germanici belli Oceanum septentrionalem primus Romanorum ducum navigavit transque Rhenum fossas navi et immensi operis effecit, quae nunc adhuc Drusinae vocantur*), a statement best suited to this great attempt than to the limited navigations of the Ems.

A poetic fragment of Albinovanus Pedo transmitted by Seneca the Elder, *Suas.* 1.15ff., which describes (along the lines of an involuntary discovery of the ends of the world, it is true) a storm that destroyed a Roman fleet: this is, in all likelihood, the one that destroyed Germanicus's fleet in A.D. 16 (Tacitus, *Ann.*, 2.23–24). On the other hand, if the *Consolatio ad Liviam* does not formally mention the expedition to Jutland, in the Elder Drusus's favor, many passages refer in general terms to the *novae terrae,* knowledge of which is owed to him (20, 309: *in orbe novo,* 391, 437, the Ocean). For a better reading of the text, see E. Pianazella, "Au-delà des frontières du monde," *REL,* 1984, 192.

There still remains the problem of Strabo's silence or statements. There is not a word in his work about a Roman navigation up to Jutland. He even affirms (7.2.4) that the Germans "are only known up to the Elbe" and that, beyond, everything is unknown: none of the "ancients" went east up to the mouth of the Caspian Sea, and the Romans until now have not yet gone beyond the Elbe: Τῶν *δὲ* Γερμανῶν, *ὡς εἶπον οἱ μὲν προσάρκτιοι παρήκουσι τῷ ὠκεανῷ, γνωρίζονται δ' ἀπὸ τῶν ἐκβολῶν τοῦ* Ῥήνου λαβόντες *τὴν ἀρχὴν μέχρι τοῦ* Ἄλβιος, *τούτων δ' εἰσὶ γνωριμώτατοι* Σούγαμβροί τε καὶ Κίμβροι, *τὰ δὲ πέραν τοῦ* Ἄλβιος *τὰ πρὸς τῷ ὠκεανῷ παντάπασιν ἄγνωστα ἡμῖν ἐστιν. οὔτε γὰρ τῶν προτέρων οὐδένα ἴσμεν τὸν παράπλουν τοῦτον πεποιημένον πρὸς τὰ ἑωθινὰ μέρη τὰ μέχρι τοῦ στόματος τῆς* Κασπίας *θαλάττης, οὔθ' οἱ* Ῥωμαῖοί *πω προῆλθον εἰς τὰ περαιτέρω τοῦ* Ἄλβιος· *ὡς δ' αὔτως οὐδὲ πεζῇ παρωδεύκασιν οὐδένες. ἀλλ ὅτι μὲν κατὰ μῆκος ἰοῦσιν ἐπὶ τὴν ἕω τὰ κατὰ τὸν* Βορυσθένη *καὶ τὰ πρὸς βορρᾶν τοῦ* Πόντου *χωρία ἀπαντᾷ, δῆλον ἐκ τῶν κλιμάτων καὶ τῶν παραλλήλων* διαστημάτων. Is this simply ignorance? Yet, he is aware of the embassies sent by the Cimbrians, which Augustus mentioned, and which were visibly the consequence of the expedition (7.2.1): Περὶ δὲ Κίμβρων τὰ μὲν οὐκ εὖ λέγεται, τὰ δ' ἔχει ἀπιθανότητας οὐ μετρίας. οὔτε γὰρ τὴν τοιαύτην αἰτίαν τοῦ πλάνητας γενέσθαι καὶ ληστρικοὺς ἀποδέξαιτ' ἄν τις, ὅτι χερρόνησον οἰκοῦντες μεγάλῃ πλημμυρίδι ἐξελαθεῖεν ἐκ τῶν τόπων· καὶ γὰρ νῦν ἔχουσι τὴν χώραν, ἣν εἶχον πρότερον, καὶ ἔπεμψαν τῷ Σεβαστῷ δῶρον τὸν ἱερώτατον παρ' αὐτοῖς λέβητα, αἰτούμενοι φιλίαν καὶ ἀμνηστίαν τῶν ὑπηργμένων. And, moreover, his expression πρὸς τὰ ἑωθινὰ μέρη is very similar to Augustus's *ad solis orientis regionem*, or Tacitus's "the Pillars of Hercules," = τὰ μέχρι τοῦ στόματος τῆς Κασπίας θαλάττης. I would be more willing to believe that it was an omission aimed at concealing what had surely been a Roman failure. What were the causes? As both Pliny (*umore nimio rigentia*) and Tacitus (*obstitit Oceanus*) state, it was due to navigational difficulties brought on no doubt by the glacial climate.

18. Dionysius, 1.3.3: "but Rome rules every country that is not inaccessible or uninhabited, and she is mistress of every sea, not only of that which lies inside the Pillars of Hercules but also the Ocean, except that part of it which is not navigable; she is the first and only State recorded in all time that ever made the risings and the settings of the sun the boundaries of her dominion." (ἡ δὲ Ῥωμαίων πόλις ἁπάσης μὲν ἄρχει γῆς ὅση μὴ ἀνέμβατός ἐστιν, ἀλλ' ὑπ' ἀνθρώπων κατοικεῖται, πάσης δὲ κρατεῖ θαλάσσης, οὐ μόνον τῆς ἐντὸς Ἡρακλείων στηλῶν, ἀλλὰ καὶ τῆς Ὠκεανίτιδος ὅση πλεῖσθαι μὴ ἀδύνατός ἐστι, πρώτη καὶ μόνη τῶν ἐκ τοῦ παντὸς αἰῶνος μνημονευομένων ἀνατολὰς καὶ δύσεις ὅρους ποιησαμένη τῆς δυναστείας·) Those last words could allude precisely to an obstacle in the navigation produced not by the existence of a continent but by the conditions of the sea itself. As is known, Dionysius was writing before 7 B.C. If he had knowledge of anything, it was before this date. Contra Thomson, *Hist. of Anc. Geogr.*, 220.

19. See below p. 109 (Pliny, *NH*, 4.81).

20. I will not elaborate on the debate concerning the date of the geographer Philemon (E. Norden, *KS*, 191–96; F. Gisinger and W. Kroll, *RE*, XIX no. 2 [1938], 2146); concerning the problem of the amber, G. Kolendo, *A la recherche de l'ambre baltique* (Warsaw, 1981), esp. 68; A. Grilli, "La documentazione sulla provenienza dell' ambra in Plinio," *Acme*, 1983, 5–17.

21. The sources of the Danube, like the Nile, are still unknown to Horace in 16 B.C. (*Odes* 4.14.45: *fontium qui celat origines / Nilusque et Hister* . . .); see A. von Premerstein, "Ein elogium des M. Vinicius cos. 19 v. Chr.," *JOAI*, 1904, 215–39; A. Moczy, *Pannonia*, Hist. of the Prov. of the Roman Empire (London, 1974); G. Alfoldi, *Noricum* (same collection) (London, 1974); and finally, E. Toth, "*Protulique fines Illyrici*," *Acta Archaeol. Ljubljana*, 1977, 278; R. Dion, *Aspects politiques* . . . (Paris, 1977), 237–45.

22. See below, p. 154.

23. For a recent update on the links with China, M. Poinsotte, "Les Romains et la Chine: réalités et mythes," *MEFRA*, 1979, 472.

V

Representation of Space: Agrippa's Geographical Work

Military surveys or diplomatic overtures—mentioned or not in the *Res Gestae*—give an account, in their own way, of the ecumenical claims made by Roman power. They extended to boundaries (the North Sea, or the Caspian regions) that had both strategic and highly symbolic value because they were consistent with the scientific concepts of the time and touched, in short, the cosmic order. However, it is not enough to draw approximately a world destined for Rome's domination: it is also necessary to govern it, as both Virgil and Velleius (2.89) stated, even if differently.[1] But to govern it, it must be known, measured, and above all drawn. Consequently, precisely in the Augustan period there was a series of undertakings of geographic, cartographic, and administrative nature. There was an increase in the number of partial or global censuses, in the publication of cadastral books or maps in numerous regions, and in the establishing of road itineraries. Most of these have left behind evidence that is sufficiently accurate; in particular, there was a most remarkable geographical achievement: Agrippa's famous map, which we will consider first.

Before starting this examination, it is necessary to mention a more problematic and uncertain undertaking, which would have taken place shortly before Agrippa's map, and which would be—if authentic—of a spectacular nature.[2] Two late geographical texts[3] report, as a preface to a description of the world, a vast undertaking of the measurement of "the inhabited world" (or "the Roman world"), which would have occurred, perhaps by an official decision of Caesar's, in the years following 44 B.C. It would have been entrusted to four chosen "scholars," who would have divided the task amongst themselves, according to regions corresponding to the cardinal points rather than according to the continents, as would be expected. In addition to the names of these "geometers" (as we shall call them), the length of time for each measurement is given in a twofold manner: first by the consular date at the end of the operations, then by a precise count in years, months, and days.

Of the two ancient texts that transmit this information, the most ancient is the *Cosmographia,* said to be by Julius Honorius, which is perhaps prior to A.D. 376, and which in any case was known to Cassiodorus. The second, known as the Pseudo-Aethicus, belongs prior to the eighth century and is similar to the former, except for a few rhetorical embellishments. The first text is seen as a compilation of notes taken (without his teacher's knowledge) by a student of Julius Honorius or Orator, who had in front of him a round map (here called *sphaera*) of the world, with geographical names for the seas, islands, mountains, provinces, towns, peoples, and rivers. These names, arranged irregularly, could be misread, and so the teacher had made a selection of them. The importance given to rivers on the original map is remarkable (reminiscent of Vitruvius's map?).[4] This type of map (round, or elliptical, with abundant toponomastic notes) then becomes well known in the Medieval period, but had definite ancient precedents.

The history of the four geometers is of course more original. It is given as follows, for example in Julius Honorius's version:

> In the consulship of Julius Caesar and Mark Antony, four chosen scholars had covered the entire earth: Nicodemus in the East, Didymus in the West, Theodotus in the North, and Polycletes in the South. From the above consulship to the fourth consulship of Augustus and Crassus's first, the East was measured in twenty-one years, five months, and nine days [etc.]. And from the above consulship to Augustus's seventh consulship and Agrippa's third, the western part was measured in twenty-six years, three months, seventeen days. From the above consulship to Augustus's tenth consulship, the northern part was measured in twenty-eight years, eight months, and (ten) days. From the above consulship to the consulship of Saturninus and Cinna, the southern part was measured in thirty-two years, one month, and twenty days.[5]

At first sight the information appears accurate and authentic, yet upon examination it is doubtful. First of all, the consular dates and the reckoning in years do not coincide.[6] But the differences can be explained: the consular dates would shorten the duration of operation by seven, eight, or nine years. It could therefore be supposed that the first version preserved traces of two stages in the completion of the operations—which, each having been started in 44 B.C., would have been finished in some way in 30, 27, 24, and 19 B.C. respectively; but supplementary operations would have prolonged each until 23, 18, 16, and 12 B.C.

Then, there must certainly have been an error in the calculation for the

South. The texts give *ad consulatum Saturnini et Cinnae* as the consular date: no consular colleagues are known by these names. The consuls of 19 B.C., C. Sentius Saturninus and Q. Lucretius Vespillo, would do: the date would coincide very well with that of other operations. But the *cognomen* Cinna is not usually attested for Lucretius Vespillo.

The same problem is seen elsewhere: the year 19 B.C. is attributed to a Cinna and a Saturninus not only in late compilations of the *Fasti* (*Fasti Hydatiani*) but again, and especially, in the *Chronicles* of St. Jerome (p. 143 Sch.; 165 Helm), who gives this year for Virgil's death. Therefore the error already existed when Jerome, ca. A.D. 378, made his compilation. What is the explanation? It has long been noted that a Saturninus and a Cinna follow each other in two very close consulships, in A.D. 4 and 5. Such a date brings to mind the famous problem of the census taken by Quirinius in Syria and Palestine in A.D. 6, which was of great interest to Christian tradition. Already in the second century A.D., Tertullian mentions a census carried out in Judea by Sentius Saturninus (whom he perhaps confused with a L. Volusius Saturninus): the error would have consisted in mistaking a legate of Syria for a consul, then in confusing two consecutive consuls in A.D. 4–5 with consular colleagues of 19 B.C. As far as we are concerned, adulteration with the widespread tradition concerning the famous "universal census" that was contemporaneous with the birth of Christ.

The second element of confusion is the names of the geometers. Their banality seems to discourage any inquiry. However, two among them could recall personages who had some link with geography or geometry: a Didymos is attested as a metrologist writing in Egypt at the beginning of the Roman period. One Theodosios is attested as a mathematician, inventor of a type of portable *gnomon*, as cited by Strabo and Vitruvius. But this would be very weak testimony. As to the vocabulary of geographical or geometrical nature in our passage, either it is banal or else—when the words are rarer, such as *admetiri* (72, 13 R) or *occidus*—it denotes a later usage, from the fourth or fifth century A.D.

This isolated tradition is therefore very difficult to interpret, and its success in the Middle Ages is not proof of authenticity. The names could as easily have been imagined as actually researched. As far as we know, the division of the task in regions north, south, east, and west does not correspond to the canonical divisions of geography according to the continents, in the time of Caesar and Augustus. There remain those precise computations, with the (unexplained) discrepancy between the consular dates and the duration given, which could not be explained if all the evidence had been invented. Thus it was believed that actual facts underlay the eventually problematic discrepancy. It brought to mind survey operations, indeed well attested as we shall see, in the time of Caesar, the triumvirate, and Augustus. But the surveys are not "mensurations": as great as they are, they involve only limited zones.

Perhaps in reality we have been blinded by hypercriticism. While no operation as global and spectacular as the measurement of the world is directly attested by another source for this period, it should not be forgotten that there is one whose existence cannot be doubted: the one that Agrippa inevitably undertook in order to achieve the publication of his *Commentarii* and his map.[7]

Of all the attempts dating from the Augustan period that touch upon or deal with the knowledge and the mastery of space, none, apparently, is clearer than Agrippa's.[8] Yet upon closer examination, there are many uncertainties about its nature, its aims, and its methods; there are even more, perhaps, regarding its actual significance—whether scientific, political, or symbolic.

The data are scanty but not negligible. Pliny provides the most explicit information. On the one hand Pliny cites Agrippa specifically more than thirty times in Books 3–6 as the author of geographic measurements concerning the dimensions of the provinces and of the regions of the world, the seas, the islands.[9] Yet the manner in which he refers to an "author" (3.86), the verbs that he uses (*prodit, tradit, credit, existimavit, sententia, colligit, fecit*), the mention of some hesitation over the *numeri* (6.207), and above all, the more developed notes on the Punic origin of the coast of Baetica (3.8) or on the known part (*qua cognitum est*) of the Caspian Sea (6.37)—all this leads us to believe that Pliny consulted a text. We shall have to consider that later.[10]

Elsewhere Pliny twice mentions in an incontestable fashion a map-like work—the famous map of the *Porticus Vipsania*[11] (Pliny, 3.16–17):

> The total length (of Baetica) according to Marcus Agrippa is 475 miles, and its breadth 258 miles, but this was when its bounds extended as far as Cartagena. . . . At present the length of Baetica from the frontiers of the town of Castulo to Cadiz is 250 miles, and from the sea-front of Murgi 25 miles more; its breadth . . . is 234 miles. . . . Who therefore could believe that . . . Agrippa, a very painstaking man, particularly for such a work, when intending to set before the eyes of the City a map of the world, made a mistake, and with him also the deified Augustus? For it was Augustus who completed the *porticus*

containing a plan of the world that had been begun by his sister in accordance with the design and memoranda of Marcus Agrippa.[12]

Proponere orbem spectandum means "to set before the eyes, so it can be seen"; this is a reference to something visual, like those *tableaux* that Agrippa wanted to exhibit in galleries (Pliny, 35.25).[13] Indeed, Pliny makes another precise allusion to the map of the *Porticus*. He remarks, concerning the town of Spasinou Charax (at the mouth of the Euphrates), that its distance from the sea has greatly increased recently: "Charax was previously ten *stades* from the coast, and the *Porticus Vipsania* even has it near the sea; but in the time of Juba it was fifty miles from the sea" (6.139).[14] The manuscripts all read *Vipsanda,* which can legitimately be corrected to *Vipsania,* and the majority read *porticus*. It should be noted that the reading *etiam ipsa portum* by certain modern editors is not valid since the subject of the sentence is the *oppidum*, Charax, in the neuter. Therefore it is a cartographic reference ("in fact a maritime town") contained in the *porticus,* which was named after either Agrippa or his sister. It would seem that Pliny mentions here a direct verification.[15]

The history of the *Porticus* is fairly well known.[16] Agrippa had specified in his will that it be built on lands that were located to the east of the *Campus Martius,* the *Campus Agrippae,* bequeathed by him to the people (Dio, 54.29.4). This wish was not realized before 7 B.C. (Dio, 55.8.9),[17] and so there was time enough for Augustus to lay out the garden and to finish the *Diribitorium,* at this date the *porticus* begun by Polla was not yet completed (ibidem). But it certainly was completed during Augustus's lifetime, as Pliny states, and, I would add, before 2 B.C.—the date of the dedication of the Temple of Mars Ultor.

This is all we know positively about the map itself. It has been shown (Chapter 3, above) that the use of flat geographical maps (*tabulae, πίνακες*) that were drawn and painted is well attested in the Greek world and at Rome from at least the fifth century—unlike "spheres," which were certainly much rarer. Some were already in the *porticus* of the *Lyceum* in Athens and were used for pedagogical purposes (Diogenes Laertius, 5.51).[18] At Rome itself, a *forma* (that is, a map, often of a large scale, especially among the *agrimensores*) of Sardinia had been placed by Ti. Sempronius Gracchus in 174 B.C. in the Temple of Mater Matuta as a memorial of his victories: *Sardiniae insulae forma erat, atque in ea simulacra pugnarum picta* (Livy, 41.28.10).[19] Thus it is both a map and painted scenes. Circa 59 B.C., there was an *Italia picta* on a wall in the Sanctuary of Tellus (Varro, *RR,* 1.2.1); the context (see the geographical discussion on the *orbis terrae* of Eratosthenes in Chapters 3–4) leads one to believe that there really was a map, whatever its nature, whether this is a cavalier view or not.[20] There also were more official *formae* placed in the archives, those drawn by the *agrimensores,* which showed the *ager publicus*: as for example the map of Campania in the *Atrium Libertatis* ca. 80 B.C. (Granius Licinianus, 10.2; see the *formae regionis,* p. 293, 5 L).[21] Closer in date to Agrippa, Vitruvius, who was writing at the beginning of Augustus's reign, enumerates in Book 8 some great rivers of the known world whose descriptions he claims to have borrowed from maps—*capita fluminum, quae orbe terrarum chorographiis picta itemque scripta . . . inveniuntur* (8.2.6)[22]; unfortunately there is no indication from the text whether they are posted monumental maps (like in the *porticus* of the *Lyceum*), or maps circulating as books. In any case, for chronological reasons he cannot mean *the* map of Agrippa, and further, Vitruvius uses the plural. As will be shown, the practice of displaying wall maps within *porticus* would continue: we will deal later with the map at Autun dating from the third century A.D.

The map of Agrippa located in the *Porticus Vipsania* in the *Campus Martius* therefore certainly existed; Pliny saw it and said so. But was it called "Agrippa's map"? When he mentions it specifically, Pliny calls it only by the name of the *porticus,* and he states that it was finished by Augustus, no doubt between 7 and 2 B.C. The ancients themselves therefore could have been uncertain about the true name of its author.

What was its actual nature? The ancients, we have seen, differentiated between two types of diagrammatic representations of a geographical nature: γεωγραφία, which drew in the whole of the earth (we would call them global maps), and chorography, which gives regional details (known regions, useful regions; Strabo, 1.1.1).[23] Both words can describe *schemata,* maps, or written texts: Strabo uses the words τόν γεωγραφικὸν πίνακα to refer to the map *itself* (2.5.13). The two procedures differed not only in size or scale but in type of layout, as well as in remarkable details, as Ptolemy stresses quite clearly (*Geogr.,* 1.1): the geographical map only records gulfs, large cities, nations, and major rivers; the chorographic map, on the other hand, sets out in detail ports, towns, districts (δήμους), river tributaries, etc. Chorography, Ptolemy adds, is related to the art of painting; geography, with its distances, its axes, and, speaking for himself, astronomical and mathematical procedures, could do without this talent. But Strabo, a century and a half earlier, made the same distinction: in Book 2.5.10, he describes the geometric projection systems necessary for a geographical map; in 2.5.17, he notes that it is the outline of the coasts that "draws" (γεωγράφει) the Earth. Furthermore, he includes rivers, mountains, and all those details of "varied colors," which fill a "chorographic" map. This passage is often commented upon in an attempt to see in the expression ὁ χωρογραφικὸς πίναξ a precise allusion to our map of Agrippa (or of Augustus), which would thus be referred to without naming it. And, in fact, the passage is ambiguous, because it seems to suggest that it could be possible to have maps that were both chorographic and geographic. We shall come back to this.[24]

First of all, Agrippa's map was truly geographic: it described the whole of the *oikoumene*—the *orbis terrarum* (Pliny, 3.17)—and not only the *orbis Romanus* and its provinces, since Spasinou Charax (specifically seen by Pliny within the *porticus*) is definitely in Parthian territory. Furthermore, we can confidently use the numerical data provided by Pliny (and perhaps by Strabo) as coming from Agrippa, in order to reconstruct the map, since it is in connection with some of these figures that Pliny mentions the map, the *porticus*, and the fact that Augustus completed it (3.17). Agrippa left some *commentarii*, and when Agrippa is referred to as *auctor*, it is to these *commentarii* that reference is being made. The map was drawn "in accordance with" them. The word *commentarii*, as we know, indicates all sorts of memoranda, often made by or for magistrates. Agrippa had also left some notes for the water works that he organized in Rome (as well as a master plan, or *forma*; Frontinus, *Aq.*, 99). Sometimes a *commentarius* is an illustrated set of instructions (Vitruvius, 9, *praef.* 14), but most often it is the accompanying text of a thing to be used (Vitruvius, 1.1.4; 7, *praef.* 11; 7, *praef.* 17), or more generally a treatise (Pliny, 17.234). The term *commentarii* is found once in a context very similar to ours, since it involves texts accompanying the map (*forma*) of a city's territory drawn up by the *agrimensores*, and which were written by the man responsible for the organization of a colony: *auctor divisionis . . . voluntatem suam edicit commentariis aut in formis . . .* (Sic. Flaccus, p. 125 Th = 160 L). These specify—as did the *forma*—the dimensions, the names, and the nature of the lands allotted.

Such were Agrippa's *Commentarii*: a written text (certainly brief but discursive) from which the map was drawn.[25] Therefore there was a definite link between them and the map; and it is quite legitimate to try to reconstruct the latter from preserved textual fragments. It has been successfully done, and so it is not necessary to go over it in detail here.[26] Suffice it to say that for this reconstruction, use was made of thirty or so citations in Pliny, as well as seven passages in Strabo concerning Corsica, Sardinia, Sicily, and Italy, where the distances are given in μίλια. Following Schweder, two late geographical texts were also employed—the *Dimensuratio provinciarum* and the *Divisio orbis terrarum* (by which Dicuil was inspired), which offer striking parallels with Agrippa's regions and measurements.[27] This resulted in the reasonably accurate *tableau* set up by Kubitschek (*RE*, X (1919), s.v. "Karten," col. 2105). There are twenty-four "regions," of which the first nineteen (with the exception of regions eight: Dacia, and nine: Sarmatia, Scythia, and Taurica) correspond to the *orbis Romanus* itself and most often, but not always, to its provinces. But the last five regions make up the rest of the *oikoumene*: *Caspium Mare, Armenia; India, Media, Parthia, Persis; Mesopotamia; Aethiopum terra universa cum Mari Rubro et superior Aegyptus*. Thus it was indeed the entire *orbis terrarum*.

For all these regions (*partes*) measurements (*dimensiones*) are given in length and width (*longitudo, latitudo*), but these terms have nothing to do with longitude or latitude or with exact coodinates, expressed in degrees, as Ptolemy would give them. Nor, as has been too quickly claimed, are the lengths always oriented precisely from West to East, or widths from North to South. Syria, for example, demonstrates the opposite case (Pliny, 5.67, without Agrippa's name; but cf. the "Agrippan" *Divisio* 19: *Dimensuratio* 4).[28] In fact, these measurements, defined by identifiable geographical points, are often oblique in relation to north-south and east-west orientations, of which Agrippa was surely aware, at least in following his predecessors (e.g., for Baetica, Brittany, Gaul; see Sallmann p. 209 and map p. 213). This very general information suffices to make us aware, at least very schematically, of the general appearance of Agrippa's map. Two certainties emerge that allow us to refute two erroneous interpretations that are occasionally maintained.

First of all, it was not exclusively an itinerary map, a prototype of the famous Peutinger Table.[29] It is true that Agrippa used itinerary measurements to arrive at certain of his dimensions, but not for the maritime distances that he often gives (frag. 15 R = Pliny, 4.60). Moreover, certain errors in the estimation, standard for that matter, like the narrowness of the Anatolian isthmus (Pliny, 5.102), would not be explicable if itineraries had been used. But most notably, the itinerary maps, as far as we can reconstruct them from the surviving *itineraria,* do not allow the representation of the length and width of territories since they are juxtapositions of a series of lines.[30]

One of the arguments often brought forward to prove the resemblance, and even the relationship, between Agrippa's map and the Peutinger Table calls upon the form and dimensions of the latter. It is, as we know, excessively long (6.82 × 0.34 m), which leads to considerable distortions in the depiction of continents and countries, as well as in their relative positions. Some scholars cite this distortion as proof that it is a copy of an original papyrus roll, and this is, I believe, the right hypothesis, given the dimensions: the height is that of a roll. But others (recently E. Weber) attribute this distortion to the original model, which would be none other than the *Saulenhalle,* the *Porticus Vipsania.* Thus they imagine the map stretched out along the *Porticus,* with its length out of proportion to its height. There is no point in stressing the arbitrariness of this conception. First of all, the exact dimensions of Agrippa's *Porticus* are unknown. There is nothing to suggest that the map covered every side, or the entire length, of the building. *Porticus* were built to shelter many different works, without any apparent connection between their dimensions and those of the building. Therefore, the dimensions and the appearance of the Peutinger Table should not be taken as indications that the Table is an exact replica of Agrippa's map. This said, it is probable that certain characteristics or details of this great cartographic compilation (dated certainly from the fourth or fifth century A.D.) could be traced back, through many intermediaries, to the map of the *Porticus.* It is possible, for example (although we have no evidence for this), that all Italian roads, radiating out from Rome were indicated on the map, as on the Peutinger Table (4.5); Agrippa and Augustus had definitely taken an interest in this highway system, and the golden milestone in the *Forum* recorded distances to the major towns of the empire (Dio, 54.8; Pliny, *NH,* 3.66).

Secondly, Agrippa's map was not what had been termed, since the beginning of cartography, a round map (Agathemerus, 1.1.2: *οἱ μὲν οὖν παλαιοὶ τὴν οἰκουμένην ἔγραφον στρογγύλην*). Konrad Miller has defended this view for two equally erroneous reasons.[31] First of all, he tends to find an ancient and especially Roman origin in round maps, which are so frequent in the Middle Ages,[32] either independently or in manuscript illuminations (especially in the manuscripts of Sallust). Moreover, the phrase "round map" is a misinterpretation, or at least a mistaken interpretation, of the Roman word *orbis,* which originally indicated roundness but which, according to Miller, always kept this significance. This last statement is erroneous. The word *orbis* evidently did not keep its original sense of "circle of the horizon," since Pliny (for example, see *NH* 2.242) writes of the "length" and "width" of this *pars nostra terrarum* that he calls *orbis terrarum* (e.g., 3.3; 3.5). The Romans in the Augustan period, like the Greeks then and before, were well aware that the known dimensions of the inhabited world, estimated by Eratosthenes and corrected by Hipparchus, Posidonius, and Artemidorus, made a rectangular or ellipsoidal shape: Strabo explains this quite clearly (2.5.9, 116 C). In order to represent the rectangle, for lack of a sphere, a *pinax* (or *tabula*) at least seven feet long is required.

Of course, the old-fashioned Ionian round maps could have continued, but Augustus's contemporaries were well aware of their inconveniences. This is clearly shown in a passage by Geminus, an author of a book on astronomy (*Intr. to Astr.*, 16.3–5), who could quite possibly have been a contemporary of Cicero and Augustus. In this text, the inconveniences of the round map, which Herodotus had already ridiculed, are clearly indicated: the ratio of the distances is distorted.[33]

The dimensions that Agrippa's (or Augustus's) map in the *Porticus* must have reproduced—according to the written fragments that are preserved—make a circular format clearly impossible. India's dimensions alone, in the East, are terribly exaggerated (3,300 miles "long" from East to West and 2,300 "wide" from North to South) and would preclude this possibility. On the contrary, the north-south dimensions of the *oikoumene* were greatly underestimated, especially around the Caspian region (see the ridiculous dimensions for the Caspian Sea at Pliny, 6.37: 480 miles by 290; though granted that Agrippa added *qua cognitum est*).[34]

The fact remains nonetheless that Agrippa's *oikoumene* is clearly a rectangular shape. In fact, if like P. Schnabel (p. 423) we calculate the length of the world by adding Agrippa's partial measurements, the total of Roman miles is 8,595, which is quite close to the figure of 8,578 that Pliny (II, 242) attributes to Artemidorus (2.242, or 8,945 miles at 2.244). This is much less than the most recently corrected measurement Pliny had at his disposal, that of Isidorus of Charax (9,818 miles). Always according to Isidorus, the known width was about half the length. Therefore it is clear that Agrippa's map, whatever its exact measurements, was oblong ("in the shape of a *chlamys*"), a shape well attested since Eratosthenes.

Every flat representation that aims to record not only itineraries but also surface measurements (which are implied by the presence of widths and lengths) must adopt, at least implicitly, a system of projection. The most commonly used system in the time of Agrippa was the simple cylindrical projection, described succinctly by Strabo (2.5.10, 116 C):

> For it will make only a slight difference if we draw straight lines to represent the circles, that is the parallels and meridians, by means of which we clearly indicate the "climate," the winds and other differences, and also the positions of the parts of the earth with reference both to each other and to the heavenly bodies—drawing parallel lines for the parallels and perpendicular lines for the circles perpendicular to the parallels, for our imagination can easily transfer to the globular

> and spherical surface the figure or magnitude seen by the eye on a plane surface. And the same applies also, we say, to the oblique circles and their corresponding straight lines. Although the several meridians drawn through the pole all converge on the sphere toward one point, yet on our plane-surface chart it will not be a matter of importance merely to make to straight meridian lines converge slightly; for there is no necessity for this in many cases, nor are the converging straight lines, when the lines of the sphere are transferred to the plane chart and drawn as straight lines, as easily understood as are the curved lines on the sphere. And so in what I have to say hereafter I shall assume that our drawing has been made on a plane chart.[35]

It is clear from this passage that Strabo and hence his sources, as well as the *πινακογραφίαι* (referred to in 2.1.11, 71 C), already knew of the *conical* system of projection (in which the meridians are drawn as converging straight lines), one of the sytems that Ptolemy would later discuss at length. But Strabo rejects it as a useless complexity. Agrippa probably adopted Eratosthenes's old system of projection for his map. It is debatable whether he designed his map using a system of perpendicular axes, as was being done since Dicaearchus's invention of the *diaphragma* (Agathemerus, 1.5, p. 472 M)—a central parallel that passed through the Pillars of Hercules, the southern part of Asia Minor, Taurus, and so forth—because Pliny gives Agrippa's measurement of the Mediterranean, first from Gades to Issos and then in two separate measurements from the straits of Sicily to Alexandria (6.207). However, there are really two different measurements for maritime distances that often occur in Agrippa (or in Pliny). As elsewhere (Pliny, 6.164), we see that for Agrippa the northern limit of Media-Parthia-Persia was the *Taurus Caucasus,* just as in the maps of Dicaearchus and Eratosthenes: it is probable that Agrippa's map also had a *diaphragma.* In any case the concept of a parallel (and hence of latitude) was the one better known not only by scholars but also by the general public: the correct use of sundials (known at Rome since the second century B.C.), which was fixed to a precise latitude, proves this. Agrippa could not ignore this fact, since the *horologium* built between 13 and 9 B.C. in Rome by Facundus Novius was indeed designed for Rome's latitude.[36] The question is more problematic for the meridians, the north-south axes. P. Schnabel,[37] a specialist on Ptolemy, thought he could show that Agrippa had at least twice corrected, by means of astronomical measurements and geometrical calculations, his predecessors' erroneous alignments, specifically for the eastern boundary of Lusitania and for the width of the Mediterranean between Cape Tenarus and Cape Physcos in Cyrenaica. But his demonstrations have not been accepted by everyone.

According to our sources, Agrippa divided the *oikoumene* into twenty-four regions. This method recalls that of the *sphragides,* those geometric figures similar to seals (or cadastral figures, which is another meaning of the word), which the geographers and cartographers traditionally used to further the schematic visualization of the shapes of countries. Their names were strictly geographical, especially in the regions beyond the Roman Empire. Furthermore, they could coincide with the provinces: and, in this sense, the map was political as well as administrative. In fact the word *provincia,* certainly attributed to Agrippa, appears in Pliny, e.g., for Narbonensis (3.37), and several times in the *Dimensuratio* and the *Divisio,* also thought to derive from Agrippa (e.g., for Spain, *Div.* 3). The dimensions could sometimes be based upon administrative frontiers—which might have changed in the time from Agrippa to Pliny. There has been much discussion as to whether there was any change in the northeastern frontier of Cisalpine Gaul: Pliny, the *Dimensuratio,* and the *Divisio* state that the River Arsia, which surrounds Istria, is its eastern limit. The problem lies in the fact that Strabo (7.5.3, 314 C) points out that the establishment of the frontier of Cisalpine Gaul (and of Italy) is recent and no doubt connected to the enlargement of the *pomoerium* in 8 B.C. (Dio, 55.8.6), and hence came after Agrippa's death. But nothing is less certain; even the reality of the extension of the *pomoerium* by Augustus has been put in doubt.[38] Agrippa himself could have chosen the Arsia as a purely geographical limit, or the extension could have been prior to his death, or Augustus might even have completed the texts left by his son-in-law.

Just how detailed was Agrippa's map? At first glance, given its general aim (the *orbis terrarum*), it would be tempting to see it as a geographic map, according to Strabo's and Ptolemy's classifications: it encompassed the whole *oikoumene,* emphasizing especially the coasts (which "draw the map"), and only mentioning the most important rivers. In fact, Agrippa's name appears on the Hereford World Map (Miller, 4.10)—although distorted and little understood by the Christian tradition—in connection with the measurements of Gaul, borrowed from Pliny (4.105): *secundum Agrippam regem.* The Hereford Map certainly cannot be viewed as a detailed map.[39] Nevertheless several questions can be asked. First of all there is the troublesome detail about the town of Spasinou Charax: one could see that it was "by the seaside." Then, the fact that one of the two texts that surely derive from Agrippa's map and *Commentarii,* the *Divisio orbis terrarum,* specifies in its title: *Quem divus Augustus primus per* chorographiam *ostendit.*[40] Moreover, as was shown, Strabo mentions in 2.5.17 (whether in a general manner or with a specific map in mind) ὁ χωρογραφικὸς πίναξ, which contains various details (χωρογραφία would almost translate the Latin phrase *situs descriptio*). And in many other instances (at least six times),[41] he specifically uses ὁ χωρογράφος, with verbs like φησί or λέγεται and with measurements in Roman miles for Corsica, Sardinia, Sicily, and Italy.[42] He seems to be alluding in this case to a particular work, very similar to the one that through Pliny (as well as the *Dimensuratio* and the *Divisio*) is attributed to Agrippa. This leads to one of the most discussed, and most obscure, aspects of the question under examination: what were the exact connections between Strabo and "Agrippa's map," or rather with the texts (essentially Pliny) through which the map can be reconstructed? What about Augustus's own "geographical work"? And, subsequently, if it existed, what were its connections with Agrippa?

But did the word *chorographia* always have the specific technical meaning given to it by Strabo and Ptolemy? It first appears in Latin in Vitruvius (an uncertain reading should be discarded in Priscianus, 6.16.83 Keil, regarding Cicero). When Vitruvius refers to *chorographiae* that include, for the entire world, rivers that are *picta itemque scripta,* and lists the Ganges, the Indus, the Tigris, the Euphrates, the Tanaïs, the Rhône, the Nile—but also, in Italy—the Timavus and the Po, he seems to be referring to one or several maps of the world. They certainly were general enough so that one could see the sources of the Ganges and of the Nile, but detailed enough to see the Timavus, which may have been "wide and deep" (Strabo, 5.1.8), but was certainly not very long. Is it altogether impossible for the same document to be labelled both γεωγραφικός and χωρογραφικός? This question seems to depend on the work's size, its content, and in fact, on the number of details included. But fifty years later, Pomponius Mela entitled his work *De chorographia,* so condensed in comparison with Strabo, yet it is a general description of the regions of the world.

Thus, sources that were not particularly late could easily have called *chorographia* a description of the world, general yet detailed enough (not unlike the one seen on the map in the *Porticus*). They also could easily have attributed it to Augustus, since Pliny does not give Agrippa's name (6.139) when he refers to the map in the *Porticus* but rather mentions that it is Augustus who completed it (3.17).

Thus Strabo's χωρογράφος could be the author (anonymous since Agrippa is dead) who completed the map in the *Porticus,* on the order of Augustus himself. We can speculate further that Strabo had in mind (or perhaps in front of him) a general map of the world whose characteristics strikingly resembled those of Agrippa's. At the conclusion of his book, in a famous passage that is a valuable ecumenical overview of the empire, he notes that the Romans dominated the largest and most important part of the three continents. In Europe, they only lack "those regions beyond the Ister and those regions along the coast between the Rhine and the Tanaïs" (17.3.24). The furthest ends of the world in the North are evidently seen in a relatively reduced or even marginal fashion. We have seen that Agrippa's map also greatly underestimated this region of the world.

What can be said about the dimensions and orientation of Agrippa's map? In the absence of any precise information, one can only put forward gratuitous hypotheses, based for example on the alleged number of names on the map derived by a comparison with those on the Peutinger Table (6,000) or in Ptolemy (8,000). Müllenhoff ("Ueber die röm. Weltkarte," *Hermes* [1875]: 194) ventured to give arbitrary figures: sixty feet long, forty wide, on a base sixteen feet high (which yields a total height of fifty-six feet or 16.80 m, very imposing for a *porticus*). It is better to plead ignorance. The same can be said for orientation. Some medieval maps show the East at the top; the same view was held for Agrippa's map. Partsch (*Wochenschr. für kl. Phil.* [1907]: 1058), following Pliny (*NH,* 3.100), who writes about the southern coasts of Italy as if they were its "shoulders" and its "neck," assumes (as does Schweder) that its orientation is with the South at the top. K. Miller, *Mappae mundi,* 6.143ff., thinks that Roman maps usually showed the East at the top, contrary to the Greeks who, like us, showed the North. F. Castagnoli, re-examining the literary testimony in "L'orientamento nella cartografia greca e romana" (*Rend. Pont. Acc. Arch.* [1975–76]: 59–69), concluded that the orientation on Roman maps was predominantly southward (i.e., with the South at the top), but he relies on the Greek texts of Strabo or Appian. This is effectively the case for the famous *forma urbis,* a marble plan of Rome of the Severan period, partially preserved. But a recently discovered plan of much earlier date was oriented to the northeast (M. Conticello de' Spagnolis, *Il Tempio dei Dioscuri nel Circo Flaminio* [Rome, 1984]). We should recall that cadastre B at Orange is oriented to the west (the West at the top), cadastre C to the north and cadastre A, according to a recent hypothesis, to the south. The layout of the plans over three walls of a room could explain this (F. Salviat, "Orientation, extension et chronologie des plans cadastraux d'Orange," *Rev. Arch. Narb.* 10 [1977]: 107–18). Perhaps the choice of orientation depended on the orientation of its monumental backing. I am unable to add anything more.

It has been too easily assumed that Agrippa's map contributed nothing to geographical knowledge. We have seen that P. Schnabel attempted at length to demonstrate otherwise: Agrippa—who, after all, was a sailor—would have corrected some measurements of latitudes and provided a new estimation of the degrees of latitude. This is going perhaps too far. But even those scholars who deny that Agrippa made new astronomical measurements and calculations must agree that his land and sea measurements, especially for certain regions, are considerably better than Posidonius's figures as found in Strabo. This is especially true in the western regions for the outline of the coasts of Spain, Gaul, and Germany. There were also improvements in the dimensions for the Pontus Euxinus (frag. 49–52 Klotz). Certain progress in geographical knowledge is still noteworthy. Thus Agrippa seems to have known of the identification of the upper course of the Danube (the Danuvius) with its lower course, known under the Greek name Hister. If *Divisio* 10 and *Dimensuratio* 28 really recall his meaning, he gives the *Danuvius* as the northern boundary of Rhaetia, Noricum, and Pannonia. In the latter two regions, there is no doubt that it was the same river; in *Div.* 11 and *Dim.* 19 the *Danuvius* is given as the southern boundary of Germany and Dacia. It is not surprising that Pliny (4.78 and 81), for the Pontic regions, always calls this part of the river Hister, explicitly quoting Agrippa. This old name would continue to be used for a long time up to, but excluding, Tacitus. Despite the use of both names, Agrippa could not fail to identify the two watercourses—which Augustus himself would do in a chapter of the *Res Gestae* certainly written as early as 2 B.C. (*RG*, 30): *protuli fines Illyrici ad ripam fluminis Danuvi.*[43]

An interesting reference is made to the Vistula: a formal testimony by Pliny (4.81 = fr. 21 K), confirmed by *Div.* 14 and *Dim.* 8, gives the Vistula as the western boundary of Dacia; there is no reason to doubt its mention in connection to Germany in *Div.* 11 and *Dim.* 19 (= fr. 17 K). Yet certain scholars have doubted it and proposed to emend Pliny's text, basing their view on Strabo's famous statement that there is no knowledge of the coastal regions beyond the mouth of the Elbe (7.2.4, 294 C). But on this point, as we have seen, Strabo is mistaken (even if he is only following his source, he writes in the present tense). In 12 B.C., Drusus's fleet had reached Jutland. There is no reason to doubt that the name of the river was actually used by Agrippa—or, at least, in the version that Augustus possibly completed or circulated later.

Should we be surprised at the remarkable quality of Agrippa's work? Pliny describes him as a *vir tanta diligentia*, and feels that he was fully aware of the importance of his undertaking. We should recall his work as an aedile in Rome in 33 B.C., his responsibilities as admiral, his military and naval campaigns, but also his undertakings in Gaul, administrative (in taking the first census in the province) as well as technical (the construction of the road network from Lyons).[44] Such a qualified man, who proved his capabilities and the scope of his interests, possessed at least the average learning of the senators of his time who were able to read and understand Varro, Cicero, Nigidius Figulus, Cornelius Nepos, and all those who had written about geography and transmitted (directly or indirectly) the knowledge of Greek science.

But above all, Agrippa certainly did not work alone. Among the Roman officers, not all of the *praefecti fabrum* were as cultured as Vitruvius, although some might have come close. Agrippa had sailors under his command, and not all the *navarchi* were as skilled as Pytheas in making astronomical observations. Admittedly they sailed more often in the Mediterranean using the *peripli* than by plotting a bearing. Nevertheless, these sailors at least knew how to calculate distances with sufficient accuracy. Pliny records some maritime distances in Roman miles, probably derived from Agrippa, who in turn used Roman *peripli.* We know from Vitruvius (9.8.1) that his contemporaries knew how to use "sundials for each latitude," the invention of a certain Theodosius of Bithynia, whom Strabo knew (12.566). Some of these sundials were portable (*viatoria* and *pensilia*). We can get an idea of them from archaeological evidence. These instruments, well known to Vitruvius, must also have been well known to Agrippa,[45] and above all, they prove that the concept of κλίμα was sufficiently widespread.

Thus Agrippa, as the person in charge of surveying (necessary for the census), of road construction, and of the fleet, could have had access to a series of carefully taken measurements that he recorded in his *Commentarii.* For what remains—lands outside the empire—we have seen that his global measurements coincided with those provided by the Greeks, since Eratosthenes. But this is not the important point even though it was accomplished with the diligent mind of a great technician. The task planned by Agrippa, and for which he had gathered other *commentarii,* was clearly symbolic and thus political. We should first believe Pliny's words: "to show the entire world to the *urbs*" (and we must preserve the reading of the manuscripts). This is perhaps Pliny's formula: he often stresses the contrast *urbs/orbis,* always in "triumphalist" contexts. For example, when he presents in Book 36 the *urbis nostrae miracula*[46] and explains that the panel will also display the conquered world, *sic quoque terrarum orbem victum ostendere,* the parallelism between the expressions is striking. Likewise (3.40) in the famous eulogy of Italy, *una cunctarum gentium in toto orbe patria.*

Pliny, in the prefaces to his Books, often solemnly insists on the unity of the world henceforth assured by the *maiestas imperii Romani* (14.2) or by the *immensa Romanae pacis maiestas* (27.2). But, as we have seen, the theme of the contrasted apposition *urbs/orbis* appears precisely at the very end of the Republican period (Cicero, *Cat.*, 4.11), in Nepos, and then in the Augustan writers and poets, such as Propertius (3.11.57) and especially Ovid (*Fasti,* 2.684), in a very solemn passage dedicated to Jupiter Terminus: *Romanae spatium est urbis et orbis idem.*

Agrippa's project is so well integrated into the theme of the universal empire that was finally incorporated by Augustus in the City, that we can legitimately wonder if Pliny's formula does not go back for its source to Agrippa's *Commentarii,* and if the words *spectandum urbi* were not on the monument itself, not unlike the formula at the beginning of the inscription of the *Res Gestae: Index rerum gestarum, quibus orbem terrarum imperio populi Romani subiecit.*

The use of large geographical *tableaux* could certainly be scientific: this was the case for Theophrastus's πίνακες, and it has been shown that Cassiodorus recommends its pedagogical use to his monks. But we can easily go beyond this pedagogical use to an ideological and political application as far as maps publicly exhibited are concerned. This was no doubt the origin of Roman cartography: the triumphal exhibition in temples of maps of victories. Once the empire had (theoretically) been expanded to the limits of the *orbis terrarum,* a general geographical map could best illustrate this accomplishment.

A strikingly precise parallel, albeit three centuries later, allows a clearer understanding of the connection between geography, map, and imperial ideology.[47] In the speech given by the *rhetor* Eumenes in the spring of A.D. 298 at the Forum of Autun thanking the Tetrarchs, especially Constantius, for their benefactions, the peroration is devoted to the restoration of the town's schools, and ends with the famous description of the map found in their *porticus* (*Pan.*, 5.20–21):

> And, furthermore, may the youth of our city look under these porticoes, and daily consider all the lands and all the seas, all the towns restored by their goodness, the peoples conquered by their bravery, the nations paralyzed by the terror which they inspire. For there, since you too have seen it, I suppose, while teaching the young people and making them learn more clearly by their eyes those concepts which the ear has some difficulty in apprehending, there is represented the position of all the countries with their names, their extent, the distance which

> separates them, as well as all the rivers of the world with their sources and their mouths, the points where the coasts curve in to form gulfs and those where the Ocean surrounds and embraces the earth or where his heedless waves make incursions. (XXI.) And may this map, because it indicates opposing regions, permit them to review the magnificent deeds of our valiant *principes,* making them see, when couriers arrive continuously, covered with sweat and proclaiming victory, the twin rivers of Persia, the parched plains of Libya, the curve of the Rhine's branches, the manifold mouths of the Nile, and inviting them to contemplate each of these countries, whether it be Egypt, recalled from its madness and calmed under your mild rule, Diocletian Augustus, or whether it be at you, invincible Maximian, hurling thunder against the now-cursed Moors, or whether, thanks to your mighty armies, Emperor Constantius, Batavia and Brittany raising their soiled heads above rivers and forests, or at you, Maximian Caesar [Galerius], trampling underfoot the bows and quivers of the Persians. Now indeed we have true pleasure in studying the map of the world, now at last we see that no country is foreign.[48]

The expressions used by the Gallic *rhetor,* although of a different century and land, must be closely examined. He begins by stating (19.4) that the restoration of education is, for the emperors, the only means to revive that far-off time when, "according to our reading, Rome was preeminent on land and sea" (*ut legimus Romana res plurimum terra et mari valuit*), which goes back at least to the golden age of the empire, if not to the time of its foundation. How can we avoid recalling the words of *Res Gestae,* 13: "when victories had secured peace by land and sea throughout the whole empire of the Roman people" (*cum per totum imperium populi Romani terra marique esset parta victoriis pax*); or at Livy, 1.19.3: "after the battle of Actium, when the emperor Caesar Augustus had brought about peace on land and sea" (*post bellum Actiacum ab imperatore Caesare Augusto pace terra marique parta*)?

The description of the Autun map recalls closely the canonical descriptions of maps of all the lands and all the seas (*omnes terras et cuncta maria*), and the more strictly geographical information: "their positions, their extent, the distance that separates them, as well as all the rivers of the world with their sources and their mouths, the points where the coasts curve in to form gulfs and those where the Ocean surrounds and embraces the earth or where his heedless waves make incursions" (*situs, spatia, intervalla, quidquid ubique fluminum oritur et conditur, quacumque litorum sinus flectunt, qua vel ambitu cingit orbem vel impetu inrupit oceanus;* Eumenes, *Pan.*, 20.3).

Strabo's cartography has been recognized in his use of classic data (the coasts), but also Vitruvius's *chorographiae,* especially for the river sources. The *spatia et intervalla* naturally recall Agrippa's measurements rather than itineraries, which no doubt would have been mentioned. They are *descripta,* which indicate (as in Vitruvius again) that they are accompanied by written notes. The *flumina* also bring to mind the *Cosmographia* of Julius Honorius and of the Pseudo-Aethicus. The *situs* ("positions" or "sites" of certain regions) recall the maps of the Caucasian regions sent by Corbulo to Nero (Pliny, 6.40: *situsque depicti . . .*). But Eumenes, before recalling these geographic characteristics, had stated the basic points (20.2): "all the lands and all the seas, all the towns restored by their goodness, the peoples conquered by their bravery, the nations paralyzed by the terror that they inspire" (*cuncta maria et quidquid invictissimi principes urbium, gentium, nationum aut pietate restituunt, aut virtute devincunt, aut terrore defigunt*). And this theme is taken up again at length in 21: "because it [the map] indicates opposing regions, (it) permit(s) them [the young people] to review the magnificent deeds of our valiant *principes*" (*fortissimorum imperatorum res gestae per diversa regionum argumenta*).

When the "messengers of victory" would arrive, it could be possible to see on the maps where these victories took place and even to imagine allegorical scenes, where the image of Roman triumphal reliefs could easily be recognized. *Nunc enim, nunc demum iuvat orbem spectare depictum, cum in illo nihil videmus alienum:* we might recognize an echo of Pliny's formula concerning Agrippa's map: *orbem urbi spectandum.* Can a similarity between situations, through the centuries, be proof of imperial history rooted in its own *topoi?* Is it a direct echo of Pliny? Or an indirect echo of that famous map set up in the very heart of Rome?

If this was the case, as seems likely, we have the most valuable "instructions" to Agrippa's and Augustus's work. It was some sort of triumphal monument, but on a plan that is no longer symbolic, as was the Theater of Pompey with its Herculean mystique, or Augustus's *Forum* laying out the allegories of the *provinciae* (beginning with the West, like Agrippa) and the *gentes* as an *orbis* surrounding the triumphal chariot of the emperor. The map was on a totally different level, rational and human and no longer symbolical and theological. We have seen that the students of Autun could locate on the map the emperors' *res gestae.* Could not Augustus likewise have ordered Agrippa to carry out this "painted world map" in order to serve as a learned illustration to his own *Res Gestae,* which he then had to complete himself after the premature death of his son-in-law? If it is true that in 2 B.C., when he received the title of *Pater Patriae,* which Ovid glosses as "Father of the World" (*Fasti,* 2.130: *iampridem tu pater orbis eras*), he had already recorded the greatest and most triumphant of his achievements, is it not tempting to believe that Augustus had Agrippa's work (not yet finished in 7 B.C.) completed in time so that men could conveniently see on the map the names that he had listed or the statues that he had placed around the Temple of Mars during the inauguration of his *Forum* in 2 B.C.? Is it a coincidence that the first occurrence of the famous linking of *orbis* and *urbs* appears precisely in the Augustan period, in the work of a poet in Augustus's entourage, on the occasion of the great *naumachia* contemporaneous with the dedication of the Temple of Mars that served as a symbolic prelude to the Eastern campaign of C. Caesar: *atque ingens orbis in urbe fuit* (Ovid, *Ars Am.,* 1.174), a formula that strangely foreshadows that used by Pliny about Agrippa's map?

To set forth his *Res Gestae* with a description of the *situs* of his victories, the rivers, the mountains, the "barbarian" kingdoms, the victories won over the entire world, the *pax* attested to by the closing of the doors on the Temple of Janus and of Rome that under his principate made the Parthians tremble—this was also the offer that Augustus had made, directly or indirectly, to Horace[49] ca. 15 B.C. It is a subject worthy of an epic poem. But it would be fulfilled not in poetry, but by means of the *Res Gestae,* the *Forum Augustum*—and the map of Agrippa.

NOTES

1. Virgil, *Aen.,* 6.851: *tu regere imperio populos, Romane, memento;* Velleius, 2.38: *paucis percurrere quae cuiusque ductu gens ac natio redacta in formulam provinciae . . . ;* 89: *pacatusque victoriis terrarum orbis.*

2. For a bibliography, an update, and a detailed study of the prologue and of the translation of this text, see C. Nicolet and P. Gautier Dalché, "Les 'quatre sages' de Jules César et la mesure du monde selon Julius Honorius: réalité antique et tradition médiévale," *Journal des Savants,* 1987, 3–50.

3. These are found in A. Riese, *Geogr. Lat. Min.* (Heilbronn, 1878) under the name *Cosmographia Julii Caesaris,* 21–55, and *Cosmographia* (of the Pseudo-Aethicus), 71–103; in fact it involves two traditions of the same original source, as was seen by W. Kubitschek, "Die Erdtafel des Julius Honorius," *Wiener Studien* 7 (1885): 1–24, 278–310; and id., "Julius Honorius," in *RE,* X no. 1 (1919), 614–28. Concerning all these points, see from now on P. Gautier Dalché, *op. cit.,* n. 2 above.

4. Vitruvius, 8.2.6: *capita fluminum, quae orbe terrarum chorographiis picta itemque scripta plurima maximaque inveniuntur. . . .*

5. *Iulio Caesare et Marco Antoni<n>o consulibus omnis orbis peragratus est per sapientissimos et electos viros quattuor: Nicodemo orientis, Didymo occidentalis, Theodoto septemtrionalis, Polyclito meridiani.*

A consulibus supra scriptis usque in consulatum Augusti IIII et Crassi annis XXI mensibus quinque diebus novem oriens dimensa est. Et a consulibus supra scriptis usque in consulatum Augusti VII et Agrippae III annis XXVI mensibus III diebus XVII occidui pars dimensa est. A consulibus supra scriptis usque in consulatum Augusti X annis XXVIII mensibus VIII septemtrionalis pars, dimensa est. A consulibus supra scriptis usque in consulatum Saturnini et Cinnae annis XXXII mense I diebus XX meridiana pars dimensa est.

6. This problem of chronology has intrigued all the editors since K. A. Pertz, *De cosmographia Aethici . . .* (Berlin, 1853); see Kubitschek's figures, in *RE,* X no. 1 (1919), 626; and A. Riese's explanations in *GLM,* XXIII. I summarize here the conclusions of my contribution, cited above, n. 2.

7. For very different conclusions (he believes in the authenticity of a project of measurement that can be attributed to Caesar and that would have implied the realization of a map in the *Saepta Julia*), see T. P. Wiseman, "Julius Caesar and the Hereford Map," *History Today,* 1987, 53–57, a copy of which the author provided me.

8. See the recent synthesis by J.-M. Roddaz, *Marcus Agrippa* (Rome, 1984), esp. 291–93 and 572–87; but one should also refer to W. Kubitschek, "Karten," *RE,* X no. 2 (1919), 2100–2112; Schanz-Hosius, *Geschichte Röm. Literatur*[4] (1935) 2:329–35; R. Hanslik, "M. Vipsanius Agrippa," in *RE,* IX A no. 1 (1961), 1226–75, esp. 1269–72; O. A. W. Dilke, *Greek and Roman Maps* (London, 1985), 41–53.

9. Any research regarding Agrippa's map is useless if one refuses to admit an equation, or at least a strong link among three things: (1) the geographical texts effectively preserved in Agrippa's name, or those that we can, according to the rules of philology, attribute to him with the greatest probability; (2) the *Commentarii* he left behind at his death (according to Pliny, 3.17) and (3) the map itself (*orbis Urbi spectandus*), which Pliny also mentions, and which was completed with Augustus's guidance. If this evidence is not taken as a whole, denying any link between the texts and the drawing, excessive hypercriticism cuts short all discussion: one sentence would then suffice to say that the *Commentarii,* and the map for which they led the way, are forever unrecognizable.

On the contrary, it is necessary to bear in mind (1) that the fragments preserved by Pliny (or by the *Divisio* and the *Dimensuratio*), if they contain some slightly developed phrases or expressions, essentially give *frontiers* and measurements—which would be too restrictive for a written geographic work, as dry and succinct it be (for a contrasting view, see Varro, Pliny, and Mela); (2) that no geographical work by Agrippa is attested (Schanz-Hosius, *Geschichte Röm. Literatur,* 334); the attempts by certain modern scholars to confuse the "statistical" sources of the Augustan period concerning the series of towns or of other information of this type with Agrippa's writings are not convincing; see below, chap. 8, p. 171. For an update and an exposé of the various theories, see K. G. Sallmann, *Die Geographie des älteren Plinius,* (Berlin, 1971), 91–107; contra J. Desanges, *Pline l'Ancien,* Book 5 (Paris, 1980), 20–27. I am unable, due to considerations of length, to provide a translation of all the fragments, although even with those from the *Dimensuratio* and the *Divisio* it would run to perhaps a dozen pages only. Concerning the whole of this question, see below, n. 27.

10. Pliny, *NH,* 3.86 writes about Sicily: *circuitu patens, ut auctor est Agrippa;* in any case, Agrippa is mentioned four times among the *auctores* in the *index* of Book 1: for Books 3, 4, 5, and 6 (and twice differentiated, for Books 3 and 4, from *Divus Augustus*): all the names are certainly those of authors, in the literary sense of the word (Sallmann, *Die Geographie des älteren Plinius,* 185). Nothing in Pliny's vocabulary, especially the verbs, suggests anything more than a literary source, or at least a written one: he uses the same words when he refers to Polybius and to Varro. When in Book 6.207 he states: *Agrippa . . . in quo haud scio an sit error numeri,* he refers explicitly to the written form of numbers. But Agrippa's text, whichever it might be, did not only include the names of areas and the figures of measurement but also, in certain places, more substantial statements. Therefore Book 3.8: *oram eam in universum originis Poenorum existimavit M. Agrippa;* 4.37: *Agrippa Caspium mare gentesque quae circa sunt . . . patere qua cognitum est* etc.; 6.39: *oram omnem a Caso praealtis rupibus accessum negare . . . auctor est Agrippa.* Thus, traces of a more elaborate exposé can be seen which had been published as a work (entitled *Commentarii*?), of which, unfortunately, Pliny had wanted to retain only the numbers. However, it is equally possible that this type of text (names, measurements, some descriptive or anecdotal sentences) had appeared on the map itself. This is a habit already attested by the Peutinger Table (although it is made up essentially of itineraries), where are found formulas such as *Nilus qui dividit Asiam et Libiam* or *hi montes subiacent paludi simili marotidi quem Nilus transit* or *hic cenocephali nascuntur;* Vitruvius (8.2.6) mentions *capita fluminum . . . picta itemque scripta;* a habit which is highly widespread on medieval maps: e.g., the Mabada Map (K. Miller, *Mappae Mundi, die ältesten Weltkarten* (Stuttgart, 1895), 6:152ff.). Regarding medieval maps, see, for example, the text of the Hereford Map, Miller, *Mappae Mundi,* 4:6–46, a text where measurements (*Longitudo Europe ab ostio Meotis . . . ,* etc.) and commentaries (13: *Roma caput mundi tenet orbis frena rotondi,* etc.) and many other examples are found, as with Agrippa. Regarding all these questions, see the useful summary by A. Klotz, *Quaestiones Plinianae geographicae, QFGG* (Berlin, 1906), 11: 13–15.

11. The bibliography is extensive, often confused with the one that deals with the *commentarii;* the main works are still F. Ritschl, "Die Vermessung des röm. Reichs unter Augustus, die Weltkarte des Agrippa," *Rh. Mus.,* (1842), 483–522 (= *Opusc.,* III, 743); F. Philipp, *Zur Rekonstrucktion d. Weltk. des Agrippa* (Marburg, 1880); E. Schweder, "Uber die Weltkarte und Chorographie des Kaisers Augustus," *Neue Jahrb. Phil. Päd.* 145 (1892): 113–32; "Uber die Weltkarte und Chorographie des Kaisers Augustus, I, Uber die römische Weltkarte," *Philol.,* 1895, 319–44; II

(cont.), *Phil.*, 1896, 528–59; III (cont.), *Phil.*, 1897, 129–62; K. Müllenhoff, *Deutsch Altertumk.* (Berlin, 1892), 3:212–95; id., "Ueber die röm. Weltkarte," *Hermes* 9 (1875): 182–95; D. Detlefsen, "Ursprung, Einrichtung und Bedeutung der Erdkarte Agrippas," *QFGG* (1906) 13:1–117; C. Pallu de Lessert, "L'oeuvre géographique d'Agrippa et d'Auguste," *Mém. Soc. Ant. Fr.*, 1909, 215–98 (a very useful update); A. Berthelot, "Les données numériques fondamentales de la géographie antique d'Eratosthène à Ptolémée," *Rev. Arch.*, 1932, 1–34; id., "L'Europe occidentale d'après Agrippa et Strabon," *Rev. Arch.*, 1933, 9–12; P. Schnabel, "Die Weltkarte des Agrippa als wissenschaftliches Mittelglied zwischen Hipparch und Ptolemaeus," *Philologus*, 1935, 405–40; J.-J. Tierney, "The Map of Agrippa," *Proc. Irish Roy. Acad.*, 1963, 151–66; concerning Agrippa's medieval influence, see K. Miller, *Mappae Mundi,* and R. Uhden, "Zur Ueberlieferung der Weltkarte des Agrippa," *Klio,* 1933, 267–78.

12. Pliny, *NH,* 3.17: *Baeticae longitudo nunc a Castulonis oppidi fine Gadis* $\overline{\mathit{CCL}}$ *et a Murgi maritima ora* $\overline{\mathit{XXV}}$ *p. amplior, latitudo a Carteia Anam ora* $\overline{\mathit{CCXXXIIII}}$ *p. Agrippam quidem in tanta viri diligentia praeterque in hoc opere cura, cum orbem terrarum urbi spectandum propositurus esset, errasse quis credat et cum eo divum Augustum? is namque conplexam eum porticum ex destinatione et commentariis M. Agrippae a sorore eius inchoatam peregit.* The reading *urbi* is adopted by Detlefsen in his edition of Pliny's geographical works, in *QFGG* (Berlin, 1904), 9:10; C. E. Gleye, "Die Weltkarte des Agrippa," *Philol.*, 1909, 318, proposed to emend *ex destinatione* to *ex delineatione;* certainly *delineare* can be said for the drawings of painters; but *ex destinatione* can easily be said of a will: see *Dig.* 50.17.76, 25.7.4, 31.77.10.

13. Pliny, 35.25: *exstat certe eius (sc. M. Agrippae) oratio magnifica, et maximo civium digna de tabulis omnibus signisque publicandis.* Note the vocabulary used in the passage: *cum orbem terrarum urbi spectandum propositurus esset.* It is not "he had proposed to . . . ," but "he would exhibit (*propositurus*) so that it could be seen"; see Pliny, 35.23: (*L. Hostilius Mancinus*) *situm eius oppugnationesque depictas proponendo in foro et ipse . . . enarrando;* 35.22: *proposuit* meaning "exhibited."

14. Pliny, *NH,* 6.139: *flumina id oppidum expugnavere. postea restituit Antiochus quintus regum et suo nomine appellavit, iterum quoque infestatum Spaosines Sagdodonaci filius, rex finitimorum Arabum, quem Iuba satrapen Antiochi fuisse falso tradit, oppositis molibus restituit nomenque suum dedit emunito situ iuxta in longintudinem* $\overline{\mathit{VI}}$ *p., in latitudinem paulo minus. prius a(f)uit a litore stadios* $\overline{\mathit{X}}$ *et maritimum etiam Vipsan(i)a porticus habet, Iuba vero prodente* $\overline{\mathit{L}}$ *p. nunc abesse a litore* $\overline{\mathit{CXX}}$ *legati Arabum nostrique negotiatores qui inde venere adfirmant. nec ulla in parte plus aut celerius profecere terrae fluminibus invectae. magis id mirum est, aestu longe ultra id accedente non repercussas.* (*Vipsania porticus:* Detlefsen and Mayhoff, following Urlichs (1853); *uipsanda* [inps. E^5]: DR; *portum: p,* ms. from Munich, copied in 1459).

15. S. B. Platner and T. Ashby, *A Topographical Dictionary of Ancient Rome* (London, 1929), 430; F. Coarelli, *Guida di Roma* (Bari, 1981), 241 and 263;

through Martial (4.18. 1–2) we know that it was bordered by the *aqua Virgo;* it was located during chance excavations, east of the *Via Lata,* during works in the Galleria Sciarra (*NS,* 1915, 35; 1917, 9–20; *Bull. Com.*, 1914, 209; 1915, 218; 1917, 220); it consisted of gardens (Martial 1.108.1); troops camped there in A.D. 69 (Plutarch, *Galba,* 25; Tacitus, *Hist.*, 1.31). See however E. Rodriguez-Almeida, *"Forma urbis marmorea,"* in *MEFRA,* 1977, 219–56.

16. Pliny is aware of a great number of Roman monuments and mentions them. But his methodology, according to his nephew's famous testimony, is that of an encyclopedia.

17. Dio, 54.29.4: "at any rate, even at his death he left them gardens and the baths named after him"; 55.8.4 (in 7 B.C.): "The *Campus Agrippae,* except the porticus and the *Diribitorium,* were made public property by Augustus himself"; (5) "The portico in the *Campus,* however, which was being built by Polla, Agrippa's sister, who also adorned the race-courses (given for Augustus's return that same year) was not yet finished" (no more so than the *Diribitorium,* as Dio mentions it above).

18. Dilke, *Greek and Roman Maps,* 31; Diogenes Laertius, 5.2 (*Life of Theophrastus:* the author quotes his will): ἀναθεῖναι δὲ καὶ τούς πίνακας, ἐν οἷς αἱ τῆς γῆς περίοδοι εἰσιν, εἰς τὴν κάτω στοάν. ("Place the panels, on which are found the maps of the world, in the lower *porticus*.") Πίναξ designates, like *tabula,* the wooden frame of a painting or a map; Strabo uses this word when he mentions the projections on a flat surface (2.5.10) "he should sketch his map on a plane surface of at least seven feet"; cf. the use of πίναξ for "map" together with the text of Dionysius "Periegetes," in Cassiodorus, *Inst.*, 25: *penacem*. The Greek words used by Diogenes Laertius, αἱ τῆς γῆς περίοδοι, can certainly indicate a written text; but one should not think, as many have done, that they indicate astronomical charts: περίοδοι can mean "orbit"; but it would be the orbit of the stars and not of the earth; see F. Prontera, "La geografia come genere letterario," *Strabone* (Perugia, 1984), 1:243.

19. Dilke, *Greek and Roman Maps,* 148; the representations of battle scenes, the capture of towns, whether during triumphs or not, are attested prior to this date: Pliny, *NH,* 35.22 (M. Valerius Messalla for the siege of Messina); regarding the *forma* of Sardinia, one can hesitate between a map and an allegory: *forma* can mean both (*TLL,* col. 1082); but the technical uses for "principal schema" or "map" are more prevalent. It has been shown in Pliny, 12.19, that *forma Aethiopiae* describes a map.

20. Here again the existence of a map was considered doubtful and an allegorical image was considered in its stead. But why would the interlocutors, ready to speak of agriculture, contemplate (*spectantes*) this image? On the other hand, there is nothing in Book 1 of Varro to indicate any reference to this map and he certainly had *seen* some geographical representations of Italy. He is quoted by Pliny (*NH,* 3.45) for distances, right after the general exposé (43) of the mapped silhouette of Italy, in the shape of an oak leaf.

21. See below, chap. 7, p. 158.

22. On the expression *orbis depictus* (Suetonius, *Dom.*, 10), see above chap. 4, p. 86, and P. Arnaud, "L'Affaire Mettius Pompusianius . . . ," *MEFRA*, 1983, 677ff.

23. Fundamental difference: Strabo 1.1.16 (the "chorographers" were interested in specific regions, India, Aethiopia, etc.); especially 2.5.17, where *γεωγράφειν* and the *χωρογραφικὸς πίναξ* are set in opposition, which mentions, in contrast to *γεωγραφικὸς πίναξ* (2.5.13) the details: peoples, sites of towns, the numerous coastal islands, etc. But, naturally, *χωρογραφία* can also mean a *written work* of regional geography (2.5.1); see G. Aujac, *Strabon* (Paris, 1969), 2154–58. Ptolemy 1.1 clearly makes this distinction (Aujac, *Strabon*, 2:180–81): "Geography is the imitative and representative description of the whole known part of the world, with everything which generally belongs to it. It differs from chorography in that the latter, considering the areas separate from one another, shows each of them with an indication of their harbors, their villages, and the smallest habitations, the derivations and detours of all the rivers, of the peoples and similar details. The actual aim of geography is solely to show the world in all its expanse, how it functions as much by its nature as by its position. It is concerned only with general descriptions, like those of gulfs, large towns, nations, great rivers, and everything which deserves to be shown as such. Chorography is concerned with the description of a part of the whole, as one would show an ear or an eye. But geography embraces the totality of things as the image of a head depicts it in its entirety" (Ptolemy, *Geography*, 1.1). See also Eustathius, *Ad Dion. Per.*, 1.212–20 (= Müller, *Ptolem.*, 2).

24. See below pp. 171 and 184. In the language of ancient specialists of military cartography, *chorographia* describes engraved maps; see *CIL* 8, suppl. pt. 1, 12914 and especially *AE*, 1947, 61 (with my forthcoming comment); *IGR* 1.1365.

25. Concerning the word (of extremely diverse usage), but principally for its literary meaning, see F. Bömer, "Der *Commentarius*," *Hermes*, 1953, 210–50, who also examines the word *ὑπομνήματα*. He does not specifically deal with the use of the word in geography or cartography. It is used essentially of "written memo-dossiers": the uses mentioned by Vitruvius are, in this regard, clear as are those of the *agrimensores*. Another interesting point is that Ptolemy (1.18.2) uses *ὑπομνήματα* to name the long series of coordinates of remarkable points (with a few descriptive sentences inserted) that form the crux of his geographical work, but are conceived so that a map could be drawn from them. One might assume that the same link could exist between Agrippa's *commentarii* and his map.

26. Detlefsen (quoted above, n. 11); however see J. Partsch's criticisms, *Wochenschrift für kl. Philol.* 1907, 1054–62; and A. Klotz, *Quaest. Plin.*, 13; for the reconstitutions of the map, Sallmann, *Die Geogr. des ält. Plinius*, 209; and recently R. Moynihan, "Geographical Mythology and Rom. Imp. Ideology," in *The Age of Augustus*, ed. R. Wilkes (Providence/Louvain, 1985), 149–62.

27. The *Divisio orbis terrarum* was edited for the first time, following the manuscript *Vat. Pal.* 1357, by E. Schweder, *Beiträge zur Kritik der Chorogr. des Augustus* (Kiel, 1878) (at the same time as Dicuil), 1:3–16; reedited by A. Riese, *GLM* (Heil-

bronn, 1878), 15–20; and by P. Schnabel, "Die Weltkarte des Agrippa," *Philol.*, 1935, 432–39; like Pliny's text, it begins with the West (Spain), then the North, the East, the South (Africa) (for a good schema, see Sallman, *Die Geogr. des ält. Plinius*, 104). The *Dimensuratio provinciarum,* known from the same manuscript, had already been edited by Schelstrate, *Antik. Eccles. II,* 525; and by A. Mai, *Class. Auct.* (1831) 3:410; Schweder also gives it, op. cit., 15–125; Riese, *GLM,* 9–14; Schnabel, op. cit. 425–31. It begins with the East. The similarity with Agrippa's fragments in Pliny is striking. A. Klotz, wanting to edit Agrippa, had included in his edition the corresponding fragments of these two texts ("Die geographische *Commentarii* des Agrippa und ihre Ueberreste," *Klio,* 1931, 38–58, 386–466), from now on the authoritative edition. Detlefsen used the argument of the difference in order to claim that Agrippa's *commentarii* were inscribed on the map (they could therefore be reproduced in any order) and had not been circulated in written form.

28. Kubitschek, "Karten," *RE,* X no. 2 (1919) 2103; this absurd case has often been discussed. Detlefsen and Partsch believed that it arose from an error in the maritime distances of the Mediterranean, which placed the gulf of Issos more to the east than the eastern mouth of the Nile and which led to a line W/SW-N/NE for the coast and thus to the notion that between Cilicia and Arabia there was a *longitudo.* Contra, Klotz, "Die geographische *Commentarii,*" 429–30.

29. See for example A. Berthelot, *Rev. Arch.*, 1932, 23; and more recently, the majority of scholars who dealt with the Peutinger Table: A. and M. Levi, *Itineraria picta* (Rome, 1967), 24; L. Bosio, *La Tabula Peutingeriana* (Bologna, 1983), 156–59; E. Weber, *Tab. Peut. codex Vindobon. 324* (Graz, 1976), 21–23.

30. On this point, see the useful remarks by A. and M. Levi, "Map Projection and the Peutinger Table," in *Coins, Culture and History in the Ancient World,* ed. L. Casson (*Studies Bluma Trell*) (Detroit, 1981), 139–47; in fact the juxtaposed itineraries involve some variable projections and some flexible orientations.

31. K. Miller, *Mappae mundi,* 6:108ff; 145 (with an erroneous interpretation of the word *orbis*).

32. It is not my intention to discuss them here: yet any study concerning ancient cartography must deal with them; a large number are reproduced in the album of M. de Santarem, *Atlas composé de Mappemondes* (Paris, 1849); but especially M. Destombes, *Mappemondes* A.D. *1200–1500* (Amsterdam, 1964). See also G. Kish, *La carte* (Paris, 1980), 18 and pls. 27–46; Numa Broc, "Hiérarchies," in *Cartes et figures de la Terre* (Paris, 1980), 76–77; I. Kupčik, *Cartes géographiques anciennes* (Paris, 1981), 25 (pl. I,. p. 17).

33. It has been shown above (p. 59) that the round map is of Ionian origin: they were the "old maps" of which Agathemerus speaks. Since Eratothenes at least, it was known that the *oikoumene* could not be included in its entirety. Geminus sums it up, *Intr. to Astr.*, 16.1.4–5: *Διαιρεῖται δὲ ἡ καθ' ἡμᾶς οἰκουμένη εἰς μέρη τρία* 'Ασίαν, Εὐρώπην, Λιβύην.

Διπλάσιον δέ ἐστιν ὡς ἔγγιστα τὸ μῆκος τῆς οἰκουμένης τοῦ πλάτους. Δι' ἣν αἰτίαν οἱ κατὰ λόγον γράφοντες τὰς γεωγραφίας ἐν πίναξι γράφουσι παραμήκεσιν, ὡς διπλάσιον εἶναι τὸ μῆκος τοῦ πλάτους. Οἱ δέ στρογγύλας γράφοντες τὰς γεωγραφίας πολὺ τῆς ἀληθείας εἰσὶ πεπλανημένοι. ἴσον γὰρ γίνεται τὸ μῆκος τῷ πλάτει, ὅπερ οὐκ ἔστιν ἐν τῇ φύσει. ἀνάγκη οὖν μὴ τηρεῖσθαι τὰς τῶν διαστημάτων συμμετρίας τὰς ἐν ταῖς στρογγύλαις γεωγραφίαις. ἔκτμημά τι γάρ ἐστι σφαίρας τὸ οἰκούμενον μέρος τῆς γῆς διπλάσιον ἔχον τὸ μῆκος τοῦ πλάτους, ὅπερ οὐ δύναται ἀποτερματίζεσθαι κύκλῳ. "The length of the inhabited world is almost double its width. This is why one uses a panel (*πίναξ*) that is longer than it is wide, with a length double its width to draw maps on a scale. Those who draw round maps (*οἱ δὲ στρογγύλας γράφοντες*) are further from the truth, for the length is equal to the width. . . . One should be wary, in round maps, of taking into account the ratio of distances, for the inhabited part of the world cannot be restricted by a circle." Geminus (Pompeius Geminus) is almost certainly the scholar (the addressee of the *Letter* by Dionysius of Halicarnassus) who lived at Rome ca. 50 B.C.; the passage, contrary to the opinion of certain scholars, is not interpolated (the word *ἀποτερματίζεσθαι* is not as late as stated): whence the interest in it.

34. This is one of the reasons, according to R. Dion (in *Mél. Carcopino* [Paris, 1966], 262–63), for Augustus's optimism when launching his fleet to the East from the mouth of the Rhine. Pliny's passage (6.37) is problematic. As was seen by the editors (Detlefsen, p. 35), the numbers give the reduced dimensions, above, of the sea itself "there where it is known." But Pliny mentioned in his sentence neighboring peoples "up to the Northern Ocean and the *Sericus* Ocean," for whom he does not give a number; this is awkward. But it is clear that, for him as for everyone, the North Sea is not very far in latitude.

35. *Διοίσει γὰρ μικρόν ἐὰν ἀντὶ τῶν κύκλων, τῶν τε παραλλήλων καὶ τῶν μεσημβρινῶν οἷς τά τε κλίματα καὶ τοὺς ἀνέμους διασαφοῦμεν καὶ τὰς ἄλλας διαφορὰς καὶ τὰς σχέσεις τῶν τῆς γῆς μερῶν πρὸς ἄλληλά τε καὶ τὰ οὐράνια, εὐθείας γράφωμεν, τῶν μὲν παραλλήλων παραλλήλους, τῶν δὲ ὀρθῶν πρὸς ἐκείνους ὀρθάς, τῆς διανοίας ῥᾳδίως μεταφέρειν δυναμένης τὸ ὑπὸ τῆς ὄψεως ἐν ἐπιπέδῳ θεωρούμενον ἐπιφανείᾳ σχῆμα καὶ μέγεθος ἐπὶ τὴν περιφερῆ τε καὶ σφαιρικήν. Ἀνάλογον δὲ καὶ περὶ τῶν λοξῶν κύκλων καὶ εὐθειῶν φαμεν. Εἰ δ' οἱ μεσημβρινοὶ οἱ παρ' ἑκάστοις ⟨διὰ⟩ τοῦ πόλου γραφόμενοι πάντες συννεύουσιν ἐν τῇ σφαίρᾳ πρὸς ἓν σημεῖον, ἀλλ' ἐν τῷ ἐπιπέδῳ γε οὐ διοίσει πίνακι τὰς εὐθείας μικρὸν συννευούσας ποιεῖν μόνον τὰς μεσημβρινάς· οὐδε γὰρ πολλαχοῦ τοῦτ' ἀναγκαῖον, οὐδ' ἐκφανής ἐστιν ὥσπερ ἡ περιφέρεια οὕτω καὶ ἡ σύννευσις, μεταφερομένων τῶν γραμμῶν εἰς τὸν πίνακα τὸν ἐπίπεδον καὶ γραφομένων εὐθειῶν. Καὶ δὴ καὶ τὸν ἑξῆς λόγον ὡς ἐν ἐπιπέδῳ πίνακι τῆς γραφῆς γινομένης ἐκθήσομεν.*

36. See above, chap. 1, p. 16; Pliny, *NH*, 36.72.

37. P. Schnabel, "Die Weltkarte," *Philol.*, 1935, 412ff., 420, etc.; contra, P. Tierney, op. cit., in *Proc. Ir. Roy. Ac.*, 1963, 155ff.

38. Dio, 55.8.6; Boatwright in *Historia*, 1986, 13–27.

39. On this point, see C. Nicolet and P. Gauthier Dalché, "Les quatre sages de Jules César," *Journ. Sav.*, 1987:3–50.

40. At the exclusion of Augustus's alleged "chorography," this word can only

allude to the nature of Agrippa's work (completed by Augustus). But it is true that *chorographia,* from the time of Pomponius Mela, can describe a general geographical work, not necessarily very detailed (although Mela gives 1,700 names).

41. Strabo, 5.2.7; 6.2.1 (ἐν δέ τῇ χωρογραφίᾳ); 6.2.11; 6.1.11; 6.3.10.

42. Gathered by Riese, *GLM,* 8.

43. Similarly (as seen above, p. 86), Agrippa, who was aware of the results of the expedition by Cornelius Balbus among the Garamantes in 19 B.C., took these into account for the dimensions of Cyrenaica (Pliny, *NH* 5.38: *qua cognitum est;* 6.299: *qua noscebatur).*

44. Strabo, 4.6.11, 207 C.

45. Regarding the sundials, see above p. 68; concerning Theodosius, see C. Nicolet, n. 39.

46. 36.101.

47. W. Kubitschek, "Karten," *RE,* X no. 2 (1919), 2122 (school maps). See Ausonius, *Grat. Act.,* 2.9.

48. Eumenius, *Pan.,* 5.20–21: *Videat praeterea in illis porticibus iuventus et cotidie spectet omnes terras et cuncta maria et quidquid invictissimi principes urbium, gentium, nationum aut pietate restituunt aut virtute devincunt aut terrore defigunt. Siquidem illic, ut ipse vidisti, credo instruendae pueritiae causa, quo manifestius oculis discerentur quae difficilius percipiuntur auditu, omnium cum nominibus suis locorum situs, spatia, intervalla descripta sunt, quidquid ubique fluminum oritur et conditur, quacumque se litorum sinus flectunt, qua vel ambitu cingit orbem vel impetu inrumpit oceanus.*

Ibi fortissimorum imperatorum pulcherrimae res gestae per diversa regionum argumenta recolantur, dum calentibus semperque venientibus victoriarum nuntiis revisuntur gemina Persidos flumina et Libyae arva sitientia et convexa Rheni cornua et Nili ora multifida dumque sibi ad haec singula intuentium animus adfingit aut sub tua, Diocletiane Auguste, clementia Aegyptum furore posito quiescentem aut te, Maximiane invicte, perculsa Maurorum agmina fulminantem aut sub dextera tua, domine Constanti, Bataviam Britanniamque squalidum caput silvis et fluctibus exerentem aut te, Maximiane Caesar, Persicos arcus pharetrasque calcantem. Nunc enim, nunc demum iuvat orbem spectare depictum, cum in illo nihil videmus alienum.

49. Horace, *Ep.,* 2.1.250 (a letter to Augustus): *Nec sermones ego mallem / repentis per humu quam res componere gestas / terrarumque situs et flumina dicere et arces / montibus impositas et barbara regna tuisque / auspiciis totum confecta duella per orbem . . .*" (And for myself, I should not prefer my "chats," that crawl along the ground, to the story of great exploits, the tale of distant lands and rivers, of forts on mountain tops, of barbaric realms, of the ending of wars under your auspices throughout the world . . .).

VI

Control of the Human Sphere: The Census

It is not enough to have conquered the world, or even to declare its conquest. The inhabitants of the *urbs,* flattered by this idea since the triumphs of Pompey in 61 B.C. and Caesar in 46 B.C., were no doubt content with the proof provided by the arrogant litany of geographic names in the *Res Gestae,* by the symbolic layout of Augustus's Forum, or by the map of the *oikoumene* in Agrippa's *Porticus.* But those in power had to face a less flattering reality. It was not sufficient to know the approximate extent and limits within the *oikoumene* of the world that they had to govern—they had actually to take possession of it. By the end of the Republic and especially by the beginning of the empire, the Romans were becoming more conscious of the strict limitations of their imperial domination and, in some ways, of its fragile nature: on several occasions they had perceived that it might exceed the capacity of their strength and resources.[1] They knew very well[2]—Cicero, for example, often reminds them[3]—that it could only endure if it was actually accepted, that is to say, if their government represented a clear advantage for its subjects.

The first benefit was internal peace, which, since 36 B.C. (Appian, *BC,* 5.54),[4] was the very basis of Octavian's politics, program, and ideology, and which would be the first and last good deed for which he would be lauded by the Alexandrian fleet's sailors in August A.D. 14 on the eve of his death (Suetonius, *Aug.* 98.2).[5] But also there was prosperity, along with good administration and the attempt at sparing—as much as possible—the lives and possessions of the subject peoples.[6] In short, it meant that resources had to be adjusted to the government's expenditure in the most exact and bearable way possible. This is the meaning given to Augustus's actions in the funerary eulogy that Dio attributes to his successor, and whose authenticity we have no reason to doubt. Not only does Dio take it up again in his own name, but these themes coincide exactly with those found in Velleius concerning Augustus (2.89.3–4) and Tiberius (2.103.5). Such was the goal, but also the condition, for the maintenance of the empire.

To achieve this, it was not enough to be complacent about old victories.

It was necessary to act and govern. And for this it was necessary to have clear and precise ideas of the empire's resources, and of the expenses required for its maintenance. Before any action could be taken, there was the problem of information available to the government. This was not a new problem; the Late Republic had had the same difficulties. Cicero often insisted upon the need for comprehensive information and for a real "science" of government.[7] The orator's most remarkable text is *De leg.*, 3.41:

> I have also added the injunction: "He shall be conversant with public affairs." It is obviously necessary for a senator to be familiar with the condition of the republic. And this rule has a wide application; he must know the number of troops available, the condition of the treasury, who our allies, friends and tributaries are, and what laws, agreements, and treaties apply to each. He must also understand the customary procedure in the passage of a decree, and know the precedents which our ancestors have handed down to us. Thus you can form a conception of the wide knowledge, the great industry, and the excellent memory which are absolutely indispensable for a senator who is prepared for the performance of his duties.[8]

Unfortunately Cicero does not mention where his ideal statesman should get his information and his science. Apparently everything is considered from an individual point of view: the individual should train and inform himself as best he can. In fact, we know very well that in this oligarchic republic, many things were of the private and familial sphere: the statesmen often counted on their network of clients, on their personal links with a particular province, and on the information (learned or otherwise) that their literary or social circles could provide. Their success or supremacy rested upon this.[9]

Yet there were also public sources of information. The Republic did not manage its day-to-day affairs—as some have suggested—without archives or administration.[10] There were public archives (*tabulae publicae*) for every type of affairs that were the responsibility of competent magistrates.[11] Many among these—such as financial accounts and affairs, but also texts of decisions, laws, and *senatus consulta*—were, in theory, kept in the Treasury of Saturn, in the quaestors' care. But before the construction (or reconstruction?) of the *Tabularium* in 78 B.C., other document-depots existed, including the ταμιεῖον ἀγορανόμων on the Capitoline, the *Atrium Libertatis,* and various temples.[12] In this way, the archives were indeed scattered throughout Rome.

Furthermore, their upkeep at the end of the Republic was in a state of abandonment and neglect, concerning which there is much proof, and which was deplored by the more conscientious statesmen. As quaestor in 65 B.C., Cato the Younger undertook a spectacular reordering of the Treasury's accounts, which had been allowed to be plundered with the complicity of scribes and of certain important persons. In spite of this, in order to continue his surveillance after leaving office, Cato had to buy (for the enormous sum of five talents) the registers from Sulla's time, which proves that they had previously been sold or robbed.[13]

But negligence was not the only problem. Entire sections of the administration—especially in the financial sector—escaped state control (at least directly): that is, the accounts of tax-collecting societies. Even if a copy of a five-year contract were deposited in the censors' archives, the annual and monthly breakdown (which alone was probable) of the accounts of taxes was found only in the local accounts of provincial *promagistri,* and eventually, as copies in the hands of the *magistri* and ex-*magistri* of the societies.[14] Cicero's difficulties in acquiring documents for his case against Verres in 70 B.C. show that this was a great weakness in the system (2 *Verr.,* 2.169–82; 187).

We have seen that Augustus, throughout his reign, sought to make knowledge and representation of the imperial sphere more precise, which ultimately implied the creation of a geography, a chorography, and even a cartography that were coherent and progressively improving. But there is not only the physical sphere to be considered: there is also the human sphere in administrative and economic terms, whose control depends on the mastery of statistical information concerning it. That is to say, the preparation and the consultation of *documents*, at all levels of power, is necessary in order to know and to command, in order to be correctly informed and to keep one's subordinates well informed. Therefore, an administrative history of the empire at the crucial moment of its foundation must proceed first, it seems clear, with an inquiry about its concrete and logistical functioning.

First of all, we need to set forth a history of the documents on which the administration was based, how they circulated between the center and the periphery, as well as their final concentration in the hands of one man—and then their eventual publication or diffusion. But it is not my aim in this chapter to deal with this question in its entirety. I will only consider the documentary sources that are essential for the control of men and their resources, that is, the various censuses of people and goods, and the global evaluations they made possible. They are the precise mark of the change that the foundation of the empire represents.[15] I will deal successively with the census which, strictly speaking, concerns people; and, regarding goods, the famous question of "cadastres" (to use a modern term not entirely pertinent). The two institutions can only be separated for the convenience of this exposé. In most cases, the two were inextricably intertwined. A census was never taken at Rome without including possessions, and the possessions (landed or otherwise) came under so many different statutes (from the fiscal point of view) that their owners almost always had to be taken into account.

The complex operations to the census were the keystone of the Roman civic system.[16] It made possible both the knowledge of the city's resources—in terms of available men and goods—and the ranking of citizens according to various criteria (the most important of which was patrimony), so as to divide up the responsibilities and the advantages of state policy (especially war). This solemn operation that, in the literal sense, *organizes* the city and gives it life, also punctuates its history with majestic continuity, for least as long as its dimensions remain true to its nature, and makes it possible to master these operations easily. From the fifth to the second century B.C., the main characteristics of the census operations were its meticulousness, its solemnity, and its physical repressiveness. The citizens (at least those who were *sui iuris*) were required to present themselves before the censors and their employees to declare under oath, their age, family, and all of their goods.

The lengthy operations took place at Rome in the *Campus Martius* in an enclosed space, where the citizens were summoned by tribes, thus in successive groups. Until the second century B.C., physical presence was obligatory except in rare, legally defined cases.[17] Originally, absence was punishable by loss of civil rights, loss of liberty, and the sale of one's belongings (Cicero, *Pro Caec.*, 99). Thus during the Republic, the Roman state was always able to update the general size of its population and the extent of its resources.

The number of *capita civium* exceeded 300,000, which yielded in 169–168 B.C. a total civic population three to four times greater (Livy, *Per.*, 45); by 115–114 B.C. this figure bordered on 400,000 (Livy, *Per.*, 60). This definitely represented a highly imposing documentation (running to thousands of register "pages"), because the information given by everyone for his children, his slaves, and his possessions was relatively detailed. But the concentration of this information at Rome, in prescribed locations, suggested that the people were exceedingly mobile (attested again for 70 B.C.; Cic., 1 *Verr.*, 54)[18] No doubt, in the third and second centuries B.C., the operations were probably carried out locally in those cities of the Roman state that had a truly municipal organization: in the Latin colonies (certainly), in the Roman colonies (probably, if one interprets correctly Velleius, 2.7.7–8), and perhaps, in the true *municipia*.[19] But the inhabitants of Rome, of the nearby *ager Romanus* and of all the villages without civic organization (*pagi, vici, praefecturae, conciliabula,* and *fora*), had to travel (Livy, 43.14.10). It was people rather than documents who circulated.

This system was burdensome and rather archaic, and would fall apart by the second century B.C. This was a result, first of all, of the fact that the needs to which the census responded were felt less from the moment when the Treasury's resources, inflated by conquests, allowed the State to avoid direct taxation of citizens. Voluntary recruitment also made it less necessary to update lists of those available for military service.[20] But, especially, when every free inhabitant of Italy received the citizenship after the Social War, the number of citizens (having nearly tripled) made traditional operations very difficult, if not impossible. These simple reasons—without mentioning civil wars or political unrest—would suffice to explain the collapse and virtual disappearance of the census between 89 and 49 B.C., with the possible exception of 70 B.C. (*pace* Brunt, *Italian Manpower,* 104–5).

Be that as it may, it is not by chance that considerable changes were introduced in the manner of taking the census and in its results precisely during the last years of the Republic and during the reign of Augustus. The first change is indicated by an epigraphic document of the greatest importance, the *Tabula Heracleensis*. The date of this inscription is all the more controversial as the document contains legislative regulations (all of Roman origin and some, as will be shown, concerning Rome in particular) which, whatever the date of their collection into a single *corpus,* could easily be borrowed from earlier documents.[21] But, in any case, the text we possess (and which must have concerned a municipal city like Heraclea, since it was engraved at that site) is later than Sulla's dictatorship and earlier than 45 B.C. It is quite probable that the whole inscription was written in the time of Caesar. In fact, the date of the inscription hardly matters. For it is certain that henceforth the proceedings for the census of Roman citizens in all of Italy would be decentralized.

From now on, every time Rome decided to take a census, the highest magistrate of each municipality would have sixty days following notification of the proceeding to carry out, in that area, a census (with everything this implies), according to the same procedure and criteria decided upon and published for Rome. This information would be transcribed and preserved in local, public registers. But a copy (or the original in the hands of local magistrates) would be officially sent to Rome by envoys who had been chosen by the local Senate, sixty days before the end of the census. There, within five days, the censor would have the information in these documents transcribed, copied into Roman registers, and preserved with Roman censorial documents (*Tabula Heracleensis,* ll. 142–55). Only those citizens who had their domicile in several *municipia* (a difficult notion to define for this period), and who were enumerated at Rome remained unaffected by this new procedure.[22]

The need of the central power at Rome for census information from the non-Roman communities of Italy was certainly not new. These communities had to supply troops for each *dilectus* and to provide funds to pay for their wages and their maintenance, both before and after 167 B.C. In order to calculate the number of troops, in each case, the Roman authorities had to know what each community (city or people) was able to contribute. Above all, they had to know the number of men capable of military duty, the equivalent of those *qui arma ferre possunt* in the Roman census. It is highly probable that the document used for these determinations, available at least by 225 B.C., is none other than the *formula togatorum* attested in a legislative document of 111 B.C. (*lex agraria,* ll. 21, 50), but certainly in use earlier (Livy, 22.57.10; 27.3).[23] However, as I believe, those figures sent to Rome did not represent the total number of the civic population or even the total number of adult males.

Furthermore, the various criteria (essentially timocratic) that were used by each city to determine the obligation to serve were of no interest to the Romans; these could vary in principle as well as in disposition according to local traditions.[24] In short, centralization that resulted from *formula togatorum* was limited and relative. The general and unified measure attested by the *Tabula Heracleensis* had only one precedent, and a highly significant one at that. It consisted of a regulation imposed on the twelve Latin colonies in 204 B.C. that, five years earlier in 209 B.C., had refused to fulfill Roman requisitions and that were not able to be punished immediately. In 204 B.C., Rome added new measures to a retrospective sanction (requiring that the rebels furnish twice the original contingent for five years):

> As for the census of these colonies, it will be taken according to a formula furnished by the Roman censors (and it was decided that it would be exactly the same as for the Roman people), and the results will be taken to Rome by the colonies' censors, before they will be released from the obligation. (Livy, 29.15.9–10)

This sanction was effectively carried out (Livy, 29.37.7). This was without precedent, as Livy points out. This was the procedure, as we have seen, that was extended to include all the citizens of the *municipia* and the colonies (old and new Roman citizens) by the ruling of the *Tabula Heracleensis*. It was no longer simply a case of knowing what each community could contribute in men and money. Rather, it was a case of centralizing at Rome, by the circulation of written documents, all the information required of citizens by the census: complete civil status (surname, name, filiation or patron, tribe, and age) and a financial accounting (*rationes pecuniae*). It seems clear that the new text certainly does not preclude the use of the old census procedure (no matter which magistrate was chosen to carry it out), but that it now included a new distinction based on domicile. The Roman census thereafter would only be concerned with Roman citizens living at Rome (if it was still taken according to the old procedure of convocation and personal presence, which has yet to be proven). Roman citizens residing in any municipality of Italy would only have to appear in person before their local magistrates. The circulation of documents thus replaced the circulation of people.

There are reasons to doubt that there was a general census of all citizens in Caesar's time, for the testimony of Livy (*Per.*, 115), Appian (*BC*, 2.102), and Plutarch (*Caes.*, 55.3) is ambiguous and stems from confusion.[25] But on the other hand, Caesar certainly had time to concentrate on the population of Rome. He wanted first of all to reduce the number of those eligible for free grain, a number that had increased to 320,000 since Clodius's measures in 58 B.C. He reduced it to 150,000. But this new and original method implied knowledge of the total size of the urban population: henceforth, this would be obtained from declarations required from owners of tenements, street by street: "He conducted a partial census (for the urban population) not in the usual place or in the usual manner, but street by street, by the owners of rented buildings, and he brought the number of those receiving public grain down to one hundred and fifty thousands" (Suetonius, *Jul.*, 41.5).[26]

We shall see later that this new method, indirect as it were, has a striking parallel in Roman Egypt. Contrary to what has generally been thought, it was not necessarily borrowed from a Ptolemaic institution but was, in all likelihood, a Roman initiative. The idea of simplifying the census operations first appeared in the enormous agglomeration that was Rome, by considering that every inhabitant was either an owner or a tenant (the position of slaves evidently remained doubtful). Such a system might seem simple or expeditious, yet we shall see that it inevitably involved the existence of many types of documents: at least the list of *domini insularum*, and no doubt a cadastral book or the beginnings of such a book. In any case, as far as Rome was concerned Augustus maintained the procedure. Suetonius describes it in the same terms used for Caesar:

> he made it [the partial census of the urban population] street by street, and, so that the plebs would not be diverted from their work too often, he planned to have *tesserae*, valid for four months, handed out three times a year. But the plebs preferred the old system, and so he allowed the distributions to be made once a month, as before (*Aug.*, 40.3).[27]

These censuses evidently differed from the general ones that were taken under Augustus. But there is no reason to believe that they were later than the city's administrative reform and the creation of the fourteen wards in 7 B.C., since they go back to at least 46 B.C. Their date is difficult to determine, but one of these censuses must have been taken in 2 B.C., when Augustus in turn reduced the number of plebeians receiving free grain.[28]

With the establishment of the Principate, the government's attention shifted away from Rome. Once peace was reestablished in an empire henceforth worldwide, the need for knowledge and control was felt on a global scale. With or without censorial powers officially conferred (I will not consider this question here)[29] the emperor had legal methods of accomplishing these operations whenever it seemed necessary to him. Augustus recalls, in the *RG*, three general censuses that led to a global count:

> = 28 B.C. In my sixth consulship with M. Agrippa as colleague, I carried out a census of the people, and I performed a *lustrum* after a lapse of forty-two years; at that *lustrum* 4,063,000 Roman citizens were registered. Then a second time I performed a *lustrum* with consular *imperium* and without a colleague, in the consulship of C. Censorinus and
> = 8 B.C. C. Asinius; at that *lustrum* 4,233,000 citizens were registered. Thirdly I performed a *lustrum* with consular *imperium*, with Ti. Caesar, my son, as colleague, in the con-
> = A.D. 14 sulship of Sex. Pompeius and Sex. Appuleius; at that *lustrum* 4,937,000 citizens were registered.[30]

These figures are problematic. First of all, a fragment of the *Fasti Ostien-*

ses (Ehrenberg-Jones, 40 = *AE,* 1946, 169)[31] for A.D. 14 gives a total of 4,100,900 citizens, almost 800,000 fewer than the number given by Augustus. It has been suggested that the difference might be due to the fact that the compilers of the *FO* would not have known the number of *cives Romani* outside Italy. It could also be a result of an error in transcription. But most importantly, these figures contrast sharply with those furnished by the last-attested Republican census, for 69 B.C. (910,000, Phlegon of Tralles, frag. 12 Jacoby; Livy, *Per.*, 98: 900,000). It is inconceivable that the Roman civic population had quadrupled in forty-two years. It is therefore clear that a change occurred: we can probably assume that after 28 B.C. the entire civic population—including women and children—is given, while in 70–69 B.C. only adult males were listed.

The three censuses mentioned by Augustus were not the only ones which were taken by him: Dio mentions census-type operations for 29 / 28, 22, 18, 13, 12 / 11, and 8 B.C. as well as for A.D. 4 and 14. They reappear regularly (partial or complete) every five years, in conjunction with the granting or renewal (since 18 B.C.) of the ten-year or five-year "powers." But these operations were not always general, not even for the *cives*. For example, in A.D. 4, the census pertained only to those *cives* residing in Italy who had a patrimony of at least 50,000 denarii (= 200,000 HS) (Dio, 55.14.4). This operation was clearly linked to the establishment of a fourth *decuria* of *ducenarii* judges (Suetonius, *Aug.*, 32.3).

As far as the citizens in Italy and the provinces were concerned, the operations were now decentralized. Several facts support this. First of all, there is the widespread presence of "quinquennial" magistrates in the *municipia* and colonies, who appear there only every five years and who obviously have all the powers and responsibilities of censors.[32] Moreover, they appear by the end of the Republic.[33] In some cases, when we have dated coins, as at Pella, Buthrotum, or Corinth,[34] or even fragments of municipal *Fasti* such as those for Venusia, Cupra Maritima, Nola, and Interamna dated by consular years, we can fix the date of the exercise of the censorial magistracy in those cities, and sometimes (as at Pompeii) go back to its introduction (*ILLRP,* 645:C. Quinctius Valgus, from Sulla's time). Sometimes we can see, as at Venusia (*CIL,* 9.422 = *ILS* 6123), that it coincides with a Roman census (for 29 B.C.); but this is not the case (in 32 B.C.) at Cupra Maritima (Degrassi, *Inscr. It.,*13, no. 7).

It would seem that the situation had changed since the stipulations included in the *Tabula Heracleensis:* the municipalities are carrying out their own census not only when one happens at Rome but according to their own rhythm. But we can assume that whenever there were operations involving all *cives,* as certainly was the case in 29/28 B.C., 12/11 B.C. (Dio, 54.35.1), 8 B.C. (*RG,* 8), in A.D. 4 (Dio, 55.13.4), and A.D. 14 (*RG,* 8), the municipalities had to follow suit. Perhaps, if this coincided with one of their own recent operations, they were content to collect the lists. We can be quite certain that the centralization of documents at Rome, at the disposal of the State, continued to function according to the injunctions of the *Tabula Heracleensis.* In the first edict of Cyrene, in 7/6 B.C., Augustus gave directions to appoint in Cyrenaica a class of judges recruited according to criteria that were based on census information.[35] Thus, Augustus knows the number of Roman citizens who possess more than 10,000 HS: "Since I find that there are in the province of Cyrene *in toto* two hundred and fifteen Romans of any age who have a census valuation of twenty-five hundred denarii . . ." (1.1.4–6). Yet, as will be shown, he does not know the number of Greeks with an equal or higher amount of property. *Εὑρίσκω,* says the emperor: this is the word used when personally consulting a document. This is not hearsay. It is quite likely that he actually had the results of the census of 8 B.C., which, incidentally, proves that the figures given in the *Res Gestae* include overseas citizens.[36]

The obligation of taking the census also extended to non-Romans, *municipia* or colonies with Latin rights. In fact, the *lex Irnitana,*[37] recently discovered in Baetica, and deriving from a municipal *lex Julia* slightly later than the *lex de iudiciis privatis* (thus to 18 B.C.), stipulates (cap. 86) that the *duumvir* will select the judges from "among the free inhabitants of the *municipium* [other than the *decuriones* and *conscripti*], provided that they be over twenty-five years of age and that they, their father, their paternal grandfather, and great-grandfather, or their adoptive father, possess capital amounting to no less than 5,000 sesterces . . ." These clauses (which strongly reflect those of the *lex repetundarum* of 123 B.C.) prove that the results of the censuses were assumed to be known, and that both the local magistrates and the province's governors[38] had access to them. There are good reasons to believe that these documents, or at least the ensuing figures, were sent to Rome.

Another innovation dates to the Augustan period that must have had important consequences from the point of view of demographic statistics: obligatory birth registrations.[39] These were introduced in a roundabout way. The *leges Aelia Sentia* and *Pappia Poppaea* (and perhaps even the *lex Julia de maritandis ordinibus,* of 18 B.C.) which concerned emancipation and succession, stipulated exceptions based on the age and number of legitimate children. Those concerned had to be able to prove their age or the number of children (registration of illegitimate children was made obligatory under

Antoninus; *SHA, Vita Marci,* 9.7–9). We see from papyrological documents (*FIRA,* 3, no. 2) that in each province—no doubt in the governor's *tabularium*—there was a *tabula professionum* from which interested parties could obtain exact copies. We also know of death registrations,[40] but these certainly had existed at Rome already from 46 B.C., since Caesar had made provisions to replace the recipients of free grain by lot after their death—it was therefore necessary to keep track of them (Suetonius, *Jul.,* 41.5: *in demortuorum locum*). It remains to be known whether, for provincial citizens, a copy of the lists was regularly sent to Rome—which would have been one way to keep the copies of the census registers up to date. We have no proof of this.

Another type of document concerning the *cives* had been kept up to date and centralized at Rome for a long time. These were the *commentarii civitate donatorum,* the lists of those who had personally been given citizenship. These had already been listed in a special register under Caesar (Cicero, *Fam.,* 13.36.1): correspondence between Pliny and Trajan attests that these *commentarii* still existed in A.D. 110, as does the *Tab. Banasitana* in A.D. 177: *in commentarios nostros referri.* The last two cases involve provincials: an Egyptian man from Alexandria (Pliny, *Ep.,* 10.6), the daughter of a centurion (ibid., 107), and finally, dignitaries of the Zegrenses tribe in Mauretania Tingitana.[41]

But what do we know concerning the subjects, the entire population of the Roman world? Everything that has been discussed so far concerns only citizens and Latins. But what about all the others: the allies, the towns and peoples who were free, the federates, or the subjects? This question is one of the most perplexing because of the unfortunate interference of scriptural sources that report the famous census held at the time of the birth of Christ. These sources have given rise to "theological passions," to borrow Mommsen's term.[42] The problem comprises two main difficulties. We know that Luke (and almost the whole of Christian tradition after him) has the birth of Christ coincide with a census taken in Palestine "while Quirinius was governor of Syria."[43] But elsewhere (Luke, 1.1), he dates the birth of Christ to the reign of Herod, who died in 4 B.C. We know from Josephus, whose many allusions are precise and definite, that P. Sulpicius Quirinius, *cos. ord.* in 12 B.C., was legate of Syria in A.D. 5/6, and that he in fact carried out a census in his entire province (Josephus, 18.1.1, confirmed by *ILS,* 2583) as well as in Judea, newly annexed after the death of Archelaos, Herod's successor.[44] In order to preserve Luke's consistency, scholars have employed boundless ingenuity, suggesting either that Quirinius held an earlier legateship of Syria, around 4 B.C., or, as we shall see, that there was an earlier census, taken not by him but by L. Sentius Saturninus, who was legate of Syria in 9–8 B.C.[45] and to whom a secondary Christian tradition (Tertullian, *Apol.,* 4.19) attributes the census contemporary with the birth of Christ. These chronological difficulties should now be considered settled (thanks to R. Syme) at least as far as Quirinius is concerned. Quirinius was governor of Syria only once, in A.D. 6, and was responsible for the first census taken in Judea.

But the real problem that concerns us lies elsewhere, in the expressions used by Luke and taken up and expanded by Christian tradition.[46] They are striking both because of their technical aspect and their solemnity:

> At that time an edict of Caesar Augustus was published, ordering the census of the entire world. This census, the first, took place while Quirinius was governor of Syria. And everyone was to be registered, each in his own town.

It is impossible to understand grammatically, as certain scholars would have it (see Millar, 406–7), "this census, the first before the one taken by Quirinius" or "the first of those taken by Quirinius," etc.[47] It has often been noted how precise the vocabulary is. Ἀπογραφή is the word that the papyri and the authors (Dio, Plutarch)[48] use to designate first the declaration (*professio*) pertaining to any census, then the census itself. The reference to obligatory travel "to their own city" by those being enumerated also recalls some characteristics of the Roman census in Egypt. From this comes our interest in Luke's other assertion that it was Augustus's edict that ordered a general census "throughout the *oikoumene*"—meaning, of course, the *orbis Romanus*. What else do we know about this subject?

It is evident that provincial censuses were taken in the empire before the time of Augustus.[49] Even if the Romans' fiscal policy had been extremely cautious and empirical, and had generally followed previous tax systems, it was nevertheless almost always based on a direct land tax, generally imposed on products (*tributum soli*; see Appian, *BC*, 5.4), and on a personal tax or a poll tax (*tributum capitis*; see *Digest*, 50.15.8.7; Appian, *Pun.*, 135; Dio, 52.3.2–3). I am leaving aside all indirect taxes.

The two forms of taxation were not always imposed at the same time. The poll tax generally passed by everything that, directly and indirectly, benefited by a civic organization—except in periods of heavy fiscal demands (Caesar, *BC*, 3.32 in Asia in 49 B.C.). But it is attested in Africa (Appian, *Lib.*, 135) and in Cilicia (Cicero, *Att.*, 5.16.2). This tax on individuals can sometimes be a true poll tax, paid by certain adult males (as was the case in Egypt and in Syria), or a tax on personal fortunes. Both cases implied something equivalent to a census. It is known that by the end of the Republic, Rome had given certain provinces a coherent censorial organization. There is definite proof of this for Sicily, under the *lex Rupilia* in 132 B.C. (Cicero, 2 *Verr.*, 2.131; 138), and for Bithynia under the *lex Pompeia* in 63 B.C. (Pliny, *Ep.*, 10.70; 80; 112; 114; 115; Strabo, 12.3.1; Dio, 37.20.2, etc.).

This fiscal system was highly varied in detail but had a base that was relatively constant. In order to function, this system implied at least on the local or provincial level a knowledge of the number of taxpayers and of their possessions, mainly land, with (and especially without) buildings. In older provinces they had to maintain and update the existing lists, while in new provinces, if necessary, they had to draw them up (see below regarding cadastres). In fact, it is contrived, for the provincial census just as for Roman citizens, to try to distinguish too rigidly between persons and things. In at least one province, Egypt, there was one operation that combined both aspects, the *κατ' οἰκίαν ἀπογραφαὶ*,[50] which, as the name indicates, were censuses of all the inhabitants (including Roman citizens), but were conducted house by house, by declaration of the owner or the tenant. Each of the latter had to make a declaration at his official domicile (*ἰδία*),[51] where he had to go if he did not reside there (see the edict of Vibius Maximus, A.D. 104, *Pap. Lond.*, 3.904 = Wilcken, *Chrest.*, 2021 = *ESAR*, 2.250).[52]

Deeds to the building had to be provided, specifying its location, and followed by a list of its inhabitants, their age, their relationship to the taxpayer, their qualifications, and possibly the taxpayer's other properties. These individual declarations were filed with various offices whose business it was to know about them. What is interesting to us is that they are filed in topographical order: by village, and, in the cities, by districts. This strongly recalls Suetonius's expression concerning Caesar's and Augustus's urban censuses: *per dominos insularum vicatim*. Within the registers (*tomoi*), the declarations are sometimes classified in alphabetical order by owners, but most often in chronological order. Here too, the comparison with the *professio* of the *Tabula Heracleensis* is striking. Of course, these documents were used mainly to draw up population lists by categories. But there is proof that the offices, in order to verify these lists, had access to topographic lists of houses, which, in turn, were used for verification.[53] It is not known whether these lists corresponded to graphic documents or to a cadastral map.[54]

We have almost 250 complete or fragmentary declarations. The latest dates to just before Diocletian's fiscal reform.[55] The earliest—as we are now certain—dates to Augustus's reign, more precisely to A.D. 5 / 6. By this date, the fourteen-year rhythm was attained (*Pap. Med.*, 1.3 = Montevecchi, pl. 37; Mélèze, *Symposium 1982*, 266). It is surely linked to the age at which individuals who were non-*immunes* had to pay the poll tax, λαογραφία. It thus seems clear that this method of simplified census-taking was introduced to Egypt by Rome, and this should not surprise us since the same system was used by Caesar as early as 46 B.C. for Rome itself.

So much for Egypt: but there is nothing to suggest that such a system was not used by the Romans elsewhere, especially in Syria or in Judea (if we did not have the papyri, we would know nothing of this institution from other sources). A text that is admittedly late—an excerpt from the *forma censualis* cited by Ulpian (*Dig.*, 50.15.4.8)—mentions in passing that the owners who must otherwise declare their *fundi* must also declare the *inquilini vel coloni*.

We have some evidence regarding the workings of the census in the provinces under the empire (see below, for the cadastres). Brunt has provided us with a useful outline (*JRS*, 1981, 171–72). The documentation is dangerously incomplete; so much so that we must admit that the absence of evidence concerning any province does not prove that there was no census. Despite the undeniable diversity of fiscal statutes until the time of Diocletian, certain dispositions seem to have had universal application, like those transmitted by Ulpian (*Dig.* 50.15.4.8).

Under these conditions, it is useless readily to accept or deny the statement found in Christian sources concerning Augustus's edict and the decision, which these sources attribute to him, to order a general census of the *orbis Romanus*. Mommsen, Marquardt, and other modern scholars (Millar, Neesel, and Brunt) have definitely rejected this.[56] As far as Judea is concerned, the first census of A.D. 6/7 might have been the one that marked the direct takeover of a new territory by the Romans: the same thing would happen in Cappadocia under Tiberius (Tacitus, *Ann.*, 6.41.1; cf. 2.42). But an inscription[57] (*ILS*, 2683) shows that there was another census taken in Syria by the same Quirinius. The census of Gaul, decided upon by Augustus in 27 B.C., begun by Agrippa, and continued in 12 B.C. by Drusus, was still in progress in A.D. 14/15.[58] It is highly unlikely that any province would have been deliberately excluded by Augustus; the case of client kingdoms is different. As will be shown, as early as 23 B.C. he had written a document that was already available and that summarized, among other things, the public revenues (τὰς προσόδους τὰς κοινὰς; Dio, 53.30.2). It is thus not improbable that a general decision—at least in principle—had been taken, perhaps as early as 27 B.C., when the regime was established and the provinces divided up.

Essentially, we have been obsessed by the obvious error made by Luke (and repeated by Orosius, 6.22.5, and probably Isidorus, *Etym.*, 5.36.4) of identifying the census of A.D. 6/7 in Judea as a universal census. But the other "Christian" sources, which have been thought to depend on the same single source, are perhaps more cautious and perhaps refer to something else. Cassidorus (*Variae,* 3.52) simply states concerning the geometers' art: "In Augustus's time, the Roman world saw its territories divided and a census was taken" (*Augusti si quidem temporibus orbis Romanus agris divisus censuque descriptus est*). Although this is without an exact date, it is certainly not false. The *Suda* mentions two distinct points. First, *s.v.* Αὔγουστος, it alludes to a count (ἀριθμεῖ) of all the inhabitants (subjected?) to the Romans, in order to know their size: "we find 411,700" (p. 851 Bern). This is an echo of the census taken in A.D. 14 but is misinterpreted as if referring to all the inhabitants of the empire. Next, *s.v.* 'Απογραφή, there appears the following passage:[59]

> Apographè, enumeration. Caesar Augustus, the emperor, having chosen twenty individuals outstanding in their lives and morals, sent them into all the provinces, and by their intermediary he took a census of people and possessions, a part of which was allocated to the Treasury. This census was the first, those in power before Augustus not having demanded anything from the owners, in such a way that wealth was shameful for the wealthy.

The "declarations of men and goods" (ἀπογραφαὶ τῶν τε ἀνθρώπων καὶ οὐσιῶν) have nothing outrageous: it is the aim of the *professiones censuales,* of every age. The date has not been specified, but the reference to twenty chosen individuals sent "to all subjected regions" (ἐπὶ πᾶσαν τὴν γῆν τῶν ὑπηκόων) is intriguing. There are clearly signs of the existence of another source besides the evangelical one. A distorted and desperate echo of this is perhaps found in Malalas (p. 226 Dindorff).[60] There may very possibly be a confusion (due to the consular dates) with the tradition concerning the geometric and geographic measurement of the world. But, apart from the attribution of a measure of general census to a single occasion in the reign of Augustus, there is nothing false here as well, for the censuses must surely have been taken everywhere.

The questions of the results of these operations, their centralization, the way in which they were used, and how they sometimes were published are much more central to our discussion. No doubt, *no* global estimation of the population of the empire has been preserved, except the number of citizens, as has been shown. It is worth noting Augustus's innovation: with him begins the custom (a statistical improvement, Beloch, p. 350)[61] of counting the *total* population and not only men available for military duty.

On the other hand, similar figures (that is, the total population) have been preserved for the provinces, or for certain parts of the provinces: first, in Syria, for A.D. 6/7. Q. Aemilius Secundus, *praefectus cohortis,* following the orders of Quirinius, had "carried out the census of the city of Apamea and found 117,000 citizens" (*ILS,* 2683).[62] Furthermore, Pliny has provided us with figures for the total population for three districts in northwest Spain: for the Asturi, 240,000 "free men"; the Lucenses, 166,000; and the Bracari (?), 285,000.[63] Surely the list of the cities proves that this calculation dates from the Flavian period, and perhaps goes back to the census taken by Vespasian and Titus in A.D. 73/74. Moreover, Flavius Josephus (2.16.4) in a well-known passage of which a portion at least proves that he referred to an official statistical and geographical work (where some have tried to find a trace of Augustus's *Breviarium imperii),* gives the total population of Egypt as 7,500,000 *ὡς ἔνεστιν ἐκ τῆς καθ' ἑκάστην κεφαλὴν εἰσφορᾶς τεκμήρασθαι*. This proves—whatever the merit of his calculation, disclaimed by Beloch[64]—that it came from fiscal documents of some sort. Of course, not everything goes back to the Augustan period in this famous "speech of Agrippa," but, by definition, these facts are pre-Flavian. Still, the census taken by Vespasian and Titus relates interesting information about "centenarians" (and people who are even older) and individual occurrences of remarkable longevity, which have been recorded by Pliny (*NH,* 7.157; 159; 162–64) and Phlegon of Tralles (frag. 37 Jacoby = 29 M). Let us note that Pliny also mentions the census taken by Claudius in 47 B.C. in his comment on Titus Fullonius of Bologna, whose age he had verified *collatis censibus quo ante detulerat.* For an old man of 150, such documents should go back at least to those censuses of A.D. 14, and 8 and 28 B.C. He could not possibly have been registered in the census of 70 B.C.! We could believe that these lists (Pliny only provides examples for the eighth region, *NH* 7.162) only include *cives Romani.*[65] Likewise, Tacitus preserves the total citizen population from the Claudian census: 5,944,000 (Tacitus, *Ann.,* 11.25.8). But along side the larger number of northern Italians, taken no doubt from Pliny's source, Phlegon clearly cites non-Roman cases from cities in Macedonia, Lusitania, and Pontus-Bithynia.

It seems clear that, since at least the reign of Augustus, the Roman authorities had access to the results of detailed statistical counts belonging to different series: the traditional census of all citizens throughout the empire; birth and death registrations at Rome and in the provinces either of individual citizens or of all the inhabitants, as in Egypt; and partial censuses of the entire subject population—as for Apamaea, Spain, or for the Greeks of Cyrenaica and Crete.

This documentation was essential for the establishment of tax brackets, at least for the subject peoples. But that was not the only purpose; the knowledge of the total number of *cives* might be important from the point of view of taxation after the introduction in A.D. 6 of the *vicesima hereditatium,* yet most of them were exempted. In fact, the results themselves interested the authorities for their statistical value: such information gave them an exact idea of the empire's resources and size. This is what the emperor Claudius expressed with a mixture of candor, curiosity, and scientific spirit. At the end of his speech to the Senate in which he had remarked upon the Gauls' docility during the census taken (between 12 and 9 B.C.) by his father Drusus, *novo tum opere et inadsueto Gallis,* he cried: "How arduous for us even now is the census, although nothing more than to make known to the world at large our resources is required, we know from all too vivid experience" (*ILS,* 212, col. 2, ll.38–40).[66] "To make known to the world at large"—the spirit of his undertaking is not so different from that of Augustus and Agrippa, who had also wished "to show the world to the *urbs.*"

NOTES

1. Parallel to the traditional arguments regarding Rome's vocation to dominate the world (which certainly began in the second century B.C.), we find, as a counterpoint, the pessimistic warnings of those who were opposed to expansion, or who wanted to show at what price the empire could be preserved or expanded. Their motives were varied: the need to maintain a menacing foreign enemy in order to preserve internal unity and discipline (this is the famous *metus hostilis:* see M. Gelzer, "Nasicas Widerspruch gegen die Zerstörung Karthagos," *Philol.* 86 (1931): 261–99); the moral danger of the advantages and bad habits that victory brought to the people, etc. Some comments concerning this facet are found in the recent works on imperialism: W. V. Harris, *War and Imperialism in Republican Rome* (Oxford, 1979), 266–67; P. Brunt, "*Laus Imperii,*" in *Imperialism in the Ancient World,* ed. P. Garnsey and C. R. Whittaker (Cambridge, 1978), 159–92. But this theme should be systematically studied.

2. For example, the Gracchi's adversaries who called upon the "hatred of the

provinces," Diodorus, 34.25; see C. Nicolet, ed., *Demokratia et Aristokratia, à propos de Caius Gracchus* (Paris, 1983), esp. 45–49.

3. For example in *De Rep.*, 3.41: "If this habit of lawlessness begins to spread and changes our rule from one of justice to one of force, so that those who up to the present have obeyed us willingly are held faithful by fear alone, then, though our own generation has perhaps been vigilant enough to be safe, yet I am anxious for our descendants, and for the permanent stability of our commonwealth, which might live on for ever if the principles and customs of our ancestors were maintained." Here Cicero has Laelius speak. Elsewhere, in judicial speeches (such as the *Verrines*) or political speeches (in favor of Pompey), or in letters (e.g., to Quintus), he often links, in his own name and quite forcefully, justice (fiscal, among others) and the empire's permanence. See some references in E. Costa, *Cicerone Giureconsulto* (Bologne, 1927), 406–10; and in P. Boyancé, "Cicéron et l'empire romain en Sicile," *Kokalos*, 1964/1965, 333–58 = *Etudes sur l'hum. Cicér.*, Coll. Latomus, 121 (1970), 140–59.

4. Appian, *BC*, 5.540: Octavian has canceled all extraordinary charges imposed since 43 B.C. and, in a speech, hurled the slogan εἰρήνην καὶ εὐθυμίαν; it is true that Dio (49.15.3–4) claims that he was making a virtue of necessity (we must, despite Mendelssohn, keep the reading εὐθυμίαν and not εὐθηνίαν (= abundance): concerning the text, see E. Gabba, *App. lib. V*, 217); P. Grenade, *Essai sur les origines du principat* (Paris, 1961), 79–80: C. Nicolet, "Augustus, Government and the Propertied Classes" in *Caesar Augustus*, ed. F. Millar and E. Segal, (Oxford, 1984), 108–11 and 127; regarding *pax et securitas*, Velleius, 2.89.3–4; 103.5; Dio, 56.40.1; 43.4.

5. Suetonius, *Aug.* 98.2: *per illum se vivere, per illum navigare, libertate atque fortunis per illum frui.*

6. We are familiar with Tiberius's statement to Aemilius Rectus, prefect of Egypt: "that it was the part of a good shepherd to shear his flock, not skin it": Suetonius, *Tib.* 32.2; Tacitus, *Ann.*, 4.6.7; Dio, 7.10.5.

7. *De oratore*, 1.159; 201; 2.337: *ad consilium autem de re publica dandum caput est nosse rempublicam;* regarding the problem of a senator's ideal culture (or of the ancient "science of the city"), see C. Moatti, *Science juridique, politique et société à Rome aux deux derniers siècles de la République*, unpub. thesis (Paris, 1987) and statements by E. Lepore, *Il princeps ciceroniano* (Naples, 1954), 289.

8. *Quodque addit: "causas populi teneto," est senatori necessarium nosse rem publicam—idque late patet: quid habeat militum, quid valeat aerario, quos socios res publica habeat, quos amicos, quos stipendiarios, qua quisque sit lege, condicione, foedere; tenere consuetudinem decernendi, nosse exempla maiorum. Videtis iam genus hoc omne scientiae, diligentiae, memoriae, de quo non paratus esse senator nullo pacto potest.*

9. There is a useful analysis concerning foreign policy in G. Clemente, "Esperti, ambasciatori del senato e la formazione della politica estera romana tra il III° e il II° secolo a. C.," *Athenaeum* 64 (1976): 319–52.

10. The personnel was more numerous than was stated: see Mommsen, *Droit Public,* I, 362–421; B. Cohen, "Some neglected *Ordines,*" in *Des ordres à Rome,* ed. C. Nicolet (Paris, 1985), 23–60; N. Purcell, "The *apparitores:* A Study in Social Mobility," *PBSR* 51 (1983): 125–73; E. Gabba, "Lineamenti di un commento alla *lex Cornelia de XX quaestoribus,*" *Athenaeum,* 1983, 487–93.

11. There is little (except for the bibliography) in E. Posner, *Archives in the Ancient World* (Cambridge, Mass., 1972). G. Cencetti, "*Tabularium principis,*" in *Studi Manaresi* (Milan, 1953), 131–66, is, on the other hand, informative, especially for the Late Empire. It is always necessary to refer to the three articles in *RE:* Kornemann, "*Tabulae publicae,*" *RE* 4A no. 2 (1932), 1957–62; Sachers, "*Tabularium,*" *RE* 8 (1932), 1962–69; von Premerstein, "*Commentarii,*" *RE* 4 no. 1 (1900), 726–59. There are interesting facts in R. Sherk, *Roman Documents from the Greek East* (Baltimore, 1969), 4–19; and J. Reynolds, *Aphrodisias and Rome* (London, 1982), 65ff.

12. C. Nicolet, "Le Temple des Nymphes et les distributions frumentaires à Rome à l'époque républicaine," *CRAI,* 1976, 29–51; id., *Le métier de citoyen*[2], 1976, 435–55.

13. Plutarch, *Cato Min.,* 16–18.

14. V. Ivanov, *De societatibus vectigalium publicorum* (Saint Petersburg, 1910), 86ff; 51ff.; C. Nicolet, *Le métier de citoyen*[2], 236ff.; concerning the State's accounts (and fiscal archives) see R. Knapowski, *Der Staatshaushalt der röm. Republik* in *Unters. z. röm Gesch.,* ed. F. Altheim, vol. 2 (Frankfurt, 1961); and id., *Die Staatsrechnung der röm. Rep. in den Jahren 49–45 v. Christ,* same series, vol. 4 (Frankfurt, 1967) (to be used with caution); E. Fallu, "La première lettre de Cicéron à Quintus et la *lex Julia de repetundis,*" *REL,* 1971, 180–204; C. Nicolet, *Les structures de l'Italie romaine*[3] (1987), 236–69.

15. I have dealt with these problems at two colloquia of the CNRS on the theme "*Genèse de l'Etat moderne*": "L'Empire romain est-il un Etat moderne?" in *Actes du Colloque d'Aix* (1984); and "Centralisation d'Etat et probleme du recensement dans le monde gréco-romain," in *Culture et Idéologie dans la genèse de l'Etat moderne* (Rome, 1985), 9–24.

16. T. Mommsen, *Droit public,* IV, 1–108; VI, 180–223; J. Suolahti, *The Roman Censors* (Helsinki, 1963), 20–79; G. Piéri, *L'Histoire du cens jusqu' à la fin de la République romaine* (Paris, 1968); T. P. Wiseman, "The Census in the 1st Century BC," *JRS,* 1969, 59–75; C. Nicolet, *Le métier de citoyen*[2], 71–121; id., *Les structures de l'Italie romaine*[3], 190–95, 332–39.

17. On these points, see especially P. Brunt, *Italian Manpower 225 BC–AD 14* (Oxford, 1971), 33ff.; 38; 61–83, etc.

18. *Haec frequentia totius Italiae quae convenit uno tempore undique comitiorum, ludorum, censendique causa* ("these multitudes that have simultaneously assembled, from all parts of Italy, to attend the elections, the games, and the census").

19. If following M. Humbert, *Municipium et civitas sine suffragio* (Rome, 1978), 320–25.

20. C. Nicolet, *Le métier de citoyen*[2], 509ff.

21. *CIL*, 1[2].593; Bruns, no. 18; *ILS*, 6085; *FIRA*, 1. no. 13; until the new edition and new commentary I am preparing for the *Group for the Revision of the Texts of Roman Laws*, see the examination of the question in E. Lo Cascio, "Mazocchi e la questione della *Tabula Heracleensis*," *Studi Lucani*, 1976, 77–107; and "*Praeconium et dissignatio* nella *Tabula Heracleensis*," *Helikon* (1975–76), 351–71; for a later date (ca. 75 B.C.), see W. Seston, "La lex Julia de 90 av. J.-C. et l'intégration des Italiens dans la citoyenneté romaine," *CRAI*, 1978, 529–42. See also "Centralisation d'Etat," *Culture et idéologie dans la genèse de l'Etat moderne* (Rome, 1985), 18–21.

22. *Tab. Her.* 1.142ff. (text by H. Legras): *Quae municipia coloniae praefecturae c(ivium) R(omanorum) in Italia sunt erunt, quei in eis municipicis coloneis / praefectureis maximum mag(istratum) maximamve potestatem ibei habebit tum, cum censor aliusve / quis mag(istratus) Romae populi censum aget, is diebus LX proxumeis, quibus sciet Romae censum populi // agi, omnium municipium colonorum suorum queique ejus praefecturae erunt, q(uei) c(ives) R(omanei) erunt, censum / agito, eorumque nomina praenomina patres aut patronos tribus cognomina et quot annos / quisque eorum habet, et rationem pecuniae ex formula census, quae Romae ab eo, qui tum censum / populi acturus erit, proposita erit, ab ieis jurateis accipito; eaque omnia in tabulas publicas sui / municipi referunda curato; eosque libros per legatos, quos major pars decurionum conscriptorum // ad eam rem legarei mittei censuerint tum, cum ea res consuleretur, ad eos, quei Romae censum agent, / mittito; curatoque utei, quom amplius dies LX reliquei erunt ante quam diem ei, queiquomque Romae / censum agent, finem populi censendi faciant, eos adeant librosque ejus municipi coloniae praefecturae / edant; isque censor, seive quis alius mag(istratus) censum populi aget, diebus V proxumeis, quibus legatei ejus / municipi coloniae praefecturae adierint, eos libros census, quei ab eis legateis dabuntur, accipito // s(ine) d(olo) m(alo), exque ieis libreis, quae ibei scripta erunt, in tabulas publicas referunda curato, easque tabulas / eodem loco, ubei ceterae tabulae publicae erunt, in quibus census populi perscriptus erit, condendas curato/.*

Qui pluribus in municipieis coloneis praefectureis domicilium habebit et is Romae census erit quo magis / in municipio colonia praefectura h(ac) l(ege) censeatur, e(jus) h(ac) l(ege) n(ihilum) r(ogatur)/.

(In the *municipia,* colonies, and *praefecturae* of Roman citizens, present and future, in Italy, the one who will hold the highest magistracy or exercise the highest power, while the censor, or some other magistrate, will take a census of the people at Rome, within the 60 days, since becoming aware that a census of the people is being taken at Rome, should take a census of all the members of his *municipium,* of his colony, or of his *praefectura,* who are Roman citizens, and should require of them a declaration under oath giving their *nomina, praenomina,* fathers or patrons, tribe, *cognomina,* their age, an account of their wealth, according to the censorial edict, posted at Rome by the one who will take the census of the people; all of these declarations, he will make sure that they are recorded in the public registers of his *municipium;* these records of the operation, he will send them by the intermediary of delegates, whom the majority of decurions and *conscripti* will have delegated, to send for this purpose, when this matter will be deliberated upon, to the ones who will be taking the census at Rome; he will make sure that there is an interval of 60 days between the day on which those, whoever they are, who will be taking a census at Rome (16), will complete the census of the people, and the day, on which those delegates will come forward and provide them with the records of that *municipium*, of that colony or of that *praefectura;* the censor, or any other magistrate taking the census of the people, within the five days since the delegates of that *municipium,* of that colony or of that *praefectura* have come forward, should take delivery *sine dolo malo* of these records of the census, which will be given to him by these delegates; the contents of these records, he will make sure that they are recorded in the public registers, and he will make certain that these registers are placed in the same premises as all the other public registers, in which the results of the census of the people have been registered.

He who will have a domicile in several *municipia,* colonies, or *praefecturae,* and as such will have been enumerated at Rome, will not also be subjected to a census in compliance with the present law in a *municipium,* a colony or a *praefectura*: on this point, the present law does not go against the established law.)

23. V. Ilari, *Gli Italici nelle strutture militari romane* (Milan, 1974).

24. C. Nicolet, "Le *stipendium* des alliés italiens jusqu'à la Guerre sociale," *PBSR* 46 (1978): 1–11.

25. P. Brunt, *Italian Manpower,* 92–106; he could not have seen J. Carcopino, "Sur un passage de la chronique de saint Jérôme," *Mél. Martroye,* 1940, 73–79 (which gives for 86 B.C.: *descriptione Romae facta inventa sunt hominum CCCCLXIII milia,* 133 Schöne); C. sees in the use of *hominum* instead of *civium* proof of a purely urban census; and he compares the Scholia of Este to Lucan 1.318 (ed. Weber, 3:53), which would give (by arbitrary calculations) a population of 486, 666 [*sic*] inhabitants in 55 B.C. for Rome; this reasoning, seductive but not convincing, is repeated in *Des Gracques à Sylla,* 397, n. 178; and *Jules César*[5], 518; see the recent work by Z. Yavetz, *Julius Caesar and his Public Image* (London, 1983), 156ff.

26. Suetonius, *Jul.*, 41.5: *Recensum populi nec more nec loco solito, sed vicatim per dominos insularum egit atque ex viginti trecentisque milibus accipientium frumentum e publico ad centum quinquaginta retraxit; ac ne qui novi coetus recensionis causa moveri quandoque possent, instituit, quotannis in demortuorum locum ex iis, qui recensi non essent, subsortitio a praetore fieret.*

27. Suetonius, *Aug.*, 40.3: *Populi recensum vicatim egit, ac ne plebs frumentationum causa frequentius ab negotiis avocaretur, ter in annum quaternum mensuum tesseras dare destinavit.*

28. Suetonius, Aug., 42.3: *impetum se cepisse scribit frumentationes publicas in perpetum abolendi* (no doubt in A.D. 5/6); 40.2 (the census); Dio, 55.10.1: "Augustus limited the number of people to be supplied with grain, a number not previously fixed, to two hundred thousand"; *RG,* 15: "In my thirteenth consulship (2 B.C.) I gave 60 *denarii* apiece to the plebs who were then in receipt of public grain; they

comprised a few more than 200,000 persons." For the chronology and the significance of Augustus's frumentary measures, see C. Virlouvet, *Famines et émeutes à Rome des origines de la République à la mort de Néron* (Rome, 1985), 17–18; and idem, *Tessera frumentaria,* thesis (Paris, 1986).

29. This point is especially studied by F. Blumenthal, "Zur zensorischen Tätigkeit des Augustus," *Klio,* 1909, 493–500, (the *Res Gestae* deals with the consulship or the *imperium consulare,* for three censuses (28, 8 B.C., and A.D. 13); since Augustus refused the censorship and even the *cura legum* (Suetonius, *Aug.,* 27), it is in virtue of an *imperium* specially voted (in 13 or in 19) that he assumes these powers; a conclusion confirmed, in my opinion, by Suetonius, *Tib.,* 21: *lege. . . lata, ut. . . cum Augusto censum ageret);* F. de Martino, *Storia della Cost. Rom.* (Naples, 1974), 4:196–207 (who refutes A. v. Premerstein).

30. *RG,* 8: *Senatum ter legi, et in consulatu sexto censum populi conlega M. Agrippa egi. Lustrum post annum alterum et quadragensimum feci, quo lustro civium Romanorum censa sunt capita quadragiens centum millia et sexaginta tria millia. Tum iterum consulari cum imperio lustrum solus feci C. Censorino et C. Asinio cos., quo lustro censa sunt civium Romanorum capita quadragiens centum millia et ducenta triginta tria millia. Et tertium consulari cum imperio lustrum conlega Tib. Caesare filio meo feci Sex. Pompeio et Sex. Appuleio cos., quo lustro censa sunt civium Romanorum capitum quadragiens centum millia et nongenta triginta et septem millia.*

31. For the census of 28 B.C., the Greek translation of the *RG* (8.3) gives, by error, 4,603,000 instead of 4,063, 000; Saint Jerome (140 Schoene) gives 4,416,000 (Syncelle, 593.5: *μυριάδες υις´ καὶ ͵δ . . .*): the difference between these figures is the simple outcome of the ancients' method of numeration. This is no doubt why we should not draw too many conclusions from the discrepancy between the *RG* and the *Fasti Ostienses* for A.D. 14: *c(ensa) s(unt) c(ivium) R(omanum) k(apita) XXXXI DCCCC* (4,100,900); both Brunt *(Italian Manpower,* 119–20) and Beloch believe that the two totals are authentic, one of them including the Romans from overseas; on the contrary W. Seston ("Remarques sur la tradition épigraphique des cens augustéens," in *Mém. Soc. Nat. Ant.,* 1954, 17–21) uses paleography to explain the divergence.

32. There is little decisive work since J. Neumann, *De quinquennalibus coloniarum et municipiorum* (Leipzig, 1892) (which was ignored by the author of the article "*Census*" in *DE,* II [1900], 175–76); a useful synthesis in H. Legras, *La Table latine d'Héraclée* (Paris, 1907), 144–49, with the list of municipal censuses (attested by calendars or *quinquennales* known at that time); regarding the Republican period, see H. Galsterer, *Herrschaft und Verwaltung im republikanischen Italien* (Munich, 1976), 110ff.; M. Humbert, *Municipium* (Rome, 1978), 310ff. I will give elsewhere the complete inquiry on the subject; see for the time being A. Degrassi, *ILLRP,* II, 473–75; and M. Gervasoni-Cébeillac, *Les magistrats municipaux du Latium et de Campanie,* thesis (Paris, 1987).

33. Concerning the empire, in addition to Neumann, the bibliography is wide-

spread: J. Marquardt, *L'organisation de l'Empire romain* (French trans. 1889), 216–26; Mommsen, *Droit public,* IV (French trans. 1894) 47; 100: but Mommsen was more explicit in *CIL,* 1, p. 471 (*Fasti Venusini*); *CIL,* 9.422; 10.5405 (= *ILS,* 6125, *Fasti Interamnates*); 10.7954; W. Liebenam, *Städtverwaltung in röm. Kaiserreiche* (Leipzig, 1900), 257–60, relying on Neumann; recent update by A. Degrassi, *Inscr. Ital.*, 13, no. 1 (Rome, 1947): 256 (and 247); and concerning Pompei, see P. Castren, *Ordo populusque Pompeianus,* Acta Inst. Finl. (Rome, 1975), 90–91; 97.

34. V. Imhoof-Blumer, *Monnaies grecques* (Amsterdam, 1883) 87, no. 100; 101 (Pella), 139–40; nos. 30, 34, 37 (Buthrotum); p. 33, Neumann wrongly cites Corinth instead of Pella; concerning Corinth (Neumann, 59), Mionnet, 4.374.

35. F. De Visscher, *Les Edits d'Auguste découverts à Cyrène* (Brussels, 1940), 17, 56–58.

36. Above, n. 31.

37. J. González, "The *lex Irnitana:* A New Flavian Municipal Law," *JRS* 76 (1986): 147–243, esp. 196, 231–32. The author believes that the mention of the tribe in the nomenclature of these nondecurion judges (l. 21) proves that the inhabitants of the Latin *municipium,* although not Roman citizens, had the *tria nomina* and the *tribu* in common with the latter among other things. This is a mistake: it is evidently the tribe of "those inhabitants" who were already Roman citizens (148–49).

38. The governor must know the global size of the population and the relative number of those who possess the census of a decurion, or HS 5,000, since he is the one who decides on the number of judges to be selected either in or out of the Senate.

39. This question is well known among papyrologists, and there is a large bibliography (up to 1973, see O. Montevecchi, *La Papirologia* [Turin, 1973], 179–80); see especially F. Schultz, "Roman registers of Birth and Birth certificates," *JRS,* 1942, 78–91; 1943, 55–64; J.-P. Lévy, "Les actes d'état civil romains," *Rev. Hist. Dr.*, 1952, 449–86; id., "Nouvelles observations sur les *professiones liberorum,*" in *Etudes J. Macqueron* (Aix, 1970), 439–49; for an updated list, B. Frid, *Ten Uppsala Papyri* (Bonn, 1981), 64 (I thank J. Melèze for this information).

40. O. Montevecchi, "Ricerche di sociologia . . . V. Le denuncie di morte," *Aegyptus* 26 (1946): 111–29; P. J. Sijpestein, *ZPE* 52 (1983): 282–84; an updated list is found in A. Martin, *Chron. Eg.* (1980), 276–83 (see n. 39).

41. W. Seston and M. Euzennat, "Un dossier de la chancellerie romaine: la *Tabula Banasitana,*" *CRAI,* 1971, 468–90 = W. Seston, *Scripta Varia,* 85–107; esp. 97 n. 2.

42. See pp. 96–97; and for more detail, C. Nicolet and P. Gautier Dalché, "Les quatre sages de Jules César et la mesure du monde selon Julius Honorius: réalité antique et tradition médiévale," *Journ. Sav.*, 1987; Mommsen's quotation is from his edition of the *Res Gestae*[2] (1883), 176.

43. Luke, 2.2.1 (see below, n. 47); Jesus was born during Herod's reign (Matthew 2.1.1; cf. Luke, 1.5: the Annunciation).

44. Josephus, *AJ,* 18.12.5: *τῆς δὲ 'Αρχελάου χώρας ὑποτελοῦς προσνεμηθείσης τῇ*

Σύρων πέμπεται Κυρήνιος ὑπὸ Καίσαρος . . . ἀποτιμησόμενος τὰ ἐν Συρίᾳ . . . ; 18.1.1; 2.1, the end of the census, "thirty-seven years after Actium" = A.D. 6/7; *BJ,* 2.8.1 (Coponius's prefecture, and the revolt of Judas of Galilee because of the census, after Archelaos's death; see *Acta Apostles,* 2.35).

45. Groag, *RE,* 2 A no. 2 (1923), 1521. Josephus, *Ant. Jud.* 16.9.1; 17.1.1, etc.; R. Syme, *Historia,* 1964, 156 = *Roman Papers,* 2:605–15; and *Roman Papers,* 3:869–84; R. Szramkiewicz, *Les gouverneurs de province à l'époque augustéenne* (Paris, 1976), 2:439.

46. On this overworked problem as a whole, see Mommsen, *RG*[2] (Berlin, 1883), 176; H. Braunert, "Der röm. Provinzialzensus und der Schätzungsbericht des Lukas Evangelium," *Historia,* 1956, 192–214; F. Millar, "The Census of Quirinius," in the revised edition of *The History of the Jewish People in the Age of J.-C.,* ed. E. Schürer (Edinburgh, 1973), 1:399–427; R. Syme, "The *Titulus Tiburtinus*" = *Roman Papers,* 3:869–84.

47. Luke, 2.1: Ἐγένετο δὲ ἐν ταῖς ἡμέραις ἐκείναις ἐξῆλθεν δόγμα παρὰ Καίσαρος Αὐγούστου ἀπογράφεσθαι πᾶσαν τὴν οἰκουμένην. αὕτη ἀπογραφὴ πρώτη ἐγένετο ἡγεμονεύοντος τῆς Συρίας Κυρηνίου. καὶ ἐπορεύοντο πάντες ἀπογράφεσθαι, ἕκαστος εἰς τὴν ἑαυτοῦ πόλιν.

48. See for example Dio, 39.24.2–3; 43.25.2 (C. Nicolet, "Le temple des Nymphes," *CRAI,* 1976, 146).

49. A complete discussion (for the period) in J. Marquardt, *L'organisation financière,* French trans. (Paris, 1888), 266–78; see the recent synthesis by L. Neesen, *Untersuchungen zu den direkten Staatsabgaben der röm. Kaiserzeit* (Bonn, 1980), with the very extensive review by P. Brunt, *JRS,* 1981, who provides (172–73) a complete *corpus* of provincial censuses attested for the empire.

50. I have spoken about this in "La Table d'Héraclée et les origines du cadastre romain," in *Actes du Colloque L'Urbs: Espace urbain et histoire* (Rome, 1985), 22–25; see M. Hombert and C. Préaux, *Recherches sur le recensement en Egypte romaine, Pap. Lugd. Bat.* (Leiden, 1952) 5:40ff. (with an update in O. Montevecchi, *La papirologia* [Turin, 1973], 179); idem., "Il censimento romano d'Egitto," in *Aevum,* 1976, 72–84; J. Mélèze, "Entre la cité et le fisc: le statut grec dans l'Egypte romaine," in *Symposion 1982* (Valentia, 1985), 265–68.

51. O. Montevecchi, *La papirologia,* 178; S. Le Roy Wallace, *Taxation in Egypt from Augustus to Diocletian* (Princeton, 1938) 106; the penalties for nondeclaration appear in *Gnomon de l'Idiologue,* chaps. 58 to 63 (*Les lois des Romains* [Naples, 1977], 542–43).

52. This is translated in A. Chester Johnson, *Roman Egypt,* in Tenney Frank, *Economic Survey of Ancient Rome* (1936), 2:250.

53. Hombert-Préaux, *Rech. sur le recensement,* 129, 132–33, 142.

54. For the only known example of a cadastral plan in the Hellenistic period, see W. Spielgelberg, *Catal. génér. Ant. ég. Musée du Caire: Die demotischen Denkmäler,* vol. 2: *Die dem. Papyrus, Text* (Strasbourg, 1908), 261, no. 31163 (Tafel 105), "Flurkare von Aphroditopolis": fragments of cadastral books (for example: ἔδαφος ἀ[μ-]/πελῶν/Ἀφροδίτ[ης], with plans and colored drawings).

55. The last census was taken in A.D. 257–58 (*Stud. Pal.*, 2:32); see O. Montevecchi, "Censimento," 77–83; J. Mélèze, "Entre la cité et le fisc," 266; the same for the date, now fixed, of the first census in 6/7, ibid. 266 n. 95.

56. Mommsen, *Staatsr.*, 2:415–17: in fact, he does not deny that "at one time or other" we could have obtained or insisted upon the total number of inhabitants in the empire; but "the results were not publicly declared"; H. Braunert, loc. cit., *Historia,* 1956, 193; P. A. Brunt, "The Revenues of Rome," *JRS,* 1981, 163–64.

57. Preserved at Venice (*Eph. Ep.*, 4.537; see Mommsen, *RG*[2], 161ff.): . . . *idem iussu Quirini censum egi Apameae civitatis millium hominum civium CXVII. . . .*

58. Marquardt, *Org. fin.*, 267–68; Livy. *Per.*, 134; Dio 3.22.5; in A.D. 12; Livy, *Per.*, 138, 139; in A.D. 16; Tacitus, *Ann.*, 1:31; 2.6.

59. *Suda,* p. 293 Adler.

60. "In the thirty-ninth year . . . of his reign . . . he ordered, by an edict, that a census be taken of all territories conquered by him, and those which were already in the possessions of the Romans, this during the second consulship of Agrippa and Donatos (?). In this way, the entire Roman Empire was enumerated by Eumenes and Attalus, both of senatorial rank; this aroused great fear and much anger." We can see the uncertainty regarding the chronology (the thirty-first year after Actium? or from 27?) which, anyway, would be A.D. 1 or 4: but Agrippa's second consulship is in 28 B.C. *Δουάτου* has been changed to *τὸ* Ϝ *αὐτοῦ* (= "his sixth consulship") by K. Petersen, "Die Kosmographie des Kaisers Augustus und die Commentarien des Agrippa," *Rh. Mus.,* 1853, 161–205, 377–442, esp. 187.

61. Concerning all these points, despite all the criticism against them see J. Beloch's conclusions in *Die Bevolkerung* (Leipzig, 1886) (Ital. trans., *La popolazione del mondo greco-romano* [Milan, 1909], 350).

62. See above, n. 57.

63. Pliny, *NH,* 3.28; regarding this passage, see P. Le Roux, *L'armée romaine et l'organisation des provinces Ibériques* . . . (Paris, 1982), 94 n. 788 (a form from the Flavian period). Concerning Spain's administrative organization under Augustus (and therefore Pliny's sources), ibid., 54ff.; Beloch, *Popolaz.*, 401.

64. Beloch, *Popolaz.*, 259–60; regarding the worth of "Agrippa's speech," the essential comments have already been stated, albeit quickly, by L. Friedländer, *De fonte quo Josephus BJ, II, 16, 4 uteretur* (Königsberg, 1873), III–IV; C. Jullian, "Le *Breviarium totius imperii* de l'Empereur Auguste," *Mél. Arch. Hist.,* 1883, 149–82; the historians of the Roman army, like those of the provinces, have often used it.

65. The only ones really to have used and discussed these texts are Mommsen, *Droit public,* IV, 100–101; and O. Cuntz, *De Augusto Plinii geographicorum auctore* (Bonn, 1888), 46–47.

66. *CIL,* 13.1688; *ILS,* 212; *FIRA*[2] I, n. 43: . . . *et quidem cum ab census tum opere et inadsueto Gallis ad bellum avocatus esset; quod opus quam arduum sit nobis, nunc cum maxime, quamvis nihil ultra, quam ut publice notae sint facultates nostrae, exquiratur, nimis magno experimento cognoscimus;* see P. Fabia, *La Table claudienne de Lyon* (Lyons, 1930).

VII

Control of the Fiscal Sphere: The Cadastres

We have seen that in the provinces, populated for the most part by noncitizens (subject to taxation), the census operations regarding individuals could hardly be distinguished from a parallel inventory of their property—especially real and landed property. On this last point, the Romans of the Late Republic and the Augustan period had at their disposal proven techniques and a long tradition.[1] In progression with Eastern, Egyptian, and Greek techniques, the Romans, like other peoples of Italy, for centuries organized their territory—especially their newly conquered territory—in light of its agricultural exploitation. They did this not only by surveying it and determining the boundaries between private and public property, but also by actually "constructing" it on the terrain. They enclosed it within vast systems of roads intersecting at right angles and defined by a precise orientation around two axes, which extended to the limits of the territory in question. These geometrically defined roads outlined square or rectangular units (centuries) which then served as the basis for the distribution of lots or parcels to future recipients. The existence of roads and of relatively close boundary stones fused and perpetuated, to some degree, the collective framework of the possession of land and of its development in the landscape itself.[2] For the Romans, these operations were linked directly to conquest, to the adjustment of the status of those who had been conquered, and to the eventual or actual expropriation that resulted in the redistribution of land to Roman colonists or to individual recipients.[3] The major phases of Roman colonization or of individual grants of land to Roman citizens had spanned the history of Italy, Cisalpine Gaul, provinces like Spain, Africa, and Narbonensis, and soon of the entire Roman world.

Since it was necessary to determine what belonged to the Roman people (for distribution) and what could be given back to the previous inhabitants, and—in addition—to revise what had been done each time a new operation affected an old territory, the network of "centuriation" gradually spread out, sometimes superimposing itself upon large territories. These operations were all the more necessary (and in the eyes of the ancients they derived all their meaning) on account of the status of lands, which—in a society that was inegalitarian in principle—was among the most varied.

The status of persons was equally varied. First, the recipients, whether veterans or civilians, were privileged individuals; their lots (which they received free of charge from the State) had to be exempt of all taxation and rent. When the assigned or granted lots formed part of a collective foundation (most often a colony),[4] the responsible officials in turn gave this new community collective land, in addition to the "divided" lots, which it could exploit by renting, leasing, or giving away. Whence came the necessity to define clearly not only the boundaries but also the legal nature of the land. In principle, and at the outset, this type of description of a territory, with its diverse allotments, was devised to be permanent and to settle various categories of farmers on the land who, the government hoped, would carry on. During the foundation of most of the colonies and in certain large settlement projects (those of the Gracchi and Caesar) the lots were even inalienable in principle.[5] However, these legal stipulations were not respected for long. In time, interventions of all kinds would occur—sales, inheritances, exchanges, rentals—but the original status of the land was often retained. And in all cases where the property of the State (or of the local community) had not been formally alienated for the profit of specific beneficiaries of the *ius Quiritium,* the possibility of recovery always remained.

This explains the important role played in the Roman civic system (which spread out gradually, on provincial soil, to the edges of the empire) by specialists responsible for defining the physical space and the legal nature of the land and for specifying its rights.[6] Following Greek and Eastern practices, the Roman State employed indispensable technicians, the *mensores,* for this task: the *mensores aedificiorum* for the built-up urban spaces and the *agrimensores* for the open countryside.[7] Of course, these men were first of all *geometrai* and as such, they were specialists in surveying techniques, in centuriation, and even, as we shall see, in the distribution of lots on the land itself. But these *mensores* also had legal responsibilities;[8] not, of course, in the actual granting of lots (Agennius Urbicus, p. 8, 26 L), which fell within the competence of the Senate, the people, and the magistrates; or in trials concerning questions of ownership, boundaries, etc., which in principle fell under the jurisdiction of a judge. But they were legally responsible for the definition of the boundaries and of the private or public nature of the lots: they made an evaluation (*renuntiatio*) which, eventually, would support legal action. Thus they were personally responsible and could be liable to an action *de dolo malo* (*Dig.*, XI, 6). And as we shall see, they were required to back up these appraisals with certain documents.

This is roughly the situation at the end of the Republic. At this time, the *mensores* (or the *finitores* for the plots) fell into two categories. Some were private and employed by the *privati* (and were often of humble means); others belonged to the military—soldiers or officers who often specialized in castrametation, and who sometimes played a role in political history (like those of Antony scolded by Cicero). Still others might—temporarily or not—be employed by magistrates; this group (e.g., the 200 *finitores ex equestri loco* of the *rogatio Servilia* in 63 B.C.) was entrusted, on authority, with a great power of appraisal and of arbitration, for example for the recovery of public land.[9]

But later, in the Early and especially the Late Empire, the ties between the administration (even justice) and the *agrimensores* grew stronger. In some regions, the military authority was entirely responsible for the centuriation and the division of land (i.e., in Africa, *CIL,* 8.22786; 22789). Elsewhere, a *mensor* who was designated by the emperor brought in a verdict (*CIL,* 10.8038). Finally, at least from the time of Constantine, there was a corps of official *mensores* recruited by competition (*professiones,* see p. 273 L), with a *primicerius* (the first mentioned on the first page of an official document)[10] at their head. This hierarchy of technicians naturally implied a culture, [11] a transmission of all types of required knowledge, and perhaps, later on, an organized training program.

Our knowledge of this, indirect and incomplete but still impressive, comes from the collection of technical texts which modern scholars have gathered as the *Corpus agrimensorum* or the *Gromatici.* In general, these were school texts compiled quite late. But—even if they are badly preserved—some treatises go back to the first and second centuries A.D. Most embrace the whole of the required knowledge of the *ars:* the module for defining boundaries, names and types of measurements, diverse statuses of land; techniques for defining boundaries, for centuriation, and for calculation in the field; types of controversies; summaries of great historical projects of allotment and colonization, especially in Italy; finally—and this is what interests us—transcription into graphic documents (plans, maps, etc.) of surveys or operations done in the field (codes, signs, letters, common abbreviations, etc.) and drafting techniques. It is remarkable that the most complete or the most ambitious of these manuals intentionally puts the art of the geometer back into the complete body of knowledge (according to the model found in Vitruvius for architecture, and in Strabo for geography), first linking it to cosmogony (the knowledge of the *mundus,* of the Universe), and then to cosmography (the knowledge of the *orbis terrarum*) (p. 61; 181–84; 187–88; 393–95 L),[12] and then to mathematical geometry. In these parallels (of which there are traces in Cassiodorus and in Pseudo-Boethius), reference to the Augustan period turns up insistently. We shall come back to this.

Two points are of particular interest to us: first, everything that deals with the elaboration of documents that must have accompanied all aspects of the *ars* of the *agrimensores* mentioned above; then, the development of a bureaucratic aspect taken by the whole of these operations in the time of Caesar, and especially under Augustus.

It is clear that these operations had always been translated into written and graphic documents.[13] We learn that in 172 B.C. the task of recovering land parcels usurped from public land in Campania, entrusted to P. Cornelius Lentulus, led to the engraving of a *forma*[14] (a plan or a map) on bronze, which was placed in the *Atrium Libertatis* (Granius Licinianus, p. 10 F: *formamque agrorum in aes incisam ad Libertatis fixam reliquit*). This location must have been chosen for its link with the censors' *tabulae publicae*. We also know that these registers included the list of public lands—fixed in geographical, or at least in administrative order, province by province; Rullus's agrarian law of 63 B.C., which provided for their sale, listed the lands in the actual order found in these documents.[15] But we do not know whether, in this case, maps or plans of them existed or not; it is likely but not certain.

Another series of public documents also contained landed, if not cadastral, information; these were the *leges* given to colonies (or to *municipia*) by their founders[16] or by those responsible for the distribution of land. They had to determine, among other things, the status of the road system, the boundaries of the collective land of the foundation, etc. (see the general text of the *lex Mamilia*, p. 264 L, and specific cases, pp. 164–65 L; p. 165 regarding the limits of the local magistrates' jurisdiction, and especially Hyginus, *De condicionibus agrorum*, pp. 118–25). These *leges* could be modified by *edicta, epistulae,* and *commentarii* (for example Augustus's edicts, p. 119 L).[17] We shall deal with these texts and their classification in the archives later.

The *mensores* had to be able to draw up actual maps of the lands for which they had done the cadastration. Their manuals often describe these operations. The generic term for these plans is *forma,* but there are many synonyms: *tabula, pertica, typon, metatio,* etc. These *formae* were drawn up on flexible materials (parchment or paper),[18] but they were also engraved on bronze, and only the latter could really be trusted: *illa tantum fides videatur quae aeris tabulis manifesta est.* A treatise like the *De limitibus constituendis* of Hyginus Gromaticus (188ff.) is entirely devoted to the method of transcription and to the technique of drawing up these *formae:* geometrical techniques (p. 190), then conventional notations and symbols, the same as on the boundary-stones (pp. 194–95, 196–97: *quatenus erit, inscriptione replevimus, ut et in forma loci latitudinem rarior litterarum dispositio demonstret*).[19] When it is a question of land distribution, there are *codices* that correspond to the *forma* of the land in question, made up of several pages or registers, on which are written the names of recipients chosen by lot (pp. 200–201). This results in the following formula:[20]

> For example the century D(extra) D(ecumanum) XXXV U(ltra) K(ardinem) XLVII: this is the one which the three (veterans) on page one should receive; we shall thus register in the book of the map: on the first page: DD XXXV UK XLVII: to Lucius Terentius son of Lucius of the Pollia tribe 66.66 *iugera;* to Gaius Numisius son of Gaius 66.66 *iugera;* to Aulus (. . .) son of Numerius of the Stellatina tribe 66.66 *iugera* . . .

Let us note the expression *libri aeris.* These cannot be "bronze books," but books (registers) that would accompany the map; they differed from *codices,* also called *tabulae* or registers, which were used for the draw by lot (p. 200 L). Rather, they were documents in which were written, before the allotment, the names of recipients who had been drawn by lot and listed in groups of three. They were divided up in pages (p. 200, 14: *a prima cera primam tabulam appellaverunt*). They were also different from the *commentarii* mentioned on p. 154, 26 L, which were no doubt the founder's dossiers and reports (as on p. 118 L, see n. 17). Thus the books and the map together formed a document of paramount importance. This document had to bear the "signature" of the colony's founder or of the official responsible for the distribution (p. 203) and had to be deposited in the imperial archives:[21]

> We shall write all these notices both on the map and in the books which accompany it: "given," "assigned," "granted," "withheld," "returned," "exchanged against one's own," "restored to the previous owner," and all other abbreviations in use; and this would be shown permanently on the map. We shall deposit the books of the map and the ground-plan [typum?] of all the rural land, with lines marking the boundaries and the neighbors' names, in the imperial archives. And if some land has been granted (as a *beneficium*) or assigned to the colony either in close vicinity, or in other cities, we shall write this in the

"book of *beneficia*"; and in a general way everything which will have to be preserved not only in the colony, but also in the imperial archives, countersigned in the founder's handwriting. The plan will have been made in such a way that the limits of all the measures taken and the drawing of the lands left outside the limits will appear on it.

The falsification of these maps was perhaps already punished under the *lex Julia peculatus (Dig.*, 48.13.10).

We see, however, that a copy had to be kept in the colony itself (see p. 155 L). The *formae* are attested in inscriptions,[22] as early as the *lex agraria* of 111 B.C., at l. 80i for the lands belonging to the Temple of Diana Tifatina, which were given by Sulla and restored by Vespasian *ex forma divi Augusti (CIL,* 10.3828 = *ILS,* 251). In A.D. 69, the proconsul of Sardinia, L. Helvius Agrippa, rendered a decree in a suit concerning the boundaries between two cities, of which one asked for a delay in order to get a *forma* (also called a *tabula)* from the *tabularium* of the *princeps (CIL,* 10.7852 = *ILS,* 5947).[23] The same inscription refers to a *tabula ahenea* that dated from the time of M. Metellus, consul in 155 B.C. Another text, by Hyginus, mentions certain improvements introduced by an *agrimensor* when he was making the cadastral plan during the distribution of new lands in Pannonia under Trajan (Hyginus, *De cond. agr.* p. 121 L):

> Recently a veteran of the emperor, skilled in military art and outstanding in our profession, while assigning lands to veterans in Pannonia by the orders and at the expense of the emperor Trajan, was not content to mark in abbreviation on the bronze [that is to say, on the map] the number of the assigned area, but he also drew the outline of each lot: he inscribed the number of the length, of the width, and the surface [of the parcel of land]. In this way there could be no dispute or contestation between the veterans.[24]

O. A. W. Dilke has discussed this passage (*Roman Land Surveyors,* p. 42) but I believe he is mistaken. Note should be taken of A. Déléage (*Cadastres antiques,* p. 191), who argues that *extrema linea* is an ablative that depends on *compraehendit:* "he surrounded it with an exterior line."

This text sheds some light on the true nature of these Roman cadastral documents. We see that ordinarily the plan consisted of an indication of the boundaries of the centuriation. It was only in exceptional cases—in Pannonia under Trajan, on the initiative of an anonymous *evocatus*—that the exact outline of the periphery of each lot was shown (*sed et extrema linea uniuscuiusque modum compraehendit),* in addition to a note on the surface area *(modus)* allotted to each recipient. Thus, it is unusual for a Roman cadastral map, which rightly deserves this name since it reproduced the layout of the boundaries on the land itself, to show individual parcels of land; the only known case figures in the text mentioned above. On the other hand, this map corresponded to what might be called a register of lots, since the names of the owners of each cadastral unit and the acreage of their possessions were given.[25]

In fact, there were doubtless two categories of register for each centuriated territory, which could accompany the same map. Some were registers of distribution, which contained the names of the recipients and the acreage each one had received; others were registers of the public land belonging to the community that was rented out (or whose revenue was leased) to purchasers. As we shall see, only the initial state of a cadastral unit was recorded in this kind of document: its periodic update was apparently not foreseen. In any case, it was often necessary to resume the entire operation—both on the site and in the books—when evidence was required, as was the case at Orange (see below). In other situations, in order to clearly establish property rights, it was necessary to undertake a lengthy investigation to establish the original title because changes were not registered in every regions or in every case (see Hyginus, *De cond. agr.,* pp. 130–31):

> Indeed here is what I have found in Samnium. The lands which the divine Vespasian had assigned to veterans were already no longer possessed in the same manner by those themselves to whom they had been assigned; a few in fact have purchased some land and have rounded off their lot, bordering it by a road, a water course or another exterior landmark.

In short, the evolution of the property—through purchase, sale, exchange, or inheritance—could profoundly modify the cadastre and might lead to confusion between land that had been surveyed and land that had not, making any inquiry exceedingly difficult (Siculus Flaccus, p. 151 L). This is why individual landowners, even for lands that, in principle, were not centuriated and thus not drawn on a *forma,* had plans drawn up at their own expense. However, such plans would have no legal force (Siculus Flaccus, p. 138 L).[26]

Two types of documents give us an idea of these cartographic documents or land registers. First, there is a unique and famous document: the—or rather the *three*—cadastres at Orange[27] engraved on large marble slabs, on the occasion of a restoration ordered by Vespasian in A.D. 77. These were originally kept in the *tabularium* of the city; the largest slab measures 7.56 × 5.90 m, and cadastre B, for example, could cover a surface of 44 × 19 km. In the background of a large-scale topographical map, showing river beds among other things, appears the grid pattern of the centuriations, along with the name of the purchaser or purchasers who have taken the lease on the *vectigal.* This document has only one equal on the level of technical skill, the well-known marble plan of Rome, to which we shall return.

Perhaps even more interesting are the illustrations (miniatures) that accompany certain manuscripts of gromatic texts,[28] as examples. These manuscripts and drawings are no doubt Medieval in their final phase (*Arcerianus A,* sixth century; *Pal.* 1564, ninth century), but it has been shown that they derive from models in the Late Empire, and in all likelihood from earlier ones. Depicting cities, their territory (with topographical landmarks), roads, the centuriated network or, on the contrary, the *subsiciva* or the *compascua,* they serve as illustrations to the texts cited above: they reproduce the conventions (letters and symbols) to which the latter refer. Some are true plans with vertical projection; others follow different conventions such as "cavalier" views in false perspective.[29] Since both types of representation were known from antiquity (Vitruvius, *praef.,* 7; 1.2), it is impossible to make any chronological distinction between them. Recalling that the true *formae* had to be drawn to scale—and to a large scale, if they could show individual parcels of land as we have seen—and that they must therefore have been closer in appearance to the model of the Orange inscription than to the miniatures, we shall consider them rather as models or explanatory *schemata.* Perhaps they were intended for the books themselves *(tabulae)* that accompanied the actual *formae:* a kind of "how-to" map.[30]

The *formae* and *libri* (with or without graphic documents), set up at least in a double copy, were tremendously bulky and, as Déléage stated, "le bureau central du cadastre devait être un service énorme" (p. 194). Everyone agrees with this—for the Late Empire. Yet, important indications allow us to go back even earlier and see that starting at the time of Augustus—or perhaps even before—there probably was a large number of centralized documents; this proves that the authorities, in Rome itself, were beginning to use extensive and detailed information.

We shall begin with allusions or details in the gromatic texts. Pseudo-Boethius (p. 395 L), after discussing the origin of the *ars* of geometry, alludes to an *epistula Julii Caesaris* that "concerns the origin of our art" and then mentions Caesar's historically well-attested colonization projects in Italy and in the provinces. We have seen that the facts provided by late texts (such as the *Cosmographia* said to be by Julius Honorius) about the great edict on the measurement of the world, attributed to Caesar, are unconfirmed and perhaps arise out of a confusion with Agrippa's surveys and the Augustan censuses. But Caesar's colonial legislation is not to be doubted: the constitution of his colony *Julia Genetiva* of Urso, in Baetica, has provided us with an example of this. We shall see that another document concerning all of the colonies, the *Liber coloniarum,* also contains parts that are clearly Caesarian; there are some references to the *leges Juliae.* More definite still is the existence of one or several Augustan constitutions, which are attested by Hyginus Gromaticus, (p. 194 L): *limitibus latitudines secundum legem et constitutionem divi Augusti dabimus.* Certain measuring units used for centuriation must certainly date to the Augustan period, for example, the *pes Drusianus* in Germany (p. 123, 9 L).

Finally, the *corpus* of the *agrimensores* mentions an author (thus someone who wrote professional or pedagogical treatises) from the Augustan period, one Balbus *mensor (Liber coloniarum,* p. 239 L): "from the books of the geometer Balbus who, in the time of Augustus, collected in dossiers plans and measurements, made by him, of cities of all the provinces" (*[ex libris] et Balbi mensoris, qui temporibus Augusti omnium provinciarum et formas civitatum et mensuras compertas in commentariis contulit. . .* [see also pp. 225, 249 L; and in Pseudo-Boethius, pp. 402–3]).[31] We also have a complete text under the name of Balbus: *Balbi ad Celsum expositio et ratio omnium formarum* (pp. 91–108 L). Mommsen had no difficulty showing that the author of this text, who alludes to Dacian victories, wrote under Trajan or Domitian (p. 92, 2 L = p. 147, t. II). But can we be certain that there were not two authors of the same name, and that Balbus *mensor* is the same as the author of the *expositio?*[32]

In actual fact, there is no doubt that general instructions, archival documents, and theoretical treatises existed from the time of Augustus. This is quite apparent from an examination of the compilation known as the *Liber coloniarum* (of which we shall speak later when we discuss the reform in Augustus's administrative geography). In its present state, it dates to the fourth century A.D. (it follows the administrative divisions of Italy in this period), and a little later, it undergoes a rewriting in certain sections (the *Liber coloniarum* 2, pp. 252–62 L): there is a long series of headings giving details on centuriation, boundary-markers, topography, and the allotment of a large number of Italian cities, as well as historical information from the Gracchi to the end of the second century A.D.[33] But we must note that most of the facts concern allotments of the Caesarian, Triumviral, or Augustan periods. It is more than likely that the origin of such a compilation goes back to the Augustan period: the title of the *Arcerianus A* (sixth century) is *Liber Augusti Caesaris et Neronis*—but other headings allude to a *commentarius Claudi Caesaris* (211, 23 L; 229, 12; 239, 15: *libri Augusti et Neronis Caesarum*). Certainly, Nero sent out colonies. But it has been proved[34] that the Nero to whom these passages refer is very likely Tiberius, before his adoption by Augustus.

In 13 B.C., Augustus had in principle decided to end the system of colonial donations or allotments of land to veterans. And, in fact, it was between 31 and 14 B.C. that the majority of Augustus's colonies were founded (see the summary in *RG,* 16.1). It is thus possible, in the wake of these numerous allotments (each one having produced its own *forma* and *libri,* deposited in archives both on site and at Rome), that there was a *commentarius* that summarized, usefully and succinctly, the crux of legal and topographic information (such a book is attested, *Liber Colon.,* p. 229 L, in the time of Claudius); there might also have been *libri,* later attributed to Augustus.[35] Also in the Augustan period—no doubt from 7 B.C.—falls the reorganization of these registers under a new classification, that of the eleven Augustan regions (p. 229, 12: *ex libro regionum;* 258, 2; see below, p. 203). Finally, I maintain the probability that a "manual" or a *liber* existed written by an *agrimensor* of this period, who might have been called (why not?) Balbus.[36] Thus, there were centralized cadastral archives with varying degrees of elaboration, based on basic dossiers.

But there is more. We have good reason to believe that documents of a cadastral nature existed at Rome and in Italy earlier still. First of all let us begin with Rome itself. The famous *forma urbis,* of which impressive fragments survive,[37] proves that detailed plans of Rome (and certainly of other cities) did exist. Of course, it is not a cadastral plan, but rather a prestigious monument connected to the Prefecture of the City and displayed on a wall of the Library of the Temple of Peace. It was engraved between A.D. 203 and A.D. 208, but it certainly derives from an earlier model. It is oriented with the South at the top—a convention often applied in descriptions of Rome[38]—at a variable scale, often 1/240 (but in other sectors 1/189 or 1/413). The plan gives everything: the road system, public monuments, private houses and buildings, with coherent symbols to show staircases and second floors. Finally, the names of monuments or neighborhoods were included. But this is not a cadastre: there are no measurements or parcels of land.

We do know of other documents in the same class that must have contained information of a cadastral nature. A marble slab recently discovered on the right bank of the Tiber, on the *Via Anicia,* shows the plan of part of the left bank of the Tiber, in the area of the Circus Flaminius.[39] Dating to the second century A.D., it shows *porticus* and warehouses belonging to private individuals (with their names: *Corneliae et soc[iorum])* and, most importantly, a series of numbers that indicate the width of the property (in feet), or other information of this order. *Formae* of this kind must have existed in the time of Claudius: it was by referring to such maps that Claudius, as censor, recovered public land that had been usurped by private individuals.[40] Also, it seems evident that such a cadastral plan is implicitly suggested by the content of a famous inscription from Orange (contemporary with those of the cadastre), called "of the *merides" (FIRA,* 3, no. 109). Schulten was the first to recognize that it involved urban land, "rented" to private individuals for a fairly high sum (one denarius per foot); according to Piganiol, it involved the rental of a right-of-way along the public road (no doubt under some *porticus).*[41] What is intriguing is that these "sections" (note the word *merides,* of Greek origin)[42] are numbered (from II to VI) without any other specification, unlike the "zones," *areae,* occupied by private individuals in another series of inscriptions from Orange.[43] In order to identify these sections, it must have been necessary to refer to a master plan or to a cadastral matrix.

But we can go back still farther in time. It is more than likely that documents of a cadastral type existed in Rome in the Late Republic, around 75 B.C., or by 45 B.C. at least. The collection of laws or of municipal regulations of Roman origin transmitted by the famous *Tabula Heracleensis* (later incorporated into the municipal constitution of this Lucanian city) contains a series of stipulations regarding the maintenance and the repair of urban public roads.[44] The general principle is as follows: maintenance and repair were the responsibility of the (private) owners of properties that border on the public road.

> Whichever roads now exist and will be built in the future, in the city of Rome and in the suburbs located close than 1000 feet from the city of Rome, each landlord of a building abutting onto one of these roads must maintain this road in keeping with the instruction of the aedile in charge of this quarter of the city, according to the present law; this aedile will ensure that all the landlords of the buildings abutting onto one of the streets which the present law obliges them to maintain, will maintain this road in accordance with these instructions, and that no water will collect on this road in such a manner as to render the road less easy of access.[45]

If the owner did not accomplish these tasks immediately, the aedile concerned would have to hold a public auction and entrust the maintenance of the roads in question to a contractor—but at the expense of the defaulting owner, who would be considered in debt to the Treasury. The procedure was as follows:

> Each time that a landlord obligated under the present law to maintain a public street before a building belonging to him does not maintain this street in accordance with the instructions of the concerned aedile, the aedile in violation of whose instructions the owner failed to maintain the street will assert the duty to maintain this street; at least ten days before the farming out of the contract for the maintenance of the street, the aedile will affix in front of his tribunal in the Forum a poster indicating the street to be maintained, the day of the farming out of the contract, and the landlords of the buildings abutting onto the street; to these landlords of buildings abutting onto the street, or to their representatives, he will make clear at their residence his intention of farming out a contract for the street, and the day on which he intends to farm it out; he will have the maintenance contract farmed out publicly in the Forum by the urban quaestor or the magistrate in charge of the administration of the Treasury. The urban quaestor or the magistrate in charge of the administration of the Treasury will ensure that the names of the landlord or landlords of the buildings abutting onto the stret will be entered in the rolls of debtors of the State, up to the sum for which the street will be farmed out, each in proportion to that portion of the street, both in length and width, which lies in front of his own building. He will assign without penalty for the payment of this sum the landlord or landlords to whom the maintenance of this street should have been tendered. If the assigned landlord, within the thirty days since he himself or his representative learned that his debt has been assigned, has not paid the sum nor put down a guarantee to the debt collector, he must turn over to the debt collector the entire assigned sum plus half as much again; for his business, each magistrate to whom this business is referred, appoints a judge and organizes legal proceedings, as he would be obligated to appoint a judge, and organize legal proceedings for a debt expressed in money.[46]

This text proves quite obviously that the aedile had to know at any given moment the names, the residences, and the representatives of owners of buildings abutting onto the roads, as well as the exact buildings that they owned, their placement, and their dimensions, at least for those facing onto the roads. In fact, he must have had access to relatively elaborate documents, since he had to post these in the Forum ten days before the auction. This information and these documents are indeed cadastral. We have seen that, at least from the time of Caesar, the censuses for the inhabitants of Rome were done "through the intermediary of owners of all the buildings" (*per dominos insularum,* Suetonius, *Jul.,* 41.5; *Aug.,* 40.2), street by street, which implies a statistical list of those owners of tenement houses. This evidence, along with the *Tabula Heracleensis,* confirms the existence of books, if not of plans, of a cadastral nature.

In each case, in order to contact the actual owners it was necessary to be aware of property transfers, and not, as in the agrarian *formae,* the original recipients. Registration of transfers of urban properties is attested, from the beginning of the first century A.D., for the allotment of rights to water from the aqueducts (Frontinus, *De aqu.,* 107; 109): "as soon as any water-rights are vacated, this is reported, and entered in the records" *(cum vacare aliquae coeperunt aquae, adnuntiatur et in commentarios redigitur. . .).*[47] Likewise, we have seen that death registrations are implied in Caesar's legislation concerning grain distribution (Suetonius, *Jul.,* 41.5: *in demortuorum locum).* Here too, we must assume that there was a declaration of transfer. As far as the *Tabula Heracleensis* is concerned, such declarations might very well have been part of the regulation itself. The first twenty lines of the inscription (whose beginning is missing) concern mysterious "declarations" that must be issued periodically by individuals who, as we have seen, could be citizens (minors or majors); declarations that are clearly of a patrimonial nature. I propose that among the individuals to whom this document is directed are included those of line 20,[48] "the ones before whose building one of these public roads is located" (*ii quoius ante aedificium earum quae via erit).* If this hypothesis is correct, we would have proof not only of the existence of a cadastre, but also of a declaration and registration of transfers of property (cf. Cicero, *Att.,* 13.33.1; and *Fam.,* 16.23.1).[49]

Such declarations and registrations are far from being unknown practices in the ancient world. I will mention only the famous inscription of Tenos,[50] listing forty-seven registrations of sales of land and of houses, over a period of a year and a half (it is too far removed from the Roman context to allow a useful comparison). A passage in Theophrastus[51] shows that the concern officially to register property sales was relatively widespread in Greek cities. The case of Tenos is doubtless explained by the special and quasi-fictitious character of these sales, since they concerned, in most cases, the lifting of mortgages that generally involved the management of dowries or of inheritances. Apparently there is no question of taxation or of a distribution of expenses. It is not a cadastre.

But it is essential, on the other hand, to compare the conclusions that we have drawn from the *Tabula Heracleensis* and the testimony of Cicero and Suetonius with what the papyrological documents teach us concerning the practices in Egypt. Two types of declarations, resulting in the collection of documents whose usage can be compared to the practice in Rome, are of interest to us. On the one hand, as seen above,[52] there were the well-known *κατ' οἰκίαν ἀπογραφαί*, introduced into Egypt in Augustus's reign.

On the other hand, there was the obligatory declaration of transfer of ownership, which had to take place in offices called *βιβλιοθῆκαι τῶν ἐγκτήσεῶν*[53] located in each administrative center. It was the subject of a regulation by the prefects of Egypt, as attested by the edict of M. Mettius Rufus (A.D. 89), which was far from being the first on this subject.[54] This regulation saw to the quality and regularity of the registrations. The declarations had to be made by the owners but also by mortgage creditors and, in a general way, by all those who had rights to a property. The sales and transfers were thus officially registered by the administration for its own use. These declarations could equally serve to solve private disputes. There was a permanent obligation to make these declarations: a "regular" declaration resulted solely from this obligation. But the prefects could order a periodical revision of all these documents, from which we have "general" declarations, made in accordance with this injunction.[55]

It is generally thought that the public registration of private acts,[56] which is at the origin of our notary profession, was a characteristic peculiar to the Greek provinces of the empire (including Egypt) and that it did not extend over Roman law until the fifth century. Maybe so. But it seems quite probable that, for certain acts that might have important consequences for the use of a property (like taxation, maintenance, water concessions, or population control), the State—at Rome, in Italy, and in the provinces—must have been keep informed long before that late date. This was already the case when the section of the law at the beginning of the *Tabula Heracleensis* was written that implies the identification, at all times, of owners of urban buildings and the knowledges of the size and value of their property. To achieve this, a regular system of declaration and registration of the shifts in property had to be devised. In my opinion, cadastral matrices and an office of acquisitions or mortgages, or probably both at the same time—in one form or another—must have existed at Rome at least by the first century B.C. Documents must have existed that are forerunners of those of which copies or echoes of a much later period have come down to us, like the

Forma Urbis or the *Regionaries*. The *Tabula Heracleensis* is proof of this, and it can prompt us to shade the primitivist vision often presented to us concerning Roman administration during the Republican period.

NOTES

1. For the Romans, the question was not only the setting up of plans and of cadastral books, but the transformation of the landscape itself by the establishment of a network of roads and boundaries. All the necessary information is found in the five volumes, magnificently illustrated and completely up-to-date, of *Misurare la Terra* (in pt. 1: *Centuriazioni e coloni nel mondo romano*) (Modena, 1985), which also gives an excellent historiographical survey of the rediscovery of Roman centuriations in the nineteenth century in Northern Italy and in Africa. An exposé of the question, a critical bibliography, and various studies are found in M. Clavel-Levêque, ed., *Cadastres et espace rural* (Paris, 1983). Of course, this does not exclude the classic works by A. Schulten, "*Gromatici,*" *RE*, VII, no. 2 (1912), 1886–96, and "*centuriatio,*" *DE*, II (1900), 189–92 (or by M. Cantor, *Die römischen Agrimensoren und ihre Stellung in der Gesch. der Feldmesserkunst* [Leipzig; 1878]); of J. Bradford, *Ancient Landscapes* (London, 1937); and recently, of O. A. W. Dilke, *The Roman Land Surveyors* (1971); Dilke; "Archaeological and Epigraphic Evidence of Roman Land Survey," *ANRW* II, 1 (1974): 564–73; F. T. Hinrichs, *Die Geschichte der gromatischen Institutionen* (Wiesbaden, 1974).

2. On the terms *scamnatio* or *strigatio*, which indicate forms of allotments (some extended to the greatest width of the territory, others to the greatest length), see the enlightening updates by A. Déléage, *Les cadastres antiques jusqu' à Dioclétien*, Etudes de Papyrologie, 2 (Cairo, 1934), 73–228, esp. 103–4; F. Favory, "Propositions pour une modélisation des cadastres ruraux antiques," in *Cadastres et espace rural*, ed. M. Clavel-Lévêque (Paris, 1983), esp. 55 n. 12 (Hinrichs, *Geschichte*, 23), and 109ff., and his thesis *Les cadastres romains* (Besançon, 1982), 116 n. 215, 119ff.

3. See the recent work by E. Gabba, "Per un interpretazione storica delle centuriazione romane," in *Misurare la Terra*, 1: 20–28; id., "Sulle strutture agrarie dell' Italia Romana fra III e I secolo a.C.," in E. Gabba and M. Pasquinucci, *Strutture agrarie e allievamento transumante nell' Italia romana* (Pisa, 1979), 7ff.

4. See the exhaustive update by L. Keppie, *Colonisation and Veteran Settlement in Italy, 47–14 B.C.* (Rome, 1983), 87ff. ("the settlement process").

5. Appian, *BC*, 1.121; Cicero, *De leg. agr.*, 2.78; Appian, *BC*, 3.2.

6. Our knowledge of these questions depends precisely on a *corpus* of specialized texts probably destined for the professional training of these employees in the Late Empire: the *corpus agrimensorem*, often called *Gromatici Veteres*. There are two editions, one as insufficient as the other: F. Blume, K. Lachmann, and A. Rudorff, *Gromatici Veteres* (*Die Schriften der röm. Feldmesser*) 2 vols. (Berlin, 1848–52)

(with Mommsen's comments to the *Libri coloniarum*, 2:143–226); and C. Thulin, *Corpus agrim. rom.*, vol. 1. (Leipzig, 1913); on these texts, their merit, and tradition see L. Toneatto, "Tradition manuscrite et éditions modernes du *C.a.R.*," in *Cadastres et espace rural*, ed. M. Clavel-Lévêque (Paris, 1983), 21–50.

7. M.-C. Panerai, "Le *agrimensores romani*," in *Misurare la Terra* 1:109–21; and G. Martines, R. Friggeri, and A. Toro, "L'agrimensura," *ibidem*, vol. 5: *Città, agricolt., commercio: materiali da Roma e dal suburbio*, 23–37.

8. Studied in his time by G. Brugi, *Le dottrine giuridiche degli agrimensores* (Verona, 1897); and recently, by F. T. Hinrichs, *Geschichte der gromatischen Institutionen*, 84ff., 171ff.

9. See C. Nicolet, "Les *finitores ex equestri loco* de la loi Servilia de 63 av. J.-C.," *Latomus*, 1970, 72–103.

10. Regarding schools and examinations, the constitutions of Theodosius and of Valentinian, 273 L; A. Dilke, *Roman Land Surveyors*, 44–45. For the *primicerius*, *Cod. Theod.* 6.34 (after two years, he can become an *agens in rebus*).

11. M.-C. Panerai in *Misurare la Terra*, 1:113; Dilke, *Roman Land Surveyors*, 47–65; Toneatto, in *Cadastres et espace rural*, 38–39, for the links with geometry in the early Middle Ages.

12. Agennius Urbicus, 61 L; Hyginus Gromaticus 181–84 L, 187–88 (with the quotation from Lucan); Pseudo-Boethius 393–95 L (cf. Cassiodorus); for the place of mathematics, geometry, and astronomy (of Greek tradition, certainly, but integrated by the Romans after Varro) in the late Middle Ages, P. Courcelle, *Les Lettres grecques en Occident* (Paris, 1948), 325–36.

13. Déléage, *Les cadastres antiques*, 190ff. (already found in Mommsen, *Gromatici Veteres*, 2:152; Rudorff: in Lachmann, *Gromatici Veteres*, 405): but the most complete study (with those of Dilke cited n. 1) remains that of F. Castagnoli, "Le *formae* delle colonie romane e le miniature dei codici dei gromatici," *Mem. Acc. Lincei, Sc. Mor.*[7] (1944): 83–118, which began by gathering the significant passages of the *Gromatici* concerning the *formae* (or *typus* or *aes*), according to various aspects (for example as an orientation map, p. 90; as a legal document, p. 91; epigraphical texts, p. 94); F. Castagnoli's conclusions are very negative. While A. Schulten, "Römischen Flurkarten," *Hermes*, 1898, 534–65, and then "Vom antiken Kataster," *Hermes*, 1906, 1–44, wanted to see in the plan-miniature exact representations going back to collections of *formae coloniarum* from the time of Agrippa or Augustus, Castagnoli thinks that he can prove (1) that some are only illustrations *a posteriori* of the actual text they accompany; (2) that even when they include details from other literary sources, these are often erroneously interpreted; and (3) that, in any case, if they sometimes depend on ancient cartographic documents, they cannot be actual *formae coloniae* (which were on an exact scale and were much more precise as far as centuriations were concerned). The recent conclusions of O. A. W. Dilke, *Roman Land Surveyors*, 109–25; and *Greek and Roman Maps*, (London, 1985), 88–101, insist upon the diversity of the origin and merit of miniatures.

14. For the role of the *Atrium Libertatis* in this regard, C. Nicolet, "Le temple des

Nymphes et les distributions frumentaires à Rome à L'époque republicaine," *CRAI*, 1976, 29–51.

15. *De leg. agr.*, 1.4: *Vendit Italiae possessiones ex ordine omnis . . . Persequitur in tabulis censoriis totam Siciliam*; 1.5: *deinde agros in Macedonia regios* etc.; 2.48.

16. These are the *leges datae*, whether from the foundation of the colony or after the Social War, when the Italian cities—having all become *municipia*—were able to give themselves, or to have proposed to them, local statutes: *Tab. Her.*, *CIL* 1^2.593, 159ff.; law from Tarentum, *CIL* 1^2.590; see W. Seston, "La lex Julia de 90 av. J.-C.," in *CRAI*, 1978, 529–42.

17. Hyginus, *De cond. agr.*, p. 118 L: "it is therefore always necessary to consider the statutes of colonies and *municipia*, and also to check if, after the granting of the statute, something has been added or removed by the (founder's) reports, letters or edicts"; 119: Augustus's *edicta*.

18. Siculus Flaccus, *De cond. agr.*, p. 154.13 L: "The maps are given various names: some are set up on wooden tablets, others on bronze, still others on skins, although 'map' is their generic term, they are sometimes called 'territory,' 'centuriation,' 'demarcation,' 'limitation,' 'grid-pattern,' 'figures'. . ."; ibid., 154.23: "Only the map which figured on the bronze tablets could be trusted; if someone challenged this, one usually had recourse to the imperial archives."

19. Hyginus, *De limit. const.*, p. 196, 7 L: "so that on the map, the width of the area is made evident by the larger spacing of the letters."

20. Hyginus, *De limit. const.*, p. 201 L: *Sit forte centuria D.D. XXXV V.K. XLVII: hanc ex prima tabula tres accipere debebunt quod in aeris libris sic inscribemus. TABVLA PRIMA. D.D. XXXV V.K. XLVII LVCIO TERENTIO LVCI FILIO POLLIA IVGERA LXVIs˜, GAIO NUMISIO G.F. IUGERA LXVIS˜ AVLO . . . NVMERII FILIO STELLATINA IVGERA LXVIs˜ eodem exemplo et ceteras sortes.*

21. Hyginus, *De limit. const.*, p. 202–3 L: *Omnes significationes / et formis et tabulis aeris inscribemus, data, adsignata, concessa, excepta, reddita commutata pro suo, reddita veteri possessori, et quaecumque alia inscriptio singularum litterarum in usu fuerit, et in aere permaneat. Libros aeris et typum perticae totius lineis descriptum secundum suas determinationes adscriptis adfinibus tabulario Caesaris inferemus. et si qua beneficio concessa aut adsignata / coloniae fuerint, sive / inproximo sive inter alias civitates, in libro beneficiorum adscribemus. et quidquid aliud ad instrumentum mensorum pertinebit, non solum colonia sed et tabularium Caesaris manu conditoris subscriptum habere debebit / typum totius pertice sic ordinavimus ut omnes mensurae actae limites et subsicivorum lineas ostendat. /*

22. See J. Kapp, *s.v.* "Forma," in *TLL*, VI, 1, 5 (1973) 1082–83; agr. law (*CIL* 1^2.585), 1.7, 78, 80 (*formae publicae*).

23. *FIRA*, I, n. 59; "Nouveau Girard" (*Les lois des Romains*), 377 (see Mommsen, *Romische Geschichte* 5.325 58), 1:14–15: *tabulam se ad rem pertinentem ex tabulario principis adlaturos*; 1:17: *nisi forma allata esset . . .*; 1:7: *ut in tabula ahenea a M. Metello ordinati essent* [it is not certain that this is a map but it is

possible—otherwise, the text of M. Metellus would have been defined legally as *sententia* or *edictum*].

24. Hyginus, *De cond. agr.*, p. 121 L: *Nuper ecce quidam evocatus Augusti, vir militaris disciplinae, professionis quoque nostrae capacissimus, cum in Pannonia agros veteranis ex voluntate et liberalitate imperatoris Traiani Augusti Germanici adsignaret, in aere, id est in formis non tantum modum quem adsignabat adscribsit aut notavit, sed et extrema linea unius cuiusque modum compraehendit: uti acta est mensura adsignationis, ita inscribsit longitudinis et latitudinis modum quo / facto nullae inter veteranos lites contentionesque ex his terris nasci poterunt.*

25. On these distinctions, see Déléage, *Les cadastres antiques,* 190–91, 202.

26. Siculus Flaccus, p. 138 L: *Horum ergo agrorum nullum est aes, nulla forma, quae publicae fidei possessoribus testimonium reddat . . . Quidam vero possessionum suarum privatim formas fecerunt, quae nec ipso vicinis nec sibi vicinos obligant, quoniam res est voluntaria.*

27. Note, with Castagnoli, the differences with the initial *formae* described and drawn up by the *agrimensores:* (1) these "cadastres" are on marble and not on bronze; (2) among the names of the owners is the name of a woman—therefore this is not, in any way, a replica of the original allotment; (3) finally, the figures given for the rents show its (local) fiscal aspect. Nevertheless, it is evident that such a document has close links with the *formae.* See A. Piganiol, "Les documents cadastraux de la colonie latine d'Orange," *Gallia,* supp. 16 (1962); J. H. Oliver, "North, South, East, West at Arausio and elsewhere," in *Mél. Piganiol* (Paris, 1966), 1075–79; O. A. W. Dilke, "Arch. and Epigr. Evidence of Roman Land Survey," *ANRW* II, 1 (1974): 573–80; but essentially (for the definitive solution of the orientation of cadastres and their disposition), F. Salviat, "Orientation, extension et chronologie des plans cadastraux d'Orange," *Rev. Arch. Narb.* 10 (1977): 107–18.

28. See above, n. 13.

29. From the graphic and pictorial point of view, the best study is that of J. N. Carder, *Art Historical Problems of a Roman Land Surveying Manuscript: The Codex Arcerianus A, Wolfenbüttel* (Pittsburgh, 1978) who distinguishes a "diagrammatic" tradition, that is, cartographic (vertical view, scale, etc.) from a "pictural" tradition (cavalier view, perspective, etc.). On perspective in antiquity, see from now on A. Rouveret, in her new edition of A. Reinach, *Recueil Milliet* (Paris, 1985), 447–48 (complete bibliography).

30. Some identified miniatures—for example the one representing *Minturnae* (*Palat.,* 1564, 88r) are interesting because they have details (here, the river crossing the city) that cannot come from a simple illustration of the text itself. In fact, this detail stems from a misinterpretation by Pliny, *NH,* 3.39 (*colonia Minturnae Liri amne divisa*), and thus, cannot go back to an authentic *forma* (Castagnoli, "La *formae* delle colonie romane," 103).

31. Pseudo-Boethius, 225 L: *ex libro Balbi provincia Piceni*; 249 L: *ex libro Balbi;* Pseudo-Boethius, 402 L: *iubente Augusto Caesare Balbo mensori . . .*; 403 L: *Balbi mensoris.*

32. Mommsen, *Gromatici,* 2:147, 176–77; to distinguish the two, Bubnov, *Gerberti . . . opera mathematica* (Berlin, 1899) 424; *contra* Pais, *Storia della colonizzazione,* 1:XXIII; but recently L. Keppie, *Colonisation,* 10–12.

33. Mommsen, *Gromatici,* 2:143–220; E. Pais, *Storia della colonizzazione,* vols. 1 and 2 (Rome, 1923) (who prefers to call them *libri regionum*); F. Castagnoli, "Note al *Liber coloniarum*," *Bull. Comm.,* 1946/48, 49–58 (again closer to Mommsen's severity, for the "mistakes" in the *Liber,* than to Pais's optimism); the new topographic research seems to confirm, in general by the revelation of centuriations that are earlier than those that had long been known in certain sectors, the documentary value of the text (see for example G. Chouquer and F. Favory, "Cadastrations antiques de Campanie, du Latium méridional et de Romagne," in *Cadastres et espace rural,* ed. M. Clavel-Lévêque, 318–21 (Paris, 1983).

34. R. Thomsen, *The Italic Regions from Augustus to the Lombard Invasion* (Copenhagen, 1947), 271.

35. The extremely precise and detailed inventory of all these dossiers and registers, of their "archival" locations and their filing system, will be completed soon by C. Moatti. I do not know, for example, if the *liber beneficiorum* mentioned by Hyginus Grom., p. 203 L is the same as the *liber beneficiorum regionis illius* of M. Iunius Nipsus, p. 295 L: the former is situated—if I understand the text correctly—in the imperial *tabularium,* and the *agrimensores,* who were responsible for leaving the *forma* there, registered in that book the lands that had been given to the colony as *beneficia.* The *liber beneficiorum regionis illius* had to be consulted by an *agrimensor* before showing a "surplus land" (*subsicivum*) on the map, in order to be sure that the emperor had not given it as a *beneficium* to someone else. It is nevertheless possible that these are one and the same document, also classified by *regions* after 7 B.C.

36. Contra, but with caution, Dilke, *Roman Land Surveyors,* 38, but see L. Keppie, *Colonisation,* 10–12; for the Augustan period on the other hand, the geographical work by C. Julius Hyginus, Augustus's librarian, had a topographic character: Servius, 3.553: *de situ urbium Italicarum,* etc. Where did his documentation come from?

37. G. Carettoni, A.-M. Colini, L. Cozza, and G. Gatti, *La Pianta Marmorea di Roma antica,* 2 vols. (Rome, 1960); E. Rodriguez Almeida, *Forma Urbis Marmorea, Aggiornamento generale 1980* (Rome, 1981).

38. F. Castagnoli, "L'orientamento nella cartografia greco e romana," in *Rend. Pont. Accad. Arch.,* 1975–76, 64 (parallel with Tacitus, *Hist.,* 3.82, which is not conclusive, in my opinion, because Tacitus describes the troops' entry by the north); Dilke, *Greek and Roman Maps,* 105.

39. Marisa Conticello de' Spagnolis, *Il Tempio dei Dioscuri nel Circo Flaminio* (Rome, 1984), esp. 30. The numbers are: XCVIII / VI / LIII / I.

40. *CIL,* 6. 919 – *ILS,* 211: [*Ti. Claudius Caes. Aug. / L. Vitellius P. f. / ex*] *s.c. / [ce]nsores, [l]oca a pilis et colum [nis] / quae a privatis / possidebantur causa / cognita ex forma / in publicum restituerunt.*

41. E. Espérandieu, *Inscriptions de la Gaule Romaine* (Paris, 1929), 2: 186; A. Schulten, "Vom antiken Kataster," *Hermes,* 1906, 1; V. Arangio-Ruiz, "Sull. iscrizione superficiaria di Arausio," *Epigraphica* 3 (1941): 98–102; id., *FIRA,* 13, no. 109; A. Piganiol, "Les documents cadastraux," 329–36, whose interpretation must be followed.

42. It is also the word used on the *Tabula Veleia* (3.2: *fundum . . . cum meridibus,* etc.).

43. A. Piganiol, " Les documents cadastraux," 343ff.

44. I resume my demonstration "La table d'Héraclée et les origines du cadastre romain," *L'Urbs: Espace urbain et histoire* (Rome, 1985), 1–25; I give the text and translation by H. Legras, *La Table latine d'Héraclée* (Paris, 1907), 16ff.

45. *Quae viae in urbem Rom(am) propiusve u(rbem) R(omam) p(assus) M ubei continente habitabitur, sunt erunt, quojus ante aedificium earum quae / via erit is eam viam arbitratu ejus aed(ilis), quoi ea pars urbis h(ac) l(ege) obvenerit, tueatur; isque aed(ilis) curato, uti quorum / ante aedificium erit quamque viam h(ac) l(ege) quemque tueri oportebit, ei omnes eam viam arbitratu ejus tueantur, neve eo / loco aqua consistat, quominus commode populus ea via utatur/.*

46. *Quemquomque ante suum aedificium viam publicam h(ac) l(ege) tueri oportebit, quei eorum eam viam arbitratu ejus aed(ilis)/, quojus oportuerit, non tuebitur, eam viam aed(ilis), quojus arbitratu eam tueri oportuerit, tuendam locato; / isque aed(ilis) diebus ne minus x, antequam locet aput forum ante tribunale suom propositum habeto, quam / / viam tuendam et quo die locaturus sit, et quorum ante aedificium ea via sit; eisque, quorum ante aedificium / ea via erit, procuratoribusve eorum domum denuntietur facito, se eam viam locaturum et quo die locaturus / sit; eamque locationem palam in foro per quaes(torem) urb(anum) eumve quei aerario praeerit, facito. Quamta pecunia eam/viam locaverit, tamtae pecuniae eum eosque, quorum ante aedificium ea via erit pro portioni, quamtum / quojusque ante aedificium viae in longitudine et in latitudine erit, q(uaestor) urb(anus) queive aerario praeerit in tabulas / publicas pecuniae factae referundum curato. Ei quei eam viam tuemdam redemerit, tamtae pecuniae eum eos / ve adtribuito sine d(olo) m(alo). Sei is, quei adtributus erit, eam pecuniam diebus XXX proxumeis quibus ipse aut pro/ curator ejus sciet adtributionem factam esse, ei, quoi adtributus erit, non solverit neque satis fecerit, is / quamtae pecuniae adtributus erit, tamtam pecuniam et ejus dimidium ei, quoi adtributus erit, dare debeto, / inque eam rem is, quo quomque de pecunia credita / [judicem] judiciumve dari oporteret /.*

47. I owe this remark to Mrs. Catherine Virlouvet.

48. "The one before whose building one of these public roads is located."

49. While awaiting the new edition of the text that I am preparing for the *Group for the Revision of the Texts of Roman Laws,* I mention only, in an enormous bibliography, the works that concern the *professiones*: E. Muttelsee, *Unters. über die lex Julia municipalis,* Diss. (Freiburg-im-Bresgau, 1911); J. Elmore, "The *Professiones* of the Heraclean Table," *JRS,* 1915, 125–37; J. S. Reid, "The So-called *Lex Julia Municipalis,*" *JRS,* 1915, 207–48; E. Hardy, " The *Professiones* of the Hera-

clean Table," *CQ*, 1917, 27–37; J. Elmore, "Ciceronian and Heraclean *Professiones*," *CQ*, 1918, 38–45.

50. *IG*, 12. 5.872; R. Dareste and B. Haussoulier, *Inscr. Jur. Gr.* (1895), 63–106. I thank Mr. Roland Etienne for allowing me to read the unedited chapter of his unpublished thesis devoted to this inscription. On its problems, see L. Germain, *La publicité des sûretés foncières . . .*, thesis, (Paris, 1968).

51. Cited by Stobaeus, *Floril.*, 44.22 (= 1: 167–68 Meinecke): "Everywhere where the official transcription of transfer deeds concerning properties and contracts, etc." It is a passage (doubtless book 17 or 18) of his *Laws*. It can be read, in the French translation and with comments, in R. Dareste, "Le Traité des Lois de Théophraste" in *Rev. Lég. Anc. et Mod.* (1870), completed in *La science du droit en Grèce* (Paris, 1893), 301–13: "partout où est établie la transcription officielle des actes translatifs des propriétés et des contrats," etc. (Yet, Cicero, *Pro Flac.*, 74, is not to be quoted: it is not a question of registration but judgments that have invalidated purchases).

52. Above, p. 129.

53. O. Montevecchi, *La papirologia* (Turin, 1973), 184–87; Déléage, *Les cadastres . . .* 141–47; A. Piganiol, *Les documents cadastraux . . .* 404–5.

54. *Pap. Oxyr.*, II, 237, col. VIII, 27–43; *FIRA*, 1:324, n. 60; *Les lois des Romains*, 381–85 (with a translation by J. Mélèze).

55. A good example of a declaration with the registration of transfers of mortgages: Mitteis, *Chrestom.*, II, 193 = Grenfell-Hunt, *Pap. Oxyr.*, II, 274 = *FIRA*, III, n. 104.

56. E.g., E. Cuq, *Institutions juridiques des Romains*, 425, n. 8, 688; see finally J. Mélèze in "Papyrologie juridique," *SDHI* 49 (1983), 685–86.

VIII

The "Geographical" Work of Augustus

We must now turn to a subject that is extremely complicated yet essential to our argument: the question of what is sometimes called the "geographical" work of Augustus. This subject has generated an enormous bibliography, and an entire volume would not suffice[1] if we desired to treat it in depth. We might, if need be, simply ask the question, for the mere fact that anyone was entitled to speak of it is, in itself, a sign of the new concern about space and its distribution that appears precisely at the time of Augustus. However, we must examine the question more closely. The problem arises, as usual, from ambiguities and gaps in our sources.

We have already seen above,[2] in relation to Agrippa (p. 99), that several sources link Augustus's name with Agrippa's work, whether referring strictly to the map in the *Porticus Vipsania* or to the texts (*commentarii*?) that were, in one way or another, connected with him. This is what Pliny seems to say when he writes (3.17):[3]

> Agrippa was a very painstaking man, and also a very careful geographer; who therefore could believe that when intending to set before the eyes of Rome a survey of the world he made a mistake, and with him the late-lamented Augustus? for it was Augustus who completed the portico (containing a plan of the world) that had been begun by his sister in accordance with the design and *commentarii* of Marcus Agrippa.

Such a link between a clearly geographical work that, for us, is embodied in a graphic monument (a map, *orbis spectandus*) and a text giving the measurements of regions (Agrippa's "fragments" quoted in Pliny, see above p. 100) is positively attested by only one source, the *Divisio orbis terrarum*:[4] "The world is divided under these three names: Europe, Asia, Libya or Africa. The divine Augustus was the first to show the entire world through a chorography" (see Dicuil, *Liber de mensura*, p. 5 Letronne; E. Schweder, *Beiträge zur Kritik der Chorographie des Augustus*, I:6). What does the word *chorographia* mean in such texts? It has been shown above[5] that, in the language of the classical geographers (Strabo and Ptolemy), χωρογραφία and γεωγραφία are opposed essentially from the point of view of scale: *chorography* is more detailed, it is regional as opposed to general. Both terms have the same ambiguous meaning: they can indicate a drawing–therefore a map—as well as a geographical text. This is the obvious meaning of *chorographia* in the middle of the first century A.D., if *De chorographia libri tres* is the actual title of the work of Pomponius Mela, as attested in the earliest manuscript.[6] But is this the most common meaning in Latin? None of the occurrences of the word reported by the grammarians (Priscian[7] or Servius[8]) in literary contexts is really convincing, except perhaps for the *Chorographia* of Varro Atacinus. On the other hand, we have seen that, in the common language, especially in epigraphy, it clearly indicates a map: a praetorian is called *chorographiar(um) caelatori,* an engraver of maps.[9] And in Vitruvius (8.2.6),[10] the word concerns the "painted" and "described" sources of rivers on or through chorographies, which seems again to indicate maps. Therefore, it seems that this meaning has to be given to the word in the passage of *Divisio orbis terrarum* under discussion. Moreover, the use of the preposition *per* encourages us to do so: Augustus showed (*ostendit,* in the literal sense of the word) the division of the world "by means" (*per*) of a map:[11] this word would not be used in Latin to refer to a text. It seems clear to me that Augustus's chorography is none other than the map in Agrippa's *porticus,* which was in fact completed by the emperor as Pliny assures us. It is not in any way a written geographical work.

Of course, this does not mean that there were not texts or documents under the name of Augustus that were akin to it, yet different. But the evidence is indirect and difficult to interpret, because it relies essentially on Pliny's geographical books—confirmed by several less coherent references in Strabo. Apparently, they suggest a geographical work (a description or an inventory of the inhabited world) in a literary form, that is written. Augustus appears explicitly as one of the "authorities," one of the *auctores* consulted and used.[12] In this context the use of the word *auctor* seems clear: apparently it is always used of authors in the modern sense of the word, that is, individuals who have left written works.

This is what Pliny seems to be saying in the key passage of Book 3, which is worth citing before any discussion can ensue. Having dealt in Book 2 with the world and the elements (and having ended with the "measurement of the entire world," *terrae universae mensura*), in Book 3 Pliny goes on to what he calls the "sites, nations, seas, towns, ports, mountains, rivers, distances, past and present peoples" (*situs, gentes, maria, oppida, portus, montes, flumina, mensurae, populi qui sunt aut fuerunt*)—the plan, in fact, of Books 3 to 6. This subject matter is strictly geographical. Book 3 follows the division of the *oikoumene* (*orbis terrarum*) in three parts, Europe, Asia, and Africa. He begins with the West (the Spains, 3.5.6–30; Narbonensis, 3.5.31–7). He then takes up Italy; paragraphs 38–45 contain a first, general inventory of its peoples followed by a famous *elogium* of the whole of Italy, then generalities about its shape and dimensions. Finally, Pliny begins a detailed description that he announces as follows:

> We will now give an account of a circuit of Italy, and of its cities. Herein it is necessary to premise that we intend to follow as "author" the deified Augustus, and the division that he made of the whole of Italy into eleven regions, but to take them in the order that will be suggested by the coastline; it being indeed impossible, at all events in a very cursory account, to keep the neighboring cities together; and so in going on to deal with the inland districts we shall follow the emperor's alphabetical list, adopting the enumeration of the colonies that he set out in that list.[13]

We see that Augustus (now deceased) is cited as an authority (i.e., an author) from whom Pliny states that he will draw his inspiration. He says that he will do this by following "a" or "the" division of all of Italy (*discriptio Italiae totius*), which Augustus accomplished by dividing it into eleven regions. Pliny's terminology in these lines should be considered carefully. But Pliny adds three important comments: 1) in listing the cities, he will follow "the order that the coastline suggests"; 2) he will not be able to keep the neighboring cities strictly together; 3) in dealing with the inland cities, he will use "the alphabetical order followed by Augustus" (*digestio in litteras*), following "the mention of colonies which the latter introduced within the list of cities."

Before examining in detail what these expressions imply for the lists of towns or peoples attributed to Augustus—problems that we shall encounter again for regions other than Italy—we must observe that there is another source that surfaces implicitly from Pliny's statement: the source that would follow the order of the coastline (*sed ordine eo, qui litorum tractu fiet*). This way of describing the coasts is found again in the whole of Pliny's geographical works. This has been well observed for Africa in Book 5, and likewise in the entire work of Pomponius Mela; this is a clear indication of the importance of the *periplus* genre in ancient geographical literature.[14] It has been possible to prove that Mela and Pliny depend, for the major portion of their coastal descriptions, on a common source datable to 44–29 B.C., and which might very well be Varro.[15] But a *periplus* by definition does not deal with inland territory (*interiore parte*). Pliny thus warns his reader (at least for Italy) that he will use lists of towns that he attributes to Augustus: *digestio in litteras* (with specific reference to colonies; we shall return to this).

But in what manner? Pliny has mentioned *Augustum . . . discriptionemque ab eo factam Italiae totius in regiones XI*. But his phrase is doubly ambiguous. On the one hand, there is the *-que*: Pliny does not say "Augustus's *discriptio*," but rather "Augustus and his *discriptio*." On the other hand, the basic meaning in Latin of *discriptio* is the act or decision of dividing into smaller units; it is an abstract term, a word from an administrative vocabulary.[16] This is how the division of citizens into tribes and centuries is described (Cicero, *De rep.*, 2.39: *Tusc.*, 4.1), or Clodius's division of slaves into *decurias* (*De domo,* 129), or simply the division of troops between legions and auxiliaries (Suetonius, *Tib.*, 30). It is thus certain that Augustus created new divisions of Italy, namely, the eleven regions. But has this division ever taken the form of a coherent text?

To answer this question, it is necessary to know what needs were met by this novelty, this creation of regions. Pliny is practically the only ancient writer who refers to this. As we shall see in the following summary (by E. Malcovati), Pliny mentions in Book 3 each of the eleven regions. Just as he stated, he follows the order of the coastlines: he begins with Liguria, roughly following the western coast, and then returns along the eastern coast of Italy—the only exception being the eleventh region, which did not border the sea[17]:

> 3.49: Under the partition of Augustus [the coast of Liguria] this is the ninth region.
> 3.50: The adjoining region is the seventh, in which is Etruria.
> 3.62: . . . The distance by sea from Cerceii is 78 miles. This region, beginning from the Tiber, under the partition made by Augustus is regarded as the first region of Italy.
> 3.97: [The town of Metapontum,] at which the third region of Italy ends.
> 3.99: Adjoining the region is the second region of Italy, embracing the Hirpini, Calabria, Apulia, and the Salentini.
> 3.106: There follows the fourth region, which includes the very bravest races in Italy [the Frentani, the Marrucini, the Peligni, the Marsi, etc.].
> 3.110: The fifth region is that of Picenum, which formerly was very densely populated.

> 3.112: Adjoining to this will come the sixth region, embracing Umbria and the Gallic territory this side of Ariminum.
> 3.115: The boundaries of the eighth region are marked by Ariminum, the Po, and the Apennines.
> 3.123: The eleventh region receives from the river the name of Transpadana; it is situated entirely inland, but the river carries to it on its bounteous channel the products of all the seas.
> 3.126: Next comes the tenth region of Italy, on the coast of the Adriatic Sea. . . .

We see that these regions, besides their numbers (which no doubt go back to their creation), generally have traditional ethnic names (Etruria, Piceni, Umbria); often they include several "regions" or ethnic groups; only one has a geographical name (the *Transpadana* region). Indeed, when we examine in detail Pliny's description of each of these regions, we can—not without difficulty—fix their precise boundaries, either by using geographical landmarks (such as rivers), or by partitioning the territories that must be allocated to specific cities. It is remarkable that their names come mostly from old Italian peoples; this is quite clear for southern and central Italy.[18] The only exception is found in northern Italy, where neologisms occur, like Aemilia (for the eighth region: see Martial, 3.4.1; 6.85.5), or Transpadana.[19] These are new groupings that reassemble men and peoples. To what does this taxonomy correspond?

First let us note that this classification breaks away from the tribe list, the only administrative division that was in use—at least up to the years following the Social War. Until Caesar's time, Italian communities were divided exclusively according to tribes. We know that this division had no geographical continuity: cities belonging to a particular tribe could be separated by great distances. It seems certain that one of Augustus's aims in the creation of the regions was to substitute for these lists of tribes (which corresponded to a classification in the public registers), without abolishing them, another system based on geographic proximity and on the coherence of the population. If we follow Pliny, we see that these ethnic groups, these "peoples," justify the new regions by their juxtaposition. The only exception is that of the Samnites, who were divided between the first, second, and fourth regions.[20] It has long been observed[21] that the description of Italy had also been given in this manner—a simple catalog of peoples—by two quite different geographers, Strabo and Ptolemy.

Although Ptolemy adds the astronomical coordinates of cities or of remarkable points that he cites, he divides them into ethnic regions—which fit easily into the Augustan *tableau*. Neither he nor Strabo names the regions. It has sometimes been hastily concluded that Strabo did not know about or rather did not use the *discriptio* by regions, because it had been introduced late in the reign of Augustus, in A.D. 6.[22] Strabo's documentation, as we know, contains unquestionable gaps for the period between 2 B.C. and A.D. 14. In fact, his ethnic order seems to be based above all on the Greek geographical sources that he uses, Artemidorus and Posidonius. This coincidence with the basic ethnic grouping of Augustan regions is interesting in itself: it shows that geographical inspiration (with its ethnographic traditions) was not foreign to him. Nevertheless, let us not make too much of these comparisons; the regions often followed topographical landmarks. These are divisions of the land. We shall return to this.

But if we cannot for the moment consider the *discriptio Italiae* as a text, and even less as a work by Augustus, the fact remains that Pliny categorically cites him as a source. The text is clear: Augustus is the author of a list, or rather of a series of *alphabetical* lists of cities, among which are mentioned "the" or "some" colonies. We are dealing with documents signed by, or attributed to, Augustus himself. And in fact, as has been seen for a long time—Pliny's text often provides such lists in accordance with his program, e.g., for Etruria (3.52) or Campania (3.63).

Many details in these lists are problematic and have been the subject of discussions and corrections, such as Pliny's frequent practice of referring to the cities by their ethnic groups. This must have been the original form of the document, but as a correction he has sometimes introduced the name of the city.[23] Moreover, Pliny made some errors: he cites certain cities twice and he sometimes adds information or names definitely later than the time of Augustus.

Thus, it is clear that Pliny (or his sources) has incorporated information from later documents in an Augustan document. The fact remains, nonetheless, that Augustus is cited as *auctor* in Book 3. He is mentioned twice in the text (3.49; 62) as well as in the famous *index* of sources in Book 1 (*ex auctoribus . . . M. Agrippa, M. Varrone, divo Augusto*). Augustus is also identified as the source in the *index* of Book 4, which covers Greece, the Balkans, and northern and western Europe (Belgico, Lugdunensis, Aquitania, Hispania Citerior, and Lusitania). But here the name of Augustus does not appear in the text nor do the frequent alphabetical lists (but see 4.118 for the alphabetical list of tributary cities of Lusitania).

On the other hand, in the sections of Book 3 that deal not with Italy but with Baetica, Tarraconensis, and Narbonensis, it has been observed[24] that lists of cities appear frequently; these are alphabetized within legal categories, such as colonies, cities with Latin rights, tributary cities, and so on.

The same situation applies for Illyricum, Africa, and Sicily. All these lists have been gathered and criticized by the successive efforts of D. Detlefsen, O. Cuntz, A. Klotz, and others. Cuntz has systematically extended his inquiry to include the eastern regions—Syria, Egypt, and the provinces of Asia Minor and Mauretania. For most of these series, he has been able to show that these lists could be dated between 31 B.C. and the end of Augustus's reign. There are a few rare exceptions that can be shown to be an update by Pliny, in line with recent legal or administrative changes. Several of these series for the East could not be later than 20 B.C. (Cuntz, *NJPhP,* Sup. 17 [1890] 523).

We can conclude that for almost all the provinces of the empire, with the notable exception of Egypt and a few districts, there was a series of statistical lists *(digestiones)* of communities, classified according to their status, and within each status listed in alphabetical order; almost certainly they had general summary figures, as they appear in Pliny. And we can conclude that such lists, which could have been (and almost certainly were) completed or corrected as changes occurred, date from the reign of Augustus. In one way or another, they carry his name; this is why Pliny can cite Augustus as *auctor.*

We can only speculate about their titles and the manner in which they were drawn up. But it seems probable that these alphabetical lists (ending with a summary account) could only be a résumé excerpted from much longer documents. Let us consider the following example: we see that Pliny mentions separately the colonies that Augustus had specifically cited in his Italian lists. There are fifty in all;[25] this number greatly exceeds the number of colonies actually founded by Augustus and in which he takes great pride (*RG,* 28.2; cf. Suetonius, *Aug.,* 46). But Pliny found information on this subject in his geographical and historical sources (Cato and Varro, for example), especially for the oldest colonies. Did the colonies appear separately in Augustus's lists or in those lists attributed to him? This is not specifically stated in Pliny's text: there is only a special reference to the colonies among the total number of cities. We shall see later the probable reasons for this. Nevertheless, this leads us to distinguish clearly between these implicit lists of colonies (a simple title or a marginal reference) and the works or documents of which we have spoken above (p. 158), concerning cadastres: the *libri coloniarum* or the *libri regionum* found in the gromatic texts. The latter gave the lists of colonies, classified by regions (for example, p. 229 L for the *regio* of Campania, region I), and in the interior by alphabetical order. But they also contained succinct facts of a cadastral nature, which do not seem to have appeared in Pliny's Augustan lists. The gromatic *libri coloniarum* are of course late. But I have stated above that a first collection from the Augustan period (the one by Balbus *mensor*) should not necessarily be exlcuded. It must nevertheless be distinguished from the Augustan lists.

Finally, which were the documents and texts explicitly attributed to Augustus that are cited and used by Pliny (likewise Strabo, 4.1.1)? We must resist the temptation to give them the title *Discriptio totius Italiae in regiones XI,* because the primary meaning of the word *discriptio* is abstract rather than concrete (although an exception to the rule is always possible). Pliny in fact uses the words *digestio in litteras.* The phrase is found frequently in his work (1.6.39; 1.9.14; 1.9.36; 1.10.13; 1.17.80; 18.216) and is clearly from the scientific field: it is a "classification" (likewise for example in Rufius Festus, 12.1). While the form of this word ending in *-tio* is rare in classical Latin (only Pliny and Velleius use it), and while *digestus* and *digestum* do not appear in their well-known meanings in the jurists' vocabulary until the second century (Aulus Gellius, 7.5.1), the verb *digerere* is already used in this sense by Cicero *(De inv.,* 1.49). I wonder if this was not indeed the title, or subtitle, of the Augustan lists. In any case, the words "list" or "classification" define closely enough the nature of these texts and documents. We shall discuss below their connections with public archives and documents. But their existence seems to be established. It is not impossible that a *princeps* who had given a *novus status* to the State, who had written historical memoirs and even philosophical works (Suetonius, *Aug.,* 85.1; Malcovati, p. xli), had also written such a digest himself or had ordered one to be written[26].

At any rate, the emperor definitely left behind another document that is of great interest to us without being specifically geographical, and which had important consequences later: the *Breviarium totius imperii.*

Augustus had prepared this work before his death, and had sealed and deposited it with the Vestal Virgins along with other documents,[27] with instructions for his successor to have them opened and read before the Senate. First of all, there was his will, contained in two *codices* written in part by himself and in part by his freedmen Polybius and Hilarion. Then there were three sealed *volumina:*

> In the first he had written the instructions for his funeral; in the second was the list of works which he had completed and which he ordered to be engraved on bronze tablets to be set up in front of the Mausoleum; in the third was a description of the "state of the empire," noting how many soldiers there were under each standard, and their

> placement, how much money was in the Treasury and in the different coffers, and what was owed to the public Treasury. He also added the names of his freedmen and slaves from whom debts could be reclaimed. (Suetonius, *Aug.*, 101)[28]

These are Suetonius's words: their accuracy is guaranteed by similar terms used by Tacitus and Dio. Tacitus (*Ann.*, 1.11.7) calls the document a *libellum* and says that "it contained the public resources, the number of citizens and allies under arms, the fleets, the kingdoms, the provinces, the amount of tribute or income, the necessary expenses and benefactions. Augustus had written all of these details in full and in his own hand." Finally, Dio writes that "the third (book) contained the condition of the military forces, the public income and expenses, the amount of money in the accounts, and, in a general way, everything which concerned the governing of the empire (ἐς τὴν ἡγεμονίαν) (56.33.2).

As we see, the three texts complement each other without being contradictory. They allow us to get a precise idea of the contents of the document, provided that we pay sufficiently close attention to the terms used by the historians. The first detail to be examined is the condition of the military forces: Augustus recorded the total strength of the military but he also distinguished among the legions, the auxiliaries, and the fleet; he indicated their stations, certainly in the provinces. The latter were listed, as well as the *regna* and the vassal or allied kingdoms (Tacitus). Next, the financial situation was recorded. Suetonius mentions the money stored in the Treasury and in the various *fisci* (and Dio confirms it by writing "the amount of money in the treasuries"—τό τε πλῆθος τῶν ἐν τοῖς θεσαυροῖς χρημάτων), but includes the *residuae pecuniae,* that is (as Forcellini realized, p. 935), not "what remained of the public revenues" but what was owed to the State, the unpaid money or arrears. This, of course, had to be credited to the Treasury.[29] Tacitus specifies the nature of the Treasury revenues: *tributa aut vectigalia;* that is, generally speaking, direct taxation on the one hand and indirect taxation or rents on the other. Note further his use of these words at *Ann.*, 13.50, but he also adds the expenses: *necessitates,* financial terminology used since Livy's time at least (23.48.10), the "regular expenses" of the Treasury, and *largitiones,* the benefactions—no doubt these are of a repetitive and provisional character.

In short, these are the *opes publicae:* all the resources of the empire (*imperii,* ἐς τὴν ἡγεμονίαν), in men, in arms, and in money. It was, therefore, a document of an administrative and accounting nature. But it also seemingly possessed a demographic and statistical aspect. It is highly unlikely that the number of citizens known from the latest censuses were not mentioned in it. The *provinciae* and the *regna* were at least listed but probably with information about their inhabitants, and perhaps also their resources, doubtless not under the form of the exhaustive and detailed lists of cities that are found in Pliny but perhaps under the shorter form of recapitulations of numbers. It is almost certain that the financial data were summarized for each province, providing the total figure that each contributed (see below). Thus, this document included figures. A detail that has not been sufficiently studied proves it; Tacitus writes *quae perscripserat sua manu. Perscribere* does not only mean "to write completely from one end to the other," to transcribe: when dealing with numbers it can also mean "to write out in words," so that there is no possibility of error.[30] The figures given were, therefore, not rough estimates.

When we try to imagine all the details involved, such a document must have been particularly impressive. The solemn reading of it at the first meeting of the Senate after the death of the *princeps* was certainly calculated to produce a profound effect on the public. At the same session, the text of the *Res Gestae,* destined to be preserved for posterity, was read—a text whose cosmocratic significance we have seen, and which illustrated for the Romans the figured representation of the *orbis terrarum* completed (at least fifteen years before) in the *Porticus Vipsania.* The *Breviarium,* by another enumeration of provinces and subject-states, of military forces, and of income and expenses (this one, a financial enumeration), completed and clarified the inventory of conquered space that the *Res Gestae* recalled, by an inventory of their strength and wealth. Several days later, the emperor's funeral, with its quasi-triumphal pomp, would once again parade before the eyes of the Romans the allegories of the conquered peoples (τά τε ἔθνη πάνθ' ὅσα προσεκτήσατο, Dio, 56.34.3).

To our knowledge, such a document had no exact precedent. Yet, it has sometimes been compared to two earlier measures. In 35 B.C., after his victory over Sextus Pompey, Octavian "gave a public accounting" of his actions, then proclaimed an abolishment of taxation with cancellation of debts owed to the Treasury (Appian, *BC,* 5.540; Dio 49.15.3). This "rendering of accounts," initially verbal, was certainly written down afterwards. But it does not have much to do with the *Breviarium;* it is more closely related to an anticipated form of the *Res Gestae.* The exemption from taxes definitely implies bookkeeping: but the Roman Republic had had that for a long time. More interesting perhaps is its comparison with the episode of 23 B.C.: this time the *princeps* (still consul at this time), believing himself on the point of death, handed over to his colleague in the consulship, Calpurnius Piso, "a booklet that contained the military forces and the state resources" (*τάς τε δυνάμεις καὶ τὰς προσόδους τὰς κοινὰς ἐς βιβλίον ἐσγράψας ἔδωκε*, 53.30.2). This apparently was a less-detailed outline of the document of A.D. 13.

Was this something new? Cicero, as already noted above (p. 124) wished in 50 B.C. that senators *nosse rem publicam (De leg.*, 3.41). He added, "this goes a long way: to know the strength of the armies, the state of the Treasury, the allies, friends, and tributaries which the State possesses, each in relation to its own law, condition or treaty." At the same time the inventory of desirable knowledge seems to discourage him and he leaves it only to the *scientia, diligentia,* and *memoria* of each senator. If a global document that was regularly updated had existed, Cicero would certainly have said so; the senators would have had only to refer to it. Surely this was not the case. Modern knowledge about the nature of the administration of the Republican period compels us to accept the notion that all this information was dispersed and not always recorded and preserved. In this sense, Augustus's "summary," destined solemnly to be published after his death, was an innovation linked intrinsically to the change of regime.

Because this text was made public in A.D. 14, scholars have searched for traces of it in our historical and geographical tradition. L. Friedländer, in 1873, was the first to make a useful comparison with the well-known passage in Flavius Josephus (*BJ,* 2.16.345–401) in which King Agrippa II persuades the Jews not to go to war against Rome.[31] Josephus takes advantage of this occasion to sketch out a vast and significant picture of Roman power, which gathers many themes we have already encountered: the succession of empires, Rome's universal domination extended to the symbolic limits of the *orbis terrarum* (*BJ,* 2.16.343), the list of barbarian peoples who obey Rome, the number of cities in Asia or Gaul, and the size of certain provinces (in walking days, admittedly). But he also gives a precise enumeration of the military forces: the number of legions in some provinces (eighteen mentioned in all), the number of men in others (3,000 in the Chersonese; 2,000 in Thrace, and 1,200 in Gaul, which is especially accurate); the mention of the *classis Pontica* consisting of forty ships; demographic information about the population of Egypt "which extends to Ethiopia and Arabia Felix"[32] and which totalled—not including Alexandria—7,500,000 inhabitants; and finally, fiscal information on the *annona* and grain supply from Egypt to Rome.

In short, this is a choice passage that recalls geopolitical information and data that we have encountered in the *Res Gestae* and geographical sources (Agrippa, the *Divisio*, and the *Dimensuratio),* but it also includes military, strategic, and financial data reminiscent of the *Breviarium*. It has long been noted that Josephus carefully updated this passage to A.D. 66—for example, he mentions the conquest of Britain. But, whatever the intermediary source, it is too reminiscent of some Augustan models not to derive from them. I do say *some* models: the *Res Gestae* and geographical and chorographic texts. Thus, it is impossible to state that this passage derives solely from the *Breviarium*, or, in other words, that the *Breviarium* had also summarized information of this type. It is possible, I must admit. There might even be an indication to support this interpretation.

Dio, as we have seen, reports that Augustus had entrusted to Tiberius not three *volumina*, as Suetonius states, but four: the fourth would have contained some *mandata* (ἐντολὰς καὶ ἐπισκήψεις) concerning the policy that he recommended be followed; among other things, it would have held the famous "recommendation to maintain the empire within the existing limits" (Dio, 56.33.5; Tacitus, *Ann.*, 1.11.4; *Agric.*, 13.2).[33] The authenticity of this document has been recently questioned, and Tiberius has been suspected of giving the impression that he possessed a text when actually he only received verbal confidences. Wrongly so, in my opinion, because Tacitus explicitly states that Augustus had added the *consilium* to the *Breviarium*. This is not incompatible with what we know about Augustus's foreign policy. Unquestionably aggressive until A.D. 9 at least, it had no doubt become more cautious, at least on a temporary basis, after the German disaster. But if this *consilium*, these *mandata*, mentioned the *terminos imperii*, it must have been necessary that the document that they completed had carefully defined them beforehand. It is quite possible that the *Breviarium* had consisted of elements borrowed from Agrippa's documents or Augustus's own lists.

But we can add other authors who, like Josephus, perhaps drew from the *Breviarium* directly or indirectly. I shall mention them quickly because a study of them and their sources would require a detailed inquiry. First, there are Strabo and Velleius, contemporaries of Augustus. From the former we can obtain military information (the three legions of Spain) or financial information (the income from customs stations in Britain, 2.5.8, 116 C) that comes from official documents. From the latter, we get precise financial information on the produce of Gaul and Egypt (2.39), which must certainly be compared to Josephus (2.16.384)—without mentioning the famous chronological list of the foundations of colonies (1.14). We can also look for parallels in later sources. The well-known battle order of the legions in Dio (55.23–24), one of the bases of our knowledge, includes a first "Augustan" state that bears traces of reorganization after Varus's disaster, and could derive from the *Breviarium* of A.D. 13.

But the most striking comparison of all is found in Appian. In his *Preface,* having given an outline of his work, he announces a projected book (which would be the twenty-fifth) that in his mind would conclude his *Roman History,* and whose content he thus summarizes: "The last book will show the present military force of the Romans, the revenues they collect from each province, what they spend for the naval service, and other things of that kind" (*Praef.,* 15).[34]

The almost exact coincidence with what we know of Augustus's *Breviarium* is striking: the armies, the fleets, the revenue of each province, and everything of this sort. In short, it is truly a "state of the empire," naturally updated to coincide with the composition of the work (between A.D. 150 and A.D. 165), or at least to the date of the last events mentioned under the reigns of Trajan or Hadrian. Was this book ever written? If so, it has not survived. A remarkable general plan is evident in the work of Appian, in which he recounted the wars of the Romans in ethnographic order (i.e., both geographical and partially chronological), then digressed in five books (13–17) to the civil wars so nearly ruinous to state and empire, and finally recaptured the thread of the conquests, in *Egyptiaca, Dacica,* and *Arabica.* In light of this, we cannot but be struck by the coincidence of this plan with the Augustan texts beginning with the *Res Gestae:* this work also unfolds in a rhythm in three movements designed to give an account of Rome's cosmocratic destiny. In planning to conclude his work with a "*breviarium* of the empire," Appian only follows the example set by the founder of the empire.

NOTES

1. See the summray in M. Schanz and C. Hosius, *Geschichte Röm. Literatur,* (Munich, 1935), 2:13–14, but also 331–35, where only are mentioned the works by Schweder; H. Malcovati, *Imp. Caes. Aug. Fragmenta*[4] (Turin, 1962), XLI–XLVI, and 81–83 (where the full dossier is compiled); V. Gardthausen, *Augustus und seine Zeit* (Leipzig, 1896), vol. 1, 2, 941ff.; vol. 2, 2, 548ff.; D. Kienast, "Augustus und Alexander," *Gymnasium,* 1969, 392 (concerning colonies); R. Thomsen, *The Italic Regions from Augustus to the Lombard Invasion* (Copenhagen, 1947), passim; K. G. Sallmann, *Die Geographie des älteren Plinius in ihrem Verhältnis zu Varro* (Berlin, 1971), 95–106; 125, 143.

2. See above, chap. 5, nn. 38ff.

3. Pliny, *NH,* 3.17: *Agrippam quidem in tanta viri diligentia praeterque in hoc opere cura, cum orbem terrarum Urbi spectandum propositurus esset, errasse quis credat et cum eo divum Augustum? Is namque conplexam eum porticum ex destinatione et commentariis M. Agrippae a sorore eius inchoatam peregit.*

4. *Divisio orbis terrarum,* 15 R: *Orbis dividitur tribus nominibus: Europa, Asia, Libya vel Africa. Quem divus Augustus primus omnium per chorographiam ostendit.*

5. Chap. 5, nn. 23 and 24.

6. V = *Vat. Lat.,* 4929 (ninth century); see P. Parroni, ed., *Pomponii Melae de Chorographie,* (Rome, 1984), 22ff. and 55–81.

7. Priscian, 2.267 (Keil), cites a passage from Cicero that is not geographical (Orelli, *Ciceronis Opera,* 4.994): some had suggested the reading *cosmographia* or *orthographia;* 2.100, on the other hand, he cites three verses: *ergo inter solis stationem et sidera septem,* etc., attributed by a manuscript to a *chorographia* by the poet Varro Atacinus; see H. Bardon, *La littérature latine inconnue* (Paris, 1952–56), 1:368; Schanz-Hosius, *Geschichte Röm. Literatur* (Munich, 1927), 1:313.

8. Servius, 3.104; 6.532; 7.363, always mentions the *chorographi* in geographical contexts (for example: *apud chorographos legimus . . . ; secundum chorographos et geometras qui dicunt terram σφαιροειδῆ esse . . . ; hunc locum umbilicum chorographi dicunt*). Certainly in Servius's time the word could have a literary meaning; yet, here again, the manuscript is uncertain, giving *cosmographi* or *historiographi.*

9. *AE* (1947) 61 = Bruna Forlati Tamaso, *Epigraphica* 7 (1945): 35–38 (I amend the commonly accepted reading, *chorographiar(io) / [ite] m*); see *IGR,* 1.1365; *CIL,* 8.12914.

10. Vitruvius, 8.2.6: *capita fluminum, quae orbe terrarum chorographiis picta itemque scripta . . . inveniuntur* (see above, chap. 5).

11. Priscian, for example, writes: *Varro in chorographia.*

12. For the *indices* of Book 1, see M. Rabenhorst in *Philol.* 4 (1906): 567–603; A. Klotz in *Hermes,* 42 (1907): 323–29; *Divus Augustus* is cited by Pliny among the *auctores* only in Books 3 and 4. But some of his citations appear (without any reference in the *index*), for example in Book 2.93 (= Malcovati, 86), for the *de vita sua.*

13. Pliny, *NH,* 3.5.46: *Nunc ambitum eius* [Italiae] *urbesque enumerabimus, qua in re praefari necessarium est auctorem nos divum Augustum secuturos discriptionemque ab eo factam Italiae totius in regiones XI, sed ordine eo, qui litorum tractu fiet; urbium quidem vicinitates oratione utique praepropera servari non posse, itaque interiore exin parte digestionem in litteras eiusdem nos secuturos, coloniarum mentione signata, quas ille in eo prodidit numero.*

14. J. Desanges, ed. of *Pline l'Ancien, N.H., V,* (Paris, 1980), 14–15.

15. Rather than the L. Vetus accepted by A. Klotz, "*Quaestiones Plinianae geographicae,*" *QFGG,* 1906, 88.

16. It is true that *discribere (discriptio)* means etymologically "to distribute while writing": see for example *lex repet., CIL* 1^2.583, l. 14: *eos . . . in tabula scriptos . . . tributimque descriptos*; in Vitruvius, 8.2.8: *omnia flumina in orbis terrarum discriptionibus* seems to refer to the chorographies (= maps) recalled above.

17. Malcovati, *Aug. Fragm.*, 82; Pliny, *NH,* 3.49 (*de ora Ligurtica*). *Haec regio ex descriptione Augusti nona est.* 50. *adnectitur septima, in qua Etruria est.* 62ff. *navigatio a Circeis duodeoctoginta milia passuum patet. regio ea a Tiberi prima Italiae servatur, ex descriptione Augusti.* 97. *oppidum Metapontum, quo tertia Italiae regio finitur.* 99. *connectitur secunda regio amplexa Hirpinos Calabriam Apuliam Salentinos.* 106. *sequitur regio quarta, gentium vel fortissimarum Italiae* [Frentanorum, Marrucinorum, Pelignorum, Marsorum, etc.]. 110. *quinta regio Piceni est, quondam uberrimae multitudinis.* 112. *sexta regio Umbriam complexa agrumque Gallicum citra Ariminum. 115. octava regio determinatur Arimino Pado Appennino.* 123. *Transpadana appellatur ab eo regio undecima, tota in mediterraneo, cui marina cuncta fructuoso alveo importat.* 126. *sequitur decima regio Italiae Hadriatico mari adposita.*

18. Marquardt, *Organisation de l'Empire Romain* (Paris, 1889), 13–15.

19. Marquardt, *Organ. Empire,* 10 nn. 3 and 4.

20. H. Nissen, *Italische Landeskunde* (1883–92), 2.775.

21. Mommsen, "Die italischen Regionem," in *Kiepert Festschriften* (Berlin, 1898), 95–109 = *GS,* 5:268–85. For books 5 and 6 of Strabo and their sources, see F. Lasserre, CUF (1967), 10ff. (Polybius, Artemidorus, and Posidonius); for the question of the *chorographer,* 21ff. (Lasserre believes that it is the map in the *porticus* and the text, whatever it might be, that accompanied it). I stress the importance of passage 5.3.9 where it is a question of "demarcating," of "distinguishing" the towns of Latium: some, due to the roads, others to the γνωρίσμασι. Can not the word γνώρισμα —a token of recognition—indicate a mark on a map? This remains to be examined. In any case, Strabo never mentions the Augustan regions. As for Ptolemy, in Book 3, we must note two things: he too ignores the regions and follows a division of ethnic type. On the other hand, he gives his coordinates of remarkable locations in two distinct series, first along the coasts, then (but elsewhere in the text) in the "mésogée" (for example, for Etruria, 3.4 and 43); see R. Thomsen, *The Italic Regions,* 47ff. who shows the origin of some of Ptolemy's errors (the map that serves as his model); Ptolemy can also erroneously attribute a particular town to a particular ethnic group. See the recent work by O. and M. Dilke, "Italy in Ptolemy's Manual of Geography," in *Imago et mensura mundi,* Atti del IX congr. intern. di storia della cartografia (Rome, 1987), 353–60.

22. R. Thomsen, *The Italic Regions,* 149–50.

23. For example, 3.52: *Clusini veteres, Florentini . . . Faesulae, Ferentinum . . . Perusia, Suanenses.*

24. O. Cuntz, *De Augusto Plinii geographicorum auctore* (Bonn, 1888), 7, 9, 13; *id.,* "Agrippa und Augustus als Schriftsteller des Plinius," *N.J. Phil. Päd.,* supp. 17 (1890): 475–526, for the east; D. Detlefsen, "Die Beschreibung Italiens in der Nat. Hist. des Plinius," *QFGG* (Berlin, 1901), 1–62; A. Klotz, "Quaestiones Plinianae geographicae," *QFGG* (Berlin, 1906), 1–227.

25. Mommsen, "Die italischen Bürgercolonien von Sulla bis Vespasian," *Hermes,* 1883, 161–213 = *GS,* 5:203–53, esp. 231–33.

26. We see that the reconstitution of the *discriptio regionum* proposed by E.

Schweder (*Beiträge zur Kritik der Chorographia des Augustus,* [Kiel, 1878] 2:25ff.) must be abandoned (as almost everyone has done; and naturally K. Petersen, "Die Kosmographie des Kaisers Augustus und die Commentarien des Agrippa," *Rh. Mus.* 8 [1853]: 161–210, 377–403; 9 [1854]: 82–106, 422–42). On the endless controversy concerning the *chorographia,* the variations of Mommsen and of Schweder, see C. Pallu de Lessert, "L'oeuvre géographique d'Agrippa et d'Auguste," *Mém. Soc. Nat. Ant. Fr.,* 1909, 213–98 who, for his part, denies the existence of any *written* work by Agrippa or Augustus (or in their name), and accepts the existence of the *formulae provinciarum,* not the original but a revised composition that would have been made after 27 (see 286ff.). For interesting errors concerning the date of his sources, see Pliny, *NH* 3.130 and 3.139, where the same towns are first given in the tenth region, then in *Liburnia,* first in ethnic form, then by their name. For Pallu de Lessert (p. 293), this proves that Pliny had two lists, one before, the other after 9 B.C. (because of the problem of variations of the northeastern frontier of Italy, see 3.127. On this question, see A. Degrassi, "Il confine nordorientale dell'Italia Romana," *Diss. Bernenses* 1, no. 6 [1954]: 47–60, 84ff.).

27. See J. Ober, "Tiberius and the Political Testament of Augustus," *Historia,* 1982, 306–28; H. Schmitt, "Tacitus und die Nachgelassenen Schriften des Augustus," *Historia Einzelschr.,* 40 (*Festschr. Bengtson*) (1983): 178–86.

28. Malcovati, *Imperatoris Caesaris Augusti Fragmenta,* (Turin, 1976) 98–103. Suetonius, *Aug.,* 101.4: *Tribus voluminibus, uno mandata de funere suo complexus est, altero indicem rerum a se gestarum, quem vellet incidi in aeneis tabulis, quae ante Mausoleum statuerentur, tertio breviarium totius imperii, quantum militum sub signis ubique esset, quantum pecuniae in aerario et fiscis et vectigaliorum residuis. Adiecit et libertorum servorumque nomina, a quibus ratio exigi posset.* Tacitus, *Ann.,* 1.11: . . . *cum proferri libellum recitarique iussit. Opes publicae continebantur, quantum civium sociorumque in armis, quot classes, regna, provinciae, tributa aut vectigalia, et necessitates ac largitiones. Quae cuncta sua manu perscripserat Augustus addideratque consilium coercendi intra terminos imperii, incertum metu an per invidiam.* Dio, 56.33.2: Τοσαῦτα μὲν αἱ διαθῆκαι ἐδήλουν, ἐσεκομίσθη δὲ καὶ βιβλία τέσσαρα. καὶ αὐτὰ ὁ Δροῦσος ἀνέγνω. ἐγέγραπτο δὲ ἐν μὲν τῷ πρώτῳ ὅσα τῆς ταφῆς εἴχετο, ἐν δὲ τῷ δευτέρῳ τὰ ἔργα ἃ ἔπραξε πάντα, ἃ καὶ ἐς χαλκᾶς στήλας πρὸς τῷ ἡρῴῳ αὐτοῦ σταθείσας ἀναγραφῆναι ἐκέλευσε· τὸ τρίτον τά τε τῶν στρατιωτῶν καὶ τὰ τῶν προσόδων τῶν τε ἀναλωμάτων τῶν δημοσίων, τό τε πλῆθος τῶν ἐν τοῖς θησαυροῖς χρημάτων, καὶ ὅσα ἄλλα τοιουτότροπα ἐς τὴν ἡγεμονίαν φέροντα ἦν, εἶχε.

29. For this meaning of *residuae,* see Livy, 33.47.2 (Hannibal in Carthage); these are the amounts that "are owed," since we can "collect" them (*exigere*); a connected meaning: amounts misappropriated (or "held") by the magistrates or tax-collectors, which explains why the expression is found in the legislation concerning misappropriation of public funds (*Dig.,* 48.13.2, 4, 9, the *lex Julia de residuis*). For Hadrian's cancellation of these "amounts owing," *CIL,* 6.967 = *ILS,* 309; Dio, 69.8; *Vita Hadr.,* 7.6. Augustus could not have indicated "misappropriated" amounts.

30. For this meaning, see Suetonius, *Galba,* 5.3: *quia notata, non perscripta erat summa* (cf. Cicero, 2 *Verr.,* 2.88; 2.5.48; *De leg. agr.* 1.2, etc.).

31. Above, chap. 6, n. 62.

32. Note the coincidence between the two regions mentioned in the *Res Gestae,* 26.5 (above, chap. 1).

33. Tacitus, *Ann.,* 1.11.4: *addideratque Augustus consilium coercendi intra terminos imperii, incertum metu an per invidiam*; *Agric.,* 13.2: *ac longa oblivia Britanniae etiam in pace: consilium id divus Augustus vocabat, Tiberius praeceptum.*

34. Appian, *Praef.,* 15: ἡ δὲ τελευταία καὶ τὴν στρατιὰν αὐτῶν, ὅσην ἔχουσιν, ἢ πρόσοδον, ἣν καρποῦνται καθ' ἕκαστον ἔθνος, ἢ εἴ τι προσαναλίσκουσιν εἰς τὰς ἐπινείους φρουράς ὅσα τε τοιουτότροπα ἄλλα ἐπιδείξει.

IX

The Administrative Organization of Space: Urban Regions and Italian Regions

Measurement of provinces in Agrippa's map; lists of these provinces in the *Res Gestae;* allusions in Pliny to a *discriptio* by Augustus of the Italian territory in eleven regions; lists of peoples, cities, and colonies that are, in Pliny or in other geographical texts, divided according to administrative criteria such as the judicial *conventus*; results of censuses given by provinces as for Syria and Judea, or by Italian regions—with all these facts, it is clear that geographical space, within the boundaries of the empire, is also and perhaps above all an administrative space. This point may seem banal; actually it marks an important change, a notable modification in the perception of space and, undoubtedly, in Roman administrative procedures. This deserves a closer examination.

That the government of men, the administration of resources, and territorial organization coincide and occur in some sense within the same space is a modern concept self-evident to us. This was not the case in Greco-Roman antiquity. Cities or kingdoms could certainly have territories precisely demarcated by zones or even boundary lines. But the concept of territory is never enough to define entirely and exhaustively their true organization and, in particular, their operation.[1] There were several reasons for this. First, in most cases, the territory was not neutral: it was viewed as having a relationship with the cosmos, religiously oriented and pervaded with sanctity.[2] On the other hand, in inegalitarian and, as the anthropologists say, "segmented" societies, the men within the territory are not interchangeable individuals. They are naturally part of their families' lineage, they belong to associations, and they possess varied status that often has no territorial basis but depends on race, religion, or specific legal standards.[3] Most often, at least in the πόλεις, these various memberships (which in fact did not coincide and which generated different classifications) determined the real structure of administrative and political life.

Rome was no exception to the rule. I shall give only two examples: until the end of the Republic and slightly later the theoretical framework of civic and administrative activity was neither the city in its topographical extension, nor the village, the territory, or the municipal towns, but the *tribe*,[4] a group that was not uniquely territorial or legal or based on voting rights, but that followed all of these criteria.

The tribes (thirty-five in number since 242 B.C.: four urban and thirty-one rural) were in fact lists of men and families among which the Roman citizens, and only they, were divided. There were no non-citizens in the tribes, and no citizens without a tribe. Of course, the tribes also had a territorial aspect: originally, no doubt, the possession of land in a certain place determined the affiliation to a tribe. But this link remained weak and vague. A citizen could be assigned a tribe for entirely different reasons: he could inherit his father's tribe or that of his patron or protector; he kept his original tribe even if he changed domicile (if he moved to Rome, for example); and, moreover, for political reasons the authorities could decide arbitrarily to assign a tribe to an individual or, on a collective basis, to a community. Thus, the tribes, insofar as they coincided with some territory, did not represent a geographical continuity; even if a community was collectively assigned one day to a particular tribe, some individuals in this community could easily, for a number of reasons, be registered elsewhere. This complex game had become by the end of the Republic and until the 50s B.C. one of the most important stakes in political life.[5]

This was because the functioning of the Roman State—although already largely imperial at this date—still rested to a large extent upon the archaic basis of the old *civitas*. Until the middle or the end of the second century B.C., for example, the tribe had remained the fundamental framework for the collection of direct tax (the *tributum*) and for army recruitment.[6] But most importantly, the tribe was still, in the first century, the basis for elections to urban magistracies—which had become, by force of circumstances, the government of the world. The assemblies took place by tribes: directly, in the *comitia tributa,* for elections to minor magistracies and to the omnipotent tribunate of the plebs; indirectly, in the *comita centuriata,* where the citizens were divided into census classes that were combined with the tribes to form voting units, or centuries. Thus we can see how the distribution of citizens and consequently the procedure of administrative and political operations were still, in principle, not totally territorial.

The same is true, moreover, if we examine the administration of the empire. The empire, that is the hegemony of Rome, still constituted until the end of the Republic a series of complex and entangled institutions where no basic principle existed, and in which territoriality was but a badly coordinated component. Here again, the preexisting nature of the legal tie that bound a community or an individual to the Roman people predominated above all: thus it was the diversity of statuses, the privilege (in the etymological sense), which was the determining factor.[7] In deed as in law, the "empire" of Rome was manifested on the one hand by alliances, which put the participants into direct contact with the only central authorities in Rome—the magistrates, the Senate, and the people in their assemblies. On the other hand, the "empire" was manifested by domination, acquired through victory over territories or groups of people (often both concurrently), which was enforced from the center (Rome) by the same authorities. But the farther one moved away from the center, where important decisions alone could be made, it inevitably became necessary that these complex relationships be centered on one man, supposedly representing Rome, its Senate, and its people with respect to its subjects (*ὑπηκόοι*). This man could only be a magistrate or a promagistrate, i.e., a former magistrate who had completed his term of office but who was fictitiously considered still to hold his legal right of command and administration.[8]

At this time there was no territorial division of the competencies of magistrates in Roman public law: no "prefect of the eastern regions" or "Secretary of State for a province" as in other contexts. On the other hand, magistrates were or could be assigned to a sphere of competency—traditional or made to measure, it mattered little: this was known as their *provincia*. The assigned *provinciae* could be jurisdiction of any type, responsibility for the Treasury or supervision of transhumant routes, census operations, or an extraordinary commission for the provisioning of Rome. The notion of territory might or might not be involved. Sometimes, it was a military command against a specific enemy in a specific sector; or else, if it was a question of a jurisdiction, it might be only for a specific area. In other cases, the territory thus understood was so greatly enlarged that it extended to the edges of the world (we have seen this for Pompey in 66 and 57 B.C.). But in the considered cases, this notion of territory was never of primary importance: it was only a corollary, a consequence of the mission entrusted.

This was originally the Roman conception of provinces, that is, territories or regions outside of Italy that historical events had given Rome the task of administering. It was only gradually that the word took on a more precise territorial significance, and overlaps on privileges continued to render this definition somewhat approximate. For even if it was usually a geographical entity that indicated the sphere and the area of competency a man was given (for example, a projected foreign war would implicitly be included in the grant of a given province, Asia for a war against Mithridates, Syria for a Parthian war), these geographical entities were in fact territorially discontinuous. Free and allied cities were enclaves within them, or contrariwise, the promagistrate was responsible for cities that were geographically outside his territory. In any case, it was only in the first century B.C. that fairly fixed boundaries on the land itself could be given to these provinces.

Moreover, it is important to recall that the real decisions, even beyond the delegation of a person to a specific place, were still made by the supreme authorities of Rome, who could only act and in the last resort could only exist in the sacred center of their power, Rome itself. The promagistrate could appear to be in some respects master or all-powerful arbitrator in his province, holder of the *imperium* granted by the Roman people. Above his head, however, there remained personal and legal links that, on several accounts, united those whom he governed with the city of Rome. Space and geography, on their own, were inadequate to draw the real map of the administration and the power.

How do the reforms and innovations that derived from Augustus fit into this tradition already more than one hundred years old?

First of all, within the Roman imperial space the concepts of center and periphery are extremely clear. There was a *caput* to the immense "body" that was the empire: it was both the city of Rome and the emperor—as everyone would repeat *ad nauseam* in A.D. 69-70, during the first great crisis of power that saw emperors proclaimed outside of Rome (Tacitus, *Hist.*, 1.4).[9] That the center of power would remain at Rome was not necessarily obvious. Augustus's first and most evident concern was the assertion that the center of power would remain fixed geographically, politically, and spiritually at Rome itself.[10]

Nicolaus of Damascus (*Vita Caes.*, 20) and Suetonius (*Jul.*, 79.3), as we know, both noticed the rumors rampant before the Ides of March concerning Caesar's supposed intention of moving the seat of the empire (*basileion* in Nicolaus; *translatis opibus imperii*, in Suetonius) to Alexandria or to Ilium. No doubt Nicolaus, who was close to Augustus, specified that Caesar refused to acknowledge his son by Cleopatra in his will. But it is clear that Caesar's Egyptian policy, where "passion and politics" were mixed (J. Carcopino), could have imprudently given support to these suspicions. Likewise, the patronage given by the Julii in favor of Ilium at least since the end of the second century B.C.,[11] despite its innocent appearance in second-rank Republican magistrates, could appear more dangerous on the part of a dictator openly preparing a Parthian war in imitation of Alexander, and to whom Nicolaus himself, concerned to exonerate him from all monarchical ambition, still attributed the plan of unifying the whole world, including the Parthians and the Indians, "under a single power" (*Vita Caes.*, 26).

It is well known and even more understandable that the same concerns, much more clearly expressed, were manifested after 36 B.C., during the last encounter between Antony and Octavian. First, an important fact must be emphasized: for the first time, the seat of the Roman power had officially been divided in two. Antony, as *triumvir reipublicae constituendae,* was certainly still a Roman magistrate, who participated at this date in the central government, since he still appointed certain magistrates. But, at the Peace of Brundisium (renewed at Misenum), his *provincia* was determined according to a geographical dividing line (the meridian of Skodra), which was an actual sharing of the world, visibly drawn on a map (Appian, *B.C.*, 5.264).[12] In 34 B.C., when he had made his great donation to Cleopatra and her children (Plutarch, *Ant.*, 54.3–5; 55.1; Dio, 49.41.1–4; Livy, *Per.*, 131; 132), he tried to obtain its ratification in Rome, but without success. The world was truly divided. And Roman public opinion could rightly be shocked by the celebration of a triumph at Alexandria (Velleius, 2.88.4).

Alexandria was a fearsome rival for Rome and an appropriate candidate for the seat of an empire that wanted to expand eastward. The Greeks of Egypt considered it "the city *par excellence*" (*Pap. Berlin,* 13045, 28). Greek scholars who were well-disposed toward Rome, like Diodorus Siculus (17.52.5; 52.6), ranked it first or second among the cities of the world, and thus in rivalry with Rome for the size of its population. Strabo praises its excellent commercial position at the meeting point of the Mediterranean and the East (17.13).

It is clear that, whether sincerely or for political reasons, Octavian chose to remove all these suspicions. The theme of the restoration of the state, customs, and the ancient religion was accompanied by the endlessly repeated assertion that hereafter Rome would never be anywhere but in Rome. The transparent symbolism of his public and official actions is well known; I only repeat it as a reminder: the possibility, briefly envisioned, of taking the name Romulus; the choice of the title Augustus, linked to Jupiter and to the growth of the empire (Ovid, *Fasti,* 1.513); the restoration of temples and of cults; and urban undertakings, destined to make the city worthy of its empire, as both Dionysius of Halicarnassus and Strabo said albeit in different ways. The seat of the government was unambiguously fixed at Rome; this is clear even if the *princeps*, in his capacity as the head of various provinces, sometimes left Rome for varying periods.[13]

A characteristic to which F. Coarelli has drawn attention has been noted less often in this context. A substantial part of the aedilician work undertaken by Agrippa and Augustus in Rome tended to reassure the Romans even more, by symbolically bringing into the *urbs* a decor inspired by Alexandrian urbanism (the *Mausoleum,* which openly copied Alexander's monument, the library, etc.).[14]

The definite choice in favor of Rome, which of course was logical in light of Italian and Roman patriotism, was actually based on a relatively ancient tradition. This is of interest because it translates a new vision of space: the *laudes Italiae,* and still more precisely the *laudes Romae*—that is, a reasoned *elogium* of the geographical location and the site of Rome in relation to its vocation as the government of the world. This was not exactly the theme developed by Cicero in his *De republica* for the location of Rome itself: he considers only the inconveniences and the advantages of maritime sites for the security and morality of cities (2.3–5; 9). When Livy, undoubtedly inspired by Augustus's politics, had Camillus give the same speech about the site of Rome after the siege by the Gauls, he too recalled first the City's religious and sacred calling, then some geographical factors that are closer to Cicero than to Varro and to Vitruvius (5.54.4). But significant changes in the expression of this theme are seen in the Augustan period. The *elogium* of Italy appears first in Varro, in Book 1 of the *Res Rusticae,* dating perhaps to 57 B.C. (R. Martin). Not without some confusion, he uses the climatic argument drawn from geographers to explain the variety of products from the peninsula. The same theme, better articulated geographically, is found in Strabo (6.4.1) and in Dionysius (1.36–7). But it cannot be by chance that it is in the work of the architect Vitruvius, completely engaged in the aedilician program of the new *princeps*, that we find between 24 and 20 B.C., but now linked to the imperial destiny of Rome, the concept that this excellence puts Rome and Italy in the center of a world that they must dominate.[15]

> Such being nature's arrangement of the universe, and all these nations being allotted temperaments which are lacking in due moderation, the truly perfect territory, situated under the middle of the heaven, and having on each side the entire extent of the world and its countries, is that which is occupied by the Roman people . . . Italy presents grounds of praise for its temperate and unsurpassed (climate) . . . Thus the divine mind has allotted to the city of the Roman people an excellent and temperate region in order to rule the world. (Vitruvius, 6.1.10–12)

As we know, Augustus was not only content with the creation of the Italian regions: he extended this reform to Rome itself and created fourteen urban regions. We are fairly well informed about them, and perhaps they will shed some light on the Italian regions. First, let us note that the date of the reform was 7 B.C. It is on this date that Dio mentions them in passing, in the context of the riots that had caused a fire in the Forum and that prompted Augustus to reorganize the police and the fire brigades:

> The blame for the fire was laid upon the debtor class, who were suspected of having contrived it on purpose, in order that they might have some of their debt remitted when they appeared to have lost heavily. They, for their part, however gained nothing from the fire; but the streets were put in charge of supervisors, chosen from the people, whom we call *stenoparchoi.* These men were allowed to use the official dress and two lictors, but only in the regions under their administration and on certain days, and they were given control over the force of slaves which had previously been associated with the aediles to save buildings that caught fire. The aediles, however, together with the tribunes and the praetors, were still assigned by lot to have charge of the whole city, which was divided into fourteen wards. This is also the present arrangement.

The fourteen topographical regions were introduced in the same year, regrouping the districts or *vici,* and the new duty of the *magistri vicorum* (στενωπάρχους)[17] responsible for the supervision of streets and fires in their respective *vici,* allowing the aediles, the tribunes and the praetors to attend to their traditional, higher responsibilities. Suetonius confirms this fact, without giving a date:[18]

> He divided the area of the city into regions and wards, arranging that the former should be under the charge of yearly magistrates selected by lot, and the latter under "masters" elected by the inhabitants of the respective neighborhoods.

Numerous inscriptions allow us to fix more precisely the chronology of the operation: they are dedications to the *Lares Augusti,* made by *collegia* of *magistri* who take up their duties on the Kalends of August. Some inscriptions for certain *vici* date from 7 B.C. (*CIL,* 6.445 = *ILS,* 3613) or allow us to derive that date from the number of the year that they indicate (*CIL,* 6.2222 = *ILS,* 6074). But the initial date for others is slightly different: 12 B.C. (*CIL,* 6.452 = *ILS,* 3620), 9 B.C. (*CIL,* 6.449 = *ILS,* 3617), 8 B.C. (*ILS,* 3090) or even 6 B.C. (*ILS,* 3308) or 2 B.C. (the Florence Base, *CIL,*

6.448 = *ILS,* 3614). We see that the operation was in fact spread over several years and that the *collegia* were not established everywhere at the same time.[19]

The connection between these *vici* and the *regiones* is clearly stated (in addition to the testimony of Dio and Suetonius) by Pliny, *NH*, 3.66: "The city of Rome is divided into fourteen regions, with 265 crossways with their guardian Lares" (*ipsa* [= *Urbs Roma*] *dividitur in regiones quatuordecim, compita Larum CCLXV*), and by a few inscriptions mentioned above, including the famous Capitoline Base, dated from A.D. 136 and dedicated to Hadrian by the *magistri vicorum Urbis regionum XIIII.* For regions I, X, XIII, XII, and XIV (in that order) it gives the name of the *curator,* the two *denuntiatores,* and then for several *vici* (63) the names of four *vicomagistri* (thus 132 names).[20]

We have seen that by 7 B.C. these *vici* and *regiones* served as a framework for the police and fire brigades, still run at that date by a servile *familia publica* (*ILS*, 1964). These positions lasted until A.D. 6, when the seven *cohortes vigilium* were created (Dio. 55.16.4–5). But we see the connection between this number and that of the regions: each cohort was obviously in charge of two regions. The *vici* and the regions also became the administrative structure for many other public services, such as the enforcement of security regulations (following the fire of 64: *ILS,* 4914 = *CIL,* 6.826); the distribution of water (*ILS,* 5791 = *CIL*, 6.3866: a *castellum* of the *aqua Claudia* for *regio I; ILS,* 8701). We have seen that Augustus and Julius Caesar had, in 46 B.C. and no doubt in 2 B.C., organized censuses of the urban population (or more precisely of the recipients of the *annona*) within the framework of the *vici.* The latter existed in the Republican period. Augustus's innovation was regrouping them into fourteen regions.

These regions thus had a uniquely topographical character. We know this by expressions used to define the domicile or the residence. Thus, on an inscription of 5 B.C. in honor of C. Caesar we read: "The urban plebs that resides in the thirteenth region and the heads of the district having combined . . ." (*plebs urbana quae habitat in regione urbis XIII et magistri vicorum . . . aere conlato; CIL,* 6.899, 39207).[21] There are many later examples expressed in a similar manner. But we know this even more clearly from much later documents, which modern scholars call the *Regionaries.* These are catalogs, or guides, to Rome in the Late Empire (the *Notitia Urbis Romae regionum XIIII* and the *Curiosum Urbis Romae regionum XIIII*).[22] These texts (their nature, date, and transmission are of no importance here) describe the city region by region, giving to each one a topographical name in addition to its number. This is no doubt a late, unofficial custom; the inscriptions only give the numbers. Furthermore, they list the remarkable monuments for each region, which allows us to specify the topographical limits of the regions with some degree of certainty. The details are not important here, but we must remember first, that the new regions, as far as their boundaries are concerned, have nothing to do with the four old regions of Rome; and second, that they do not coincide with the Servian wall or with the line of the *pomoerium*. It has been shown that the farthest limits of the new regions often went beyond the area later enclosed by the Aurelian wall. The regions included zones that were traditionally outside the *pomoerium,* such as the Aventine.[23]

But the most positive proof that the regions were destined to become administrative districts is that both *Regionaries* give, at the end of the list of monuments in each region, summary statistics of the number of *vici* and *vicomagistri,* but also of *insulae*[24] and *domus, horrea, balnea,* fountains, and bakeries, as well as the surface area of the *regio* in square feet. After the fourteenth and last region, summary statistics are found of all monuments, areas, fora, streets, columns, obelisks, thermae, aqueducts, markets, theaters, *insulae,* etc. for the entire city. We can imagine the conclusions that demographers[25] or historians of Rome have attempted to draw from these figures—with uneven success. It is not my intention to tackle these questions here. Let it merely be noted that, even if this is a late development in a period of great centralized urban services at Rome (prefectures of the city, of the *annona,* etc.), collections of the elements of these statistics must have started earlier, doubtless with the creation of the regions. Let us recall that in 46 B.C. Caesar had taken a census of the inhabitants of Rome *per dominos insularum,* and that the *Tabula Heracleensis*—dated between 75 B.C. and 45 B.C.—inevitably suggests the existence of a cadastral plan or book of the *urbs.*

The urban *regio* is thus both a new topographic and administrative framework. But what was its underlying significance? We shall perhaps understand it better if we take note of the changes that the status, the composition, and even the very definition of the civic population of Rome undergo throughout the reign of Augustus. Until then, the entire Roman civic body—I include all the citizens residing outside of Rome (already several millions in 89 B.C.)—was always officially distributed among the thirty-five tribes. But the distinction was no longer pertinent between the four urban tribes,[26] which originally had held the city's inhabitants and had corresponded to the four homonymous regions (Varro, *De ling. lat.,* 5.45; 56;

Dionysus, 4.14), and the thirty-one rural tribes: the city was now full of inhabitants, often settled there for many generations, who belonged to all tribes.

From the reign of Augustus,[27] we see new official phrases appearing: "the urban plebs from the thirty-five tribes"[28] or the "the thirty-five tribes." Perhaps surprisingly but not equivocally these indicate the *cives Romani* living in Rome. It even becomes a habit to call these groups "the urban tribes,"[29] clearly at odds with the usage of the Republican period, when *tribus urbanae* indicated exclusively the citizens registered in the Esquilina, the Palatina, the Suburana, and the Collina. It seems almost as if the concept of tribe no longer existed, or was at least of no real significance, outside the city of Rome. This is not to say that the tribes did not survive; they remained the framework and the proof of citizenship. No doubt the census of citizens, which continued to mention the tribes, preserved its tribal registers just as during the Republic.

At Rome itself, the tribes survived since they served as the framework for a new type of operations, which in turn made, of these "urban tribes" or of this "urban plebs of thirty-five tribes," a privileged body within the privileged group of Roman citizens of Italy and the empire. They benefited from the *princeps*'s generosity, in grain and in money. The tribes preserved their structure (divided into *centuriae*), their administration (*centuriones, curatores,* and employees), and their corporate existence: they formed *corpora,* they had common treasuries, they were entitled to manage common funds, and to receive gifts or bequests[30] as a corporate body. But all of this only concerned a privileged few, restricted by a *numerus clausus,* of the inhabitants of the city. The administration of the entire population, on the other hand, demanded different structures.

There remains one burning question: what about political participation? The establishment of the empire in 27 B.C. did not change the old *respublica,* at least not in principle:[31] the voting on laws and the election of magistrates continued to belong to the Roman people—the vast collectivity of all citizens, wherever they resided. But the operations themselves, as at the beginning of the Republic, could only take place in Rome, in consecrated areas, and in a legally prescribed space. This attachment to ancient forms had already produced considerable imbalances and inconveniences at the end of the Republic, when the civic body had expanded disproportionately to the limits of the Italian peninsula. It was now clear that all the citizens could not be physically present in Rome every time it was requested of them. This inconvenience also applied to the census, except that the occasions for voting were more frequent: several dozen days per year, in the case of the voting on laws.[32] Certainly we have the proof that up to the last years of the Republic (still in the 50s), part of the electorate—the well-to-do, whose vote legally carried the most weight in the tribal centuriate system—might still come from afar (from Cisalpine Gaul, for example) to meet a particular deadline. By this period, the Italian *clientela* still played an occasional but important role in the political game that could only be played at Rome.[33] But the force of circumstances had for a long time given first place, in this type of decision-making process, to what was already called the urban plebs, in the sense that we have seen: citizens living in Rome but not necessarily belonging to the four urban tribes. Geographically, sociologically, and politically, this urban plebs was far from representative of the entire *populus Romanus,* with its numerous adult male citizens firmly settled in their Italian districts or municipalities. But legally and fictively, it was authorized to speak and to decide in its name, since only it had the opportunity to do so. Such an abuse could not be perpetuated without profound difficulties.

This was the system that Augustus not only respected but apparently "restored" in 27 B.C. We must examine it more closely, and from our own point of view. After 27 B.C., the elections and the voting on laws resumed their old familiar course, at least in principle. This was not without the aftermath of crises, as in 19 B.C. under the consulship of C. Sentius Saturninus (Velleius, 2.92; Dio, 54.10), or even later still (in A.D. 7 for example: Dio, 55.34.2).[34] But it is undoubtedly significant that we hardly have any testimony for this period of the possible presence of Italian or provincial voters travelling to Rome in an attempt to appoint a candidate or to pass a law. This course of action could perhaps still be taken—e.g., by the compatriots of Q. Varius Geminus (who was the first Paelignian from Superaequum to become senator, praetor, and proconsul under Augustus), who proudly recalled his *cursus* on the base of the statue that they dedicated to him (*CIL,* 9.3305 = *ILS,* 932).[35] But we only have one formal testimony, insignificant given the exceptional and obviously symbolic character of the event. At Augustus's election as *Pontifex Maximus* in 12 B.C., "such a concourse poured in from the whole of Italy to my election as has never been recorded at Rome before that time" (*cuncta ex Italia ad comitia mea confluente multitudine, quanta Romae nunquam fertur ante id tempus fuisse; RG,* 10.2).

On the other hand, several facts taken randomly from our historiographical and epigraphical tradition demonstrate to us that there was, during the triumvirate and Augustus's reign, a keener awareness of the problems raised by the Italian political sphere and of the various attempts to solve them in a new way. Let us not forget the warning sign given by the last military rebellion in Italy against Octavian, in 41 B.C., at the appeal of the consul Lucius Antonius, brother of Marcus.[36] Octavian had learned his lesson and, after 36 B.C. following this victory over Sextus Pompeius, he had undertaken the task of winning back the favor of all the Italian cities, including the new colonies set up by Antony (Dio, 50.6.3, for Bologna). When war was declared in 32 B.C. against Egypt and Antony, the "emergency oath" (*coniuratio*) was demanded and received, city by city, which afterwards created between the *dux* and the western populations that bond of *clientela* on which the *princeps* based his future position (*RG*, 25.2: "the whole of Italy of its own free will swore allegiance to me" (*iuravit in mea verba tota Italia sponte sua*). We know this from the dispensation Octavian granted spontaneously to the city of Bologna, a client-town of Antony (Suetonius, *Aug.*, 17.2): "He also excused the community of Bononia from joining in the rally of all Italy to his standards, since they had been from ancient days dependents of the Antonii." (*Bononiensibus quoque publice quod in Antoniorum clientela antiquitus erant gratiam fecit coniurandi cum tota Italia pro partibus suis*). This is definitely an oath, city by city.[37]

But later still—at a date not precisely known—Augustus took a very curious initiative:

> After having thus set the city and its affairs in order, he added to the population of Italy by personally establishing twenty-eight colonies; furnished many parts of it with public buildings and revenues; and even gave it, at least to some degree, equal rights and dignity with the city of Rome, by devising a kind of votes which the members of the local senate were to cast in each colony for candidates for the city offices, and send under seal to Rome against the day of the elections (Suetonius, *Aug.* 46.1).[38]

We would prefer more detail, because this is a truly revolutionary procedure. While the written vote (*per tabellam*) had existed in Rome since the second century B.C., we have never found a trace of a "postal vote." The *decuriones* (and doubtless the magistrates) of the colonies represented between 3,000 and 5,500 individuals—depending on whether we estimate that the measure affected only the twenty-eight Augustan colonies or all the colonies of Italy. Each person had voted in his own city—sometimes hundreds of kilometers away from Rome. But the voters, under Augustus as well as later, were always distributed by tribes and by classes.[39] If these votes were simply to be integrated into the total of votes collected at Rome on election day, it was necessary to have them classified by tribe[40] and by centuries without opening or counting them, and to have each ballot deposited, at the correct time and place, in the appropriate urn. This is not impossible, but it would mean a very long operation that implied above all, in one way or another, the knowledge of each voter's name, tribe, and class. Thus, it would mean the loss of the anonymity of the vote—at which the use of the *tabella* aimed. This would result in a very limited gain—these 3,000 or 5,000 votes in any case only represented a minimal percentage of those cast by the urban plebs—150,000 or 200,000 potential voters.

For this reason, I wonder if there was not another method: a procedure similar to the one revealed by the *Tabula Hebana,* which was introduced for the election of consuls and praetors by the *lex Valeria Cornelia* of A.D. 5. This law instituted, under the name of *destinatio,* a preliminary vote by the 600 senators and the approximately 2,000 *equites* in service in the judicial *decuria* at Rome. In this vote they were divided up into ten (later, fifteen and twenty) "centuries," which were composed of voters who were present and who belonged to a group of tribes drawn by lot; they voted to supply the required number of magistracies.[41]

In this case, we see that the urns corresponding to each century (whose content will count as the vote of that century) are the ones that are sealed (*ad cistas suffragiis latis signandas,* 1.34) and given to the archival praetor to be transported to the *saepta* of the *Campus Martius,* where the votes were counted and proclaimed out loud before the rest of the people could vote.[42] Unfortunately, we do not know how this preliminary vote, whose result was known only on the day of the *comitia* at Rome, was integrated and counted among the votes of the regular assembly. The similarity between both procedures is nevertheless striking.

In other words, I suggest that the votes of our colonial *decuriones* were somehow already gathered before being counted and used (or proclaimed) at Rome. I would go so far as to say that they must have had a particular prerogative value, as the vote of senators and *equites* did later: otherwise, why would Suetonius have used the word *dignatione*? But I may be mistaken, and perhaps the "voting unit" was simply the colony in question. Each colony would thus have been considered as having voted for the candidates of its choice, and these twenty-eight (or fifty) votes would have been added to the others. This hypothesis is, however, less satisfactory since it would have been necessary to integrate the voters into a complex system of collective voting units, which would have unbalanced the system.

If my first hypothesis is correct—that is to say if, somehow, the votes of a colonial city were recorded together and in one single register—another comparison with the extraordinary *Tabula Heracleensis* comes to light. We have seen (p. 128 above) that, based on the stipulations of the latter, the registers of the census that had been taken locally by local magistrates according to Roman rules had to be sent to Rome and transcribed into public registers, which would be archived in the same offices as the registers of the Roman census. If we follow the particulars of the text, it seems clear that the results of the local census were not registered purely and simply in the blank spaces of Roman books, but that they consisted of separate and, in some way, autonomous registers.[43] I see no other classification for these registers than a geographical one.

The traditional classification of the census is the tribe. Formerly, the registers were those of the tribes; but what was now being brought to Rome and transcribed into other books, was not the census of, e.g., the *tribules* of the Falernian tribe, but rather the register from Heraclea or some other city where there were citizens of different tribes. How to arrange these registers, if not in a topographical order? In the same period, we have seen that the urban census ordered by Caesar was taken *vicatim;* here again, I doubt that the resulting documents could have been otherwise arranged.

Such a process was a serious break with the traditional system of tribes and centuries, which implied, by its centralization at Rome, a considerable and henceforth impossible physical mobility of people. The parallel with the somewhat earlier procedural changes in the census is certainly not fortuitous. The same answer was given to the challenge that traditional institutions faced because of the expansion of the Italian political arena: substitute the mobility of documents for the mobility of people, decentralize the operations in order to centralize the results. The empire could not function without a series of representations where the clear consciousness of space depended on the primacy of the document. Under these conditions, it is not surprising to see the gradual disappearance of the old timocratic, familial, or personal structures—like the tribes or centuries—which favored men instead of space, and social and legal status instead of topography.

With the tribes thus reduced, by convergent paths, to a purely honorific role, I believe that we can better understand the appearance of the Italian regions. In my opinion, this can only have been *grosso modo* contemporary with that of the urban regions. Their name itself—*regio*—asserts their neutral and exclusively topographic character. In fact, it is a word borrowed from the vocabulary of the geometers: a zone of space determined by lines of an astronomical character (Varro, *De ling.lat.,* 6.2; *Gromatici,* p. 47 L). It is only by extension that the word designates a "part" of space, a "region" (for example Siculus Flaccus, p. 135 L, on the extent of the jurisdiction of a municipal magistrate).

We have seen above that these regions definitely served as a new statistical framework: as in the census taken by Titus and Vespasian in A.D. 73–74 or the lists of centenarians of the eighth region (Pliny, 7. 163–64, Phlegon of Tralles, fr. 29 M). Nevertheless, these lists also mentioned the tribe (Pliny, 7. 164).

But we have also seen that the regions served as a framework—at least an archival one—for other operations, which F. de Martino[44] has recently summarized: the list of the *subseciva* of communities; deposited in the *Tabularium (Gromatici* pp. 195, 12; 202, 5 L; 203, 1; 221, 14; 226, 5; 229; 252; 259); later, the management of imperial estates; the districts of the *XX hereditatium* (*CIL,* 11.378, etc.), and the *XX libertatis* (*CIL,* 5.3351). It is important to note that such a regionalization of Italy had had remote precedents in the first century B.C. When obligatory military service for all had long since disappeared, occasionally there were levies officially limited to a particular zone: as for L. Licinius Murena in Umbria (Cicero, *Mur.,* 42: *habuit proficiscens dilectum in Umbria*), Q. Metellus Celer in Picenum in 63 B.C. (Sallust, *Jug.,* 30), and M. Licinius Crassus in Lucania in 55 B.C. (Pliny, *NH,* 2.147). Each time, it is the traditional ethnic name that indicates these zones, but we have seen that Augustus's regions in most cases coincided with these old divisions, sometimes regrouping them.

In the case of special levies, military or political reasons (such as the reputation of a particular ethnic group) clearly determined the actions of the authorities. By extending the system throughout Italy, and officially numbering his regions, Augustus on the contrary tended to erase the local character and equalize property and men in a numbered taxonomy that recalled that of the legions—or of the administrative registers. It should further be considered that the order of the numbering—like that of the regions of Rome—is indicated in spatial terms; it runs from Latium and Campania to the south (which was rather east-south-east for the Romans) down both coasts, then into the center (IV, V, VI, VII), still from one side to the other, then to the north, from east to west (VIII, IX), and then again from east to west (X, XI). We shall observe the formal intention of describing Italian space by a zigzag itinerary no longer derived from history or public law—but which, not surprisingly, holds to the requirements of the map and the traditions of the *periplus.* Administration—but not yet politics—begins to pattern itself on space more than on people. It borrows from the double tradition of ancient geography. Italy still remained, under Augustus, the *mater* of a sovereign people—but this was but a fiction. The appearance of numbered regions, which cut the land up according to the requirements of a physically unbroken space and the demands of a public accounting and administration of archives, foreshadows the day when—a mere century later—Italy would be a mere province among others.

NOTES

1. The essential works on this precise theme remain those of E. Kornemann, "Stadtstaat und Flächenstaat des Altertums in ihren Wechselbeziehungen," *Neue Jahrb.*, 4 (1908): 223–53; "Polis und Urbs," *Klio* 5 (1905): 72–92; and F. Hampl, "Poleis ohne territorium," *Klio* 32 (1939): 1–60.

2. See the important works by P. Catalano, *Contributo allo studio del diritto augurale* I (Torino, 1960), 248–320 and "Aspetti spaziali del sistema giuridico-religioso romano," *ANRW* II, 16, no. 1 (1978): 442–553; and Mommsen, *Droit public,* VI, 2, 476–85.

3. I have stressed this point, after many others, in *Le métier de citoyen*[2] (Paris, 1979), 71–121; and in *Les structures de l'Italie romaine*[2] (Paris, 1987), 190ff.; 332ff. For the Greek world, see D. Roussel, *Tribu et cité* (Besançon, 1976).

4. Mommsen, *Die romischen Tribus in administrativer Beziehung* (Altona, 1844); id., *Droit public,* VI, 1, 180–213; G. Botsford, *The Roman Assemblies* (New York, 1909); and L. Ross Taylor, *The Voting Districts of the Roman Republic* (Rome, 1960); W. Kubitschek, *De Romanorum tribuum origine ac propagatione* (Vienna, 1882).

5. L. Ross Taylor, *Roman Voting Assemblies from the Hannibalic War to the Dictatorship of Caesar* (Ann Arbor, 1966), 54ff.

6. E. Gabba, "Ricerche sull'esercito professionale romano," app. 1: "Leva per tribu e censo equestre," *Athenaeum,* n.s., 29 (1951): 171–272 = *Esercito e Società . . .* (1973), 144–50; P. Fraccaro, "*Tribules* ed *aerarii,*" *Athenaeum,* n.s., 9 (1933): 150–72 = *Opuscula* 2:149–70; C. Nicolet, *Tributum* (Bonn, 1976), 30; 46–55.

7. For a clarification see J.-M. Bertrand and C. Nicolet in *Genèse d'un empire,* ed. C. Nicolet (Paris, 1979), 817ff., 910–14; W. Dahleim, *Gewalt und Herrschaft. Das provinziale Herrschaftsystem der röm. Republik* (Berlin, 1977), 74ff.; and the thesis of J.-L. Ferrary, *Aspects idéologiques de la conquête romaine du monde hellénistique* (Paris, 1989). For the empire, see for example M. Lemosse, *Le Régime des relations internationales dans le Haut-Empire romain* (Paris, 1967), 127ff.; and F. Fabbrini, *L'impero di Augusto come ordinamento sovra-nazionale* (Milan, 1974).

8. W.-F. Jashemski, *The Origins and History of the Proconsular and the Propraetorian Imperium to 27* B.C. (Chicago, 1950).

9. The metaphor *caput/corpus,* for Rome and her empire appears precisely in the period of Augustus (*TLL,* 3:2, col. 426), in Livy and Ovid (Livy, 1.16.7: *mea Roma caput orbis terrarum sit;* Ovid, *Ars Am.,* 1.15.26; Pliny, *NH,* 28.15, 3.38, etc.). Tacitus, *Ann.,* 1.46–47, 3.47.1; Tacitus, *Hist.,* 1.4.2: *evulgato imperii arcano posse principem, alibi quam Romae fieri.* See D. Kienast, "Augustus und Alexander," *Gymnasium,* 1969, 417–18.

10. See C. Nicolet, "Rome capitale," in *Da Roma alla terza Roma* (Rome, Edizione Scientifiche Italiane 1987).

11. *OGI*, 440 = *ILS* 8770; 444.

12. J.-H. Michel, "Le méridien de Skodra et le partage du monde," *Att. Conv. Intern. Accad. Rom. Constantiniana (in on. M. Di Dominici)*, 4. no. 1 (1979 [1982]): 181–91.

13. Certainly the emperors: to begin with Augustus, at the beginning of his reign, until 8 B.C. But in fact the Julio-Claudians (and especially Tiberius) did not venture far from Rome (or Campania, with daily contacts carefully organized with Rome); the plebs dreaded their final departure: see the enlightening article of the late P. Ceausescu, "*Altera Roma*. Histoire d'une folie politique," *Historia*, 1976, 79–167.

14. See above, chap. 1, n. 7.

15. Vitruvius, 6.1.10: *Cur ego haec ita sint ab natura rerum in mundo collocata et omnes nationes immoderatis mixtionibus disparatae, veros inter spatium totius orbis terrarum regionesque medio mundi populis Romanus possidet fines . . . Italia . . . temperatas et invictas habet laudes . . . Ita divina mens civitatem populi Romani egregia temparataque regione conlocavit, ut orbis terrarum imperii potiretur.*

16. Dio, 55.8.8.

17. Στενωπός means "narrow road," "street." The "stenoparchoi" are inevitably the *vicomagistri* (D. Magie, *De Romanorum iuris publici sacrique vocabulis . . .* [Leipzig, 1905], 55): Mommsen, *Droit public*, V, 333–35.

18. Suetonius, *Aug.*, 30.1: *Spatium urbis in regiones vicosque divisit instituitque ut illas* [= the *regiones*] *annui magistratus sortiti tuerentur, hos* [= the *vici*] *magistri e plebe cuiusque viciniae lecti.* On the urban regions, see S. B. Platner and T. Ashby, *A Topographical Dictionary of Ancient Rome* (London, 1929) 444–47 (who provide references to the manuals of topography by H. Jordan [1871–85], O. Gilbert [1883–90], and O. Richter [1903]; L. Homo, *Rome impériale et l'urbanisme dans l'antiquité*[2] (Paris, 1971), 74–123, 130–32.

19. See. G. Niebling, "*Laribus Augustis Magistri Primi*. Der Beginn des Compitalkultes der Lares und des Genius Augusti," *Historia*, 1956, 303–31; see A. Degrassi, *Inscr. Ital.*, 13, no. 1, (1937): 289; A. M. Tamassia, *Bul. Comm.* 68 (1962): 158.

20. *CIL*, 6. 975 = *ILS*, 6073 (in the Museum of the Conservators).

21. *CIL*, 6.899 and 39207 (with a supplement by A. Degrassi, *Doxa*, 2 [1949]: 79 = *AE* [1949]:176); line 3, the reconstruction [*magistr*]*i vicorum* is essential. I found various examples of domicile, origin, or address using the region, in *CIL*, 6: 33899, 6: *qui manet in regione nona;* 10089 [*pistor*] *region(a)e secund(a)e;* 1956; *praeco . . . de regione Portae Capenae,* etc. Not to be confused with the *procurator Urbis a regionibus,* and his subordinates; for these see Hirschfeld, *Die kaiserlichen Verwaltungsbeamten . . .*, (1905), 260–62; H.-G. Pflaum, *Carrières*, 2:495–98, 2:727–31.

22. These can be found in R. Valentini and G. Zucchetti, *Codice Topografico della città di Roma,* I (Rome, 1940), 1:64–258; A. Nordh, *Libellus de regionibus Urbis Romae,* Acta Inst. Rom. Regn. Sueciae, 3:8 (Lund, 1949).

23. In fact, the extent and limits of the regions of imperial Rome are not well-known. See the summary and some hypotheses in A. von Gerkan, "Grenzen und Grossen der Vierzehn Regionen Roms," *Bonn. Jahrb.*, 1949, 5–65; and in L. Homo, *Rome impériale et l'urbanisme dans l'Antiquité* (Paris, 1971), 100–103.

24. Let us put aside this thorny problem of the definition of the word that was already in use in Caesar's time. The two essential articles are those of E. Cuq, "Une statistique de locaux affectés à l'habitation dans la Rome impériale," *Mém. Ac. Inscr. Bell. Lettres* 11 (1915): 279–335; and F. Castagnoli, "L'insula nei cataloghi regionari di Roma," *Riv. Fil.* 104 (1976): 45. I shall return to this in my comments on the *Tabula Heracleensis*.

25. Finally (but with some errors), see G. Hermansen, "The Population of Imperial Rome: the Regionaries," *Historia*, 1978, 129–68.

26. Always essential is L. Ross Taylor, "The Four Urban Tribes and the Four Regions of Ancient Rome," *Rend. Pont. Ac.* 27 (1952–54): 225–38.

27. We have little before this: perhaps by 44 B.C. if my interpretation of a statue of Lucius Antonius with the inscription *Quinque et triginta tribus patrono* (Cicero, *Phil.*, 6.12) is correct: see my article "Plèbe et tribus: les statues de Lucius Antonius et le testament d'Auguste," *MEFRA*, 1985, 799–839; for *tribus* = *regio*, see Varro, *LL*, 5.45; *e quis prima scripta est regio Suburana . . . quarta Palatina*.

28. This is the *formula* expression that appears in A.D. 23 (but doubtless as early as 21) in the funeral honors bestowed on Germanicus and Drusus: *CIL*, 6.910 = *ILS*, 168; 6.909 = *ILS*, 176 (Nicolet, "Plèbe et tribus," 825); *plebs urbana quae frum. publ. accipit et tribus* [XXXV], in A.D. 79 (*CIL*, 6.943 = *ILS*, 6045).

29. This is certainly the meaning of *tribus urbanae*, when Nero wanted a military levy. (Suetonius, *Nero*, 44.2; *mox tribus urbanas ad sacramentum citavit*); the same applies to Vitellius in 69: Tacitus, *Hist.*, 3.58.8: *vocari tribus iubet*.

30. On all this, see Mommsen, *Droit public*, VI, 1, 211–23; L. Ross Taylor, *Voting Districts*, 15; Nicolet, "Plèbe et tribus," 813–16.

31. Suetonius, *Aug.*, 40.2: *comitiorum quoque pristinum ius reduxit* (Velleius, 2.89.4: Dio, 56.40.4).

32. L. Ross Taylor, *Roman Voting Assemblies*, esp. 64ff.; C. Nicolet, *Le métier de citoyen*[2], 391ff.

33. Cicero, 1 *Verr.*, 54; Q. Cicero, *Comm. Pet.*, 30; Caesar, *BG*, 8.50.1–3 (Caesar's *suffragatio* in favor of Antony); L. Ross Taylor, *Party Politics in the Age of Caesar* (1949), 58.

34. Velleius, 2.92.3–4: *Egnatium . . . profiteri vetuit;* Dio, 54.10.1; for A.D. 7: Dio, 55.34.2 (Augustus, because of all the trouble, chose all the magistrates; for A.D. 8, he decided to publish the list of his *commendati;* I leave out the problem of the links between this measure and the famous *lex Valeria Cornelia* of A.D. 5, known through the *Tabula Hebana*.

35. *CIL*, 9.3305 = *ILS*, 932; *is primus omnium Paelign. senator factus est* (see R. Syme, "Caesar, the Senate and Italy," in *PBSR*, 1938, 1–31 = *Roman Papers*, 1:94).

36. C. Jullian, *Les transformations politiques de l'Italie sous les empereurs romains* (Rome, 1884), 22ff; M. Volponi, *Lo sfondo italico della lotta triumvirale* (Genoa, 1975), 85ff.

37. A. von Premerstein, "*Vom Werden und Wesen des Prinzipats,*" Abhand. Bay. Akad., 1937, 40ff.

38. Suetonius, *Aug.*, 46.1: *Ad hunc modum Urbe urbanisque rebus administratis, Italiam duodetriginta coloniarum numero deductarum a se frequentavit operibusque ac vectigalibus publicis plurifariam instruxit, etiam iure ac dignatione Urbi quodam modo pro parte aliqua adaequavit, excogitato genere suffragiorum, quae de magistratibus urbicis decuriones colonici in sua quisque colonia ferrent et sub die comitiorum obsignata Romam mitterent.*

39. This definitely appears for the *destinatio* assembly of the *lex Valeria Cornelia* of A.D. 5 (*Tab. Hebana* in Ehrenberg-Jones, *Documents Illustrating the Reigns of Augustus and Tiberius*[2] [Cambridge, 1976], n. 94, a, ll.22–30).

40. Even if we could say approximately that a particular colony is affiliated to a particular tribe, it goes without saying that for a variety of reasons some individuals (and *a fortiori* colonists) can belong to other tribes. This is clearly seen in the epigraphical corpus of Augustan veterans gathered by L. Keppie, *Colonisation and Veteran Settlement in Italy . . .* (Rome, 1983), for example, 217, for Telesia (nos. 53–54), 222–23 (nos. 94–95). Even if these cases are relatively rare, it is clear that we cannot, without being arbitrary, count all *decuriones* from a colony in one single tribe. (For an interesting case in which we find a veteran taking the tribe of a colony that differs from that of his father, see Keppie, n. 37 = *CIL,* 9.1616 (Beneventum): C. Lisidius, of the XXX legion, is in the *Stel.*; his father, Marcus, in the *Publilia*). Strangely enough Keppie shows no interest in this voting privilege of the veterans.

41. I shall not go into a discussion of this terribly confused question; the best book remains that of G. Tibiletti, *Principe e magistrati repubblicani* (Rome, 1953); see also R. Frei-Stolba, *Untersuchungen zu den Wahlen in der röm Kaiserzeit* (Zürich, 1967); M. Pani, *Comitia e senato* (Bari, 1974).

42. I referred to the excellent translation of J. Béranger (esp. 1.35–50), "La démocratie sous l'Empire romain: les opérations électorales de la *Tabula Hebana* et la *destinatio,*" *Mus. Helv.*, 1957, = *Principatus* (Geneva, 1973), 240. Unfortunately the gaps in the text do not allow us for the moment to understand how the *destinatio* vote was counted in the *comitia*. Everything depends on the following question: is the number of *destinati* candidates (after the first vote) superior, equal, or inferior to the number of positions to be filled? I assume it is equal.

43. Above, chap. 6, n. 21: l.155: *in tabulas publicas referunda curato* means that the censors at Rome will have the documents that have been brought in from the *municipia* copied in *some* Roman public registers and that they will have them deposited in the same offices as the documents of the census that they themselves have carried out.

44. F. de Martino, "Note sull'Italia Augustea," *Athenaeum,* 1975, 245–61.

Bibliography

Alföldi, A. *Die monarchische Repräsentation im römischen Kaiserreiche.* Darmstadt, 1970.

———. "Symboles syllaniens et propagande pompéienne." *REL.* 1950, pp. 45–55.

Alföldi, G. *Noricum.* London and Boston, 1974.

Almagià, R. *Monumenta cartographica Vaticana.* Vol. 3: *Le pitture murali della galleria delle carte geografiche.* Vatican City, 1952.

———. *Monumenta cartographica Vaticana.* Vol. 4: *Le pitture geografiche murali della Terza Loggia e di altre sale Vaticane.* Vatican City, 1955.

———. "Sugli autori delle pitture geografiche del Palazzo Farnese di Caprarola." *Rend. Accad. Lincei,* ser. 8, 11, nos. 5, 6 (1956): 129–33.

Anderson, R., Parsons, P., and Nisbet, R. "Elegiacs by Gallus from Qasr Ibrîm." *JRS,* 1979, 125–55.

André, J. "Des Indiens en Germanie." *Journ. Sav.,* 1982, 45–55.

Andreae, B. *L'art de l'ancienne Rome.* Paris, 1977.

Arangio-Ruiz, V. "Sull'iscrizione superficiaria di Arausio." *Epigraphica* 14 (1941): 98–102.

Arnaud, P. "L'image du globe dans le monde romain." *MEFRA,* 1984, 53–116.

———. "L'affaire Mettius Pompusianus." *MEFRA,* 1982, 677ff.

———. *Imago Mundi,* thesis of Paris IV, 1984.

Aujac, G. "La sphéropée, ou la mécanique au service de la découverte du monde." *Rev. Hist. des Sciences,* 1970, 93–107.

———. "L'image du globe terrestre dans la Grèce ancienne." *Rev. Hist. des Sciences,* 1973, 193–210.

———. "Sphérique et sphéropée en Grèce ancienne." *Historia Mathematica* 3 (1976): 441–47.

———. *Strabon et la science de son temps.* Paris, 1966.

———. "Le ciel des fixes et ses représentations en Grèce ancienne." *Rev. Hist. des Sciences,* 1976, 289–307.

———. "Regards sur l'astronomie grecque." In *L'Astronomie dans l'Antiquité classique,* 35–56. Paris, 1980.

———. Introduction to *Géminos, Introduction aux Phénomènes,* 65–77. CUF. Paris, 1975.

———. *La géographie dans le monde antique.* Paris, 1975.

Badian, E. *Roman imperialism in the Late Republic.* Ithaca, 1967.

Bagrow, L. *History of Cartography.* London, 1964.
Baladié, R. *Le Péloponnèse de Strabon.* Paris, 1980.
Bardon, H. *La littérature latine inconnue.* Paris, 1952–56.
Beazley, C. R. *The Dawn of Modern Geography.* 3 vols. 1896–1906.
Beloch, J. *Die Bevölkerung der griechisch-römischen Welt.* Leipzig, 1886. Italian trans., *La popolazione del mondo greco-romano.* Milano, 1909.
Bentham, R. M. *The Fragments of Eratosthenes.* London, 1948.
Béranger, J. "La Démocratie sous l'Empire romain: les opérations électorales de la Tabula Hebana et la destinatio." *Mus. Helv.,* 1957, 216–40.
———. *Principatus.* Geneva, 1973.
Berger, H. *Geschichte der wissenschaftlichen Erdkunde der Griechen.* 4 vols. Leipzig. 1887–91.
———. *Die geographischen Fragmente des Eratosthenes.* Leipzig, 1880.
Bernhard, M. L. "Topographie d'Alexandrie: le tombeau d'Alexandre et le Mausolée d'Auguste." *Rev. Arch.,* 47 (1956): 129–56.
Berthelot, A. *L'Asie ancienne . . . d'après Ptolémée.* Paris, 1930.
———. "Les données numériques fondamentales de la géographie antique d'Eratosthène à Ptolémée." *Rev. Arch.,* 1932, 1–34.
Besnier, M. "Les cartes vaticanes. Une vue de Rome en 1631." *Mél. Arch. Hist.,* 1900, 289–98.
Blume, F.; Lachmann, K.; and Rudorff, A. *Gromatici Veteres (Die Schriften der röm. Feldmesser).* 2 vols. Berlin, 1848–52.
Blumenthal, F. "Zur zensorischen Tätigkeit des Augustus." *Klio,* 1909, 493–500.
Bömer, F. "Der Commentarius." *Hermes,* 1953, 210–50.
Bonnefond, M. "Le Forum d'Auguste et le Capitole: transfert de fonctions et mutations idéologiques." in *L'Urbs. Espace urbain et histoire.* Colloque de l'EFR, 251–78. Rome, 1987.
Bosio, L. *La Tabula Peutingeriana.* Bologne, 1983.
Bowersock, G. *Augustus and the Greek World.* Oxford, 1965.
———. *Roman Arabia.* Cambridge, Mass., 1983.
———. "A Report on Arabia Provincia." *JRS,* 1971, 219–42.
Boyancé, P. "Cicéron et l'Empire romain en Sicile." *Kokalos,* 1964–65, 333–58.
Braccesi, L. "Una ipotesi sull'elaborazione delle RGDA." *Giorn. ital. Fil.,* 1973, 25–40.
———. *Epigrafia e storiografia (interpretazioni augustee).* Naples, 1981.
Bradford, J. *Ancient Landscapes.* London, 1937.
Braunert, H. "Der röm. Provinzialzensus und der Schätzungsbericht des Lukas Evangelium." *Historia,* 1956, 192–214.
———. "Omnium provinciarum populi Romani . . . fines auxi." *Chiron,* 1977, 207–17.
Broc, N. *La Géographie de la Renaissance.* Paris, 1980.
———. "Hiérarchies." In *Cartes et figures de la Terre,* 76–77. Paris, 1980.
Brugi, G. *Le dottrine giuridiche degli agrimensores.* Verona, 1897.

Brunt, P. "Lex de imperio Vespasiani." *JRS,* 1977, 95–116.

———. "Laus Imperii." In *Imperialism in the Ancient World,* ed. P. A. Garnsey and C. R. Whittaker, 159–91. Cambridge, 1978.

———. "Review of H. D. Meyer, *Die Aussenpolitik des Augustus* . . . ," *JRS,* 1963, 170–76.

———. *Italian Manpower 225 BC–AD 14.* Oxford, 1971.

Buchner, E. "Solarium Augusti und Ara Pacis." *MDAI* 83 (1976): 319–65.

———. "Horologium solarium Augusti." *MDAI* 87 (1980): 355–73.

———. *Die Sonnenuhr des Augustus.* Mainz, 1982.

Bunbury, E. H. *History of Ancient Geography.* 2 vols. London, 1878.

Calmeyer, P. "Zur Genese altiranischen Motive, VIII: Die statistiche landcharte des Perserreiches II." *Arch. Mitt. aus Iran,* 16 (1983): 141–222.

Canesi, L. "La produzione geografica latina e gli influssi letterari." *Historia,* 1931, 145–58, 330–50, 511–32.

Cantor, M. *Die römischen Agrimensoren und ihre Stellung in der Gesch. der Feldmesserkunst.* Leipzig, 1878.

Capelle, W. "Berges- und Wolkenhöhen bei griechischen Physikern." *Stoicheia,* 5 (1916).

———. "Die griechische Erdkunde und Poseidonios." *N. Jahrb. Kl. Altertum* 45 (1920): 305–24.

Carcopino, J. "Sur un passage de la chronique de saint Jérôme." in *Mélanges Martroye,* 73–79, 1940.

Carder, J. N. *Art Historical Problems of a Roman Land Surveying Manuscript: the Codex Arcerianus A, Wolfenbüttel.* Pittsburgh, 1978.

Carettoni, G., Colini, A. M., Cozza, L., and Gatti G., *La Pianta Marmorea di Roma antica,* 2 vols. Rome, 1960.

Cartes et figures de la Terre. Centre Pompidou. Paris, 1980.

Cary, M. *The Geographical Background of Greek and Roman History.* Oxford, 1949.

Cary, M., and Warmington, E. H. *The Ancient Explorers.* London, 1929.

Castagnoli, F. "Influenze alessandrine nell'urbanistica della Roma augustea." *Riv. Fil. Istr. Class.* 1981, 414–23.

———. "L'insula nei cataloghi regionari di Roma." *Riv. Fil.* 104 (1976): 45.

———. "Le formae delle colonie romane e le miniature dei codici dei gromatici. *Mem. Acc. Lincei Sc. Mor.* 7, no. 4 (1944): 83–118.

———. "Note al liber coloniarum." *Bull. Com.,* 1946–48, 49–58.

———. "L'orientamento nella cartografia greca e romana," *Rend. Pont. Accad. Arch.,* 1975–76, 59–69.

Castren, P. *Ordo populusque Pompeianus.* Acta Inst. Finl. Rome, 1975.

Castritius, H. *Der römische Prinzipat als Republik.* Husum, 1982.

Catalano, P. *Contributo allo studio del diritto augurale.* Vol. 1. Turin, 1960.

———. "Aspetti spaziali del sistema giuridico-religioso romano . . . ," *ANRW* II, 16, no. 1 (1978): 442–53.

Ceauseșcu, P. "Altera Roma: Histoire d'une folie politique." *Historia,* 1976, 79–167.

Cebrian, K. *Geschichte der Kartographie.* Vol. 1. Gotha, 1922.

Cencetti, G. "Tabularium principis." In *Studi Manaresi,* 131–66. Milano, 1953.

Chevallier, R. *Littérature gréco-romaine et géographie historique.* Paris, 1974.

Chouquer, G. and Favory, F. "Cadastrations antiques de Campanie, du Latium méridional et de Romagne." In *Cadastres et espace rural,* ed. M. Clavel-Lévêque, 318–21. Paris, 1983.

Claval, P. *La pensée géographique.* Paris, 1972.

Clavel-Lévêque, M., ed. *Cadastres et espace rural.* Paris, 1983.

Coarelli, F. "Il complesso pompeiano del Campo Marzio e la sua decorazione scultorea." *Rend. Pont. Acc. Arch.,* 44 (1971–72): 92–122.

———. *Roma.* Guide Archeologiche Laterza. Rome and Bari, 1981.

Cohen, B., "Some Neglected Ordines." In *Des ordres à Rome,* 23–60. Paris, 1985.

Cohen, M. R., and Drabkin, I. E., *A Source-book in Greek Science.* Cambridge, Mass., 1948.

Conticello de' Spagnolis, M. *Il tempio dei Dioscuri nel Circo Flaminio.* Rome, 1984.

Costa, E. *Cicerone Giureconsulto.* Bologne, 1927.

Courcelle, P. *Les lettres grecques en Occident.* Paris, 1948.

Crawford, M. *Roman Republican Coinage.* 2 vols., Cambridge, 1974.

Cresci Marrone, G. "Allesandro fra ideologia e propaganda in età augustea." *Giorn. Ital. Fil.,* 1978, 245–59.

Cuntz, O. *Itineraria Romana.* Leipzig, 1929.

———. *De Augusto Plinii geographicorum auctore.* Bonn, 1888.

———. "Agrippa und Augustus als Schriftsteller des Plinius." *N.J. Phil. Päd,* supp. 17 (1890): 475–526.

Cuq, E. "Une statistique de locaux affectés à l'habitation dans la Rome impériale." *Mem. Ac. Inscr. Bell. Lettres* 11 (1915): 279–335.

Dahleim, W. *Gewalt und Herrschaft. Das provinziale Herrschaftsystem der röm. Republik.* Berlin, 1977.

Dant, R. "Belli facies et triumphus," *MDAI,* 1984, 115ff.

Dareste, R. "Le Traité des lois de Théophraste." In *La science du droit en Grèce,* 301–13. Paris, 1893.

de Dainville, F. *La géographie des Humanistes.* Paris, 1940.

———. *Le langage des géographes.* Paris, 1964.

Degrassi, A., "Virgilio e il foro di Augusto." In *Scritti Vari di Antichità,* Rome and Trieste, 1962–71. 1:283ff.

———. "'Elogia' del Foro d'Augusto," *Inscr. Italiae* 13, no. 3 (Rome, 1937). 2–8.

———. "Il confine nord-orientale dell'Italia Romana." *Diss. Bernenses* 1, no. 6 (1954).

———. *Scritti vari di Antichità.* 4 vols. Rome, Trieste, 1962–71.

del Badia, J. E. *Danti, cosmographo e matematico.* Firenze, 1898.

Déléage, A. "Les cadastres antiques jusqu'á Dioclétien." In *Etudes de Papyrologie,* vol. 2. Cairo, 1934.

de Martino, F. *Storia della costituzione romana.* 4 vols., Naples, 1974.

———. "Note sull'Italia augustea." *Athenaeum,* 1975, 245–61.

de Ruggiero, E., ed. *Dizionario Epigrafico di Antichità Romane.* Rome, 1895–.

Desanges, J., *Recherches sur l'activité des Méditerranéens aux confins de l'Afrique.* Rome, 1978.

———. *Pline l'Ancien, N.H., V.* CUF. Paris, 1980.

de Santarem, M. *Atlas composé de Mappemondes.* Paris, 1849.

Destombes, M. *Mappemondes A.D. 1200–1500.* Amsterdam, 1964.

Detlefsen, D. "Die Entdeckung des germanischen Nordens." *QFGG* 8 (1904).

———. "Ursprung, Einrichtung und Bedeutung der Erdkarte Agrippas." *QFGG* 13 (1906): 1–117.

———. "Die Beschreibung Italiens in der Nat. Hist. des Plinius. . . . " *QFGG* 1 (1901): 1–62.

———. "Vermutungen über Varro's Schrift de ora maritima." *Hermes* 20 (1886): 240–65.

de Visscher, F. *Les edits d'Auguste découverts à Cyrène.* Brussels, 1940.

Dicks, D. R. *The Geographical Fragments of Hipparchus.* London, 1960.

Dihle, A. "Plinius und die geographische Wissenschaft." In *Tecnologia, economia e società nel mondo romano,* 121–37. Como, 1980.

Dilke, O. A. W. *Greek and Roman Maps.* London, 1985.

———. *The Roman Land Surveyors.* 1971. Italian trans., *Gli Agrimensori di Roma antica.* Bologna, 1979.

———. "Archeological and Epigraphic Evidence of Roman Land Survey." *ANRW* II, 1 (1974), 564–73.

———. "Italy in Ptolemy's manual of geography." In *Imago et mensura mundi,* Atti del IX Congr. Intern. di Storio della cartografia, 353–60. Rome, 1987.

Dion, R. "La géographie humaine rétrospective" (1948). In *Littérature gréco-romaine et géographie historique,* 15–30. Paris, 1974.

———. *Aspects politiques de la géographie antique.* Paris, 1977.

———. "Explication d'un passage des RGDA." In *Mélanges Carcopino,* 249–69. Paris, 1966.

———. "Où Pythéas voulait-il aller?" In *Mélanges Piganiol,* 1315–36. Paris, 1966.

Dittenberger, W. *Orientis Graeci Inscriptiones Selectae,* 2 vols. Leipzig, 1903.

Drumann, W. and Groebe, P. *Geschichte Roms.* Berlin, 1899–1929.

Dubuisson, M. *Le latin de Polybe.* Paris, 1985.

Duhem, P. *Le système du monde. Histoire des doctrines cosmologiques de Platon à Copernic.* 5 vols. Paris, 1913–17.

Dumont, J. D.; Ferray, J. L.; Moreau, P.; and Nicolet, C. *Insula Sacra, la loi Gabinia Calpurnia de Délos (58 av. J. C.).* Rome, 1980.

Edelstein, L., and Kidd, I. G. *Posidonius.* Vol. 1: *The Fragments.* Cambridge, 1972.

Eichler, F. "Zum Partherdenkmal von Ephesos." *Oester. Jahrb.* 9 (1971): 102–86.

Elmore, J. "Ciceronian and Heraclean professiones." *Cl. Quart.,* 1918, 38–45.

———. "The professiones of the Heraclean Table." *JRS,* 1915, 125–37.

Engels, D. "The Length of Eratosthenes' stade," *AJPhil.* 106 (1985): 298–311.
Ensslin, W. "Zu den R.G.D.A.," *Rhein. Mus.* 81 (1932): 335–65.
Erim, K. "Récentes découvertes à Aphrodisias de Carie." *Revue Arch.*, 1982, 163–69.
———. *Aphrodisias 1982.* V. Kazi Sonuçlari Toplantisi (Ankara, 1983) 275–83.
———. *Aphrodisias.* London, 1986.
Esperandieu, E. *Inscriptions de la Gaule romaine.* Paris, 1929.
Fabbrini, F. *L'impero di Augusto come ordinamento sopranazionale.* Milan, 1974.
Falenna, D. "Il Pompeo di Palazzo Spada." *Arch. Class.* 8 (1956): 193ff.
Fallu, E. "La première lettre de Cicéron à Quintus et la lex Julia de repetundis." *REL*, 1971, 180–204.
Favory, F. "Propositions pour une modélisation des cadastres ruraux antiques." In *Cadastres et espace rural*, ed. M. Clavel-Levêque, 51–135. Paris, 1983.
Fears, J. Rufus, "Princeps a diis electus . . . ." *Pap. Mon. Amer. Acad. Rome* 26 (1977).
Ferrary, J. L. *Aspects idéologiques de la conquête romaine du monde hellénistique.* Thesis. Paris, 1987.
Filliozat, J. Appendix to J. André, *Pline l'Ancien, VI*, 2, 143–65. CUF. Paris, 1980.
Forbiger, A. *Handbuch der alten Geographie.* 3 vols. Leipzig, 1842–48.
Forni G., and Angeli Bertinelli, M. G. "Pompeo Trogo come fonte storica." *ANRW* II, 30, no. 2 (1982): 1298–1362.
Fraccaro, P. "Tribules et aerarii." *Athenaeum*, n.s., 9 (1933): 150–72.
———. "Ancora sui processi degli Scipioni." *Athenaeum*, n.s., 17 (1939): 359ff.
Fraenkel, E. *Horace.* Oxford, 1957.
Frei-Stolba, R. *Untersuchungen zu den Wahlen in der röm. Kaiserzeit.* Zurich, 1967.
Frézouls, E. "Sur l'historiographie de l'impérialisme romain." *Ktèma* 8 (1983 [1986]): 141–62.
———. "La construction du theatrum lapideum et son contexte politique." In *Actes des Colloques du CRPOGA*, VII, 193ff. Strasbourg, 1983.
Frid, B. *Ten Uppsala Papyri.* Bonn, 1981.
Friedländer, L. *De fonte quo Josephus BJ, II, 16, 4, uteretur.* Konigsberg, 1873.
Furtwängler, A. *Antike Gemmen.* Leipzig and Berlin, 1900.
Gabba, E., "Per un'interpretazione storica della centuriazione romana." In *Misurare la Terra*, 1:20–28.
———. "Sulle strutture agrarie dell'Italia romana fra II e I secolo a. C." In E. Gabba and M. Pasquinucci, *Strutture agrarie e allevamento transumante nell'Italia romana*, 7ff. Pisa, 1979.
———. "Ricerche sull'esercito professionale romano . . . , App. I: Leva per tribù e censo equestre." *Athenaeum*, n.s. 29 (1951): 171–272.
Gagé, J. "Romulus Augustus." *Mél. Arch. Hist.*, 1930, 138–81.
———. *Res Gestae Divi Augusti.* Strasbourg, 1935. Paris, 1975[3].
———. *La montée des Sassanides.* Paris, 1964.
Galsterer, H. *Herrschaft und Verwaltung im republikanischen Italien.* Munich, 1976.

Gardthausen, V. *Augustus und seine Zeit.* 3 vols., Leipzig, 1896.
Gelzer, M. "Nasicas Widerspruch gegen die Zerstörung Karthagos. *Philol.* 86 (1931): 261–99.
Gervasoni-Cebeillac, M. *Les magistrats municipaux du Latium et de Campanie.* Thesis. Paris, 1987.
Giard, J. B. *Bibl. Nat. Catal. des Monnaies de l'Empire Rom.* Vol. 1: *Auguste.* Paris, 1976.
Gibbs, S. L. *Greek and Roman Sundials.* New Haven, 1976.
Gilbert, O. *Geschichte und Topographie der Stadt Rom in Altertum.* 3 vols. Leipzig, 1883–90.
Gisinger, F. s.v. *Geographie.* In *RE,* supp. X (1924), cols. 521–685.
———. s.v. *Oikoumene.* In *RE,* XVII, 2 (1937), cols. 2123–74.
Glacken, C. J. *Traces on the Rhodian Shore.* Berkeley, 1967.
Gleye, C. E. "Die Weltkarte des Agrippa." *Philol.*, 1909, 318.
Gonzalez, J. "The lex Irnitana: A New Flavian Municipal Law." *JRS*, 76 (1986): 147–243.
Gosselin, P. F. *Recherches sur la géographie systématique et positive des Anciens.* Paris, 1813.
Goukowski, P. "L'espace impérial de Darios Ier." In *Essai sur les origines du mythe d'Alexandre*, Vol. 1. Nancy, 1978.
Gozzoli, S. "Etnografia e politica in Agatharchide." *Athenaeum*, 1978, 54–79.
Grenade, P. *Essai sur les origines du Principat.* Paris, 1961.
Gritti, A. "La documentazione sulla provenienza dell'ambra in Plinio." *Acme*, 1983, 5–17.
Gros, P. "La fonction symbolique des édifices théâtraux dans le paysage urbain de la Rome augustéenne." In *L'Urbs; Espace urbain et histoire*, Colloque de l'EFR, 319–46. Rome, 1987.
Grueber, H. *Brit. Mus., Coins of the Rom. Rep.* 3 vols., London, 1910.
Guarnieri, G. *Le correnti del pensiero geografico nell'antichità classica.* 2 vols. Milan, 1968.
Hampl, F. "Polis ohne Territorium." *Klio* 32 (1939): 1–60.
Hardy, E. "The professiones of the Heraclean Table." *Cl. Quart.*, 1918, 38–45.
Harris, W. V. *War and Imperialism in Republican Rome.* Oxford, 1979.
Heath, Th. *Aristarchus of Samos.* Oxford, 1913.
Hellegouarc'h, J. *Velleius Paterculus.* CUF. Paris, 1982.
Hennig, R. *Terrae incognitae: Eine Zusammenstellung und kritische Bewertung der wichtigsten vorkolumbischen Entdeckungsreisen* . . . , 4 vols. Leiden, 1936–56.
Hermansen, G. "The Population of Imperial Rome: the Regionaries." *Historia,* 1978, 129–68.
Hinrichs, F. T. *Die Geschichte der gromatischen Institutionen.* Wiesbaden, 1974.
Hohl, E. "Zu den Testamenten des Augustus." *Klio*, 1937, 323–42.
Holloway, R. Ross. "The Tomb of Augustus and the Princes of Troy." *AJA,* 1966, 171–63.

Hölscher, T. *Victoria Romana.* Mainz, 1967.

Hombert, M. and Préaux, C. *Recherches sur le recensement en Egypte romaine,* Pap. Lugd. Bat. V, Leiden, 1952.

Homo, L. *Rome impériale et l'urbanisme dans l'Antiquité.* Paris, 1971.

Höningman, E. s.v. *Marinos.* In *RE,* XIV (1930), cols. 1767–96.

Hultsch, F. *Griechische und römische Metrologie.* Berlin, 1882.

Humbert, M. *Municipium et civitas sine suffragio.* Rome, 1978.

Ilari, V. *Gli Italici nelle strutture militari romane.* Milan, 1974.

Imhoof-Blumer, F. *Monnaies grecques.* Amsterdam, 1883.

Jacob, C. "La mimésis géographique en Grèce antique." In *Espace et représentation: Penser l'espace,* 53–80. Paris, 1982.

Jacoby, F. ed. *Fragmente der griechischen Historiker.* Berlin, 1923–.

Jameson, S. "Chronology of the Campaigns of Aelius Gallus and C. Petronius." *JRS,* 1968, 71–84.

Janni, P. *La mappa e il periplo, cartografia antica e spazio odologico.* Rome, 1984.

Jashemski, W. F. *The Origins and History of the Proconsular and Propraetorian Imperium to 27 BC.* Chicago, 1950.

Jodry, C. "L'utilisation des documents militaires chez Velleius Paterculus." *REL,* 1951, 265–84.

Johnson, A. C. "Roman Egypt." In *Ec. Survey Anc. Rome,* vol. 2, ed. Tenney Frank. Baltimore, 1936.

Joly, F. *La cartographie.* Paris, 1976.

Jordan, H. *Topographie der Stadt Rom in Altertum.* 3 vols., Berlin, 1871–1906.

Jullian, C. "Le Breviarium totius imperii de l'empereur Auguste." *Mél Arch. Hist,* 1883, 149–82.

———. *Les transformations politiques de l'Italie sous les empereurs romains.* BEFAR, 1884.

Kähler, H. *Die Gemma Augustea.* Berlin, 1967.

Kaimio, J. *The Romans and the Greek Language.* Commentat. Human. Litter., 69. Helsinki, 1979.

Kapp, J. s.v. *Forma.* In *TLL,* VI, 1, 5 (1973), cols. 1082–83.

Keppie, L. *Colonisation and Veteran Settlement in Italy, 47–14 BC.* Rome, 1983.

Kienast, D. "Augustus und Alexander." *Gymnasium,* 1969, 430–56.

———. *Augustus,* Darmstadt, 1982.

Kish, G. "The Mural Atlas of Caprarola." *Imago Mundi,* 1953, 51–56.

———. *La carte, image des civilisations.* Paris, 1980.

Klotz, A. *Cäsarstudien, nebst einer Analyse des Strabonischen Beschreibung von Gallien und Britannien.* Leipzig, 1910.

———. "Die geographische Commentarii des Agrippa und ihre Ueberreste." *Klio,* 1931, 38–58, 386–466.

———. "Quaestiones Plinianae geographicae." *QFGG,* 1906, 1–227.

Knapowski, R. "Der Staatshaushalt der röm. Republik." In *Unters. z. röm. Gesch.,* vol. 2. Frankfurt, 1961.

———. "Die Staatsrechnung der röm. Republik in den Jahren 49–45 v. Christ." In *Unters. z. röm. Gesch.*, vol. 4. Frankfurt, 1967.

Kolendo, J. *A la recherche de l'ambre baltique.* Varsavia, 1981.

Kornemann, E. *Mausoleum und Tatenbericht des Augustus.* Leipzig, 1921.

———. s.v. *Monumentum Ancyranum.* In *RE,* XVI (1933), cols. 211–31.

———. "Stadtstaat und Flächenstaat des Altertums in ihren Wechselbeziehungen." *Neue Jahrb.* X (1908): 233–53.

———. "Polis und Urbs." *Klio* 5 (1905): 72–92.

Kossack, G. "The Germans." In *The Roman Empire and Its Neighbours,* ed. F. Millar, 294ff., esp. 351. London, 1967.

Kraft, K. "Der Sinn des Mausoleum des Augustus." *Historia,* 1967, 189–206.

Kubitschek, W. s.v. *Karten.* In *RE,* X, 2 (1919), cols. 2022–149.

———. s.v. *Itinerarien.* In *RE,* IX, 2 (1916), col. 2310.

———. s.v. *Julius Honorius.* In *RE,* X (1919), cols. 614–28.

———. "Die Erdtafel des Julius Honorius." *Wiener Studien* 7 (1885): 1–24, 278–310.

———. *De Romanorum tribuum origine ac propagatione.* Wien, 1882.

Kupčik, I. *Cartes géographiques anciennes.* Prague, 1980. Paris, 1981.

Labrot, G. *Le Palais Farnèse de Caprarola: Essai de lecture.* Paris, 1970.

Laffranque, M. *Poseidonios d'Apamée.* Paris, 1964.

Langlouis, K. *Raumauffassung und geographische Weltbild in der röm. Politik von Pompeius bis Traian.* Tübingen, 1951.

La Rocca, E. *Ara Pacis Augustae.* Rome, 1983.

Lasserre, F. *Die Fragmente des Eudoxos von Knidos.* Berlin, 1966.

———. "Strabon devant l'Empire romain." *ANRW* II, 30, 1 (1983), 867–96.

Legras, H. *La Table latine d'Héraclée.* Paris, 1907.

Lemosse, M. *Le Régime des relations internationales dans le Haut-Empire romain.* Paris, 1967.

Leroi-Gourhan, A. *Le geste et la parole.* 2 vols. Paris, 1965.

Le Roux, P. *L'armée romaine et l'organisation des provinces ibériques. . . .* Paris, 1982.

Levi, A. and Levi, M. "Map projection and the Peutinger Table." In *Coins, Culture and History in the Ancient World,* 139–48. Detroit, 1981.

———. *Itineraria picta: contributo allo studio della T.P.,* Rome, 1967.

Lévy, J. P. "Les actes d'état civil romains." *Rev. Hist. Dr.,* 1952, 449–86.

———. "Nouvelles observations sur les professiones liberorum." In *Etudes J. Macqueron,* Aix-en-Provence, 1970. 439–49.

Liebenam, W. *Städtverwaltung im röm. Kaiserreich.* Leipzig, 1900.

Linderski, J. "Si vis pacem, para bellum: Concepts of Defensive Imperialism." In *The Imperialism of Mid-Republican Rome,* ed. W. V. Harris, Pap. and Mon. Am. Acad. Rome, 3 (Rome, 1984) 133 64.

Little, D. "Politics in Augustan Poetry." *ANRW* II, 30, 1 (1982), 357.

Lo Cascio, E. "Mazocchi e la questione della Tabula Heracleensis." 1976, 77–107.

Lugli, G. *Roma antica. Il centro monumentale.* Rome, 1946.

Lundström, Suex. *Ovids Metamorphosen und die Politik des Kaisers.* Uppsala, 1980.

Magdelain, A. *Auctoritas Principis.* Paris, 1947.

Magie, D. *De Romanorum iuris publici sacrique vocabulis. . . .* Leipzig, 1905.

Malcovati, E. *Imperatoris Caesaris Augusti Fragmenta.*[4] Turin, 1964.

———. *Oratorum Romanorum Fragmenta.* Turin, 1976.

Mancinetti-Santamaria, G. "Strabone e l'ideologia augustea." *Annali Fac. Lettere Perugia,* 16, no. 4 (1978–79): 129–42.

Maricq, A. "Res gestae Divi Saporis." *Syria,* 1958, 304–31.

Marquardt, J. *Organisation de l'Empire Romain.* French trans. Paris, 1889.

———. *De l'organisation financière chez les Romains.* French trans. Paris, 1888.

Mélèze, J. Entre la cité et le fisc: le statut grec dans l'Egypte romaine." *Symposion,* 1982, 265–68. Valencia, 1985.

Mendels, D. "The Five Empires: A Note on a Propagandistic Topos." *AJPhil.* 1981, 330–39.

Mette, H. J. *Pytheas von Massalia.* Berlin, 1952.

Meyer, H. D. "Die Aussenpolitik des Augustus und die augusteische Dichtung." *Köln Ist. Abh.* 5 (1961).

Michel, D. *Alexander als Vorbild für Pompeius, Caesar und Marcus Antonius. Archaeologische Untersuchungen.* Coll. Latomus, XCIV. Brussels, 1967.

Michel, J. H. "Le méridien de Skodra et le partage du monde. . . . " In *Atti Conv. Intern. Accad. Rom. Constantiniana,* IV, 1 [1979], 1982, 181–91.

Millar, F. "The census of Quirinius," in the reissue of E. Schürer, "The History of the Jewish people in the age of J.C.," 399–427. Edinburgh, 1973.

Miller, K. *Mappae mundi, die ältesten Weltkarten.* 6 vols. Stuttgart, 1895.

Mitchell, S. "Archeology in Asia Minor." *JHS, Arch. Reports,* 3 (1984–85): 70–105.

Moczy, A. *Pannonia.* London, 1974.

Momigliano, A. "Terra marique," *JRS,* 1942, 53–64.

Mommsen, T., *Römische Geschichte.* vol. 5: *Die römische Provinzen von Caesar bis Diokletian.* Italian trans. *Storia di Roma antica.* vols. 5: *Le province romane da Cesare a Diocleziano.* Firenze, 1967.

———. *Römisches Staatsrecht.* 3 vols. Leipzig, 1871–87. French trans. *Le droit public romain.* 7 vols. Paris, 1887–92.

———. *Res Gestae Divi Augusti.*[2] Berlin, 1883.

———. "Mamilius Sura, Aemilius Sura, L. Manlius." *Rh. Mus.*, 1861, 282.

———. "Die italischen Bürgercolonien von Sulla bis Vespasian." *Hermes*, 1883, 161–213.

———. "Die italischen Regionen." In *Kiepert Festschriften.* 95–109. Berlin, 1898.

Montevecchi, O. "Ricerche di sociologia . . . , V: Le denunzie di morte." *Aegyptus* 26 (1946): 111–29.

———. "Il Censimento romano d'Egitto." *Aevum*, 1976, 77–83.

———. *La papirologia*. Turin, 1973.

Moynihan, R. "Geographical Mythology and Roman Imperial Ideology." In *The Age of Augustus*, 149–62. 1985.

Müllenhoff, K. *Deutsche Altertumskunde*. 5 vols., Berlin, 1890–1929.

———. *Die Germanie des Tacitus*. Berlin, 1900.

Müller, C. *Geographi graeci minores*. 2 vols. Paris, 1853–61.

———. *Fragmenta Historicorum Graecorum*. 5 vols. Paris, 1841–70.

Muttelsee, E. *Untersuchungen über die lex Julia municipalis*. Diss. Freiburg-in-Bresgau, 1911.

Neesen, L. *Untersuchungen zu den direkten Staatsabgaben der röm. Kaiserzeit*. Bonn, 1980.

Neugebauer, O. "The History of Ancient Astronomy: Problems and Methods." *Journ. of Near Eastern Stud.*, 4 (1945): 1–38.

Neumann, J. *De quinquennalibus coloniarum et municipiorum*. Leipzig, 1892.

Newton, R. *The Crime of Claudius Ptolemaeus*. Baltimore, 1977.

Nicolet, C. "L'Empire romain: espace, temps et politique." *Ktèma* 8 (1983): 163–73.

———. "Plèbe et tribus: les statues de Lucius Antonius et le testament d'Auguste." *MEFRA*, 1985, 799–839.

———. *Polybe et les institutions romaines*. In *Polybe*, Entretiens de la Fond. Hardt, XV, 209–65. Geneva, 1974.

———. "Augustus, Government and the Propertied Classes." In *Caesar Augustus*, 89–128. Oxford, 1984.

———. *Demokratia et Aristokratia, à propos de Caïus Gracchus*. Paris, 1983.

———. "Le temple des Nymphes et les distributions frumentaires à Rome à l'époque républicaine." *CRAI*, 1976, 29–51.

———. *Le métier de citoyen dans la Rome républicaine*. Paris, 1979. Italian trans. it., *Il mestiere di cittadino nell'antica Roma*. Rome, 1980. English trans., 1980.

———. *Rome et la conquête du monde méditerranéen*. Vol. 1: *Les structures de l'Italie romaine*. Paris, 1979. Vol. 2: *Genèse d'un empire*. Paris, 1978.

———. "Le stipendium des alliés italiens jusqu'à la guerre sociale." *Papers of Brit. School Rome* 46 (1978): 1–11.

———. "La table d'Héraclée et les origines du cadastre romain." In *L'Urbs: Espace urbain et histoire,* Colloque de l'EFR, 1–25. Rome, 1987.

———. "Les finitores ex equestri loco de la loi Servilia de 63 av. J.-C." *Latomus,* 1970, 72–103.

———. "Rome capitale." In *Da Roma alla terza Roma*. Rome, 1987.

———. *Tributum*. Bonn, 1976.

Nicolet, C., and Gautier Dalché, P. "Les quatre sages de Jules César et la mesure du monde selon Julius Honorius: réalité antique et tradition médievale." *Journ. des Savants,* 1987, 3–50.

Niebling, G. "Laribus Augustis Magistri primi, Der Beginn des Compitalkultes der Lares und des Genius Augusti." *Historia,* 1956, 303–31.

Nora, P. *Les lieux de mémoire*. 3 vols., Paris, 1986–87.

Norden, E. *Die germanische Urgeschichte in Tacitus Germania*.[2] Leipzig-Berlin, and 1922.

Nordenskjöld, N A. *Facsimile Atlas to the Early History of Cartography*. Stockholm, 1889.

Ober, J. "Tiberius and the Political Testament of Augustus." *Historia,* 1982, 306–28.

Oberleitner, W. *Funde auf Ephesos und Samothrake, Kunsthistor. Mus*. Wien, 1978.

Oehmichen, G. *Plinianische Studien*. Erlangen, 1880.

Oldfather, W., and Canter, H. V. "The Defeat of Varus and the German Frontier Policy of Augustus." *Univ. of Illinois Studies* 4, no. 2 (1915): 1–118.

Oliver, J. H. "North, South, East, West at Arausio and Elsewhere." In *Mél. Piganiol,* 1075–79. Paris, 1966.

Pais, E. *Storia della colonizzazione*. 2 vols. Rome, 1923.

Pallu de Lessert, C. "L'oeuvre géographique d'Agrippa et d'Auguste." *Mem. Soc. Ant. Fr.,* 1909, 215–98.

Panerai, M. C. "Gli agrimensori romani." In *Misurare la Terra,* 1:109–21.

Pani, M. *Comitia e senato*. Bari, 1974.

Parroni, P., ed. *Pomponii Melae de Chorographia*. Rome, 1984.

Pédech, P. *La méthode historique de Polybe*. Paris, 1964.

———. *La géographie des Grecs*. Paris, 1976.

Pelletier, M. "L'Amérique septentrionale du globe de Louis XIV." In *Imago et mensura mundi,* Atti. del IX Congr. Intern. di Storia della cartografia, 393–407. Rome, 1987.

Pertz, K. A. *De cosmographia Aethici libri tres*. Berlin, 1853.

Peter, H. *Historicorum Romanorum Reliquiae*. 2 vols. Leipzig, 1906–14.

Petersen, K. "Die Kosmographie des Kaisers Augustus und die Commentarien des Agrippa," *Rh. Mus*. 8 (1853): 161–205, 377–442. 9 (1954): 82–106, 297n.25.

Philippi, F. *Zur Rekonstruktion d. Weltkarte des Agrippa*. Marburg, 1880.

Phillips, Ph. L. *A list of Geographical Atlases in the Library of Congress*. Washington, D.C., 1914.

Photinos, K. G. "Marinos von Tyros." In *RE,* supp. XII (1970), cols. 791–838.

Pianazella, E. "Au delà des frontières du monde . . . ." *REL,* 1984, 192.

Picard, G. "Le monument de César Cosmocrator au Capitole." *Rev. Arch*., 1973, 261–72.

Piéri, G. *L'histoire du cens jusque'á la fin de la République romaine*. Paris, 1968.

Piganiol, A. "Les documents cadastraux de la colonie latine d'Orange," *Gallia,* supp. 16 (1962).

Pinchemel, Ph. "Réflexions sur l'histoire de la géographie: histoire de la géographie, histoire des géographes." In *Histoire et épistémologie de la géographie,* Bull. Com. Trav. hist., Sect. de Géographie, 1979, 221–31.

Pinkwart, D. *Das Relief des Archelaos von Priene und die Musen des Philistos*. Kallmünz, 1965.

Platner, S. B. and Ashby, T. *A Topographical Dictionary of Ancient Rome.* London, 1929.
Poinsotte, M. "*Les Romains et la Chine: réalités et mythes.*" *MEFRA,* 1979, 472.
Polaschek, E. "Ptolemaeos als Geographer." In *RE,* Supp. X (1965), cols. 681–833.
Posner, E. *Archives in the Ancient World.* Cambridge, Mass., 1972.
Praz, M., and Faldi, I. *Il Palazzo Farnese di Caprarola.* Seat, 1981.
Prell, H. *Die Vorstellungen des Altertums von der Erdumfangslänge.* Berlin, 1959.
Prontera, F. *Geografia e geografi nel mondo antico: Guida storica e critica.* Rome and Bari, 1983.
———. "Prima di Strabone: Materiali per uno studio della geografia antica come genere letterario." In *Strabone, contributo allo studio della personalità e dell'opera,* 189–259. Perugia, 1984.
Purcell, N. "The Apparitores: A Study in Social Mobility," *Pap. of Br. School Rome,* (1983): 125–73.
Raffestin, C. *Pour une géographie du pouvoir.* Paris, 1980.
Randles, W. G. L. *De la terre plate au globe terrestre, une mutation épistémologique rapide, 1480–1520.* Paris, 1980.
Raschke, M. *New Studies in Roman Commerce with the East. ANRW* II, 9, no. 2 (1978): 604–1378.
Ratzel, F. *Anthropogeographie.* 2 vols., Stuttgart, 1882–91.
———. *Politische Geographie.*[3] Munich, 1903.
Rawson, E. *Intellectual Life in the Late Roman Republic.* London, 1985.
Rebuffat, R. "Le bouclier de Doura." *Syria,* 63 (1986): 85–103.
Reed, N. "Pattern and Purpose in the Antonine Itinerary." *AJPhil.,* 1978, 228–51.
Reid, J. S. "The so-called lex Julia Municipalis." *JRS,* 1915, 209–48.
Reinach, A. *Recueil Milliet,* ed. A. Rouveret. Paris, 1985.
Reinaud, J. J. *Relations politiques et commerciàles de l'empire romain avec L'Asie orientale.* Paris, 1863.
Reinhardt, K. "Poseidonios von Apamea." In *RE,* XXII, 2 (1953), cols. 558–826.
Reynolds, J. *Aphrodisias and Rome.* London, 1982.
———. "New Evidence for the Imperial Cult in Julio-Claudian Aphrodisias." *ZPE* 43 (1981): 317–27.
Riccobono, S., ed. *Fontes Iuris Romani Antejustiniani*[2], 3 vols. Florence, 1941.
Richard, J. C. "Mausoleum: d'Halicarnasse à Rome, puis à Alexandrie." *Latomus,* 29 (1970): 370–88.
Riepl, W. *Das Nachrichtenwesen des Altertums, mit besonder Rücksicht auf die Römer.* Leipzig, 1913.
Riese, A. *Geographi Latini Minores.* Heilbronn, 1878.
Ritschl, F. "Die Vermessung des röm. Reichs unter Augustus, die Weltkarte des Agrippa." *Rh. Mus.,* 1842, 483–522.
Robert, L. *Villes d'Asie Mineure.*[3] 1962.
Roddaz, J. M. *Marcus Agrippa.* Rome, 1984.

Rodriguez Almeida, E. *Forma Urbis Marmorea. Aggiornamento generale 1980.* Rome, 1981.

Rostovtzeff, M. *Social and Economic History of the Hellenistic World.* Oxford, 1939. Italian trans., *Storia economica e sociale del mondo ellenistico.* 3 vols. Firenze, 1966.

Roussel, D. *Tribu et cité.* Besançon, 1976.

Sallmann, K. G. *Die Geographie des älteren Plinius in ihrem Verhältnis zu Varro.* Berlin, 1971.

Salviat, F. "Orientation, extension et chronologie des plans cadastraux d'Orange." *Rev. Arch. Narb.* 10 (1977): 107–18.

Sauron, G. "Le complexe pompéien du champ de Mars: nouveauté urbanistique à finalité idéologique." In *L'Urbs: Espace urbain et histoire,* Colloque de l'EFR, 457–73.

Schanz, M., and Hosius, C. Munich, 1935. *Geschichte der Römische Literatur.* Vol. 1. Munich, 1987. 1927. Vol. 2. Munich, 1935.

Schlachter, A. *Der Globus, seine Entstehung und Verwendung in der Antike.* Stoicheia 8. Leipzig and Berlin 1927.

Schmitt, H. "Tacitus und die nachgelassenen Schriften des Augustus." *Historia Einzelschr.* (Festschr. Bengston, 1983): 178–86.

Schnabel, P. "Die Weltkarte des Agrippa als wissenschaftliches Mittelglied zwischen Hipparch und Ptolemaeus." *Philol.*, 1935, 405–40.

Schoff, W. H. *Parthian Stations of Isidore of Charax.* Reprint, 1976.

Schulten, A. *Gromatici.* In *RE,* VII, 2 (1912), cols. 1886–96.

———. *Centurio.* In *DE,* II (1900), cols. 189–92.

———. "Römischen Flurkarten." *Hermes,* 1898, 534–65.

———. "Vom antiken Kataster." *Hermes,* 1906, 1–44.

Schulz, F. "Roman Registers of Birth and Birth Certificates." *JRS,* 1942, 78–91; ibid.; 1943, 55–64.

Schweder, E. "Ueber die Weltkarte und Chorographie des Kaisers Augustus." *Neue Jahrb. Phil. Päd.* 145 (1892): 113–32.

———. "Ueber die Weltkarte und Chorographie des Kaisers Augustus. I: Ueber die römische Weltkarte." *Philol.,* 1895, 319–44; II (continued), 1896, 528–59; III (continued), 1897, 130–62.

———. *Beiträge zur Kritik der Chorographie des Augustus.* 3 vols. Kiel, 1878–83.

Seager, R. *Pompey, A Political Biography.* Oxford, 1979.

Seel, O. *Eine römische Weltgeschichte.* Nuremberg, 1972.

———. "Pompeius Trogus und Universalgeschichte." *ANRW* II, 30, 2 (1982), 1363–423.

———. *Julii Caesaris Commentarii.* Leipzig, 1961.

Seston, W. "La lex Julia de 90 av. J. C. et l'intégration des Italiens dans la citoyenneté romaine." *CRAI,* 1978, 529–42.

Seston, W., and Euzennat, M. "Un dossier de la chancellarie romaine: la Tabula Banasitana . . ." *CRAI,* 1971, 468–90.

Sherk, R. T. "Roman Geographical Exploration and Military Maps." *ANRW* II, 30, 1 (1974), 534–62.

———. *Roman Documents from the Greek East.* Baltimore, 1969.

Sieglin, W., ed. *Quellen und Forschungen zur alten Geschichte und Geographie.* Berlin, 1901–20.

Simon, E. *Ara Pacis.* Tübingen, 1967.

Simpson, J. "The Date of the Dedication of the Temple of Mars Ultor." *JRS,* 1977, 91–94.

Sitwell, N. H. *The World the Romans Knew.* London, 1984.

Sordi, M. "Timagene: uno storico ellenocentrico e filobarbaro." *ANRW* II, 30, 1 (1982), 775–97.

Soubiran, J. *Vitruve, livre IX.* CUF. Paris, 1969.

Spielgelberg, W. *Catal. génér. Ant. ég. Musée du Caire: Die demotischen Denkmäler.* Vol. 2: *Die dem. Papyrus, Text.* Strasbourg, 1908.

Stahl, W. H. *Roman Science.* Madison, 1962. Italian trans. *La scienza dei romani.* Roma and Bari, 1974.

Stiehle, R. "Der Geograph Artemidoros von Ephesos." *Philol.,* 1856, 191–244.

Stier, H. E. "Augustusfriede und römische Klassik." *ANRW* II, 2 (1975), 3ff., 16–20.

Suolahti, J. *The Roman Censors.* Helsinki, 1963.

Swain, J. W. "The Theory of the Four Monarchies: Opposition History under the Empire." *Cl. Phil.* 35 (1940): 1–21.

Syme, R. "The Crisis of 2 B.C." *Sitz. Bay. Ak. Wiss.,* 1974, 2–34.

———. *Danubian Papers.* Bucharest, 1971.

———. *History in Ovid.* Oxford, 1978.

———. "The Northern Frontier." *CAH* 10 (1934): 340–81.

———. "The Titulus Tiburtinus." In *Rom. Papers,* 869–84.

———. "Caesar, the Senate and Italy." *PBSR,* 1938, 1–31.

Szramkiewicz, R. *Les gouverneurs de province à l'époque augustéenne.* 2 vols. Paris, 1976.

Tabaronni, G. "Sfere celesti sulle monete romane." *Caelum* 26 (1956): 7–16.

———. "Globi celesti e terrestri sulle monete romane." *Physis* 7 (1965): 317–53.

Tannery, P. *Mémoires Scientifiques,* 3 vols., Paris 1912–37.

———. *Pour l'histoire de la science hellène.* Paris, 1930.

———. *Recherches sur l'histoire de l'astronomie ancienne.* Paris, 1893.

Taylor, L. Ross, *The Voting Districts of the Roman Republic.* Rome, 1960.

———. *Roman Voting Assemblies from the Hannibalic War to the Dictatorship of Caesar.* Ann Arbor, 1966.

———. *Party Politics in the Age of Caesar.* Berkeley, 1949.

———. "The Four Urban Tribes and the Four Regions of Ancient Rome." *Rend. Pont. Acc.,* 27 (1952–54): 225–38.

Temporini, H., ed. *Aufstieg und Niedergang des römischen Welt.* Berlin, 1972–.

Thiel, J. H., *Eudoxus of Cyzicus.* Hist. Stud., 23. Utrecht, 1966.

Thomassy, R. *Les papes géographes et la cartographie du Vatican.* Paris, 1852.

Thomsen, R. *The Italic Regions from Augustus to the Lombard Invasion.* Copenhagen, 1947.

Thomson, J. O. *History of Ancient Geography.* Cambridge, 1948.

———. "Marcus Aurelius and the Small Earth." *JRS,* 1953, 47–48.

Thulin, C. *Corpus agrimensorum romanorum.* Vol. 1, pt. 1. Leipzig, 1913.

Tibiletti, G. *Principe e magistrati repubblicani.* Rome, 1953.

Timpe, D. "Untersuchungen zur Kontinuität des frühen Prinzipats." *Historia Einzelschr.* 3 (1962).

Toneatto, L. "Tradition manuscrite et éditions modernes du Corpus Agrimensorum Romanorum." In *Cadastres et espace rural,* ed. M. Clavel-Lévêque. Paris, 1983, 21–50.

Toth, T. "Protulique fines Illyrici." *Acta Arch. Ljubljana,* 1977, 278.

Valentini, R., and Zucchetti, G. *Codice topografico della città di Roma.* Vol. 1. Rome, 1940.

Van Der Vliet, E. C. L. *Strabo over Landen, Volken en Steden.* Amsterdam, 1977.

Van Ooteghem, J. *Pompée le Grand bâtisseur d'empire.* Brussels, 1954.

Van Paassen, C. *The Classical Tradition of Geography.* Groningen, 1957.

Veyne, P. "Y a-t-il eu un impérialisme romain?" *MEFRA,* 1975, 793–855.

Vidal-Naquet, P. *Flavius Arrien entre deux mondes.* In *Arrien, histoire d'Alexandre,* 311–94. Paris, 1984.

Virlouvet, C. *Famines et émeutes à Rome dès origines de la République à la mort de Néron.* Rome, 1985.

Vivien de Saint Martin, M. *Histoire de la géographie et des découvertes géographiques.* Paris, 1873.

Vogt, J. *Orbis Romanus.* Tübingen, 1929.

———. *Vom Reichsgedanken der Römer.* Leipzig, 1942.

———. *Orbis.* Freiburg-im-Bresgau, 1960.

Volkmann, H. *Res Gestae Divi Augusti.*[3] Berlin, 1969.

Volponi, M. *Lo sfondo italico della lotta triumvirale.* Genova, 1975.

von Gerkan, A. "Grenzen und Grössen der Vierzehn Regionen Roms." *Bonn. Jahrb.,* 1949, 5–65.

von Premerstein, A. "Ein elogium des M. Vinicius cos 19 v. Chr." *JOAI,* 1904, 215–39.

———. "Vom Werden und Wesen des Prinzipats." *Abhandl. Bay. Akad.,* 1937.

Walbank, F. "The Geography of Polybius." *Class. et Med.* 9 (1948): 155–82.

———. *Polybius.* Berkeley, 1972.

———. *Comm. on Polybius.* 3 vols., Cambridge, 1957–79.

Wallace, S. L. *Taxation in Egypt from Augustus to Diocletian.* Princeton, 1938.

Warmington, E. H. *Greek Geography.* London and New York, 1934.

Weber, E. *Tabula Peutingeriana, codex Vindobonensis 324.* Graz, 1976.

Wehrli, F. *Die Schule des Aristoteles,*[2] vol. 1. Bâle, 1967.

Weinstock, S. *Divus Julius.* Oxford, 1971.

Welles, C. *The German Policy of Augustus*. Oxford, 1972.

Werenberg, B. "Augustus Forum and Akropolis." *Jahrb. Deutsch. Arch. Inst.*, 1984, 164ff.

Wikajak, J. "De M. Tullii Ciceronis opere geographico quid judicandum." *Meander,* 35 (1980): 541–46.

Williams, G. *Change and Decline*. Berkeley, 1978.

Wiseman, T. P. "Julius Caesar and the Hereford Map." *History Today* 37 (1976): 398.

Woelk, D. *Agathemeros von Knidos über das Rote Meer.* Bamberg, 1966.

Woodman, A. J. "Questions of Date, Genre and Style in Velleius: Some Literary Problems." *CQ,* 1975, 272–306.

Yavetz, Z. "The Res Gestae and Augustus' Public Image." *Caesar Augustus,* ed. F. Millar and E. Segal, 1–36. Oxford, 1983.

Zanker, P. *Forum Augustum*. Tübingen, 1974.

Index

Plates

Fig. 1. Farnese Palace of Caprarola. Antonio Vanosino of Varese: World Map (ca. 1574). Photo Instituto centrale per il catalogo e la documentazione, Rome.

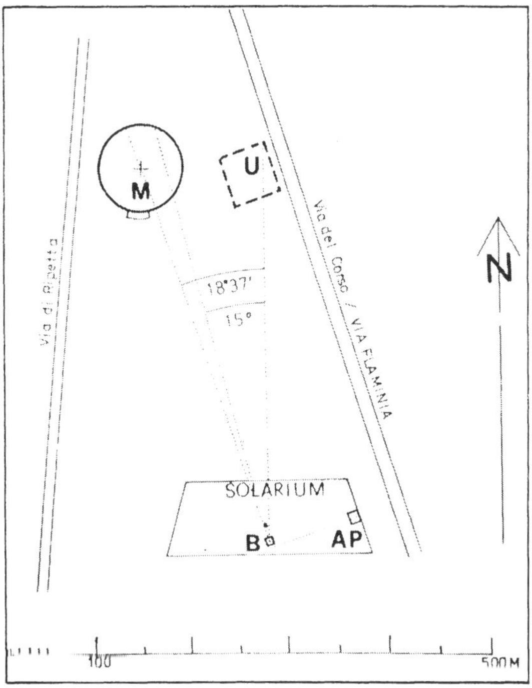

Fig. 2. The Mausoleum *(M)*, the *Horologium (B)*, and the *Ara Pacis (AP)*. (From E. Buchner.)

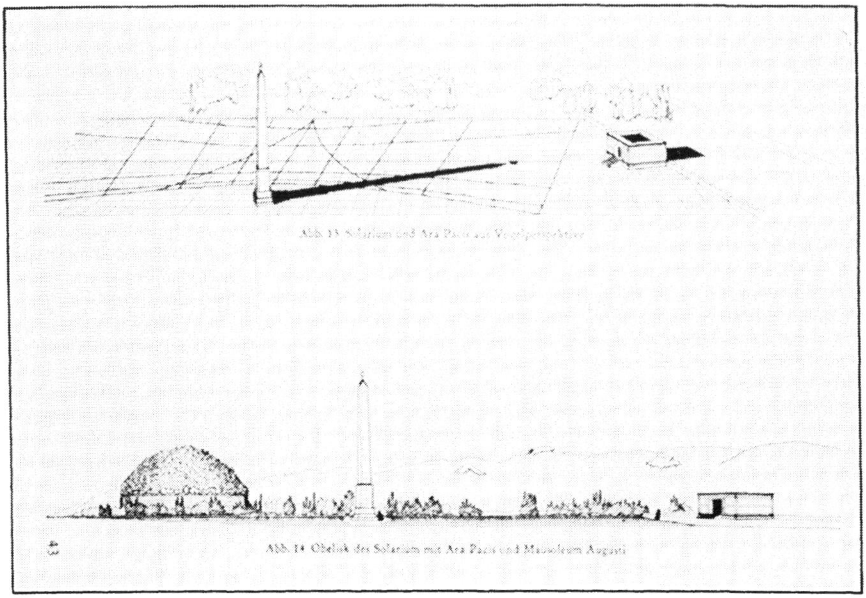

Fig. 3. Perspective view. (From E. Buchner.)

Fig. 4. The obelisk of the *Horologium* (actual site). (Photo X.D.R.)

Fig. 5. Denarius of T. Carisius: the globe. (Photo X.D.R.)

Fig. 6. Denarius of Faustus Sulla: the globe and Pompey's triumphal wreaths. (Photo X.D.R.)

Fig. 7. Coins of Augustus with the globe. (Photo X.D.R.)

Fig. 8. Coin of Trajan with the globe. (Photo X.D.R.)

Fig. 9. Statue of Pompey (from his Theater?), in the Palazzo Spada. (From F. Coarelli.)

Fig. 10. Relief of the Via Cassia (Rome, Museo Nazionale). (From S. Weinstock.)

Fig. 11. "Altar of the Parthians" at Ephesus: *profectio* of L. Verus. (*Kunstmuseum*, Vienna.)

Fig. 12. Coin of Hadrian: *orbis terrarum*. (Photo X.D.R.)

Fig. 13. The Forum of Augustus (reconstruction). (From P. Zanker.)

Fig. 14. The Forum of Augustus: caryatids and medallion. (From P. Zanker.)

Fig. 15. The *Gemma Augustea* in Vienna. (Photo X.D.R.)

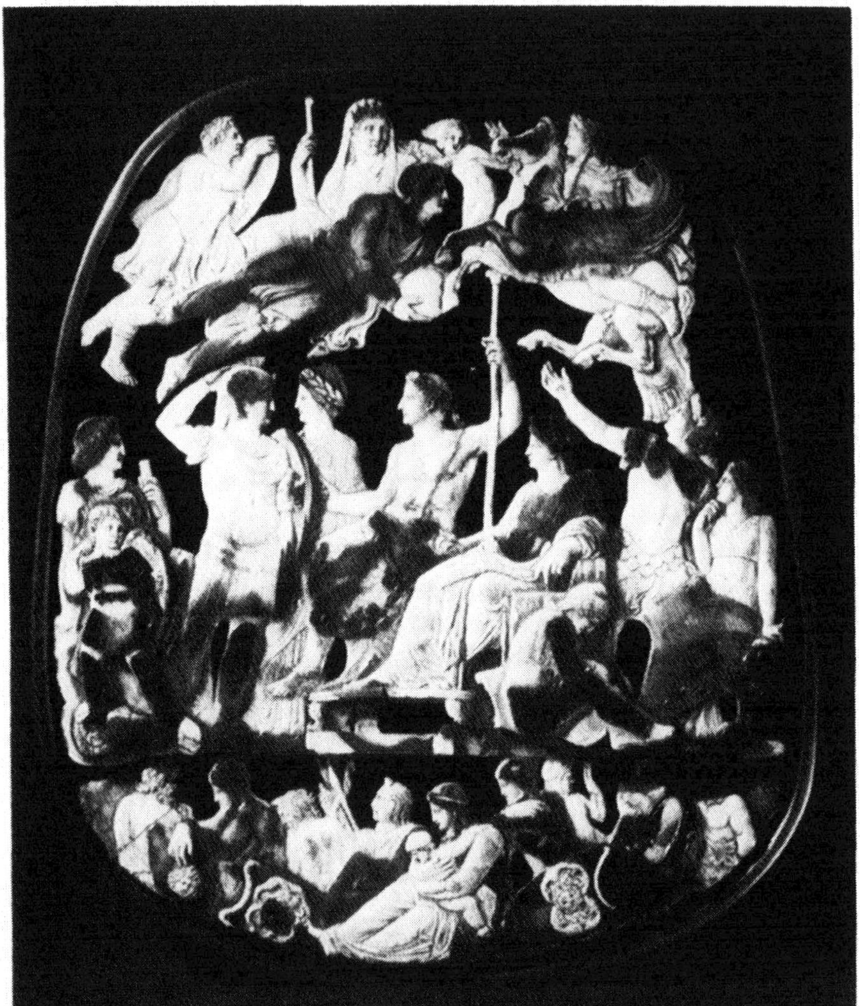

Fig. 16. The *Great Cameo of France*. (Photo B.N.)

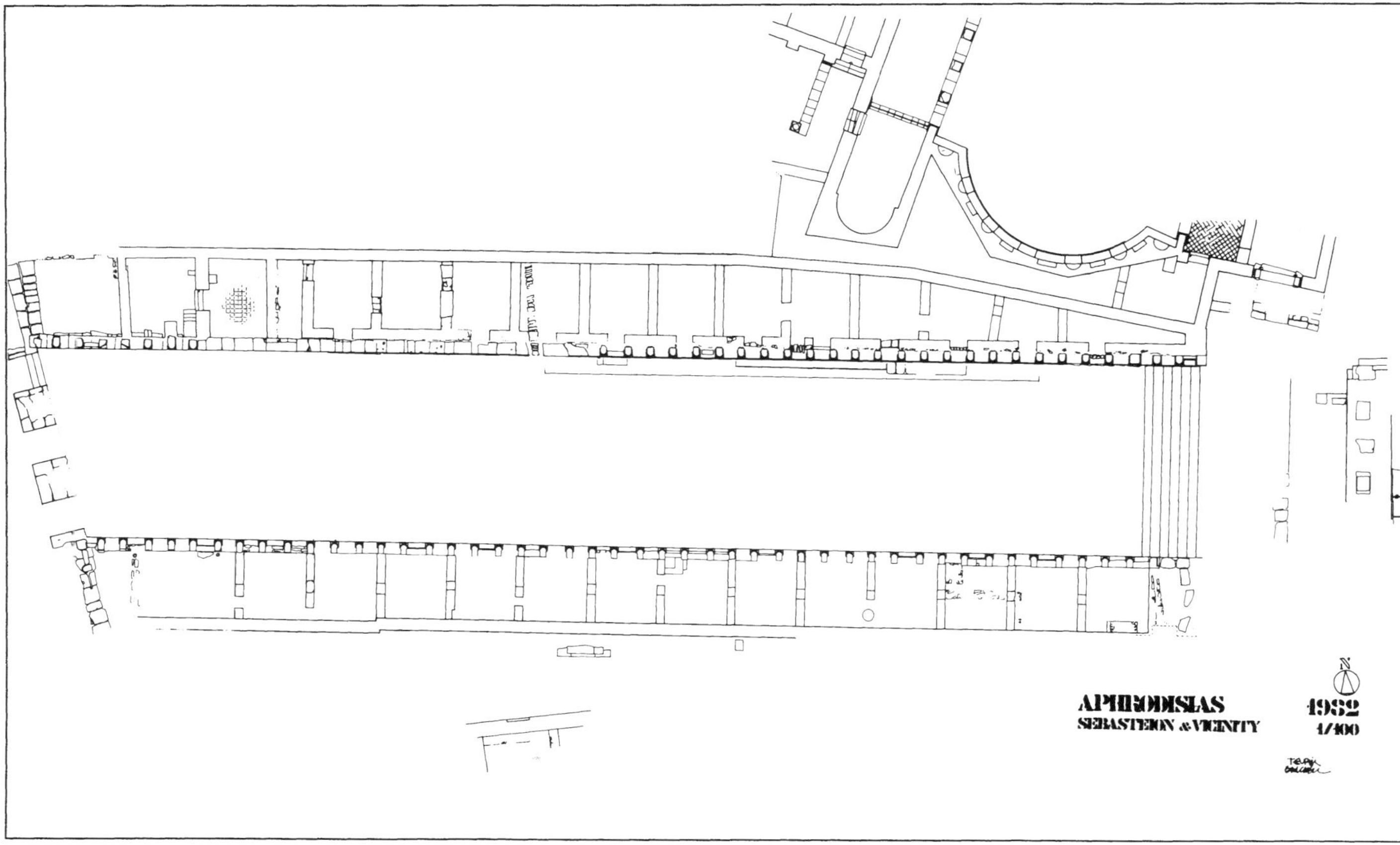

Fig. 17. Carian Aphrodisias: the *Sebasteion*, general plan.

Fig. 18. Aphrodisias, the *Sebasteion*, northern *porticus: Okeanos.* (Photo A. Dögenci.)

Fig. 19. Aphrodisias, the *Sebasteion*, southern *porticus:* Augustus as master of the worlds and of the sea. (Photo A. Döğenci.)

Fig. 20. Aphrodisias, the *Sebasteion,* northern *porticus:* allegory of the *Pirystai.* (Photo A. Dögenci.)

Fig. 21. Aphrodisias, the *Sebasteion*, northern *porticus:* base with the name of the "people of the Bessi." (Photo A. Dögenci.)

Fig. 22. Farnese Atlas. (Photo Alinari © Viollet.)

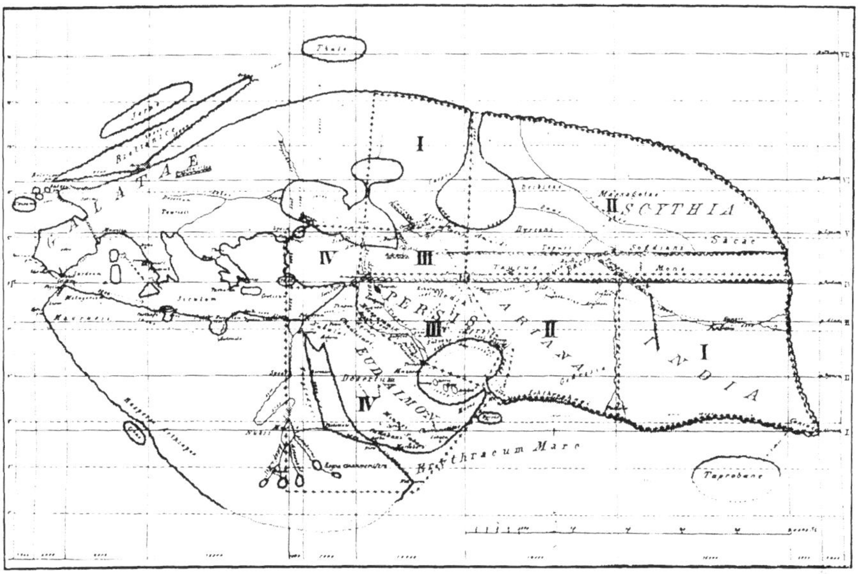

Fig. 23. The *oikoumene* of Eratosthenes. (From K. Miller.)

Fig. 24. The *oikoumene* on the globe according to Strabo. (From K. Miller.)

Fig. 25. The four inhabited worlds of Crates of Mallos. (From K. Miller.)

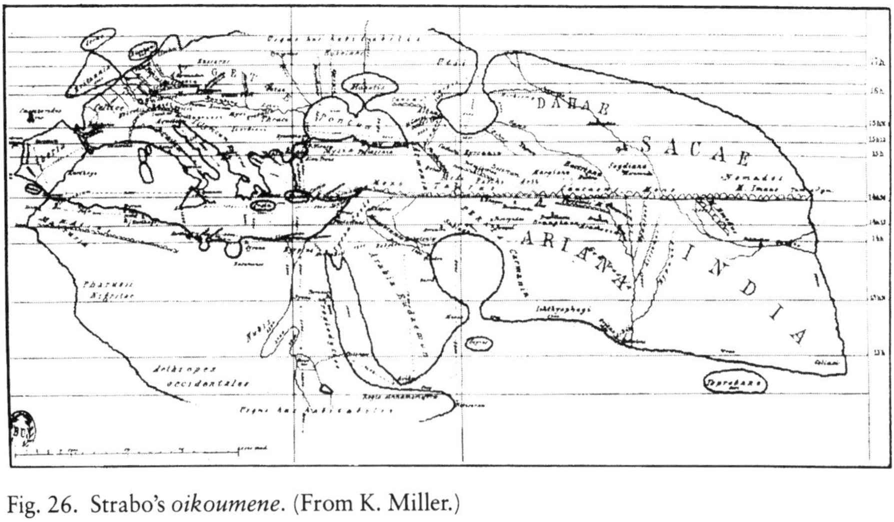

Fig. 26. Strabo's *oikoumene*. (From K. Miller.)

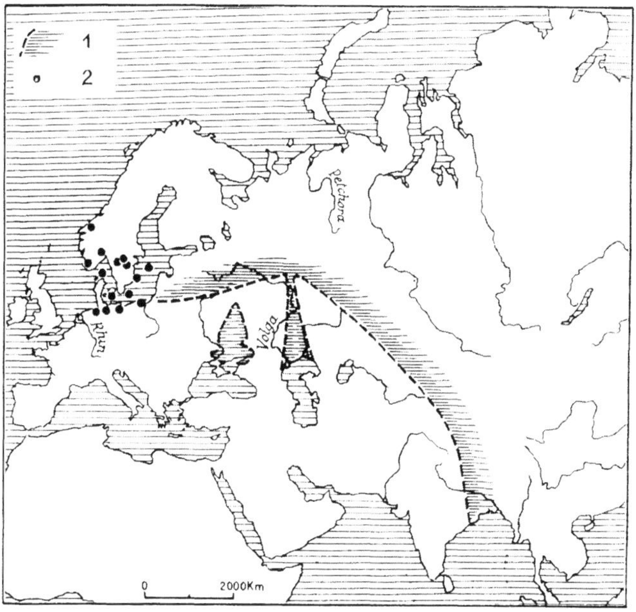

Fig. 27. The known world in antiquity. (From R. Dion.)

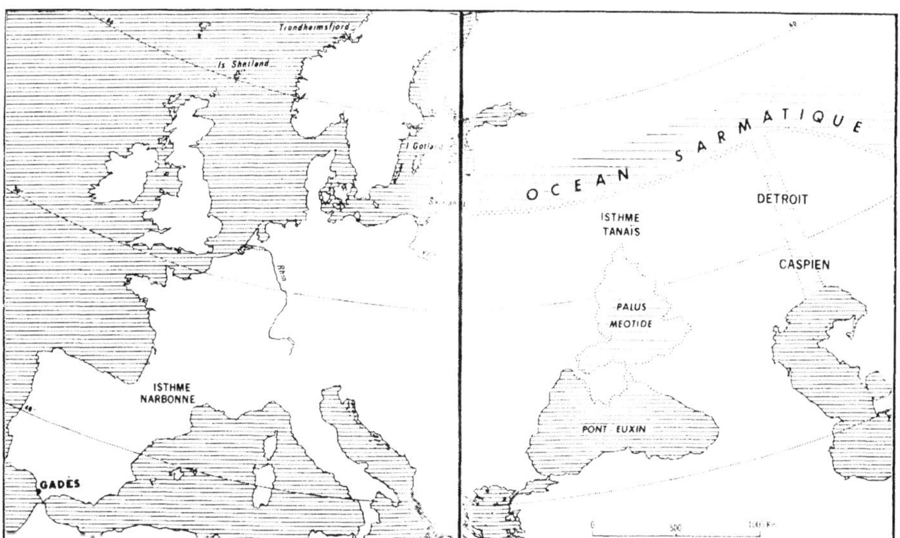

Fig. 28. The Northern Sea of antiquity. (From R. Dion.)

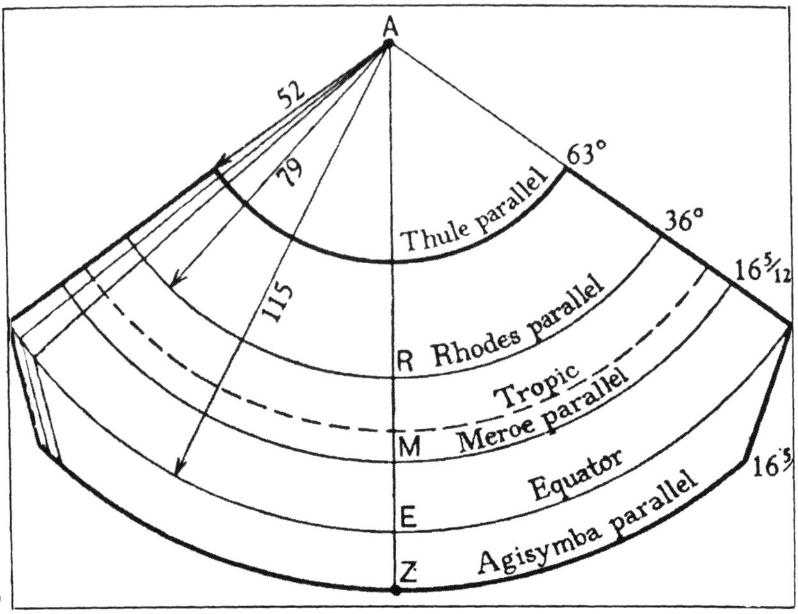

Fig. 29

Figs. 29–31. Ptolemy's systems of projections. (From J. O. Thomson.)

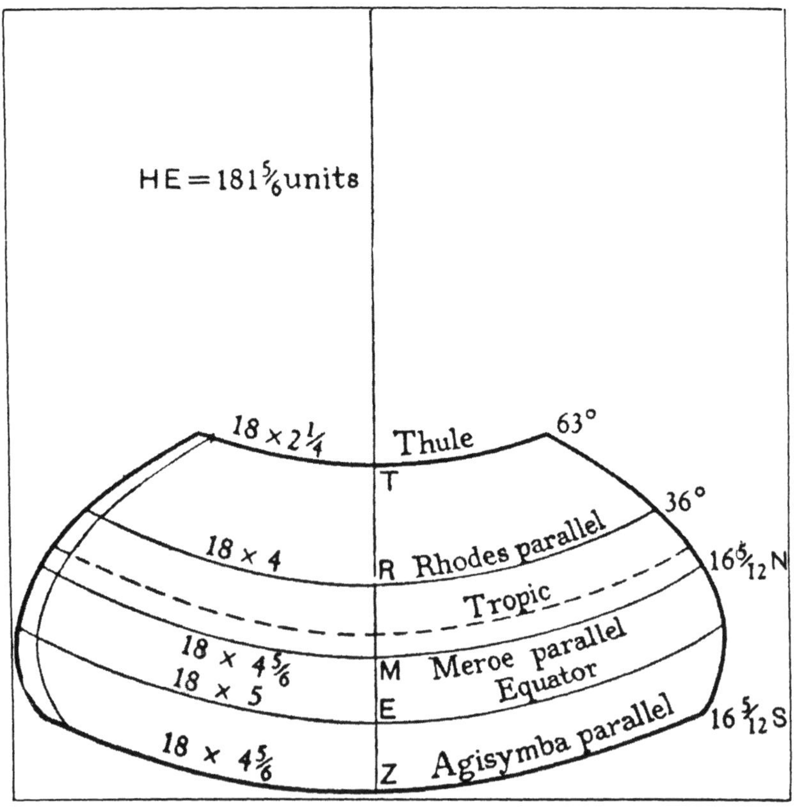

Fig. 30

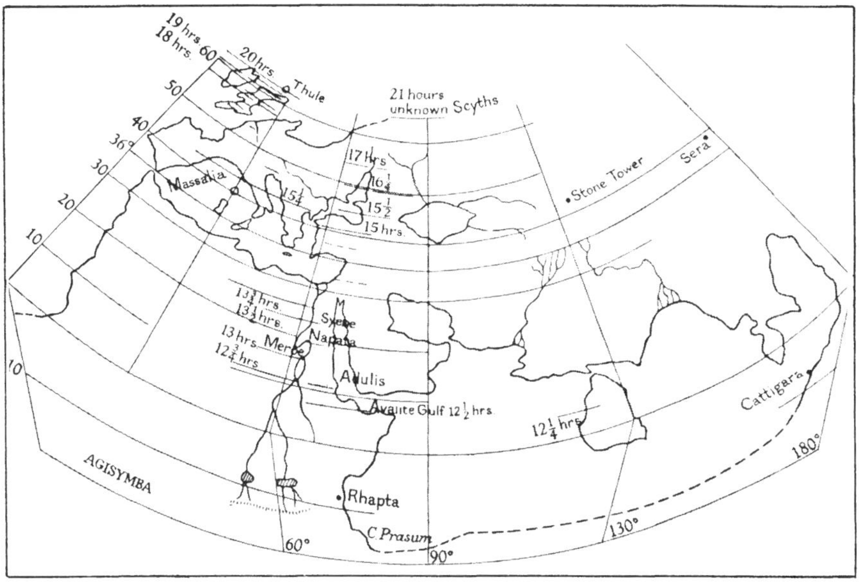

Fig. 31

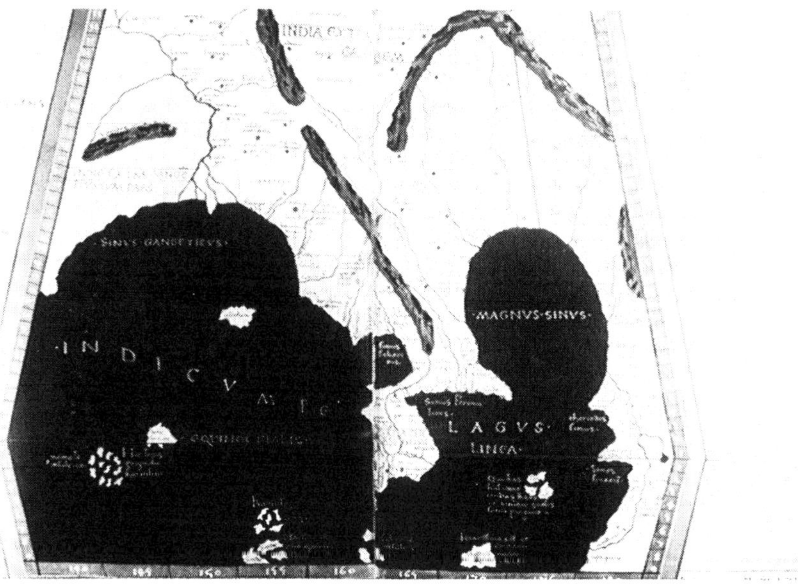

Fig. 32. Ptolemy (Naples manuscript). (Photo X.D.R.)

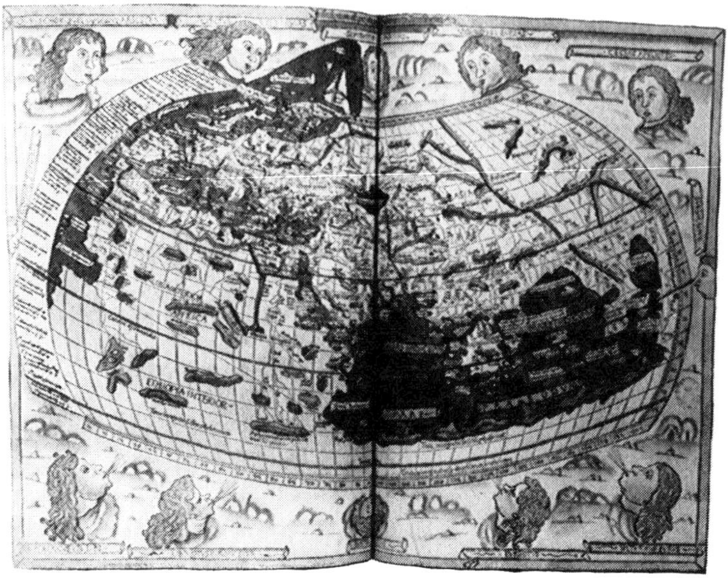

Fig. 33. Ptolemy. (Ulm edition.)

Fig. 34. Ebstorf Map. (Photo X.D.R.)

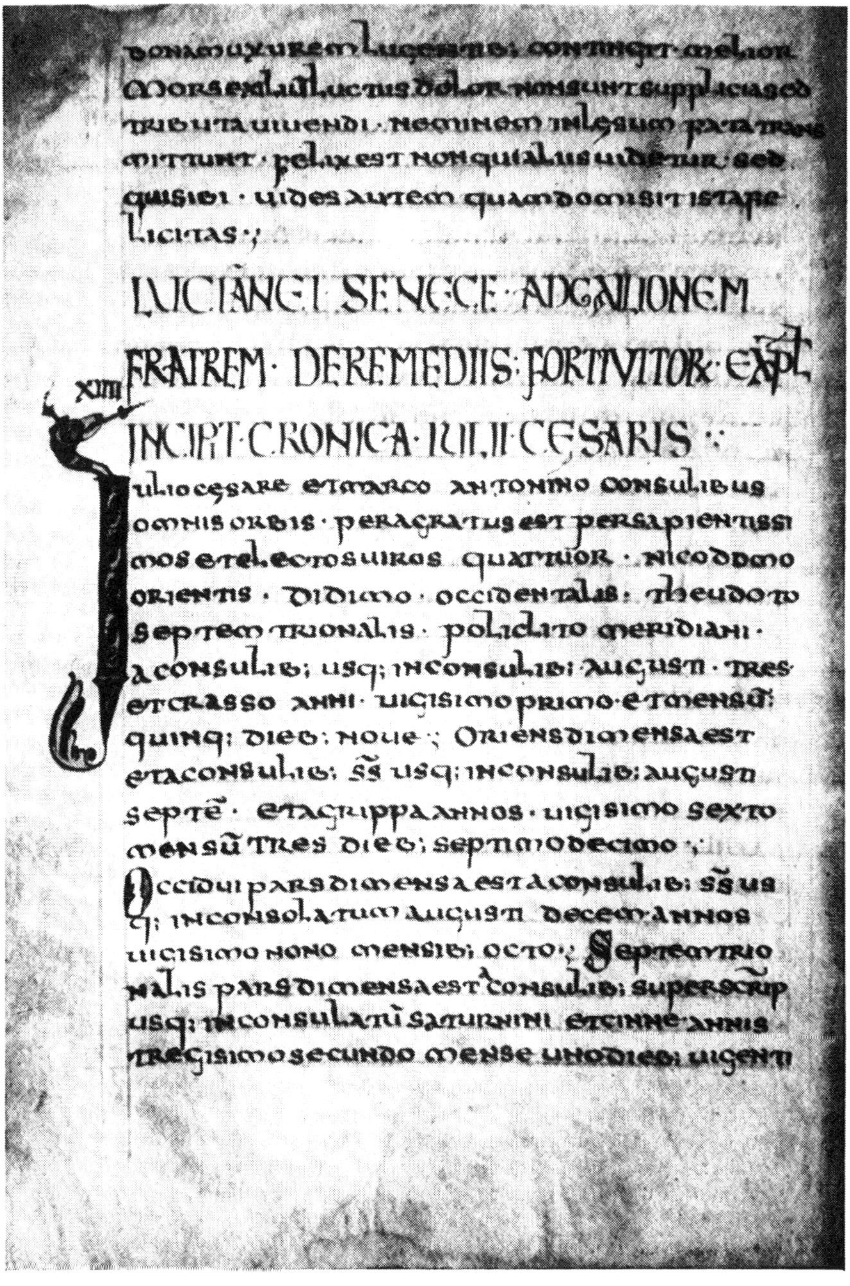

Fig. 35. The beginning of the *Cosmographia Julii Honorii* (ms. Parisinus 10318). (Photo B. N.)

Fig. 36. The Hereford map. (Photo X.D.R.)

Fig. 37. The Hereford map (detail: the emperor and three *mensores*). (Photo X.D.R.)

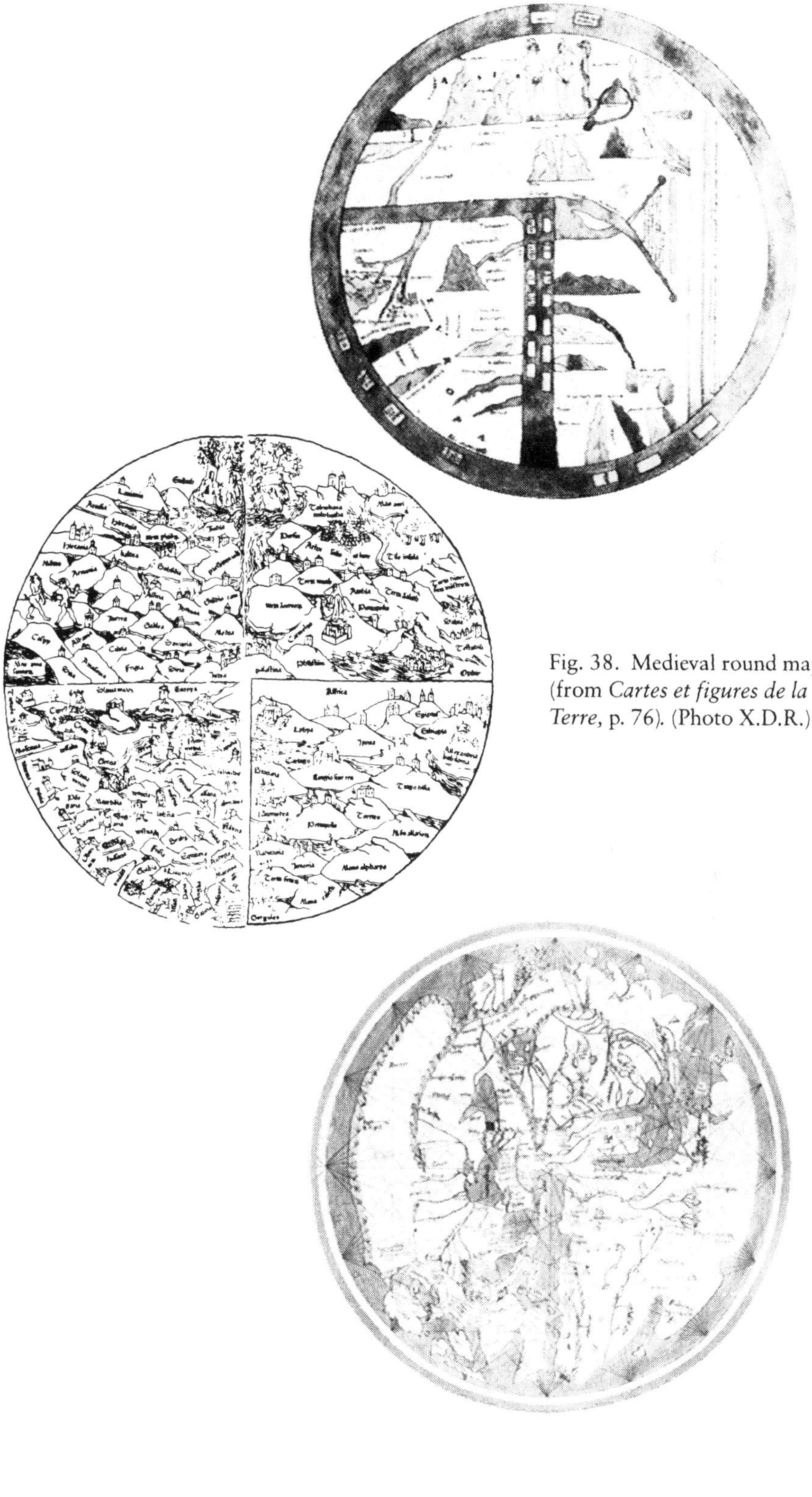

Fig. 38. Medieval round maps (from *Cartes et figures de la Terre*, p. 76). (Photo X.D.R.)

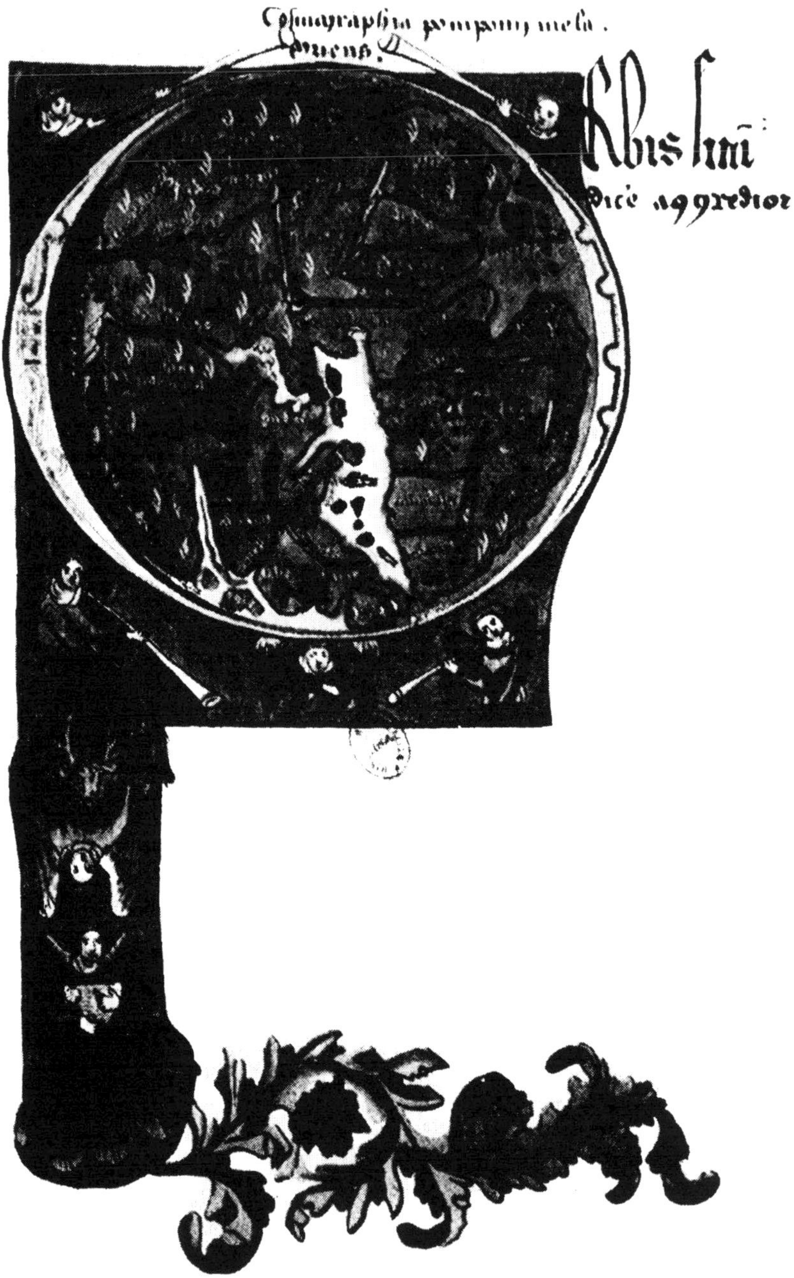

Fig. 39. Round map. Manuscript of Pomponius Mela.

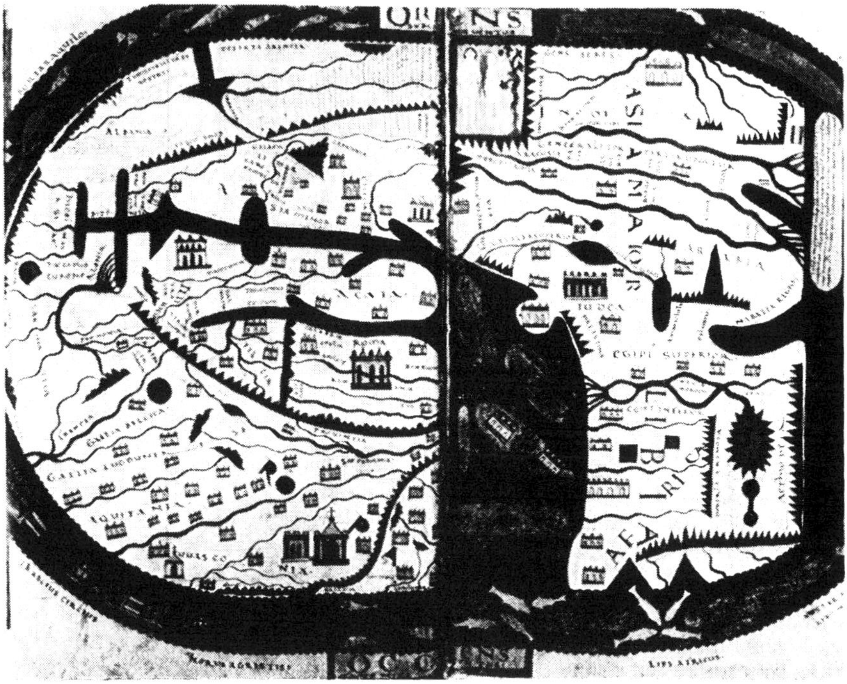

Fig. 40. The map of Beatus (Bibliotheque Nationale Latin ms. 8878, f. 45). (Photo X.D.R.)

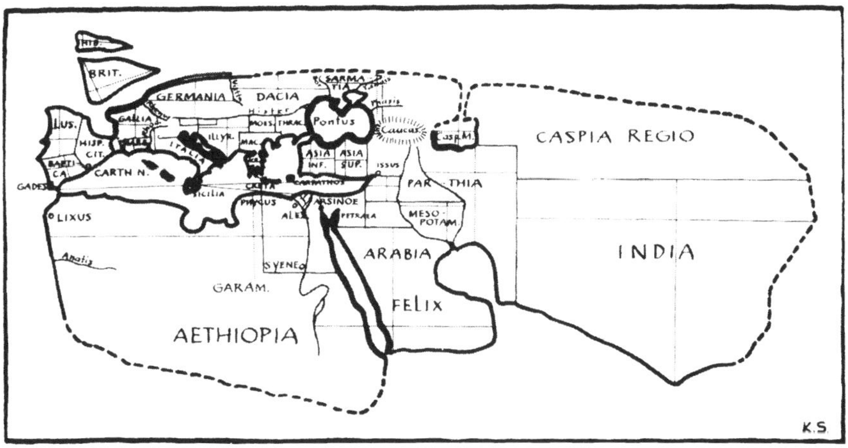

Fig. 41. Agrippa's map. (From Sallmann.)

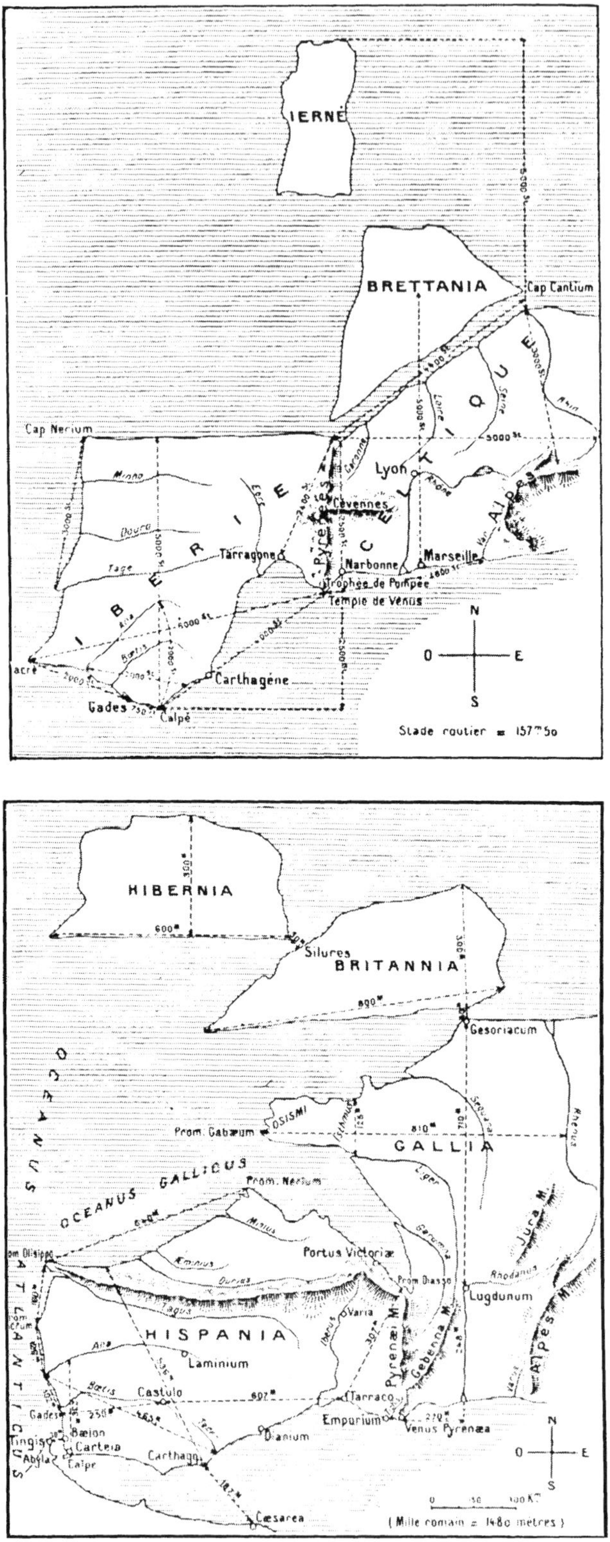

Fig. 42. Views of Western Europe of Strabo and Agrippa. (From A. Berthelot.)

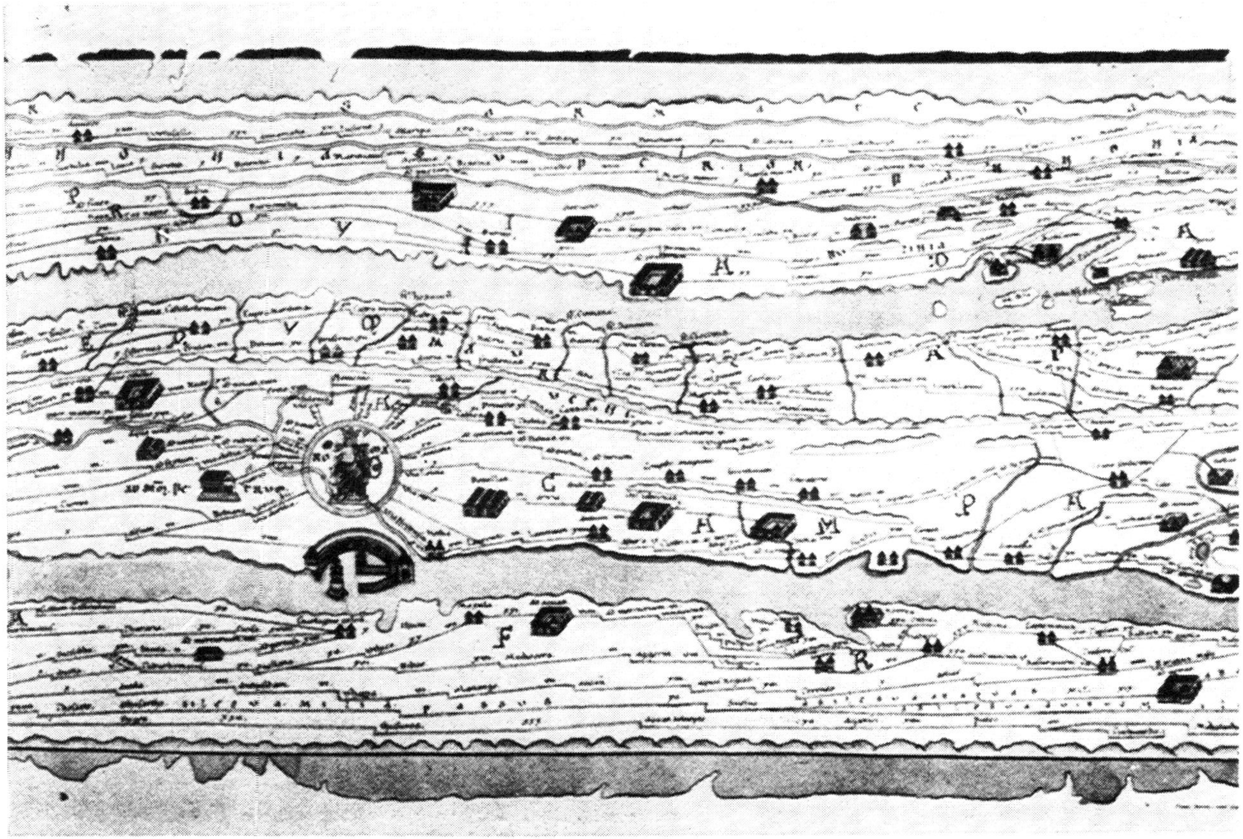

Fig. 43. The Peutinger Table (detail; facsimile).

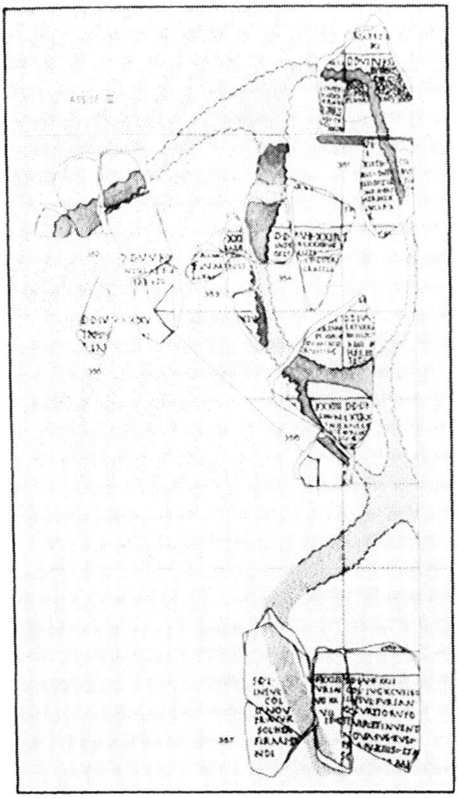

Fig. 44. The cadastres at Orange. (From Piganiol.)

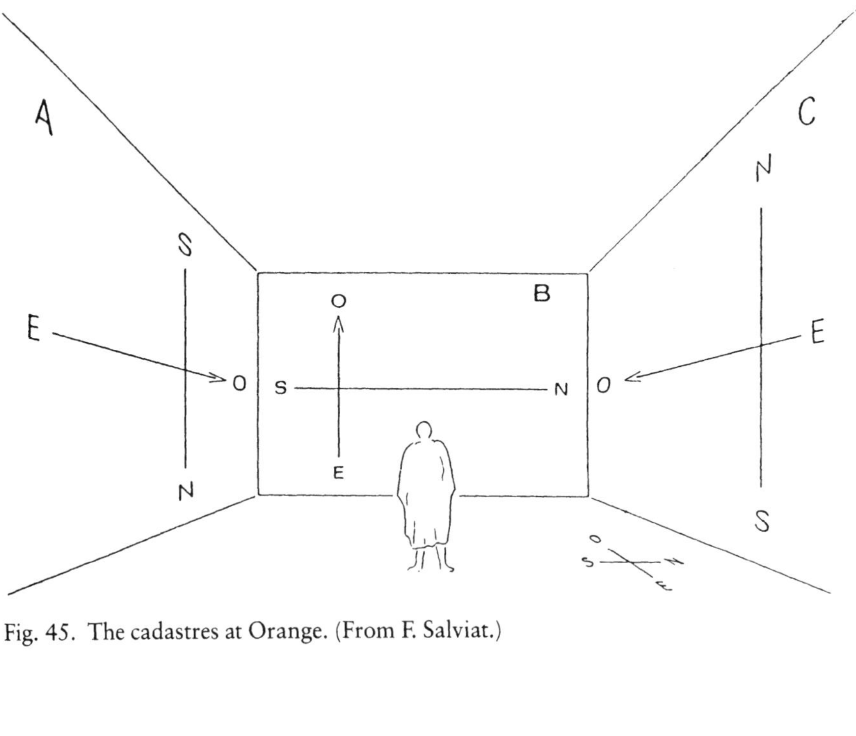

Fig. 45. The cadastres at Orange. (From F. Salviat.)

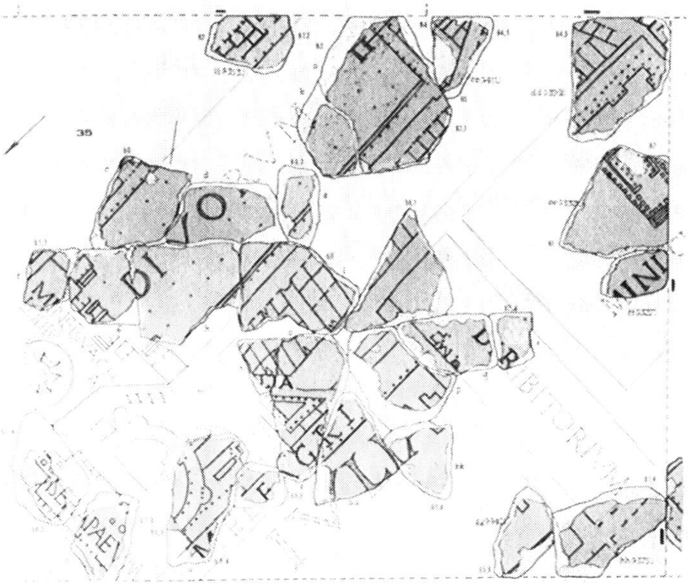

Fig. 46. The *Forma Urbis Romae* (detail).

Fig. 47. Vignette from the *Gromatici Veteres:* Terracina (Pal. 1564; from *Misurare la Terra,* p. 107). (Photo X. D. R.)

Fig. 48. Vignette from the *Gromatici Veteres:* Colonia Claudia (Pal. 1564; from *Misurare la Terra,* p. 114). (Photo X.D.R.)

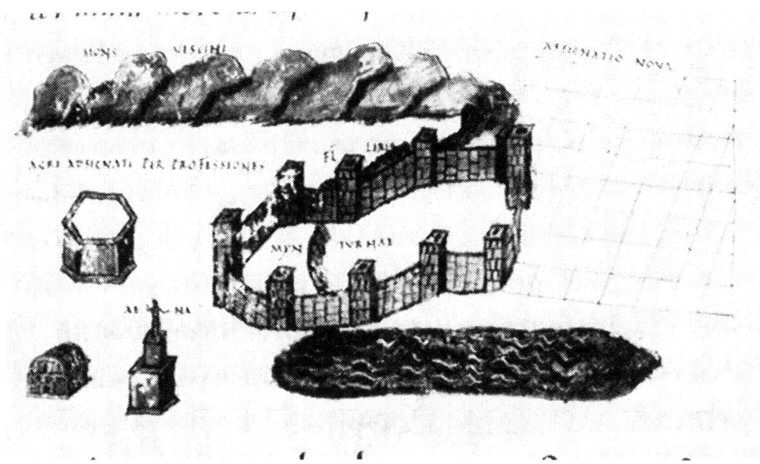

Fig. 49. Vignette from the *Gromatici Veteres:* Minturnae (Pal. 1564; from *Misurare la Terra,* p. 114). (Photo X. D. R.)

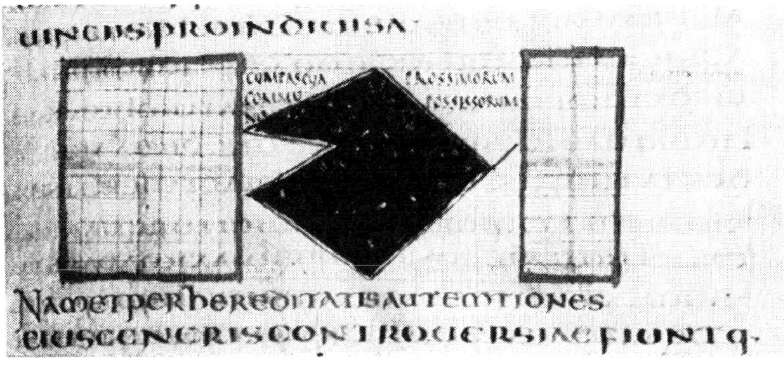

Fig. 50. Vignette from the *Gromatici Veteres:* land neither centuriated nor allotted (Arcerianus A.; from *Misurare la Terra,* p. 154). (Photo X. D. R.)

Figs. 51–52. The cadastre of the Via Anicia (from M. Conticello di Spagnolis).

Fig. 51

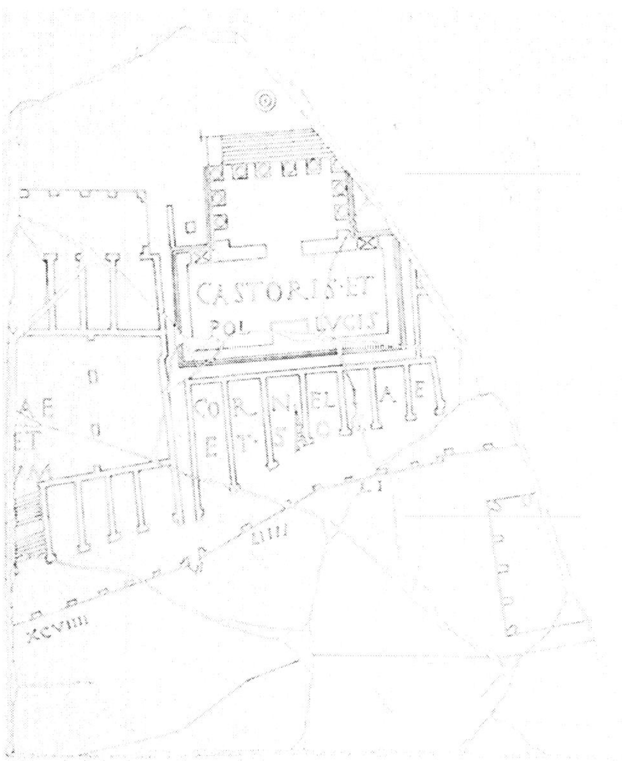

Fig. 52

Fig. 53. Orange: the *merides* inscription. (From Piganiol.)

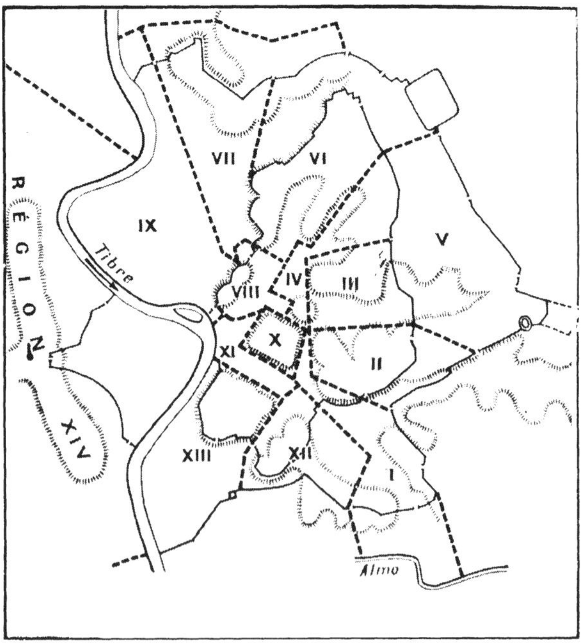

Fig. 54. The fourteen urban regions. (From Homo.)